JEWISH AND CHRISTIAN TEXTS IN CONTEXTS AND RELATED STUDIES

29

Executive Editor
James H. Charlesworth

Editorial Board of Advisors
Motti Aviam, Michael Davis, Casey Elledge, Loren Johns,
Amy-Jill Levine, Lee McDonald, Lidia Novakovic,
Gerbern Oegema, Henry Rietz, Brent Strawn

AFTERLIFE AND RESURRECTION BELIEFS IN THE APOCRYPHA AND APOCALYPTIC LITERATURE

Jan A. Sigvartsen

LONDON • NEW YORK • OXFORD • NEW DELHI • SYDNEY

T&T CLARK
Bloomsbury Publishing Plc
50 Bedford Square, London, WC1B 3DP, UK
1385 Broadway, New York, NY 10018, USA
29 Earlsfort Terrace, Dublin 2, Ireland

BLOOMSBURY, T&T CLARK and the T&T Clark logo are
trademarks of Bloomsbury Publishing Plc

First published in Great Britain 2019
This paperback edition published in 2021

Copyright © Jan A. Sigvartsen, 2019

Jan A. Sigvartsen has asserted his right under the Copyright,
Designs and Patents Act, 1988, to be identified as the Author of this work.

All rights reserved. No part of this publication may be reproduced or
transmitted in any form or by any means, electronic or mechanical,
including photocopying, recording, or any information storage or retrieval
system, without prior permission in writing from the publishers.

Bloomsbury Publishing Plc does not have any control over, or responsibility for,
any third-party websites referred to or in this book. All internet addresses given
in this book were correct at the time of going to press. The author and publisher
regret any inconvenience caused if addresses have changed or sites have
ceased to exist, but can accept no responsibility for any such changes.

Scripture quotations from the Apocrypha are from the Revised Standard Version of the Bible,
copyright © 1946, 1952, and 1971; and from the New Revised Standard Version Bible, copyright
© 1989 National Council of the Churches of Christ in the United States of America. Used by
permission. All rights reserved.

A catalogue record for this book is available from the British Library.

Library of Congress Cataloging-in-Publication Data
Names: Sigvartsen, Jan Age, author.
Title: Afterlife and resurrection beliefs in the Apocrypha and apocalyptic
literature / by Jan A. Sigvartsen.
Description: 1 [edition]. | New York: T&T Clark, 2019. |
Series: Jewish and Christian texts; 29 | Includes bibliographical references and index.
Identifiers: LCCN 2019009765 | ISBN 9780567685513 (hardback) |
ISBN 9780567689252 (epub) | ISBN 9780567685520 (epdf)
Subjects: LCSH: Apocryphal books (Old Testament)–Criticism, interpretation,
etc. | Apocalyptic literature–History and criticism. | Future
life–Biblical teaching. | Resurrection–Biblical teaching.
Classification: LCC BS1700.S548 2019 | DDC 229/.06–dc23
LC record available at https://lccn.loc.gov/2019009765

ISBN: HB: 978-0-5676-8551-3
PB: 978-0-5677-0063-6
ePDF: 978-0-5676-8552-0
ePUB: 978-0-5676-8925-2

Series: Jewish and Christian Texts, volume 29

Typeset by Forthcoming Publications (www.forthpub.com)

To find out more about our authors and books visit
www.bloomsbury.com and sign up for our newsletters.

*For
Leanne Sigvartsen
and our sons
Leif Sigvartsen
Thor Sigvartsen
Axel Sigvartsen*

Contents

Acknowledgments — ix
List of Abbreviations — xi
Figures — xvi
Tables — xvii

OUR PERENNIAL YEARNING FOR POSTMORTEM EXISTENCE
OR RESURRECTION
  James Hamilton Charlesworth — xix

FOREWORD
  C. E. Elledge — xxiii

Chapter 1
INTRODUCTION — 1

Part I
OLD TESTAMENT APOCRYPHAL WRITINGS

Chapter 2
APOCRYPHAL/DEUTEROCANONICAL BOOKS — 27

Part II
OLD TESTAMENT PSEUDEPIGRAPHICAL WRITINGS

Chapter 3
APOCALYPTIC LITERATURE AND RELATED WORKS — 88

Chapter 4
CONCLUDING OBSERVATIONS — 183

Appendix A
CLASSIFICATION AND ANTHOLOGY OF RESURRECTION TEXTS — 185

Appendix B
RESURRECTION PASSAGES IN QUMRAN, JOSEPHUS, NEW TESTAMENT,
AND EARLY RABBINIC JUDAISM   249

Bibliography   268
Index of References   275
Index of Authors   299

Acknowledgments

My interest and study into the Apocrypha and Pseudepigrapha was initially motivated by P. Richard Choi, Professor of New Testament and Chair of the New Testament Department at Andrews University, Michigan. I would like to take this opportunity to thank him for launching me on this rewarding journey.

I also wish to thank Michael E. Stone, (now Emeritus) who was my professor when I was a visiting research fellow at Hebrew University of Jerusalem, Israel, who encouraged me and set me firmly on the track of making this area of study my specialization.

I would also like to thank Casey C. Elledge, Associate Professor at Gustavus Adolphus College, Minnesota, for his invaluable review, feedback, and encouragement of this work.

Thanks also goes to my long-time professor and mentor, Jacques B. Doukhan, Professor of Hebrew and Old Testament Exegesis and Director of the Institute of Jewish-Christian Studies at Andrews University, Michigan. Enjoy your retirement – although now you will probably be busier than ever.

I also wish to convey my sincere gratitude to the administrators of Theologische Hochschule, Friedensau, Germany, where I currently work, for their support and special funding that brought this publication to fruition. Special thanks to Dekon Stefan Höschele, Rektor Roland Fisher, and Kanzler Tobias Koch.

Thank you also to Duncan Burns for all his work in preparing this manuscript for publication and for undertaking the indexing.

Thanks also to Yale University Press for allowing me to license a substantial amount of material from their translation of the Pseudepigrapha, edited by James H. Charlesworth, Executive Editor of this series. I would also like to thank Michael More from Fortress Press for allowing me to licence material from their translation of *1 Enoch* and *2 Baruch* and for waiving the licensing fee; Nicole Tilford from the Society of Biblical Literature Press and John Reeves, Blumenthal Professor of Judaic Studies, University of North Carolina, for allowing me to licence material from his translation of *Sefer Elijah* and for waiving the licensing fee; and the National Council of the Churches of Christ, USA, for their generous free use policy and for use of their translation of the Apocrypha. The support of scholarship by these organizations and individuals is much appreciated.

Finally, but most importantly, I would like to thank my wife, Leanne M. Sigvartsen, for listening to me talk endlessly about this topic, reading my manuscripts, for providing feedback, and encouraging me to complete this work.

Abbreviations

AB	Anchor Bible
ABD	*Anchor Bible Dictionary*
ABRL	Anchor Bible Reference Library
AnBib	Analecta biblica
ANEM	Ancient Near East Monographs/Monografías sobre el Antiquo Cercano
ANF	Ante-Nicene Fathers
AUSDDS	Andrews University Seminary Doctoral Dissertation Series
AUSS	Andrews University Seminary Studies
BAR	*Biblical Archaeology Review*
BCE	Before the Common Era = BC
BETL	Bibliotheca ephemeridum theologicarum lovaniensium
CBQ	*Catholic Biblical Quarterly*
CBQMS	Catholic Biblical Quarterly Monograph Series
COQG	Christian Origins and the Question of God
CE	Common Era = A.D.
CEJL	Commentaries on Early Jewish Literature
ConBNT	Coniectanea neotestamentica or Coniectanea biblica: New Testament Series
CSB	Holman Christian Standard Bible
DCLS	Deuterocanonical and Cognate Literature Studies
DEJ	Dictionary of Early Judaism
DNTB	*Dictionary of New Testament Background*
DSS	Dead Sea Scrolls
Ebib	*Etudes bibliques*
EncJud	*Encyclopaedia Judaica*
EncJud²	*Encyclopaedia Judaica*, 2nd ed.
ET	English Text
FB	Forschung zur Bibel
Hen	Henoch: Studies on Judaism and Christianity from Second Temple to Late Antiquity
HSS	Harvard Semitic Studies
HTR	*Harvard Theological Review*
HUCA	Hebrew Union College Annual
IDB	*The Interpreter's Dictionary of the Bible*
JATS	*Journal of the Adventist Theological Society*

JBQ	*Jewish Bible Quarterly*
JCTS	Jewish and Christian Texts Series
JE	Jewish Encyclopedia
JETS	*Journal of the Evangelical Theological Society*
JNES	*Journal of Near Eastern Studies*
JSJSup	Supplements to the Journal for the Study of Judaism
JSOT	*Journal for the Study of the Old Testament*
JSOTSup	Journal for the Study of the Old Testament: Supplement Series
JSP	*Journal for the Study of the Pseudepigrapha*
JTS	*Journal of Theological Studies*
JWSTP	Jewish Writings of the Second Temple Period: Apocrypha, Pseudepigrapha, Qumran Sectarian Writings, Philo, Josephus
KJA	King James Version Apocrypha
LXT/LXX	Septuagint – Ancient Greek translation of the Hebrew Bible
MGWJ	*Monatsschrift für Geschichte und Wissenschaft des Judentums*
MJT	Melanesian Journal of Theology
MT	Massoretic Text
NICNT	New International Commentary on the New Testament
NIDNTT	New International Dictionary of New Testament Theology
NIDOTTE	New International Dictionary of Old Testament Theology and Exegesis
NovTSup	Novum Testamentum: Supplements
NRSV	New Revised Standard Version
OTL	Old Testament Library
OTP	Old Testament Pseudepigrapha
RBS	Resources for Biblical Studies
SBLDS	Society of Biblical Literature Dissertation Series
SBT	Studies in Biblical Theology
Sem	*Semitica*
SVTP	Studia in Veteris Testamenti Pseudepigrapha
TaNaKh	Hebrew based acronym = Torah – Prophet – Writings = Jewish Bible
TBM	Themes in Biblical Narrative: Jewish and Christian Traditions
Tg. Onq.	*Targum Onqelos*
Tg. Ps.-J.	*Targum Pseudo-Jonathan*
TMP	The Minor Prophets – An Exegetical & Expository Commentary
TNTC	Tyndale New Testament Commentary
TRENT	Traditions of the Rabbis from the Era of the New Testament
TWOT	*Theological Wordbook of the Old Testament*
VC	Vigiliae Christianae
VT	Vetus Testamentum
WBC	Word Biblical Commentary
WGRW	Writings from the Greco-Roman World
WUNT	Wissenschaftliche Untersuchungen zum Neuen Testament
ZAW	*Zeitschrift für die alttestamentliche Wissenschaft*
ZPE	*Zeitschrift für Papyrologie und Epigraphik*

Second Temple Period Literature

Apocrypha/Pseudepigrapha

Apoc. Elij. (C)	*Coptic Apocalypse of Elijah*
Apoc. Elij. (H)	*Hebrew Apocalypse of Elijah*
Apoc. Ezek.	*Apocryphon of Ezekiel*
Apoc. Mos.	*Apocalypse of Moses*
2 Bar.	*2 Baruch*
4 Bar.	*4 Baruch*
1 En.	*1 Enoch (Ethiopic Apocalypse)*
2 En.	*2 Enoch (Slavonic Apocalypse)*
3 En.	*3 Enoch (Hebrew Apocalypse)*
2 Esd	2 Esdras
Gk. Apoc. Ezra	*Greek Apocalypse of Ezra*
Hel. Syn. Pr.	*Hellenistic Synagogal Prayers*
Hist. Rech.	*History of the Rechabites*
Jos. Asen.	Joseph and Aseneth
Jub.	Jubilees
L.A.B.	Liber antiquitatum biblicarum
Lad. Jac.	Ladder of Jacob
L.A.E.	*Life of Adam and Eve*
Liv. Proph.	*Lives of the Prophets*
2 Macc.	2 Maccabees
4 Macc.	*4 Maccabees*
Mart. Ascen. Isa.	*Martyrdom and Ascension of Isaiah*
Odes	*Odes of Solomon*
Ps.-Philo	*Pseudo-Philo*
Ps.-Phoc.	*Pseudo-Phocylides*
Pss. Sol.	*Psalms of Solomon*
Ques. Ezra	*Questions of Ezra*
Sib. Or.	*Sibylline Oracles*
Sir.	Sirach/Ecclesiasticus
T. Ab.	*Testament of Abraham*
T. Adam	*Testament of Adam*
T. Ash.	*Testament of Asher*
T. Benj.	Testament of Benjamin
T. Dan	Testament of Dan
T. Gad	Testament of Gad
T. Iss.	Testament of Issachar
T. Job	Testament of Job
T. Jos.	*Testament of Joseph*
T. Jud.	*Testament of Judah*
T. Levi	*Testament of Levi*
T. Mos.	*Testament (Assumption) of Moses*
T. 12 Patr.	*Testament of the Twelve Patriarchs*

T. Sim.	Testament of Simeon
T. Zeb.	Testament of Zebulon
Vita	Vita Adae et Evae
Wis.	Wisdom of Solomon

Dead Sea Scrolls

4Q386	4QPseudo-Ezekiel^b
4Q388	4QPseudo-Ezekiel^d
4Q416	4QInstruction^b
4Q418	4QInstruction^d
4Q504	4QWords of the Luminaries^a
4Q521	4QMessianic Apocalypse
4Q548	4QVisions of Amramf? ar

Josephus

Ant.	Jewish Antiquities
J.W.	Jewish War

New Testament

Mt.	Matthew
Mk	Mark
Lk.	Luke
Jn	John
Acts	Acts
Rom.	Romans
1 Cor.	1 Corinthians
2 Cor.	2 Corinthians
Gal.	Galatians
Eph.	Ephesians
Phil.	Philippians
Col.	Colossians
1 Thess.	1 Thessalonians
2 Thess.	2 Thessalonians
1 Tim.	1 Timothy
2 Tim.	2 Timothy
Heb.	Hebrews
Jas	James
1 Pet.	1 Peter
2 Pet.	2 Peter
Jude	Jude
Rev.	Revelation

Rabbinic Works

'Abod. Zar.	Avodah Zarah
b.	Babylonian Talmud
B. Bat.	Baba Bathra
Ber.	Berakhot
Chul.	Chullin
Chag.	Chagigah
Deut. Rab.	Rabbah Deuteronomy
Eccl. Rab.	Rabbah Ecclesiastes
Esth. Rab.	Rabbah Esther
Exod. Rab.	Rabbah Exodus
Gen. Rab.	Rabbah Genesis
Ketub	Ketubbot
Lam. Rab.	Rabbah Lamentation
Lev. Rab.	Rabbah Leviticus
m.	Mishnah
Meg.	Megillah
Nid.	Niddah
Num. Rab.	Rabbah Numbers
Pesach	Pesachim
Qidd.	Kiddushin
Rab.	Rabbah
Roš Haš.	Rosh HaShana
Šabb.	Shabat
San.	Sanhedrin
Song. Rab.	Rabbah Song of Songs
Sot	Sotah
t.	Tosefta
Ta'an.	Ta'anith

FIGURES

1.	Two Jewish Diasporas	25
2.	Death and Resurrection in 2 Maccabees	49
3.	Death and Resurrection in Wisdom of Solomon	63
4.	Three-Stage Worldview Presented in *4 Ezra*	71
5.	Death and Resurrection in *4 Ezra* (2 Esd. 3–14)	71
6.	Death and Resurrection in the *Book of Watchers*	110
7.	Death and Resurrection in the *Book of the Epistle of Enoch*	124
8.	Death and Resurrection in *2 Enoch*	130
9.	Death and Resurrection in *3 Enoch*	136
10.	Death and Resurrection in the *Apocalypse of Zephaniah*	157
11.	Death and Resurrection in the *Greek Apocalypse of Ezra*	159
12.	Death and "Resurrection" in the *Vision of Ezra*	160
13.	Death and "Resurrection" in the *Questions of Ezra*	161
14.	The Two-Stage Worldview Presented in *2 Baruch*	165
15.	Death and Resurrection in *2 Baruch*	176

Tables

1.	Order of the books in the Hebrew Bible and the Septuagint	22
2.	Classifications of the Apocryphal writings	26
3.	Literary genres of the Apocrypha	28
4.	Resurrection texts in the Apocrypha	29
5.	The literary structure of Ben Sira's list of heroes (Sir. 44:1–49:16)	34
6.	The links between Malachi 3:19-23 and Sirach 48:1-11	35
7.	The Speeches in 2 Maccabees 7	43
8.	The chiastic structure of the Book of Eschatology	55
9.	Two phases of life after death	58
10.	Parallels between Isaiah 52–53 and the *Wisdom of Solomon* 2–4	62
11.	Titles given to books associated with Ezra	65
12.	The state of the dead (*4 Ezra* 7:81-87, 92-98)	70
13.	Parallels between the resurrection passages in *4 Ezra* 7 and Daniel/Isaiah	75
14.	Judgment scenes in apocalyptic literature	79
15.	The literary genres of the Pseudepigrapha	85
16.	Jewish apocalypses	89
17.	Resurrection texts in the apocalypse category of the Pseudepigrapha	92
18.	The literary structure of *1 Enoch* 22	100
19.	The four holding compartments for the souls in *1 Enoch* 22	103
20.	The literary structure of *1 Enoch* 51	113
21.	The literary structure of *1 Enoch* 61:1-5	115
22.	The literary structure of *1 Enoch* 102:4–104:8	121
23.	The bodily forms of the soul	134
24.	The provenance of the *Sibylline Oracles*	137
25.	Classification of the resurrection texts in the Apocrypha	188

26. Classification of the resurrection texts
    in the Apocalyptic literature and related works   208
27. List of categories used in the five resurrection texts tables 250
28. List of resurrection texts: Dead Sea Scrolls   251
29. List of resurrection texts: Josephus   251
30. List of resurrection texts: New Testament   252
31. List of resurrection texts: Jewish Liturgy   259
32. List of resurrection texts: Rabbinic Literature   259

Our Perennial Yearning for Postmortem Existence or Resurrection

James Hamilton Charlesworth
Princeton

For millennia, as *homo sapiens*, we have universally yearned for a continuation of life. Death is horrifically too final. About 9000 BCE in Jericho, human skulls with clay as "skin" seem to reflect ancestor worship. These "revived skulls" perhaps harbor the dream that loved ones had not disappeared and may be experienced again. About 2400 BCE, and even earlier, in Egypt, the pyramids and the pyramid texts preserve imaginations that some life continued after death, perhaps only for those who seem to be divine, at least partly.

Humans knew that death was certain and everywhere they created beliefs that some existence continued after mortality. In the early first millennium BCE in India, sometimes the concept was a return to an ocean of being, as in Hinduism. A little later and also in India, the authors of the *Upanishads* believed the human is defined by the elements in all living things, including trees. According to one memorable text, crushing a seed a father told a son: "That art Thou." What continued after life was not the person but the elements once collected into a finite human. In a similar fashion, Greek philosophers contemplated something survived the death of a human. Sometimes it was a return to the originating and immortal "atoms," the primordial fundamental element of being.

In Mesopotamia, about the middle of the fifth century BCE (perhaps) thinkers concluded that "resurrection" was promised, for all or for only those who had lived exemplary lives. Resurrection beliefs preserved the hope that not elements but the person, in an immortal form, survived death and decay. Perhaps resurrection beliefs can be located in some later compositions in the Davidic Psalter, but the clearest evidence is in Daniel, which can be dated to the middle of the second century BCE. Daniel may have early portions from Mesopotamia but the final form appeared in ancient Palestine.

Resurrection beliefs are evident within the Dead Sea Scrolls (the Qumran Scrolls) and *On Resurrection* (or *Messianic Apocalypse*; 4Q521) is a document found in Qumran Cave IV. Within the Apocrypha and Pseudepigrapha of the Old Testament, resurrection beliefs appear more and more frequently and can be dated from the second century BCE to the second century CE.

Not everyone in Early Judaism believed in the resurrection of the body after death. Beginning in about the middle of the second century BCE, the Sadducees, who controlled the cult in the Jerusalem Temple, rejected a resurrection belief because they claimed it could not be found in the Pentateuch, which to them was the only *sacra scriptura*. Most of the authors of books collected into the Old Testament (TANAKH) reflect a belief in a lifeless abode of the dead in Sheol and offer no resurrection beliefs.

In contrast to the Sadducees, most Jews did not have a limited or closed canon. For them some of the so-called apocryphal works were also full of God's revelation and were revelatory "sacred scripture." In these compositions, now on the fringes of our canon, are found many passages in which beliefs in a resurrection "of the body" are articulated.

Daniel and the Apocalypse of John are the two apocalypses in the Christian canon. Each of them affirms belief in the resurrection of believers. In the Old Testament Pseudepigrapha and the Qumran Scrolls are many apocalypses. They are attributed to many biblical saints, including Adam, Enoch, Abraham, David, Solomon, Elijah, Isaiah, Jeremiah, and Ezra. Jews placed the abode of the dead who await resurrection in many places on earth or in one of the heavens. Some Jews believed that resurrection occurred only at the Endtime, others harbored the belief that resurrection occurred immediately or soon after death. Many Jews and Christians held to the belief that bones in graves or ossuaries (or in the bellies of beasts or the depths of the sea) did not prove the person had not been resurrected. The Creator had created *ex nihilo*, so to revive life where it had once been was not impossible for the Supernatural One.

Philosophers debate if "resurrection beliefs" are merely the wish becoming the father of the thought. Surely, virtually all humans wish that life does not end so tragically in the ebbing of energy and then life. They would add growing old is a part of dying. How can God be a loving Father if the latter years are the lesser years?

Many Jews today believe that they will be resurrected. In fact, the belief is immortalized in the *Eighteen Benedictions* recited with religious fervor in synagogues. Christians are united by the belief that God raised Jesus from the dead, and confess this common belief liturgically in churches.[1] As one of my closest friends, a surgeon, stated: "Believing in the resurrection is the best insurance policy going."

On the one hand, if there is no resurrection, I would believe in it since it enriches my life and memories of my loved ones, especially my father and mother. On the other hand, living the Jewish-Christian faith creates an existential insight that moves me from believing in Jesus' resurrection to knowing it.

Jan A. Sigvartsen reviews and offers insight into the major passages focused on resurrection in the Apocrypha and Pseudepigrapha, Qumran, Josephus, the New Testament, and Rabbinics. The appendices provide clear avenues to texts and passages. The "tables" provide clarification and point to the major texts. The "figures" provide symbolic images to explore the minds of the ancients and our own rich reflections. Sigvartsen wisely sees the influence of Zoroastrianism in the development of Jewish creative thinking on resurrection and that it is to be distinguished from the Hellenistic belief in the immortality of the soul. The book brings forward the major texts in translation with judicious use of Hebrew and Greek. The book is ideal for classes and private study.

James H. Charlesworth
Princeton
Spring, 2019

---

1. Some ecclesiastical authorities in the USA judge resurrection belief to be a relic of ancient mythology.

Foreword

Resurrection of the dead was in antiquity – and in contemporary theological studies – a celebrated, yet also controverted topic. In historical retrospect, one can appreciate how this insurgent hope that took shape in postexilic Judaism gradually emerged as a landmark eschatological doctrine within Rabbinic Judaism and Early Christianity. Much remains in darkness, however, regarding the formation, conceptual diversity, and social settings of resurrection within earlier Judaism. Monumental tomes have treated vast bodies of evidence; yet there also remains the need for more selective studies of particular features of resurrection.

It is all the more commendable that Jan A. Sigvartsen has concentrated his energies upon one select feature of the problem: the presence of scriptural language and imagery throughout a range of early Jewish and Christian expressions for resurrection. Jon Levenson, in fact, laments the lack of scholarly attention to this problem, calling for a deeper appreciation of the intertextual features of early Jewish discourse of resurrection (Levenson, *Resurrection and the Restoration of Israel*, 185). This unfulfilled desideratum is even surprising, since it has long been recognized that both Daniel 12 and 1 Corinthians 15, two of the most significant canonical expressions of resurrection, both rely heavily upon particular interpretive assumptions about underlying scriptural prophecies. Yet there has been no comprehensive study of this phenomenon among expressions of the afterlife in the broader literature of the Apocrypha, Pseudepigrapha, and other early Jewish/nascent Christian writings.

Sigvartsen's timely volume addresses this pressing need in a thorough exploration of the Pseudepigrapha, which preserve some of the most significant writings for understanding early expressions of resurrection. His study leads the reader on an enlightening journey into the rich interpretive culture that stood behind early references to resurrection. As a result, one may more fully appreciate the possibility that resurrection was not merely directed to the fate of human remains or to retribution *per se*, important as these conceptual problems were within select literary texts. Indeed, expressions for resurrection remained conceptually diverse, and the hope could offer redress to a variety of religious problems. Yet, as Sigvartsen carefully documents, one of the more unifying strands amid the often bewildering evidence is the conviction that resurrection affirmed the integrity of the divine promises to Israel, so fragile and so repeatedly endangered by the historical contexts in which resurrection originally flourished. In so doing, his focused volume presents a reservoir for more fully understanding the interrelationships between scriptural traditions, eschatological hopes, and ancient theodicies that flourish from within the writings of the Pseudepigrapha.

C. D. Elledge
Gustavus Adolphus College

Chapter 1

INTRODUCTION

When compared to ancient Near Eastern literature and archaeological remains, the Hebrew scriptures convey little regarding death and an afterlife.[1] However, it is apparent from scripture that there was certainly an interest in and concern about the topic (see, e.g., Gen. 5:24; Num. 16:33; 1 Sam. 2:6; 28:8-19; 2 Kgs 2:11; Isa. 26:19; Ezek. 37:1-14; Prov. 12:28).[2] The overall impression from a study of the TaNaKh passages relating to the afterlife is that death was not considered the start of the next life, but an end to the present life.[3] שְׁאוֹל (*Sheol*)[4] is the destiny that awaits both the righteous and the wicked (Eccl. 9:1-10), a place where everyone will be equal (Job 3:13-19; Ezek. 32:18-32).[5] The lack of articulate and consistent

---

1. For a brief overview of the Egyptian, Canaanite, Hittite, and Mesopotamian thoughts regarding death and the afterlife, see, e.g.: Volkert Haas, "Death and the Afterlife in Hittite Thought," in *Civilization of the Ancient Near East*, ed. Jack M. Sasson (New York, 1995; repr. in 2 vols., Peabody, MA: Hendrickson, 2006), 2:2021–30, and, in the same volume, Leonard H. Lesko, "Death and the Afterlife in Ancient Egyptian Thought," 2:1763–74; JoAnn Scurlock, "Death and the Afterlife in Ancient Mesopotamian Thought," 2:1883–93; Alan F. Segal, *Life After Death: A History of the Afterlife in the Religions of the West* (New York: Doubleday, 2004), 27–119; Paolo Xella, "Death and the Afterlife in Canaanite and Hebrew Thought," in Sasson, ed., *Civilization of the Ancient Near East*, 3:2059–70.

2. Editorial Staff, Encyclopaedia Judaica, "Afterlife," *EncJud* 2:337.

3. See, e.g., Philip S. Johnston, *Shades of Sheol: Death and Afterlife in the Old Testament* (Downers Grove, IL: InterVarsity, 2002), 65, and N. T. Wright, *The Resurrection of the Son of God*, COQG 3 (Minneapolis: Fortress, 2003), 97.

4. The Hebrew word שְׁאוֹל (*sheol*) is most often translated as ᾅδης (*hades*), "the underworld," in the Septuagint, as *infernus*, "hell," in the Vulgate, and as "grave, pit, hell, death," or as *Sheol* in English translations (see Table 1 in Eriks Galenieks, "The Nature, Function, and Purpose of the Term שְׁאוֹל in the Torah, Prophets, and Writings" [PhD diss., Andrews University, 2005], 4-6).

5. Laurentino Jose Afonso observes that Isa. 14:14-19 and Ezek. 32:17-32 indicate that there are several levels of *Sheol*, and Deut. 26:12, 14 (cf. Jer. 26:7; Hos. 9:4; Job 21:25) alludes to the practice of feeding the dead (even giving a tacit

religious burial rites in the Hebrew Bible may further suggest a lack of interest in the afterlife among religious leaders.⁶ The biblical writers

---

approval for such a practice as long as consecrated food was not used), suggesting that there may be some form of existence in the afterlife. However, he notes that the TaNaKh speaks strongly against the practice of necromancy (Deut. 18:11; Isa. 18:19; 1 Chr. 10:13) and sacrificing to the dead (Num. 25:2-3; Ps. 106:28). Apart from these passages, Afonso argues that "the numerous biblical references to the netherworld are vague and inspired by Ancient Near Eastern folklore" (Laurentino Jose Afonso, "Netherworld," *EncJud* 12:996). Johnston, in *Shades of Sheol*, makes several observations regarding death and afterlife in the Hebrew Scripture. He suggests that there seems to be no great concern with the ongoing fate of the dead (85), no suggestion in either textual or archaeological data indicating a continued interest in the remains of the dead (65), no evidence of a highly developed demonology (166), and no preoccupation with necromancy (ibid.). He notes further, "the Hebrew Bible does not substantiate the scholarly view that veneration of the ancestors was widespread in Israel and that evidence of it was later suppressed. On the contrary, it suggests that, while it may have occurred, it was of marginal importance" (195). Johnston concludes that although there are a few texts which seems "to affirm a continued communion with God after death" (217) or suggests a hope in an eschatological resurrection (218–39), the Israelites were firmly anchored in the present life, serving the God of the living.

Galenieks, however, categorically denies any conscious existence in *Sheol*. His exegetical examination of all the 66 references to the term *sheol* in the TaNaKh, focusing on its nature, function, and purpose, show that it is consistently "a poetic synonym of the grave" (Galenieks, "The Nature, Function, and Purpose of the Term שְׁאוֹל," 582), and, as such, is never used as a term for a literal netherworld (passim). He observes: "Sheol means no more than the place of the dead or simply the grave in general, where the dead bodies or corpses return to become the dust of the earth (Gen. 2:7; 3:19). On the other hand, the fact that not even one of the 66 references to the term Sheol contains any indication that Yahweh would somehow try to communicate with the dead is strikingly clear and does not need to be commented on" (598). The finality of *Sheol* is further supported by the fact that only two of the 66 *Sheol* passages (1 Sam. 2:6; Job 14:13) indicate that it is merely a temporary place for its habitants (see his Table 19 [600]). Matthew J. Suriano draws a similar conclusion noting that *Sheol* "has two general senses: it is used to refer to a mythologized realm of the dead, or it appears as a type of tomb" (*A History of Death in the Hebrew Bible* [Oxford: Oxford University Press, 2018], 218). He notes that it is "a liminal place, a conceptual boundary between life and death that affects the status of the individual," adding it is a part of the dying process and "the liminality is temporal, referring to the period of time within which the defunct individual is no longer a part of a living community but not yet joined to the ancestors" (246–47).

6. Elizabeth Bloch-Smith observes that the "biblical references to burial are descriptive rather than prescriptive" and "it is impossible to distinguish Israelite

focused on the present life and centered on the covenant relationship between humans and God. The Hebrew Scriptures do not present a fully developed, or rather, a complete, comprehensive, and detailed description of the afterlife. N. T. Wright notes that "the Bible mostly denies or at least ignores the possibility of a future life, with only a few texts coming

from Canaanite burials" during the MB II ("Burials," *ABD* 1:785). Archaeological evidence from the First Temple Period suggests the Israelites provided their dead with gifts and provisions (ibid., 785–9; also see Bloch-Smith's *Judahite Burial Practices and Beliefs about the Dead*, JSOTSup 123 [Sheffield: Sheffield Academic, 1992]). The only detailed description of a funeral in the Hebrew Bible, according to Xella, is that of Abner in 2 Sam. 3:31-36 ("Death and Afterlife," 3:2068). However, the TaNaKh regards proper burial with great importance (the patriarchs and matriarchs, with the exception of Rachel, were all buried in the family tomb at Machpelah [Gen. 23; 49:29-33; 50:25-26], while inappropriate or lack of burial was considered a curse [e.g. Deut. 28:26; Jer. 22:19]). Delbert Roy Hillers notes that there was a great desire by the Israelites "to maintain some contact with the community even after death, through burial in one's native land, and if possible with one's ancestors" ("Burial," *EncJud*² 4:291). This desire is perhaps voiced the strongest by Jacob (Gen. 49:29) and Joseph (Gen. 50:24-25) who both requested that their bodies should be brought back to the promised land (Gen. 50:1-14 describes the fulfillment of Jacob's request while the fulfillment of Joseph's request envelops the Exodus narrative which refers to Joseph's bones in Exod. 13:19 and Josh. 24:32). The practice of family burial gave rise to Hebrew expressions such as: "to sleep with one's fathers," "buried with his fathers," and "to be gathered to one's kin" (e.g. Gen. 25:8; 1 Kgs 11:43; 2 Kgs 8:24). Some maximalist scholars may view these Hebrew expressions and the importance placed on a burial in one's native land with one's ancestors as early evidence of resurrection beliefs. Be that as it may, however, the Second Temple period burial practices differed radically and reflect the strong resurrection hope held during this period (see, e.g., Rachel Hachlili, "Burials: Ancient Jewish," *ABD* 1:789–94, and *Jewish Funerary Customs, Practices and Rites in the Second Temple Period*, JSJSup 94 [Leiden/ Boston: Brill, 2005]).

However, Richard C. Steiner, in his *Disembodied Souls: The Nefesh in Israel and Kindred Spirits in the Ancient Near East, with an Appendix on the Katumuwa Inscription*, ANEM 11 (Atlanta: SBL Press, 2015), notes the Pentateuchal idiom וַיֵּאָסֶף אֶל־עַמָּיו, "and is gathered unto his people" (Gen. 25:8-9, 17; 35:29; 49:29, 33 [cf. 50:13]; Num. 20:24; 27:13; 31:2; Deut. 32:50), "refer[s] to something that occurs after death but before burial – either right before burial (Isaac) or long before burial (Jacob)" (94), implying "the existence of the soul or spirit that leaves the body at death, before interment, and continues to exist in disembodied form" (97).

out strongly for a different view."[7] However, there is little doubt that the Hebrew Scriptures speak of a resurrection belief, Dan. 12:2-3, 13 being the most explicit statement.[8] Collins states that "even if one takes

---

Steiner finds Jacob Milgrom's suggestion that the punishment כָּרֵת, as in the formula וְנִכְרְתוּ הַנְּפָשׁוֹת הָעֹשֹׂת מִקֶּרֶב עַמָּם, "and the souls who are doing [so] shall be cut off from the midst of the people" (Lev. 18:29), is the idiom's antonym (Jacob Milgrom, *Leviticus 1–16: A New Translation with Introduction and Commentary*, AB 3 [New York: Doubleday, 1991], 459–60) "attractive and potentially very important" (Steiner, *Disembodied Bodies*, 99) as these two archaic expressions provide evidence "that ideas about disembodied souls and their punishment in the afterlife were current among the Israelites far earlier than generally assumed" (100). Saliently, Steiner notes that the disembodied soul could still possess a bodily form or shape, adding the Hebrews may have had a hard time conceiving "souls in the shape of anything but a body – a body resembling their own" (123).

7. Wright, *The Resurrection of the Son of God*, 129.

8. John J. Collins states that "the resurrection language is certainly used metaphorically in the Hebrew Bible (e.g. Ezek. 37; Hos. 6:2), but there is virtually unanimous agreement among modern scholars that Daniel is referring to the actual resurrection of individuals from the dead, because of the explicit language of everlasting life. This is, in fact, the only generally accepted reference to resurrection in the Hebrew Bible" (*Daniel: A Commentary on the Book of Daniel*, Hermeneia [Minneapolis: Fortress, 1993], 391–92). Claudia Setzer makes an important observation regarding the use of metaphor: "metaphors cannot communicate if they have nothing to do with the way people think and live. These images in Ezekiel and Isaiah likely are metaphorical, and not literal, but would be meaningless in a context where afterlife is seen as an absurdity" (*Resurrection of the Body in Early Judaism and Early Christianity: Doctrine, Community, and Self-Definition* [Boston: Brill, 2004], 8). Bertrand C. Pryce reached a similar conclusion in his exegetical study on Hos. 5:8–6:6. His multi-faceted approach (including issues of limitation, translation, form, genre, historical context, structural analysis, and lexical survey) which presumes the reliability of the MT, suggests that the resurrection motif should be understood both metaphorically and physically ("The Resurrection Motif in Hosea 5:8–6:6: An Exegetical Study" [PhD diss., Andrews University, 1989]).

Artur A. Stele's theological study of Dan. 12 reveals that this resurrection text is structurally, linguistically, and thematically related to other passages of the book of Daniel. Furthermore, "the presence of the motifs of death, resurrection, retribution, eternal life and judgment," in addition to the "contribution to such major theological themes as the power and absolute sovereignty of God, the Kingdom of God, judgment, creation, and theology of history – all seem to support the suggestion that resurrection is indeed the theological climax of the book" ("Resurrection in Daniel 12 and Its Contribution to the Theology of the Book of Daniel" [PhD diss., Andrews University, 1996], 257–9).

a maximalist view of the evidence for resurrection in the Hebrew Bible,[9] the hope expressed in Daniel 12 was exceptional."[10]

At this point it is important to make a few comments regarding Job 19:25-27, which most Christian maximalist interpreters view as a solid resurrection text. Gordon E. Christo and Jacques Doukhan[11] argue that the book of Job not only expresses a bodily resurrection hope, but that the resurrection statement is found at the chiastic center of the book. Doukhan bases his interpretation of the key word נִקְּפוּ־זֹאת, "is destroyed, this...," on the poetic dynamics of Job 19:25-27, and on Job 10:8-12, which is structural, linguistically, and theologically related. However, Christo acknowledges that most commentaries find this passage perplexing and, as such, disagree with his interpretation,[12] as critical scholars deny any hint of a resurrection hope within the book of Job.

Interestingly, the LXX gives this text a clear resurrection meaning.[13] It translates 19:26a וְאַחַר עוֹרִי נִקְּפוּ־זֹאת, "And after my skin has been

---

9. It could be argued that some maximalist interpreters are continuing the Rabbinical exercise of searching for biblical proof-texts to support an already accepted belief, and in the process are reading more into the Hebrew text than is warranted. However, most interpreters try to stay true to the text. For maximalist interpretations, see, e.g., Andrew Chester, "Resurrection and Transformation," in *Auferstehung-Resurrection: The Fourth Durham–Tübingen Research Symposium, Resurrection, Transfiguration and Exaltation in Old Testament, Ancient Judaism and Early Christianity (Tübingen, September 1999)*, ed. F. Avemarie and H. Lichtenberger, WUNT 2/135 (Tübingen: Mohr Siebeck, 2001), 65–7; Mitchell Dahood, *Psalms*, 3 vols., AB 16-17A (Garden City: Doubleday, 1965–70); Galenieks, "The Nature, Function, and Purpose of the Term שְׁאוֹל"; Leonard J. Greenspoon, "The Origin of the Idea of Resurrection," in *Traditions in Transformation: Turning Points in Biblical Faith*, ed. B. Halpern and J. Levenson (Winona Lake, IL: Eisenbrauns, 1981), 189–240; Gerhard F. Hasel, "Resurrection in the Theology of Old Testament Apocalyptic," *ZAW* 92 (1980): 267–84; Robert Martin-Achard, *From Death to Life: A Study of the Development of the Doctrine of the Resurrection in the Old Testament* (Edinburgh: Oliver & Boyd, 1960); John A. Sawyer, "Hebrew Words for the Resurrection of the Dead," *VT* 23 (1973): 18–34.

10. Collins, *Daniel*, 395.

11. Gordon E. Christo, "The Eschatological Judgment in Job 19:21-29: An Exegetical Study" (PhD diss., Andrews University, 1992), and Jacques B. Doukhan, "Radioscopy of a Resurrection: The Meaning of *niqqᵉpû sōʾt* in Job 19:26," *AUSS* 34, no. 2 (1996): 187–93.

12. Christo, "The Eschatological Judgment in Job 19:21-29," 164–5.

13. It should be note that the LXX tends to give potential resurrection passages in the Hebrew Scripture a more clear and distinctive resurrection message. Moreover,

destroyed," with ἀναστῆσαι τὸ δέρμα μου, "God will resurrect my skin." It is clear that the translator of Job believed in a bodily resurrection since Job 14:14 and the postscript, 42:17, contain a resurrection hope. However, there are several factors speaking against a resurrection interpretation. First, there are no references to Job 19:26 in any of the Second Temple period literature, nor in early rabbinic literature, during the time when the Rabbis examined the TaNaKh for resurrection passages. Christo notes that "Clement of Rome was the first of the early church fathers on record to quote Job 19:25-27 in the context of resurrection [1 Clem 26.3]"; Origen was the first to give this passage a Christological reading (viewing the redeemer of Job 19:26 as a reference to Jesus);[14] Augustine used it as a resurrection proof-text;[15] while Jerome gave the Vulgate the following reading: *et rursum circumdabor pelle mea et in carne mea videbo Deum*, "And I shall be clothed again with my skin, and in my flesh I shall see my God."[16] Second, a strong resurrection hope at the literary center of the composition would seem to destroy the overall philosophical tension in the book as it would provide a satisfactory solution to the problem of theodicy, the core issue of the book. Third, if the book of Job is one of the oldest books in the TaNaKh, as suggested by most maximalist interpreters, who follow the rabbinic view of Mosaic authorship (*b. Bat.* 14b), it raises the question why such a developed bodily resurrection hope did not have a greater impact on later writings of the TaNaKh, especially when it comes to the question of theodicy. One could question how likely it would be to have a strong bodily resurrection hope in the earliest strata of the TaNaKh, followed by a deafening silence until the hope re-emerges and is extensively explored during the Second Temple period.

The explicit resurrection passage of Daniel 12 draws on and alludes to several older biblical passages suggesting that the author must have understood them eschatologically and saw in them a resurrection hope.[17]

---

metaphorical resurrection texts in the MT become individualized in the LXX. For further study, see, e.g., Joachim Schaper, *Eschatology in the Greek Psalter*, WUNT 2/76 (Tübingen: Mohr Siebeck, 1995), and Wright, *Resurrection of the Son of God*, 145–50.

14. Origen, *Commentary on Matthew* 17.29.
15. Augustine, *City of God* 22.29.
16. Christo, "The Eschatological Judgment in Job 19:21-29," 11–12.
17. The "book" mentioned in Dan. 12:1 is most likely the same book described in Exod. 32:32, "the Book of Life," and contains the name of the righteous, those who will survive God's judgment and become citizens of His kingdom (cf. also Isa. 4:2-6;

The most fertile source for ideas and images was the book of Isaiah[18] and, importantly, some of the language was taken directly from Isa. 26:19,[19] which describes the dead who will come back to life and the corpses that will rise up and are commanded to "wake up and shout joyfully, you who live in the ground!"[20] Segal concludes that "it looks like the resurrection prophecy of Daniel 12:1-2 is based on a visionary understanding of Isaiah 66:14 with the imagery of Ezekiel 37."[21]

The close of the First Temple period and the return of the Jews from Babylonian exile heralded much more exploration of the issues of the afterlife among the Jews during the Second Temple Period.

Mal. 3:16-18; Ps. 69:28; and see Angel Manuel Rodriguez, "The Heavenly Books of Life and of Human Deeds," *JATS* 13, no. 1 [2002]: 10–26). This resurrection passage is also using the metaphor of "sleep" for death and "dust" for the destination of the dead, both of which are used widely in the Hebrew Scripture (for sleep = death, see, e.g., 2 Kgs 4:31; 13:21; Jer. 51:39, 57; Nah. 3:18; Ps. 13:3; Job 3:13; 14:12; and for dust = final destination, see, e.g., Gen. 3:19; Isa. 26:19; Ps. 104:29; Eccl. 3:20; 12:7; Job 10:9), and it would be natural to assume that Dan. 12:2 followed this metaphor when using the word "awake" when describing the resurrection. For further reading, see Segal, *Life After Death*, 262–6; Wright, *The Resurrection of the Son of God*, 109–19.

18. The word, לְדִרְאוֹן, "abhorrence," is used only twice in the Hebrew Scriptures, Dan. 12:2 and Isa. 66:24, linking these two passages, indicating that the author of Daniel read Isa. 66 eschatologically and viewed the punishment described in Isa. 66 as the final destiny measured out to the wicked. The word, וְהַמַּשְׂכִּלִים, "the wise," of Dan. 12:3 is closely linked with Isa. 52:13 and 53:11, and the entire theme, the vindication of the persecuted righteous, follows "the scenario with which Isaiah 40–55 reaches its great climax" (Wright, *The Resurrection of the Son of God*, 115).

19. Isaiah 26:19 is a part of the larger apocalyptic unit, Isa. 24–27, which describes the cosmic judgment which will rescue the righteous and resurrect the dead. Although critical scholars may disagree on the nature of this prophesied resurrection, preferring to view this passage as a reference to the promised restoration of the nation of Israel, it is apparent that the author of Daniel understood it as a literal bodily resurrection. Moreover, John Day makes a strong case that Isa. 26:19 is dependent on Hos. 13:14 and Hos. 6 ("A Case of Inner Scriptural Interpretation: The Dependency of Isaiah xxvi.13–xxvii.10 [Eng. 9] and Its Relevance to Some Theories of the Redaction of the 'Isaiah Apocalypse'," *JTS* 31 [1980]: 309–19).

20. For further reading about allusions in Dan. 12:1-3, see Collins, *Daniel*, 391–8; George W. E. Nickelsburg, Jr., *Resurrection, Immortality, and Eternal Life in Intertestamental Judaism and Early Christianity* (Cambridge, MA: Harvard University Press, 2006), 23–42; Wright, *The Resurrection of the Son of God*, 109–19.

21. Segal, *Life After Death*, 264.

The Persian (538–331 BCE), and later the Greco-Roman Empire (331 BCE–5th/6th century CE), made a significant impact on Second Temple Period Judaism. Not only did these powers influence the culture but also the belief system. Scholars argue that increased interest in angels, the battle between good and evil, and the interest in a future bodily resurrection and judgment, as seen in these Jewish writings, were due to the influence of the Zoroastrian religion of the Persians.[22] The belief in an immortal soul, which exists separately from the physical body after the moment of death, could be due to the Hellenization of Judaism.[23]

---

22. Johnston suggests there are also several differences between the Zoroastrian eschatology and the eschatological view appearing in Second Temple Period Jewish literature (see, *Shades of Sheol*, 235–6). There is also a question of dating, most details of Zoroastrian eschatology come from late material (the *Bundahishn*, a ninth-century CE text) which makes it difficult to determine the extent of the influence it had on Judaism. Furthermore, if the date given by the author of the book of Daniel is accurate, and the book is a reliable historical document, a case could be made that Daniel could have influenced the Persians since "the earliest reference to resurrection [in Zoroastrian writings] comes from the fourth century BCE" (ibid., 236). It should not be ruled out that the Jewish resurrection belief could have evolved from the rich fertile ground of the TaNaKh, which presents God as an almighty and just God, who will reward His covenant people and show mercy towards the repentant sinners. Johnston concludes "there was no simple line of development from Persian to Israelite belief" (ibid.). This skepticism to a Zoroastrian background for the resurrection belief is also shared by, e.g., C. D. Elledge, *Resurrection of the Dead in Early Judaism: 200 BCE – CE 200* (Oxford: Oxford University Press, 2017), 45–57; Wright, *The Resurrection of the Son of God*, 124–25; and by Edwin Yamauchi, "Life, Death, and Afterlife in the Ancient Near East," in *Life in the Face of Death: The Resurrection Message of the New Testament*, ed. Richard Longenecker (Grand Rapids: Eerdmans, 1998), 47–9.

23. Wright warns against equating the Greek immortality of the soul concept with the Jewish Second Temple Period concept that the soul is stored somewhere in wait for the eschatological resurrection when it will once more rest in a physical body (Wright, *The Resurrection of the Son of God*, 194–95). The Greek notion that death is something good, since the soul will finally be liberated from its physical prison (body), contradicts the high value Jews place on God's physical creations which permeates Jewish thought (e.g. Gen. 1 states that God was well pleased with all that He had created. This appreciation for the "physical" is also seen in the many blessings, *berakhot*, which are said by observant Jews throughout the day. Interestingly, the first tractate of the Mishnah is titled "*Berakhot*," Blessings).

Steiner makes a compelling case that the ancient Israelites would most likely have been able to conceive of "a disembodied נפש" long before their interaction

1. Introduction

The question of theodicy is a central theme in the Hebrew Scriptures (e.g. Gen. 18:17-32; Lev. 16; Job),[24] but it was during this period that the problem of theodicy became more apparent for the Jews. The

with Greek culture, as they would otherwise "have been a rather sheltered soul, oblivious to the beliefs and practices found all over the Ancient Near East" (Steiner, *Disembodied Souls*, 9). He adds that "a belief that humans have a soul that survives death is not the same as a belief in disembodied souls. Nevertheless, it seems clear that the two beliefs often go together" (ibid., 22). Steiner considers Ezek. 13:17-21 as the clearest passage from the TaNaKh presenting the נפש, "soul," as something separate from the body. In this passage, Ezekiel condemns the women sorceresses who trap dream-souls with pillow casings (Ezek. 13:17-21), turning them into bird-souls who await the "imminent demise of their owners, unless the latter agree to ransom them" (ibid., 66). Steiner notes although he "clearly condemns the *behavior* of the women" there is no indication that Ezekiel rejected the underlying belief (ibid., 66–7). Based on this key passage, Steiner argues that several additional passages may also reflect a belief in a disembodied נפש, "soul" (e.g. Gen. 35:18; 1 Sam. 25:29; Ps. 116:7; and Song 5:6 – see his discussion, ibid., 68–100). He concludes, "in the light of all this evidence, it is no longer possible to insist that the Hebrew was unable to conceive of a disembodied נפש. If anything, the opposite now appears to be true. The evidence suggests that a belief in the existence of disembodied souls was a part of the common religious heritage of the people of the Ancient Near East" (ibid., 127).

Daniel I. Block makes a similar observation based on his study on Ezekiel's vision of death and afterlife, finding it noteworthy that many scholars still maintain that the ancient Israelites did not believe in a life after death. Block writes, "many believe that the Pharisaic acceptance of the doctrine (see Acts 23:6-9) derives from a limited number of late texts which reflect Persian influence, and that the Sadduceans, who rejected the notion, were the true heirs of Old Testament belief. It is encouraging to see that some have reversed the roles of these two parties and are now insisting that the Sadducean position represented a conscious departure from both Hebrew and common Semitic beliefs" (Daniel I. Block, *By the River Chebar: Historical, Literary, and Theological Studies in the Book of Ezekiel* [Eugene, OR: Cascade, 2013], 198).

24. The question of theodicy not only occupied the minds of biblical writers but was also found in ancient Near Eastern texts as early as the second millennium BCE. For further reading into the question of theodicy in ancient Near Eastern texts, Hebrew Scripture, New Testament, Second Temple Period literature (including Qumran, Philo), and Rabbinic literature, see Antti Laato and Johannes C. de Moor, eds., *Theodicy in the World of the Bible: The Goodness of God and the Problem of Evil* (Leiden: Brill, 2003). For a penetrating study on the Day of Atonement and theodicy, see Roy Gane, *Cult and Character: Purification Offerings, Day of Atonement, and Theodicy* (Winona Lake, IN: Eisenbrauns, 2005).

traditional belief that God would reward the righteous, Torah-observant Jews with a long and prosperous life while cutting short the life of the wicked needed adjustment. This was a period of foreign occupation and oppression; oppression of the righteous poor, religious persecution, and martyrdom. For the Torah-observant Jews, justice had been perverted: the righteous were receiving the curses of the wicked, while the wicked enjoyed the blessings promised the righteous. Only a belief in an afterlife could solve this acute problem. If there was an afterlife, it was argued, God could set things straight and give the righteous and the wicked their proper due.[25]

The Jews of the Second Temple Period borrowed religious and philosophical concepts from Persia and Greece and synthesized and amalgamated these views into their own religious framework. Thus, multiple afterlife beliefs developed and appeared in their literature, in an attempt to solve the problem of theodicy. By the end of this period, belief in a bodily resurrection had become mainstream in both surviving strands of Second Temple Judaism: Rabbinic Judaism and the early Christian Church. It was a central tenet for both communities. For Christians, questioning this doctrine was equated with questioning the historicity of Jesus' resurrection, which was the guarantee for the Christians' salvation hope (e.g. Rom. 6:3-6; 1 Cor. 15; 1 Pet. 1:3-4). For Rabbinic Judaism, questioning this faith would disqualify the person from any share in the world to come: "All Israelites have a share in the world to come… And these are the ones who have no portion in the world to come: (1) He who says, the resurrection of the dead is a teaching which does not derive from the Torah, (2) and the Torah does not come from Heaven; and (3) an Epicurean" (*m. Sanh.* 10:1).

As already mentioned, the literature of the Second Temple Period indicates that there was an increased interest in and speculation about the fate of the righteous and the wicked after the time of death.[26] This period saw the birth of multiple Jewish sects and also multiple views of the afterlife. These views fall into two main categories based on the opinion held regarding the nature of the soul. If the soul was believed to be mortal, the literature describes a range of views like:

---

25. Nickelsburg, *Resurrection, Immortality, and Eternal Life*.
26. J. Julius Scott, Jr., *Jewish Backgrounds of the New Testament* (Grand Rapids: Baker Books, 1995), 278–81. See also Nickelsburg, *Resurrection, Immortality, and Eternal Life*.

1. rejection of an afterlife;[27]
2. a future limited resurrection of all the righteous;[28]
3. a future limited resurrection of the most righteous and the most wicked;[29]

---

27. This view was held by the Sadducees, who belonged to the aristocracy and the priestly class (see Josephus in *Ant.* 13.5.9; 18.1.4 and *J.W.* 2.8.15 and the New Testament writings [Mt. 22:23-33; Mk 12:18-37; Lk. 20:27-40; Acts 23:6-9]). They saw no need for a resurrection to solve the problem of theodicy since they strongly believed in the two-way theology/covenant theology appearing in the Pentateuch which held that God rewards or punishes people for their behavior in the present life. Josephus writes regarding their view on fate: "they suppose that all our actions are in our own power, so that we are ourselves the causes of what is good and receive what is evil from our own folly" (*Ant.* 13.5.9). Interestingly, this view closely resembles the Greek philosophy of the Epicureans. Alan F. Segal notes that although there are no texts which can be identified as penned by the Sadducean sect, there are several biblical and Second Temple Period texts (e.g. Job, Ecclesiastes, Wisdom of Jesus Ben Sira) which harmonize well with the Sadducean philosophy. Segal concludes: "The Sadducees knew that when the Bible is interpreted literally there is scant evidence for any afterlife worth having" (*Life After Death*, 377). For further reading, see Suriano, *A History of Death in the Hebrew Bible*, and Elledge, *Resurrection of the Dead in Early Judaism*, 87–106.

28. Several New Testament passages seem to suggest that only believers in Jesus Christ will be resurrected and receive eternal life (e.g. Rom. 14:10-12; 1 Cor. 15:12-57; 1 Thess. 4:13-18).

29. Nickelsburg observes that religious persecutions during the Second Temple Period caused a problem of theodicy. The righteous, Torah-observant Jews, were martyred without receiving the promised rewards for their pious lives. In fact, it was their adherence to the Torah which caused their deaths (2 Macc. 7). However, the Hasidic Jews noticed that Hellenizing Jews, who disobeyed the Torah, prospered. The resurrection belief became the solution to this problem since God could reward the martyred righteous in the world to come (*Resurrection, Immortality, and Eternal Life*, 32). It is important to note that the clearest resurrection text in the TaNaKh, Dan. 12:1-3, describes a double resurrection, one for the righteous and one for the wicked. However, this passage does not support a universal resurrection, but only a resurrection for some righteous and some wicked (Dan. 12:2). Importantly, the most righteous and the most wicked are resurrected to receive God's justice, the blessing or the curse, suggesting that everyone else has received their just reward. Jacques Doukhan, on the other hand, in his article "From Dust to Stars: The Vision of Resurrection(s) in Daniel 12,1-3 and Its Resonance in the Book of Daniel," in *Resurrection of the Dead: Biblical Traditions in Dialogue*, ed. Geert Van Oyen and Tom Shepherd, BETL 249 (Leuven; Walpole, MA: Peeters, 2012), 850–98, argues for a universal resurrection of the righteous, but only a limited resurrection of the wicked.

4. a future universal resurrection.[30]

If, on the other hand, the soul was believed to be immortal (a separate entity from the body, which could live independently from the body) the literature describes a range of views like:

1. some form of existence in *Sheol*;[31]
2. a belief that the soul left the body to have an independent existence until the day of a universal judgment when it would return to its resurrected body;[32]
3. a belief that the soul left the body at the time of death and would live independently with no need for a future resurrection, since the good or the bad soul would receive its just reward.

---

30. E.g. *2 Bar.* 49-52; *T. Benj.* 10:2-11; *Mart. Isa.* 4:14-22; *Apoc. Mos.* 13; *Ps.-Philo* 3:10; Mt. 25:31-46; Acts 24:15, 21; Rev. 20:4-6, 12-15.

31. The Hebrew word *Sheol* is used 66 times in the TaNaKh and describes the final resting place for the dead (for a comprehensive study on *Sheol* in the TaNaKh, see Galenieks, "The Nature, Function, and Purpose of the Term Sheol") and Suriano, *A History of Death in the Hebrew Bible*, 217–48. The Septuagint translates this word with the Greek term *Hades* which is also the term used in the Pseudepigrapha (*4 Ezra* 4:7-8; 8:53; *Sib. Or.* 3:393, 458; 5:178; *T. Reub.* 4:5; *T. Levi* 4:1; *T. Benj.* 9:5; *3 Bar.* 4:4-6; 5:3) and the New Testament writings (e.g. Lk. 16:23; Acts 2:27, 31; Rev. 1:18; 20:13-14). Segal notes that "like the Greek Hades, it was neither a place of reward nor of punishment inherently, merely the final destination where the dead go" (*Life after death*, 136). Interestingly, Deut. 26:14 suggests some Israelites must have believed in some form of existence in *Sheol* and felt a need to provide food for the dead (see also Jer. 16:7; Hos. 9:4; Job 21:25). This notion is further supported by Saul's use of a medium to request a prophetic message from the dead prophet Samuel (1 Sam. 28:7-19) and ancient Jewish tomb inscriptions (Joseph S. Park, *Conceptions of Afterlife in Jewish Inscriptions: With Special Reference to Pauline Literature*, WUNT 2/121 [Tübingen: Mohr Siebeck, 2000]).

32. According to Josephus and the New Testament writings, the Pharisees were the dominant religious force of the late Second Temple Period which then evolved into Rabbinic Judaism after the destruction of the Jewish temple. They were strong believers in a bodily resurrection (Josephus, *Ant.* 18.1.3 and *J.W.* 2.8.14; Acts 23:6-9; Hippolytus, *Haer.* 28) but they were also influenced by the Greek Platonistic notion that the soul was immortal. They believed that the soul would leave the body at the time of death and exist independently from the body. However, they held that the soul would return to the body at the time of resurrection in order to be judged as one unified entity at the great judgment. This synthesized view appears in, e.g., 2 Esd. 7:32-38; *Apocryphon of Ezekiel* frag. 1.

This last view is similar to the Platonic immortality of the soul concept that strongly influenced Philo's writings.[33] Each of these views sought support in the Hebrew Scriptures, but the different sects connected and interpreted the scriptural passages differently.

Despite the emerging interest in death and the afterlife during the Second Temple Period, there is no definitive study that systematically outlines the numerous afterlife views and analyzes the biblical arguments used in support of the resurrection beliefs within the literature of the Second Temple Period, the Apocrypha and the Pseudepigrapha. Thus, the purpose of the present monograph is to fill this large gap in scholarship, to systematically outline the numerous afterlife beliefs in the Apocrypha and Apocalyptic literature, and identify and analyze the texts from the TaNaKh that support a resurrection belief within Jewish extra-biblical passages, from the Second Temple Period, the Apocrypha and the Pseudepigrapha, which imply or state a belief in resurrection. The afterlife beliefs appearing in the non-apocalyptic literature of the Pseudepigrapha are presented in the companion volume, *Afterlife and Resurrection Beliefs in the Pseudepigrapha*.

---

33. According to Josephus (*Ant.* 18.1.5; *J.W.* 2.8.11), the Essenes believed in the immortality of the soul and was the Jewish religious group which was most closely related to the Platonic afterlife belief. This is also supported by Philo in his description on the Alexandrian therapeutic sect, a branch of the Essenes (J. T. Milik, *Ten Years of Discovery in the Wilderness of Judea*, SBT 26 [London: SCM, 1959]; and Pierre Geoltrain, *Le traité de la Vie Contemplativa de Philon d'Alexandrie*, Sem 10 [Paris: Adrien-Maisonneuve, 1960], 11–29), who "thinking that their mortal life has already come to one end," thus believing that they were already partaking in the eschatological life, gave all their possessions away (Philo, *Contempl. Life* 11-13). However, the Dead Sea Scrolls and Hippolytus of Rome (*Haer.* 27.1) suggest that the Essenes did believe in a bodily resurrection. Josephus also notes that Eleazar ben Yair, the rebel leader at Masada, appealed to the belief in the immortality of the soul when promoting mass suicide instead of capture by the Romans (*J.W.* 7.8.7). It could be argued that Philo Judaeus was one of the strongest advocates of the immortality of the soul doctrine without mentioning a bodily resurrection. Segal observes that Philo attempted to synthesize Greek and Hebrew thought by giving the TaNaKh an allegorical reading, believing that "the Hebrew Bible not only illustrates Greek philosophical views through allegory (as do the *Iliad* and *Odyssey*, according to the Greek commentators) but morally surpasses them. For Philo, Greek philosophers and the Hebrew Bible told the same philosophical truth" (*Life After Death*, 368). For an insightful discussion on the Dead Sea Scrolls and the resurrection, see Elledge, *Resurrection of the Dead in Early Judaism*, 150–74.

The reader should be aware that the acronym TaNaKh is used here anachronistically as it is difficult to know what constituted "scripture" or which literary composition was considered authoritative or canonical by differing religious communities during the Second Temple Period. Even in the case of the Qumran community and the Dead Sea Scrolls, it is difficult to know whether the community considered all these scrolls sacred and authoritative, or whether the number of copies of specific scrolls reveals something regarding their authoritative standing. The Dead Sea Scrolls could even have been a part of a library collection and, as such, a certain scroll may not necessarily reflect the ethos of the community nor provide reliable insight into its authoritative nature within that community. It was only when sacred texts were collected into codices that the canon became rigid, as it became necessary to decide which texts should be included and which texts should be left out.

The canon was rather fluid during this period, at least in the earlier part thereof. Therefore, this study uses the acronym TaNaKh out of convenience as it is the most neutral term for the body of literature recognized as sacred by both present-day Jewish and Christian communities.

Why this Study Is Needed

There are several studies on the beliefs in the resurrection, immortality, and eternal life in Second Temple Period Judaism.[34] Typically they deal with aspects such as: why the views arose; how the views developed; what the different sects believed about the afterlife; the ancient Near Eastern influence on Jewish beliefs; the archeological findings in ancient Palestine regarding the notions of afterlife; the formation and development of resurrection faith in early Judaism; or the Jewish background for Paul's statements on the resurrection in the New Testament. However, there is no definitive study that systematically outlines the numerous afterlife

---

34. Hans Clements Caesarius Cavallin, *Life After Death: Paul's Argument for the Resurrection of the Dead in 1 Cor. 15 – Part 1: An Enquiry into the Jewish Background*, ConBNT 7:1 (Lund: CWK Gleerup, 1974); Elledge, *Resurrection of the Dead in Early Judaism*; Ohyun Kwon, "The Formation and Development of Resurrection Faith in Early Judaism" (PhD diss., New York University, 1984); Senzo Nagakubo, "Investigation into Jewish Concepts of Afterlife in the Beth She'arim Greek Inscriptions" (PhD diss., Duke University, 1974); Nickelsburg, *Resurrection, Immortality, and Eternal Life in Intertestamental Judaism*; Park, *Conceptions of Afterlife in Jewish Inscriptions*; Daniel Patte, *Early Jewish Hermeneutic in Palestine*, SBLDS 22 (Missoula, MT: Society of Biblical Literature and Scholars Press, 1975); Segal, *Life After Death*.

views and analyzes the texts used from the TaNaKh in support of a resurrection belief within Jewish extra-biblical passages from the Second Temple Period, which imply or state a belief in resurrection. Neither is this topic addressed within the framework of early Jewish hermeneutics. Jon D. Levenson suggests that "the language and symbolism of resurrection were present and available, perhaps even abundant, long before the literal expectation." This monograph and the companion volume will demonstrate beliefs in resurrection were indeed abundant and, in turn, address Levenson's *desideratum* regarding their abundance, ensuring scholars do not "underestimate the verbal particularity and the textual character of its appearance – points of great significance to the ancient Jewish culture itself."[35] These two monographs also attempt to provide a better understanding of how the TaNaKh was read by Jewish sects during this important period and the role the TaNaKh played in the overall development of the resurrection belief that became a central article of faith in both Christianity and Rabbinic Judaism.

Anthology and Categorization of Texts

Appendix A forms the foundation of this study as it provides a comprehensive list of resurrection passages from Second Temple Period Jewish literature, compiled from the Apocrypha and the Apocalyptic Literature. These passages are divided into tables in which they are categorized and analyzed, noting when a specific resurrection text is referring or alluding to the TaNaKh. Additionally, each table is followed by an anthology of the listed passages to show the larger context of each resurrection statement and to provide the reader easy access to these resurrection texts. These anthologies are highlighted and annotated. The "Reference to the TaNaKh" category includes both "citation" (the author quotes the TaNaKh passage verbatim and includes the textual reference) and "quotation" (the author quotes a TaNaKh passage verbatim without including the textual reference) and is the most objective category. The "Allusion to the TaNaKh" category is rather broad and more subjective as the original author does not quote the TaNaKh passage verbatim, but similarly rephrases, reshapes, or re-purposes the passage. It is apparent, and therefore assumed, that both the original author and the original target audience were aware of the primary source of the allusion.

---

35. Jon D. Levenson, *Resurrection and the Restoration of Israel: The Ultimate Victory of the God of Life* (New Haven: Yale University Press, 2006), 185.

Appendix B provides similar tables for the resurrection passages found in the Dead Sea Scrolls, Josephus, New Testament, Jewish Liturgy, and Rabbinic Literature. However, these passages will not be considered in this study (nor in the companion volume), although references to them will be made throughout this work and the companion volume, when deemed relevant.

This study bears in mind James H. Charlesworth's resurrection categories.[36] He proposes that there are several dimensions of resurrection and found it useful to categorize resurrection passages into the following sixteen categories, even if some of these are overlap. These are as follows:

1. Resurrection of the nation (Isa. 26:19; Ezek. 37:1-12; *T. Jud.* 23:3-5; *T. Mos.* 10:7-10);
2. Raising of a group from disenfranchisement (1QH^a 16.5-6);
3. Raising of the individual from social disenfranchisement (1QH^a 16 [= olim 8]);
4. Raising of the individual from personal embarrassment (1QH^a 10 [= olim 2] cf. 1QpHab 7.4-5);
5. Raising of the individual from the sickbed to health (Ps. 132:3; 1QH^a 17 [= olim 9].4-12; Mk 5:21-43);
6. Raising of the individual from inactivity to do God's will (1QH^a 14 [= olim 6].29-30, 34; cf. 1 Sam. 2:8; Ps. 44:25);
7. Raising of the individual from despondency due to consciousness of sin (11QPsa 19.10-11);
8. Raising of the individual from ignorance to divinely revealed knowledge (1QH^a 19 [= olim 11].12-14);
9. Raising of the individual from meaninglessness in this world to a realizing eschatology (= Experiencing the end time in the present) (1QH^a 11 [= olim 3].19-21; 1QS^b 5.23);
10. Both-And: The author may intentionally collapse any distinction between the present age and the future age (1QS 4.6-8);
11. Raising of Christ from *Sheol* [*descensus ad inferos*] (*Ode* 42:10-14);
12. Raising an apocalyptist into heaven (*2 En.* 1:8 [cf. *2 En.* 8]; 2 Cor. 12:1-3; Rev. 4:1);
13. A spiritual raising up or awakening of an individual (Eph. 5:1, 7-8, 14);

---

36. For more details, see James H. Charlesworth, "Where Does the Concept of Resurrection Appear and How Do We Know That?" in *Resurrection: The Origin and Future of a Biblical Doctrine*, ed. James H. Charlesworth *et al.* [New York: T&T Clark, 2006], 2–17).

14. Raising of the individual from death to mortal life (1 Kgs 17:17-24; 2 Kgs 4:31-37; 13:20-21; Jn 11:1-45);
15. Raising of the individual from death to eternal life (Dan. 12:1-3; 2 Macc. 14; *1 En.* 22–27; 92–105; *T. Jud.* 25.1, 4; 4Q521; *Amidah* [Eighteen Benedictions] 2; Acts 2:22-24; 1 Cor. 15; 1 Thess. 4:15-17; *m. Sanh.* 10; *m. Sotah* 15);
16. Intentional ambiguity.

Chapters 2 and 3 are titled "Apocryphal/Deuterocanonical Books" and "Apocalyptic Literature and Related Works," respectively. Even though the classification of the writings as Apocryphal/Deuterocanonical or Pseudepigraphical may be regarded as artificial and anachronistic, this classification will still be utilized in order to acknowledge the Apocryphal/ Deuterocanonical writings are a part of the *Septuagint* and to show sensitivity towards the faith communities who still regard these writings as a part of their sacred Scriptures (see Table 1 and Table 2). The third chapter considers the literature belonging to the first of five categories utilized by James H. Charlesworth's two-volume collection, *The Old Testament Pseudepigrapha*; they are:

1. Apocalyptic Literature and Related Works.
2. Testaments (Often with Apocalyptic Sections).
3. Expansions of the "Old Testament" and Legends, in this study labeled *Expansions of Stories and Legends*.[37]
4. Wisdom and Philosophical Literature.
5. Prayers, Psalms, and Odes.

The literature belonging to the last four categories (2-5) are considered in the companion volume. Chapters 2 and 3 of the present volume systematically outline the numerous afterlife views held and examine the passages listed in the tables of Appendix A, which are either referring or alluding to texts from the TaNaKh in support of a resurrection belief. All of these passages are a part of the anthology provided in Appendix A. This will provide a better understanding of the numerous afterlife views held during this period and the role the TaNaKh played in the development of these beliefs. In addition, it will reveal which TaNaKh passages were viewed as resurrection passages by the groups of believers who produced these texts.

---

37. It was decided to amend this category label for sensitivity reasons.

The final chapter of this monograph provides a brief concluding remark while the "Summary and Conclusion" chapter of the companion volume summarizes the main findings of both volumes, considers their implications, and concludes with some general observations.

Scope and Delimitations of the Study

There are many passages in the extra-biblical literature of the Second Temple Period which address the topic of an afterlife. However, this study only examines resurrection passages appearing in the Apocrypha and the Pseudepigrapha[38] which refer or allude to the TaNaKh in support of the resurrection belief.

Even though it would be interesting to compare the different textual variations appearing in the original language (e.g. Hebrew, Aramaic and Greek) with textual traditions witnessed in the various translations (e.g. Greek, Latin, Syriac, Coptic, Armenian, Slavonic, Georgian, Ethiopic, Arabic), this would go far beyond the scope of this study. In most cases, the English translation does suffice when determining whether a resurrection passage refers or alludes to the TaNaKh and when identifying the TaNaKh text. Thus, these two volumes primarily examine the English

---

38. Only the literary works included in James H. Charlesworth's two-volume collection of pseudepigrapha (*OTP*) are used in this study. However, these two volumes are by no means a complete collection. Thus, the pseudepigraphical writings that were not included will be a part of the two-volume collection, *Old Testament Pseudepigrapha: More Noncanonical Scriptures*, edited by Richard Bauckham, James R. Davila, and Alexander Panayotov. The first volume was published by Eerdmans in 2013 while the second volume, as of time of writing, is still yet to be published. Most of the texts included in the first volume are relatively late and do not include eschatological material relevant for this study, as such, they have not been included. *Outside the Bible: Ancient Jewish Writings Related to Scripture*, is a three-volume collection of Jewish writings composed in the period between 538 BCE and 200 CE, edited by Louis H. Feldman, James L. Kugel, and Lawrence H. Schiffman, and was published by the Jewish Publication Society of America in 2013. This work goes beyond Charlesworth's two-volume collection as it includes texts also from the Septuagint, Philo, Josephus, and Sectarian Texts. The two-volume work *Early Jewish Literature: An Anthology*, edited by Brad Embry, Archie T. Wright, and Ronald Herms was published by Eerdmans in 2018 is an anthology and provide sample of early Jewish literature, but does not add any additional Pseudepigraphical work not already appearing in Charlesworth's collection. It should be noted that the author is currently concluding a similar study identifying resurrection texts from Philo, Josephus, Qumran Community, New Testament and early Rabbinic Judaism.

translations of the Apocrypha and the Pseudepigrapha, keeping the original language in mind, and considers the resurrection passage in its original language (or in its textual tradition) if it adds value to the analysis or if the English translation is unclear.

References to any relevant passages both in the New Testament and early Rabbinic Literature are made if salient. Given that Jesus, his disciples, and first followers were Palestinian Jews, and given the Jewish educational background of Paul of Tarsus (Acts 22:3-5), who held great influence in the formative years of the early Christian Church,[39] it should be expected, therefore, that Paul's writings are influenced by Rabbinical teaching and the New Testament in general would serve as a witness to late Second Temple Period Jewish thought. Although early rabbinical writings post-date the Second Temple Period, they are still relevant since they often reflect a much earlier theological debate or contain a record of oral traditions attributed to rabbis living during the Second Temple Period. Craig Evans gives the following cautionary note: "Rabbinic literature is notoriously difficult to date. Part of the problem is that a given work, which may have been edited in the Middle Age, may contain a great deal of Tannaic tradition." As a further complication, he adds that "there is also the problem of pseudonymity. Sayings may be credited to a famous Tanna (such as Aqiba or Ishmael), but, in reality, they derive from a much later Amora."[40] Appendix B includes tables of all the resurrection passages from the Dead Sea Scrolls, New Testament, Josephus, and early Rabbinic Literature which are currently being assessed in a separate study by the present author.

---

39. According to tradition, Paul authored thirteen of the epistles of the New Testament and was one of Gamaliel the Elder's (grandson of Hillel the Elder) disciples. This suggests that Paul was educated as a Pharisee and belonged to the more liberal House of Hillel.

40. Craig A. Evans, *Ancient Texts for New Testament Studies: A Guide to the Background Literature* (Peabody, MA: Hendrickson, 2005), 220.

Part I

Old Testament Apocryphal Writings

The Old Testament *Apocrypha*[1] is the Protestant label for the additional texts included in the Septuagint that are included in the Roman Catholic, Coptic, and Eastern Orthodox canons, but not in the Jewish or Protestant canons (see the highlighted books in Table 1). These books are known as *deuterocanonical* by the Roman Catholic, Coptic, and Eastern Orthodox churches, or the *outside books* (ספרים חצונים) in Jewish traditions.[2] George W. E. Nickelsburg adds that this canon-related term is irrelevant since the texts belonging to the Apocrypha were written for, used by, and influential to the community of faith long before any decision regarding the canon was made.[3]

1. The term Apocrypha comes from the Greek word ἀπόκρυφα (neutral plural of ἀπόκρυφος), "hidden things," deriving from the verb ἀποκρύπτω, "to keep secret." It was originally a positive term describing the high value placed on these texts "which were withheld from public knowledge because they were vehicles of mysterious or esoteric wisdom which was too sacred or profound to be disclosed to any save the initiated" (R. H. Charles, ed., *The Apocrypha and Pseudepigrapha of the Old Testament in English*, 2 vols. [Oxford: Clarendon, 1913], 1:viii).

2. For the various definitions of the term Apocrypha by various faith communities and their attitudes towards these writings, see, e.g., Mary Chilton Callaway, "The Apocryphal/Deuterocanonical Books: An Anglican/Episcopal View," xxxv–xxxix; D. A. Carson, "The Apocryphal/Deuterocanonical Books: An Evangelical View," xliv–xlvii; John J. Collins, "The Apocryphal/Deuterocanonical Books: A Catholic View," xxxi–xxxiv; Demetrios J. Constantelos, "The Apocryphal/Deuterocanonical Books: An Orthodox View," xxvii–xxx; Walter J. Harrelson, "The Apocryphal/Deuterocanonical Books: A Protestant View," xl–xliii; and S. J. Tanzer, "A View from History," xxi–xxvi, all in *The Parallel Apocrypha*, ed. John R. Kohlenberger III (New York: Oxford University Press, 1997),

3. George W. E. Nickelsburg, *Jewish Literature Between the Bible and the Mishnah* (Philadelphia: Fortress, 1981), 6; deSilva, "Apocrypha and Pseudepigrapha," 60. It should be noted that these texts were first written on scrolls and not as part of a codex. As such, it becomes difficult to know how these texts were viewed by the various faith communities of the Second Temple Period. The Dead Sea Scrolls serve as a good example, since biblical scrolls were stored together with non-biblical scrolls. The question of canonicity became crucial at the moment the faith community decided to make a codex containing all the books considered inspired and authoritative.

Table 1. Order of the books in the Hebrew Bible and the Septuagint

The Hebrew Bible	The Septuagint
Torah [Law]	**Pentateuch**
Genesis	Genesis
Exodus	Exodus
Leviticus	Leviticus
Numbers	Numbers
Deuteronomy	Deuteronomy
Nevi'im [Prophets]	**Historical Books**
Former Prophets	Joshua
Joshua, Judges, Samuel, Kings	Judges
	Ruth
Latter Prophets	1 Reigns [1 Samuel]
Isaiah, Jeremiah, Ezekiel	2 Reigns [2 Samuel]
The Twelve:	3 Reigns [1 Kings]
Hosea, Joel, Amos,	4 Reigns [2 Kings]
Obadiah, Jonah, Micah,	1 Paralipomenon [1 Chronicles]
Nahum, Habakkuk,	2 Paralipomenon [2 Chronicles]
Zephaniah, Haggai,	*1 Esdras*
Zechariah, Malachi	2 Esdras [Ezra-Nehemiah]
	Esther (with additions)
	Judith
	Tobit
	1 Maccabees
	2 Maccabees
	3 Maccabees
	4 Maccabees
	Poetic Books
	Psalms
	Odes
	Proverbs
	Ecclesiastes
	Song of Solomon
	Job
	Wisdom [of Solomon]
	[Wisdom of] Sirach [Ecclesiasticus]
	Psalms of Solomon
	Isaiah
	Jeremiah
	Baruch
	Lamentations
	Epistle of Jeremiah
	Ezekiel
	Susanna
	Daniel
	Bel and the Dragon

Ketuvim [Writings]	Prophets
Psalms	The Twelve:
Job	Hosea, Amos, Micah, Joel,
Proverbs	Obadiah, Jonah, Nahum,
Ruth	Habakkuk, Zephaniah,
Song of Solomon	Haggai, Zechariah, Malachi
Ecclesiastes	
Lamentations	
Esther	
Daniel	
Ezra-Nehemiah	
Chronicles	

Sara J. Tanzer argues that while the works belonging to the Apocrypha are Jewish, these books were "never formed into one collection by Jews"; rather, they should be viewed as a Christian innovation since there is no evidence that they were ever a part of any Jewish translation of the Hebrew Bible into Greek. Moreover, all "the codices which attest a collection of Apocrypha are late (fourth and fifth centuries C.E.)...do not include all the Apocrypha, and they are Christian."[4] This view is shared by Paul D. Wegner, who concludes, based on the following, that there was no Alexandrian canon represented by the expanded Septuagint canon because:

1. Hellenistic and Palestinian Judaism were more integrated than first assumed.
2. The Apocrypha has a more diverse background than first assumed and the books were not all written in Greek.
3. The prologue of Sirach only mentions the tripartite divisions of the Hebrew Scripture, with no reference to the apocryphal books.
4. There is insufficient evidence that Jewish writers during the Second Temple Period considered the apocryphal books as inspired.[5] It is also important to note that the criteria outlined by Josephus (*C. Ap.* 1.7-8 §§37-42) and early Rabbinic texts (e.g. *m. Yad.* 4.5) would exclude the apocryphal texts from the Hebrew canon.

Regardless of the canonical status of the Apocrypha, Arye Edrei and Doron Mendels argue that the Apocrypha and the Pseudepigrapha became a part of the literary collection of the Greek-speaking Jews living in the western diaspora. In contrast, these books were rejected by the Sages of the Land of Israel and the eastern diaspora, who instead developed

---

4. Tanzer, "A View from History, xxi.
5. Paul D. Wegner, *The Journey from Texts to Translation: The Origin and Development of the Bible* (Grand Rapids: Baker Academic, 1999), 116.

and adhered to the oral tradition (Mishnah, Midrash, and Talmud). The oral tradition spread eastward from the Land of Israel and the Sages of the "Babylonian community became full partners in its development"; however, it did not reach the western diaspora until the ninth century, since they "were unable to decode it." Edrei and Mendels make a strong case that this growing rift between the Greek-speaking western and the Hebrew/Aramaic speaking eastern Diaspora caused by the destruction of the Temple in Jerusalem (the unifying center of Judaism), was due to the language divide (Greek vs. Hebrew/Aramaic) and the system of communication (written vs. oral collection of literature). It is important to note that these two Diasporas (East and West) had the Bible in common and maintained access to it in their own language, a Greek translation (LXX) in the western Diaspora and the Hebrew and an Aramaic translation (Targum) in the eastern. Yet, the two diasporas developed separate literature, written in the west and an oral in the east, which also caused a separate theological and cultural identity.[6] This rift was only healed when the oral tradition was written down and brought to the western diaspora which had by then adopted Hebrew as their "official" language of study.[7] Figure 1 shows the two Jewish Diaspora and is a simplified version of Doran Mendels' map,[8] while Table 2 shows the classification – canonical/ deuterocanonical, or non-canonical/apocryphal – of these books by Jewish sources, as well as the respective canons of the Roman Catholic, Protestant, and the Eastern Churches. It should be noted that books classified as canonical in Table 2 are considered as inspired or canonical by the religious community as the books of the Hebrew Scriptures.[9]

6. Arye Edrei and Doron Mendels, "A Split Jewish Diaspora: Its Dramatic Consequences," *JSP* 16, no. 2 (2007): 95.

7. For further study, see ibid., 91–137, and idem, "A Split Jewish Diaspora: Its Dramatic Consequences II," *JSP* 17, no. 3 (2008): 163–87.

8. Doron Mendels, "Why Paul Went West: The Difference Between the Jewish Diasporas," *BAR* 37, no. 1 (2011): 50–51.

9. Craig A. Evans, *Ancient Texts for New Testament Studies: A Guide to the Background Literature* (Peabody, MA: Hendrickson, 2005), 9. It was due to the Protestant Reformation that the Catholic Church declared these books as fully canonical at the Council of Trent in 1546. Leading up to the Reformation, Catholic scholars were divided; Jerome and Origen recognized the difference between the Hebrew canon and the collection of Old Testament texts used by the Church, referring to the former as the "canonical" texts and the latter as "ecclesiastical" texts, viewing the latter as useful and edifying, but not canonical. Clement of Alexandria and Augustine, on the other hand, considered them a part of an enlarged canonical collection and embraced "the larger collection as of uniform inspiration and value" (deSilva, "Apocrypha and Pseudepigrapha," 59).

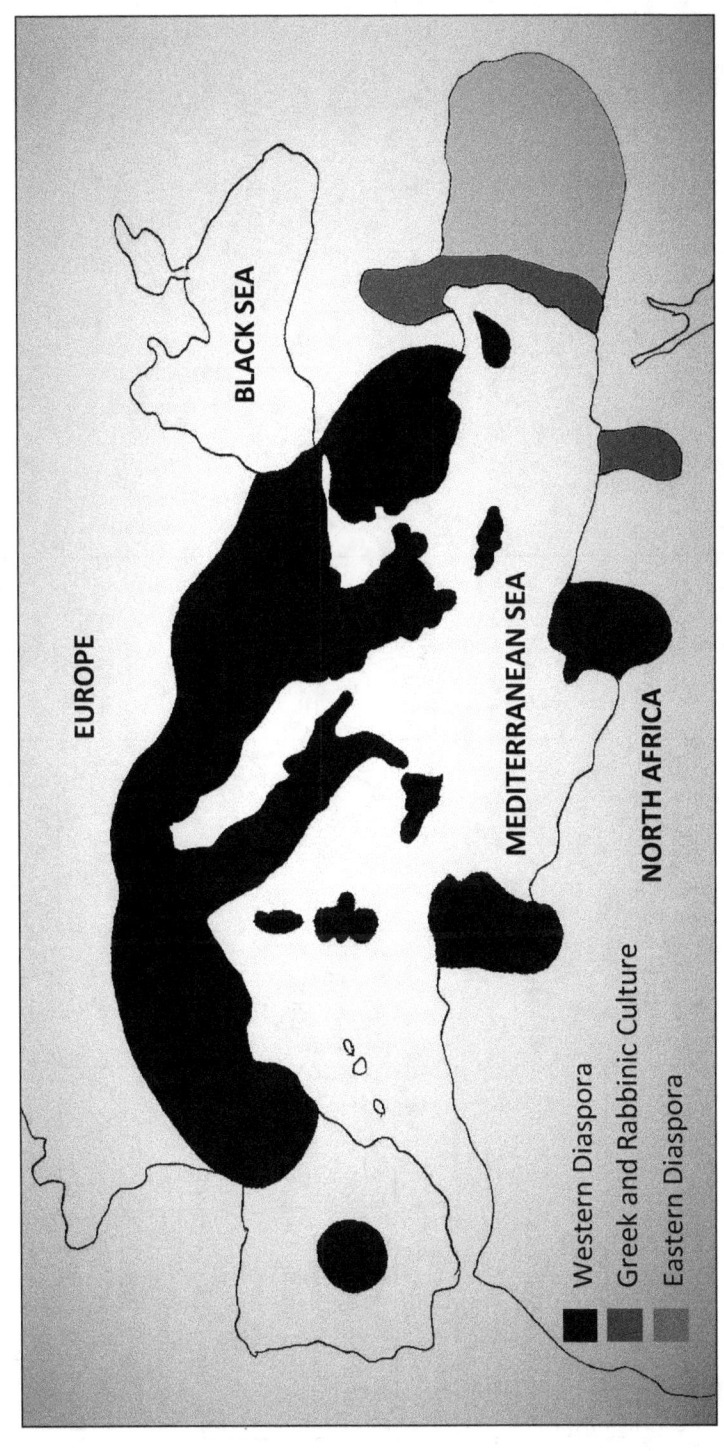

Figure 1. Two Jewish Diasporas. (Created by Leanne M. Sigvartsen.)

Table 2. Classifications of the Apocryphal writings

Book	Jewish Sources	LXX Mss. A.B.	Council of Trent (1546)	Luther	Eastern Church 17th cent.
Tobit	OUTSIDE BOOKS	CANONICAL BOOKS	CANONICAL BOOKS	APOCRYPHA	CANONICAL
Judith					
Ben-Sira					
Wisdom of Solomon					
1 Maccabees					
2 Maccabees					
Additions to Esther Addition A-F					
Book of Baruch					
Epistle of Jeremiah					
Additions to Daniel					
■ Bel and the Dragon					
■ Susanna					
■ The Prayer of Azariah					
■ The Song of the Three Jews					
3 Maccabees					APOCRYPHA
1 Esdras (3 Esdras)[a]		NON-CANONICAL	NON-CANONICAL		
Prayer of Manasseh					
Psalm 151					
4 Maccabees[b]					
2 Esdras[c]					

[a] Rejected by the Council of Trent but included in the Latin Vulgate Appendix (3 Esdras).
[b] In the Appendix to the Greek Bible.
[c] In the Slavonic Bible (3 Esdras) and in the Latin Vulgate Appendix (4 Esdras).

Chapter 2

APOCRYPHAL/DEUTEROCANONICAL BOOKS

The works comprising the Old Testament Apocrypha represent several literary genres (see Table 3) and were mostly written in Hebrew and Aramaic (with the exception of Wisdom of Solomon and 2 Maccabees) which was later translated into Greek and included in the Septuagint. Some of these books are additions to the canonical books of Jeremiah (Baruch and the Letter of Jeremiah), Psalms (Ps. 151), Esther (Additions A-F), and Daniel (The Prayer of Azariah, the Song of the Three Jews, Susanna and Bel and the Dragon), while the others are separate compositions. They are all Jewish (with the exception of the Christian prologue and epilogue of 2 Esdras), written by Jews from the land of Israel and Jews of the Hebrew/Aramaic-speaking eastern diaspora (see Fig. 1) – Israel, Antioch in Syria and Persia (e.g. Prayer of Manasseh and Ps. 151) or Jews living in the Greek speaking western diaspora (see Fig. 1) – Alexandria in Egypt (e.g. Wisdom of Solomon and *3 Maccabees*) and were composed in the period between the third century BCE and the first century CE (see Table 3).[1] Table 3 shows the literary genres of the apocrypha, the date of composition, and the books containing a resurrection belief (bolded and highlighted) based on the analysis of Appendix A. This will help the reader see the extent of this belief in the Apocryphal books.

There are only four passages from the Apocrypha that imply or state a resurrection belief which also refer or allude to the TaNaKh as its foundation for this belief; these are listed in Table 4: Sir. 48:11; 2 Maccabees 7; Wis. 3:1-13a; and 2 Esd. 7:32-38.

---

1. David A. deSilva, *Introduction to Apocrypha: Message, Context, and Significance* (Grand Rapids: Baker Academic, 2002), 16.

Table 3. Literary genres of the Apocrypha

Literary Genre	Apocryphal Texts	Date[a]
Historical Works	1 Maccabees	125–100 BCE
	2 Maccabees	124–50 BCE
	1 Esdras (= 2 Esdras in Slavonic = 3 Esdras in Appendix to Vulgate)	2nd cent. BCE–1st Cent CE
Tales	Tobit	250–175 BCE
	Judith	mid. 2nd cent. BCE
	3 Maccabees (see OT Pseudepigrapha)	1st cent. BCE
	Additions to Esther (Additions A-F)	114–77 BCE[b]
	Additions to Daniel	
	• Bel and the Dragon (LXX Dan 14)	2nd cent. BCE
	• Susanna (LXX Dan 13)	6th–late 2nd cent. BCE
Wisdom Literature	*Wisdom of Sirach (Ecclesiasticus)*[c]	196–175 BCE
	Wisdom of Solomon	220 BCE–100 CE
Pseud-epigraphical Prophetic Literature	Baruch (addition to Jeremiah)	mid. 2nd cent. BCE.
	Letter of Jeremiah (= Baruch ch. 6)	317–306 BCE[d]
Liturgical Texts	Prayer of Manasseh	200 BCE–50 CE
	Psalm 151 (addition to Psalms; see OT Pseudepigrapha)	6th cent. BCE–68 CE
	Prayer of Azariah (addition to Daniel, between 3:23 and 3:24)	175–164 BCE
	Song of the Tree Young Men (addition to Daniel, between 3:23 and 3:24)	> 100 BCE[e]
Apocalypse	*2 Esdras* (= 3 Esdras in Slavonic = 4 Esdras in Vulgate Appendix)	c. 100–3rd cent. CE
Philosophical Encomium	*4 Maccabees* (see OT Pseudepigrapha)	19–54 CE

[a] Dates provided are mainly based on deSilva, *Introducing the Apocrypha*, and to a lesser degree on Evans, *Ancient Texts for New Testament Studies*.
[b] This date is based on the identification and dating of the "fourth year of the reign of Ptolemy and Cleopatra" (Add Est. 11:1). If this verse refers to Ptolemy VIII Soter II and Cleopatra II/III, the additions would be dated to 114–113 BCE, while the additions would be dated to 78–77 BCE if identified with Ptolemy XII Auletes and Cleopatra V.
[c] In the Greek recension of the book, see the discussion on Sirach below.
[d] This date is based on Ep. Jer. 6:3, which states that they will remain in captivity for "up to seven generations." To make this an "accurate" statement, this addition would be dated to no later than 280 (7×40) years after the first (597 BCE) or second (586 BCE) deportation to Babylon.
[e] The approximate time of the completion of the Septuagint version of Daniel which contains the apocryphal additions.

2. Apocryphal/Deuterocanonical Books

Table 4. Resurrection texts in the Apocrypha

Passage		Notes	Resurrection		Classification			
			Imp.	Stat.	Ref.	Allude	Phil.	Assum.
Ecclesiasticus (Sirach)	2:9c; (7:17b); 16:22c; 19:19	These passages in the longer GII recension hints to a resurrection hope	x					x
	46:19-20	Sleep = Death	x					x
	48:11b	Ben Sira's grandson may have added this resurrection hope	x					x
2 Maccabees	6:26	No one will escape the hands of God	x					x
	7	The Martyrdom of the seven brothers		x		x	x	
	12:43-45	Made atonement for the dead. Paul uses this argument in 1 Cor. 15:29		x		x	x	
	14:37-46	Death of Razis		x				x
Wisdom of Solomon	3:1-13a	Body/Soul They will shine forth	x					x
	4:16-5:16	The triumph of the righteous and the final judgment	x			x		x
2 Esdras/ 5 Ezra	2:10-47	Exhortation to good work; Proper burial practice; Replacement theology; Resurrection/Reward of the Kingdom; Sleep ‖ Death		x				x
2 Esdras/ 4 Ezra	4:7-11	Exits of Hades – Entrances of Paradise	x					
	4:33-43	Predestined time; Hades ‖ womb; Souls in the chambers of Hades are impatient; The number needs to be filled	x					
	5:38-40	Only God knows his judgment and the goal of his love	x				x	x
	7:10-16	Two worlds, this world is the test	x					x

Table 4 continued

Passage		Notes	Resurrection			Classification		
			Imp.	Stat.	Ref.	Allude	Phil.	Assum.
2 Esdras/ 4 Ezra	7:26-51	Body + Soul = Resurrection; Universal resurrection (Individuals/nations); Detailed eschatology		×		×		×
	7:66-105	The state of the departed before the judgment		×		×		×
	7:112-115	Universal judgment	×					
	7:117-131	Future promises given to the righteous	×					
	8:1-3	Two worlds. "Many have been created, but only a few shall be saved"	×					×
	8:12-19	Ezra questions God's judgment/justice	×					
	8:37-40	The final destiny of the two ways	×					×
	8:46-54	The final destiny of the righteous	×					
	9:7-13	The wicked will acknowledge God's justice	×					×
	10:10, 15-17	"If you acknowledge the decree of God to be just, you will receive your son back"	×					
	14:34-35	Resurrection/Judgment	×					×

1. Sirach (Ecclesiasticus)

The original Hebrew composition of Sirach probably did not contain a doctrine of retribution and reward beyond death (e.g. Sir. 14:16-19; 17:27-28; 38:19-23; 41:3-4).[2] Instead, Ben Sira adheres to the traditional Deuteronomic view of theodicy, claiming that God gives a person his/her just reward based on the person's adherence to the Law and the Prophets (see, e.g., the Prologue of Sirach; Sir. 1:11–2:17) during his/her life time (e.g. Sir. 11:14-25; 16:12-14), through the way of his/her death (e.g. Sir. 11:26-28), and through his/her legacy (e.g. Sir. 41:5-13; 44:1–50:21). However, there are several passages in the longer Greek recension (GII) of the book which hint at a retribution beyond death (see Table 4)[3] and may have originated with the Greek translation of Ben Sira's grandson or in a later copy.[4] John Collins writes: "It is well known that the Greek translator of Sirach introduced a belief in resurrection at several points in the text…and that the redactor of the Greek text (GII) added further

---

2. John Collins notes that Sir. 41:3-4 provides the "most definitive statement on the finality of death and leaves no room for resurrection or a blessed afterlife" (*Jewish Wisdom in the Hellenistic Age*, OTL [Louisville, KY: Westminster John Knox, 1997], 92).

3. The Greek recension (GII) contains the following additions: "Because his reward is an everlasting gift, with joy" (Sir. 2:9c); "and he keeps them for their day of vengeance" (Sir. 12:6c); "and a scrutiny for all [will come] in the end/at death" (Sir. 16:22c); and "knowledge of the Lord's commandments is life-giving instruction those who do what pleases him will harvest the fruit of the tree of immortality" (Sir. 19:19).

It is interesting to note that the Greek translation of Sir. 46:19-20 interprets death (Hebrew original) as sleep, stating that "after he [Samuel] had fallen asleep, he prophesied" (μετὰ τὸ ὑπνῶσαι αὐτὸν προεφήτευσεν). This choice of words alludes to a resurrection hope since "sleep" suggests that death is not permanent – if you are sleeping you will also wake up from the sleep at one point in the future. This analogy became popular in later Second Temple Period Judaism and was used most famously by Jesus in the New Testament (e.g. Mt. 9:24; 27:52; Mk 5:39; Lk. 8:52; Jn 11:11-14). In the case of Samuel and Elisha (Sir. 48:13-14), Ben Sira's focus is on their powers, even after death, rather than a lasting resurrection or an eschatological resurrection hope. Still, these texts suggest that death was not necessarily final, since there are cases when people came back to life, or, according to the longer Greek recension, will be judged or rewarded after death.

4. Alexander A. Di Lella, "Conservative and Progressive Theology: Sirach and Wisdom," *CBQ* 28 (1966): 145–6; Patrick W. Skehan and Alexander A. Di Lella, *The Wisdom of Ben Sira*, AB 39 (New York: Doubleday, 1987), 201–2.

allusions to the afterlife."⁵ The most interesting of these are Sir. 7:17b and 48:11b, which allude to and quote the TaNaKh, although only the latter text states an eschatological resurrection hope.

Sirach 7:17b notes that the punishment of the ungodly is "fire and worms" (ταπείνωσον σφόδρα τὴν ψυχήν σου, ὅτι ἐκδίκησις ἀσεβοῦς πῦρ καὶ σκώληξ [LXT]), possibly drawing on the eschatological imagery of Isa. 66:22-24 (ὁ γὰρ σκώληξ αὐτῶν οὐ τελευτήσει, καὶ τὸ πῦρ αὐτῶν οὐ σβεσθήσεται [v. 24, LXT]), alluding to some kind of postmortal punishment for the ungodly. If this is the case, it would follow that there would also be some kind of resurrection for the righteous, although the fate of this group is not mentioned in the text. It would be hard to understand how the "fire and worms" could be viewed as a punishment for the ungodly, if their destiny is no different from that of the righteous. Only if the righteous were to receive a different fate, a reward beyond death as suggested by Isaiah, would the warning of Ben Sira make sense and be viewed as an allusion to the resurrection hope.⁶ Howard Clark Kee remarks that "the hellenistic translator has interpreted the reference in the Hebrew text to *fire and worms* as meaning not simply death but the inescapable divine judgment that is soon to come,"⁷ an eschatological punishment which, according to Isaiah, will take place in the newly created heaven and earth (Isa. 66:22).

Sirach can be outlined as following, the relevant section has been highlighted:

---

5. Collins, *Jewish Wisdom in the Hellenistic Age*, 95. Conleth Kearns, *The Expanded Text of Ecclesiasticus: Its Teaching on the Future Life as a Clue to Its Origin*, DCLS 11 (Berlin: de Gruyter, 2011).

6. It should be noted that Isaiah does not suggest that the wicked are in any way conscious and tormented for all eternity like the image of Hell developed later (e.g. Dante's *Inferno*). Rather, Isaiah clearly states that these wicked people are "corpses" (בְּפִגְרֵי הָאֲנָשִׁים/τὰ κῶλα τῶν ἀνθρώπων τῶν παραβεβηκότων), dead bodies. The noun פֶּגֶר appears 24 times in the Hebrew Scripture, and in the majority of these cases it refers to dead corpses (Gen. 15:11 refers to a carcass while Lev. 26:30 and perhaps Ezek. 43:7, 9 refer to idols or "stele"; see T. Alexander, "פֶּגֶר," *NIDOTTE* 3:577). This is the meaning in all the occurrence in the book of Isaiah, including Isa. 66:24 (Isa. 14:19; 34:3; 37:36; 66:24). The only two exceptions are found in 1 Sam. 30:10, 21, where the noun describes the near to death condition of David's men.

7. Howard Clark Kee, ed., *Cambridge Annotated Study Apocrypha: New Revised Standard Version* (New York: Cambridge University Press, 1994), 64, notes on v. 17; see also, John J. Collins, "Ecclesiasticus, or The Wisdom of Jesus Son of Sirach," in *The Oxford Bible Commentary*, ed. John Barton and John Muddiman (New York: Oxford University Press, 2001), 674.

Greek Prologue	
I. Wisdom sayings	(Sir. 1:1–43:33)
II. The Praise of the Fathers	(Sir. 44:1–49:16)
Introduction	(Sir. 44:1-15)
Past Heroes	**(Sir. 44:16–49:16)**
Present Heroes	(Sir. 50:1-24)
III. Conclusion	(Sir. 50:25–51:30)
Epilogue	(Sir. 50:25-29)
Song of Praise	(Sir. 51:1-12)
Alphabetic Prayer	(Sir. 51:13-30)

a. Sirach 48:10-11

In light of the above-mentioned passages, Sir. 48:11b expresses a clear resurrection hope. This verse concludes the hymn in praise of the prophet Elijah (Sir. 48:1-11) which is a part of a historical survey (Sir. 44:1–49:16) listing the great Israelite ancestors of the past (see Table 5) towards the end of the book. In his praise of Elijah, Ben Sira gives the highlights of the prophet's life[8] bracketed by an allusion (v. 1)[9] and a direct quotation (v. 10) from the eschatological conclusion of the book of Malachi (Mal. 4:1 [MT 3:19] and 4:5-6 [MT 3:23-24] respectively). The link with Malachi 4 is further strengthened by Sira's reference to Horeb, where Elijah heard God's judgments of vengeance (Sir. 48:7b || Mal. 4:4 [MT 3:22]). Table 6 highlights the links between Mal. 4:1-6 [MT 3:19-23] and Sir. 48:1-11.

---

8. According to Sir. 48:1-11, these miraculous exploits are: bringing famine by shutting up the heavens (vv. 2-3a || 1 Kgs 17:1); bringing down fire from heaven (v. 3b || 1 Kgs 18:38; 2 Kgs 1:10, 12); raising a corpse from death, Hades (v. 5a || 1 Kgs 17:17-22); sending kings down to destruction (v. 6a || 1 Kgs 21:19-24) and famous men from their sickbeds (v. 6b || 2 Kgs 1:2-4, 6, 16-17); visiting with God at His mountain (v. 7 || 1 Kgs 19:8-18); anointing his successor (v. 8 || 1 Kgs 19:16); and taken to heaven in a chariot with horses of fire (v. 9 || 2 Kgs 2:1-11).

9. כתנור, "like a furnace," describes both the eschatological day of judgment in Mal. 4:1 (MT 3:19) and Elias' prophetic message in the hymn praising prophet Elijah in Sir. 48:1 (in original Hebrew). It is important to note that Malachi gives Elijah a key role in his end-time vision, predicting his "second coming" to herald the day of the Lord. This part of the prophecy is commented on by Sira at the end of the hymn (Sir. 48:10-11).

Table 5. The literary structure of Ben Sira's list of heroes (Sir. 44:1–49:16)

INTRODUCTION – Twelve Categories of Heroes			44:1-15	
TORAH	Enoch		44:16	
	Noah		44:17-18	
	Abraham		44:19-21	Genesis
	Isaac and Jacob	5×	44:22-23e	
			44:23f–	
	Moses		45:5	Exodus–Deuteronomy
	Aaron		45:6-22	
	Phinehas		45:23-26	
	Joshua and Caleb	5×	46:1-10	
PROPHETS	The Judges		46:11-20	Time of Judges
	Samuel		46:13-20	
	Nathan		47:1	
	David		47:2-11	United Kingdom
	Solomon		47:12-22	
	Rehoboam and Jeroboam	5×	47:23-25	
	Elijah		**48:1-11**	The Northern Kingdom
	Elisha		48:12-16	
	FALL OF ISRAEL – Evaluation of History (48:15-16)			
	Hezekiah		48:17-22	The Southern Kingdom
	Isaiah		48:23-25	
	Josiah and Other Worthies		49:1-16	
	Josiah		49:1-3	
	FALL OF JUDAH – Evaluation of History (49:4-7)			
WRITINGS	Jeremiah		49:6b-7	Warning of Coming
	Ezekiel		49:8	Destruction
	Job	3×	49:9	
	Twelve Prophets		49:10	Message of Hope for Israel
	Zerubbabel		49:11	The Post-Exilic Generation
	Jeshua son of Jozadak		49:12	and National Builders
	Nehemiah	3×	49:13	
CONCLUSION – Retrospective			49:14-16	
	Enoch		49:14	
	Joseph		49:15	
	Shem – Seth – Enosh		49:16a	
	ADAM		49:16b	MOST HONORED OF ALL

Reading Sir. 48:1-11, it becomes clear that Sira summarizes all the miraculous exploits of Elijah as recorded in 1 Kings 17–2 Kings 2, and adds the only other reference to Elijah recorded in the TaNaKh, Mal. 4:5, which describes his role at the end of time, at Elijah's "second coming." According to this eschatological prophecy, Elijah will once more help reconcile the people with God, like his famous deed at Mt. Carmel (1 Kgs 18 || Sir. 48:3b), when the hearts of God's people were turned back to YHWH (1 Kgs 18:37, 39). In the typological story, this was to bring true conversion and save the people from the coming judgment of the Baal prophets (1 Kgs 18:40). In the anti-typical story, Elijah will once more bring a message of salvation before the LORD's day of Judgment, to give all people an opportunity to repent and be counted among God's righteous (Mal. 4:2-4 [MT 3:20-22]) and not share in the destiny of the wicked (Mal. 4:1, 3, 6b [MT 3:19, 21, 24b]).[10]

Table 6. The links between Malachi 3:19-23 and Sirach 48:1-11

Malachi 3:19-23 [ET 4:1-6]	Sirach 48:1-11[a]
19כִּי־הִנֵּה הַיּוֹם בָּא בֹּעֵר כַּתַּנּוּר וְהָיוּ כָל־זֵדִים וְכָל־עֹשֵׂה רִשְׁעָה קַשׁ וְלִהַט אֹתָם הַיּוֹם הַבָּא אָמַר יְהוָה צְבָאוֹת אֲשֶׁר לֹא־יַעֲזֹב לָהֶם שֹׁרֶשׁ וְעָנָף:	1עד אשר קם __נביא__ כאש ודבריו כתנור בוער:
20וְזָרְחָה לָכֶם יִרְאֵי שְׁמִי שֶׁמֶשׁ צְדָקָה וּמַרְפֵּא בִּכְנָפֶיהָ וִיצָאתֶם וּפִשְׁתֶּם כְּעֶגְלֵי מַרְבֵּק:	
21וְעַסּוֹתֶם רְשָׁעִים כִּי־יִהְיוּ אֵפֶר תַּחַת כַּפּוֹת רַגְלֵיכֶם בַּיּוֹם אֲשֶׁר אֲנִי עֹשֶׂה אָמַר יְהוָה צְבָאוֹת:	
22זִכְרוּ תּוֹרַת מֹשֶׁה עַבְדִּי אֲשֶׁר צִוִּיתִי אוֹתוֹ בְחֹרֵב עַל־כָּל־יִשְׂרָאֵל חֻקִּים וּמִשְׁפָּטִים:	7והשמיע בסיני תוכחות ובחורב משפטי נק[ם]:
23הִנֵּה אָנֹכִי שֹׁלֵחַ לָכֶם אֵת __אֵלִיָּה הַנָּבִיא__ לִפְנֵי בּוֹא יוֹם יְהוָה הַגָּדוֹל וְהַנּוֹרָא:	10הכתוב נכון לעת להשבית אף לפנ[י]. . .
24וְהֵשִׁיב לֵב־אָבוֹת עַל־בָּנִים וְלֵב בָּנִים עַל־אֲבוֹתָם פֶּן־אָבוֹא וְהִכֵּיתִי אֶת־הָאָרֶץ חֵרֶם:	10cלהשיב לב אבות על בנים ולהבין ש[ב]טי ישרא[ל][b]:
	11אשר ראך ומת. . . .ך[c]. . . . . יה:

10. Douglas Stuart, "Malachi," in *Zephaniah, Haggai, Zechariah, and Malachi*, vol. 3 of *The Minor Prophets: An Exegetical and Expository Commentary*, ed. Thomas Edward McComiskey (Grand Rapids: Baker Books, 1998), 1395–96.

¹"For indeed, the day is coming, burning like a furnace, when all the arrogant and everyone who commits wickedness will become stubble. The coming day will consume them," says the LORD of Hosts, "not leaving them root or branches. ² But for you who fear My name, the sun of righteousness will rise with healing in its wings, and you will go out and playfully jump like calves from the stall. ³You will trample the wicked, for they will be ashes under the soles of your feet on the day I am preparing," says the LORD of Hosts. ⁴"Remember the instruction of Moses My servant, the statutes and ordinances I commanded him at Horeb for all Israel. ⁵Look, I am going to send you Elijah the prophet before the great and awesome Day of the LORD comes. ⁶And he will turn the hearts of fathers to *their* children and the hearts of children to their fathers. Otherwise, I will come and strike the land with a curse." (CSB)	¹Till there arose a prophet like fire, whose words were like a burning furnace. ⁷Who heardest reproofs in Sinai, and judgments of vengeance in Horeb; ¹⁰Who art written down as ready for a season, to make anger to cease before… ¹⁰ᶜTo turn the heart of the fathers to the children, and to give understanding to the tr[ibes of Isra]el ¹¹Happy he that saw thee and died (?)… . . . .

ᵃ Hebrew and translation is taken from A. E. Cowley, and Ad. Neubauer. *The Original Hebrew of a Portion of Ecclesiasticus (XXXIX. 15 to XLIX. 11) together with the Early Versions and an English Translation, Followed by the Quotations from Ben Sira in Rabbinical Literature* (Oxford: Clarendon, 1897), 36–7.
ᵇ The Greek and Syriac version have "tribes of Jacob."
ᶜ Only the tail of the letter remains.

Di Lella suggests an additional allusion in Sir. 48:10c, noting that the phrase ולהבין ש[בטי ישרא]ל, "and to give understanding to the tribes of Israel," derives from the phrase אֶת־שִׁבְטֵי יַעֲקֹב וּנְצוּרֵי יִשְׂרָאֵל לְהָשִׁיב, "the tribes of Jacob and restoring the protected ones of Israel," appearing in the highly charged Messianic passage of Isa. 49:6.[11] Sira connects Isa. 49:6 with the eschatological work of Elijah in Mal. 4:6 (MT 3:24), making Elijah's work universal: "It is not enough for you to be My servant raising up the tribes of Jacob and restoring the protected ones of Israel. I will also make you a light for the nations, to be My salvation to the ends of the earth" (CSB).

The Hebrew of the last two lines of Sira's hymn is unfortunately fragmentary, but Émile Puech suggests the following restoration: "…for you give life, and he will live."[12] As noted earlier, the Greek translation of this verse has a clear resurrection hope and reads: μακάριοι οἱ ἰδόντες σε καὶ οἱ ἐν ἀγαπήσει κεκοιμημένοι καὶ γὰρ ἡμεῖς ζωῇ ζησόμεθα (LXT), "Blessed are those who saw you and slept/died in love; for we shall surely live."[13] Patrick Skehan notes that the corresponding Syriac reads: "Blest is he who shall have seen you and died; but he shall not die, but shall certainly live."[14] Although it is unlikely that the resurrection belief was a part of the original Hebrew hymn, the Greek and Syriac translations show that Elijah's eschatological work contains a resurrection hope. It is significant that this association became a part of Rabbinic tradition (*m. Soṭah* 9:15; *Pesiq. Rab. Kah.* 76a).[15]

b. Concluding Remarks

Allusions and references to the resurrection appear in the Greek version of Sirach (Sir. 2:9c; 7:17b; 12:6c; 16:22c; 19:19; 46:19-20; 48:11b, 13-14) and most of them were probably not a part of the original Hebrew composition. Little is revealed regarding the nature of the resurrection, only that it will happen in the eschatological age. Two texts were considered when looking at the resurrection belief in the book of Sirach. The first text, Sir. 7:17b, reveals the destiny of the wicked, alluding to Isa. 66:22-24. The second text, Sir. 48:1-11, summarizes the life of Elijah (1 Kgs 17–

---

11. Skehan and Di Lella, *The Wisdom of Ben Sira*, 534. This allusion is made even stronger in the Greek and Syriac translation, see Table 6, note b.

12. Émile Puech, "Ben Sira 48:11 et la Résurrection," in *Of Scribes and Scrolls: Studies on the Hebrew Bible, Intertestamental Judaism, and Christian Origins, Presented to John Strugnell on the Occasion of His Sixtieth Birthday*, ed. Harold W. Attridge, John J. Collins, and Thomas H. Tobin (Lanham, MD: University of America, 1990), 81–90.

13. "Fortunate are those who live to see you come, as well as those who have already died in love, for we too shall live" (TEV).

14. Skehan and Di Lella, *The Wisdom of Ben Sira*, 531.

15. Collins, *Jewish Wisdom in the Hellenistic Age*, 96.

2 Kgs 2) and places the resurrection of the righteous as a part of Elijah's eschatological work which will introduce the Messianic age, supported by quoting Mal. 4:1-6 (MT 3:19-24) and alluding to the Servant Songs of Isaiah (Isa. 49:6).

2. 2 Maccabees

2 Maccabees, originally written in Greek, covers a period of about 25 years, beginning with the reign of Seleucus IV Philopator (187–175 BCE) and ending with the defeat of Nicanor, the Seleucid general, by Judas Maccabeus in the spring of 162 BCE (2 Macc. 3:3; 15:20-37). The book easily fits the genre of apologetic historiography due to its pro-Maccabean sentiments and its theological interpretation of the historical events, mixed with the use of Greek rhetoric in its defense and exaltation of Jewish values and traditions. deSilva notes that 2 Maccabees also seeks "to demonstrate the ongoing legitimacy of Deuteronomy's philosophy of history as can be traced out in recent events, as well as the legitimacy of the Jerusalem temple as the focal point of God's protective care and concern."[16]

The two prefixed letters of 2 Maccabees (1:1–2:18), the first dated to 124/123 BCE and the second dated to 164/163 BCE,[17] are addressed to the Jewish Diaspora of Egypt, commanding them to celebrate the festival of Chanukah and make it a part of their calendar. The second part of the

---

16. deSilva, *Introducing the Apocrypha*, 266. Robert Doran argues that 2 Maccabees could also be understood as Temple propaganda, showing God's favor towards the Temple in Jerusalem (*Temple Propaganda: The Purpose and Character of 2 Maccabees*, CBQMS 12 [Washington, DC: Catholic Biblical Association, 1981]). It is important to note that, according to Josephus, there was also a Jewish temple in Leontopolis (located in the Nomus of Heliopolis) during this time-period (*J.W.* 1.1.1; 7.10.2-4), which had been founded by Onias IV who fled to Egypt after his father, high-priest Onias III (for further reading about the high-priests of this crucial period described in 2 Maccabees, see James C. VanderKam, *From Joshua to Caiaphas: High Priests after the Exile* [Minneapolis: Fortress, 2004], 188–226), had been murdered in Jerusalem (Josephus, *Ant.* 12.9.7 §387). However, Doran and Arenhoevel refute that 2 Maccabees contains a polemic against the Egyptian temple: D. Arenhoevel, *Die Theokratie nach dem 1. und 2. Makkabäerbuch* (Mainz: Matthias-Grünewald, 1967), 100–102, and Doran, *Temple Propaganda*, 11–12.

17. Since this letter is undated, some scholars argue that it should be regarded as a much later composition, dated to c. 60 BCE. See the discussion in John J. Collins, *Between Athens and Jerusalem: Jewish Identity in the Hellenistic Diaspora*, 2nd ed., The Biblical Resource Series (Grand Rapids: Eerdmans, 2000), 80.

book[18] chronicles the events preceding the Maccabean revolt, followed by the exploits of Judas Maccabeus, who, with God's help, overthrew the foreign oppressor, then purified and rededicated the Temple of Jerusalem – the key event being celebrated. This conclusion is further supported by the narrative's "universal nature." God and the Martyrs are the heroes of the salvation story as noted by deSilva: "The book's emphasis falls on God's deliverance through any and all agents God chooses, rather than on the contribution of a particular family to the well-being of Israel,"[19] as is the case of 1 Maccabeus. As such, this book serves the same purpose for Chanukah as the book of Esther serves for Purim (alluded to in the concluding remark of 2 Macc. 15:36, which refers to the day of Mordecai), in that they both present the background story for their respective "salvation festival."[20]

Following is an outline of 2 Maccabees. The bolded text specifies the location of the most explicit resurrection passage, which also serves as the turning point of the book:

I. Prefix: Two letters inviting the Jews of the Egyptian Diaspora to celebrate Hanukkah (1:1–2:18)   1st Letter (1:1-9)   2nd Letter (1:10–2:18) II. An epitome of the five-volume work of Jason of Cyrene   The Preface (2:19-32)   Pre-Maccabean Revolt (3–7)   Pre-Maccabean Episodes (3:1-40)   The Hellenistic Reforms – Apostasy (4:1-50)   Jewish Worship suppressed by Antiochus IV (5:1–6:11)   Martyrs of the Persecution (6:12–7:42)   Theological Significance of the Persecution (6:12-17)   Martyrdom of Eleazar (6:18-31)   **Martyrdom of Seven Brothers (7:1-42)**   Maccabean Revolt – Exploits of Judas Maccabeus (8:1–15:37)   Epilogue (15:38-39)

18. 2 Maccabees 2:23 states that the second half of the book is an abridged version of Jason of Cyrene's five-volume work on the Maccabean revolt, which was possibly completed before the death of Judah in 160 BCE since the author of 2 Maccabees ends his epitome with the death of Nicanor, two years earlier. The abridger of the book may have completed his work no earlier than the first letter of the book, dated to 124 BCE (see Table 4).

19. deSilva, *Introducing the Apocrypha*, 274. See also Collins, *Between Athens and Jerusalem*, 82–3.

20. R. Doran, "1 and 2 Maccabees," *DNTB* 660.

2 Maccabees struggles with harmonizing the deuteronomistic principle of just-reward based on observance of the Torah and the martyrdom of the righteous Jews, by presenting an ingenious theological structure which combines the universal aspect of the covenant with a personal eschatology. According to this book, it is the apostasy of the people led by Jason and Menelaus (2 Macc. 4–6) which brought collective punishment on the people, while the martyrdom of the righteous played a pivotal role in "bringing to an end the wrath of the Almighty" (2 Macc. 7:38) thereby reconciling the people with God (2 Macc. 6:12-17; 7:6, 32-33, 37-38; 8:5). 2 Maccabees 8–15 recounts God's miraculous work through his Torah-observant people. DeSilva writes: "They [the martyrs] suffered as part of the nation: but at the same time, their voluntary surrender of their bodies for the sake of God and God's law becomes an efficacious death on behalf of the nation… [J]ust as the sin of individuals brought collective punishment, so the covenant loyalty of individuals can effect reversal."[21]

It is important to note that 2 Maccabees introduces a faith in a bodily resurrection (see Table 4) to deal with the question of theodicy on a personal level. Although the death of the "righteous Torah-observant Jews" atones for the sins of the nation, the heroes of faith do not seem to receive their just reward in this world. Only a future reward, after their resurrection, would solve this problem, and as such, the resurrection belief becomes key in upholding Deuteronomy's philosophy and solves the problem of theodicy.

a. 2 Maccabees 7

2 Maccabees 7 is the only passage that refers/alludes to the TaNaKh when describing the resurrection belief[22] and serves as the central chapter and

---

21. deSilva, *Introducing the Apocrypha*, 275.
22. Although other passages in 2 Maccabees alludes (2 Macc. 6:26) or states a resurrection belief (2 Macc. 12:43-45; 14:37-46), they do not attempt to base this belief on Scripture. In the case of the martyrdom of Eleazar, he argues that he will not try to save his life by pretenses, since this act may lead astray the righteous (v. 25) and his less than honest behavior will be judged by God either in this life or after his death (v. 26). Although Eleazar does not mention a bodily resurrection, it is clear that he believes that he would be held accountable for his action, even after he has died.

2 Maccabees 12:43-45 is especially interesting since it supports the resurrection belief based on the actions taken by Judas' act and his troops upon realizing that their brothers in arms had fallen in the battle due to "the sacred tokens of the idols of Jamnia" worn under their tunics (v. 40). Jonathan Goldstein noted that Jason engages "in a complicated piece of logical gymnastics to prove that Judas believed in the resurrection of the dead" (Jonathan A. Goldstein, *2 Maccabees*, AB 41A [Garden

turning point of the book (see the outline in n. 20). In this chapter, all but two of the resurrection allusions/references (vv. 20c and 40b which are the words of the narrator) have been placed in the speeches given by the heroes, the mother and her seven children. Table 7 contains all the speeches of 2 Maccabees 7, Appendix A provides their full context.

Three interconnected themes emerge from these speeches. The first theme, underlined in Table 7, is introduced by the first son, probably the oldest, who speaks on behalf of his brothers. This is the core issue facing God's people during any time of religious persecution and what in the end caused the Maccabean revolt: Which command do you follow – the one given by God or the one given by the persecutor? The first brother makes his decision clear, he would rather die as a martyr than transgress the laws of God (v. 2b). This sentiment is echoed by the second brother (v. 9b), the mother (vv. 23c and 29a), and in the concluding remarks of the seventh brother (vv. 30b, 36b and 37a).

The second theme, highlighted in *italics* in Table 7, provides the lens through which this chapter, and the entire book, should be understood. According to the Deuteronomistic principle (Deut. 28–32), God blesses or curses his people based on their adherence to his covenant. The mother and her six sons (the seventh son has been so mutilated that he is not able to speak) encourage each other by remembering the Song of Moses (v. 6 || Deut. 32), which promises that God "will vindicate His people and have compassion on His servants when He sees that [their] strength is gone" (Deut. 32:36, CSB). This is the situation in which they find themselves. They have run out of options, but they have not given up on God, so they cling to his Covenant, in the hope that God will show them compassion.

City, NY: Doubleday, 1983], 449). Jason argues that Judas' act of collecting two thousand drachmas of silver to provide for a sin offering and prayers on behalf of the dead soldiers would have been foolish and superfluous unless he was expecting that this deed would somehow be helpful and bring atonement for the sin they had committed. From this, Jason concludes, Judas' intent was to expiate for their grievous acts of idolatry, so they would be able to partake in the resurrection of the righteous and receive the splendid reward awaiting them (vv. 44-45). It should be noted that Paul uses the same "logical gymnastics" when arguing for a resurrection belief in 1 Cor. 15:29 based on the practice of baptizing a person on behalf of (ὑπὲρ) the dead. For a detailed discussion on this text, see Gordon D. Fee, *The First Epistle to the Corinthians*, NICNT (Grand Rapids: Eerdmans, 1987), 762–7.

The last resurrection passage of 2 Maccabees recounts the suicide attempt and death of Jewish revolutionary Razis (14:37-46), and his great belief in a future bodily resurrection. In graphic language Razis "tore out his entrails, took them in both hands and hurled them at the crowd, calling upon the Lord of life and spirit to give them back to him again" (v. 46, NRSV).

This sentiment is restated by the sixth (v. 18) and the seventh son (vv. 32-33 and vv. 37-38), who add that their suffering is deserved since God gives the Covenant curses to the whole nation because of their lack of obedience. However, the seventh son hopes that his and his brothers' great loyalty towards God's Covenant will bring to an end God's wrath and cause him to once more show compassion on his nation (v. 38).[23]

The first and the second theme creates a theological dilemma. According to the second theme, the covenant people are being punished for not adhering to the covenant stipulations – hence the punishment befalling the community by the pagan king is deserved. The first theme, however, does not seem to apply the deuteronomistic principle to a personal level since the brothers are suffering and dying even when they uphold the secrecy of the covenant. The conundrum is that God's covenant is in stark conflict with the king's demands and the brothers are not able to adhere to them both. If they adhere to the king's demands, they break God's covenant and will be punished. On the other hand, if they adhere to God's covenant, they will still suffer punishment and death by the hand of the king.[24] The third theme, the theme of bodily resurrection highlighted in gray in Table 7, solves the predicament. It is introduced in the speech of the second brother (v. 9b) and is reiterated and expanded upon by the third (v. 11b), fourth (v. 14b), and the seventh (v. 36) brother. The most extensive resurrection statements are given by the mother in her two encouraging speeches to her youngest son (vv. 22-23 and vv. 27b-29).

---

23. Deuteronomy notes that when God vindicates his people, "He will avenge the blood of his servants...take vengeance on his adversaries...[and] will purify His land and His people" (Deut. 32:43, CSB). This aspect of the Deuteronomistic principle is also found in the speeches of the brothers, **bolded** in Table 7. The king is warned by the fourth (v. 14b), fifth (v. 17), sixth (v. 19) and three times by the seventh brother (vv. 31, 34-35, 36b) that God would hold him accountable for his heinous deeds against the righteous.

24. Both the universal and individualistic aspects of the Deuteronomistic principle are considered in 2 Macc. 7. The speeches in Table 7 moves from an individualistic view towards a universal view – from a focus on the vindication of the brothers (v. 9b) to the vindication of the whole nation of Israel (v. 38).

2. Apocryphal/Deuterocanonical Books

Table 7. The speeches in 2 Maccabees 7

Verse	LXT/LXX	NRSV
1st SON — 2b	τί μέλλεις ἐρωτᾶν καὶ μανθάνειν ἡμῶν ἕτοιμοι γὰρ ἀποθνῄσκειν ἐσμὲν ἢ παραβαίνειν τοὺς πατρίους νόμους	²ᵇWhat do you intend to ask and learn from us? For we are ready to die rather than transgress the laws of our ancestors.
HEROES — 6	ὁ κύριος ὁ θεὸς ἐφορᾷ [cf. LXX Zech. 9:1; Job. 34:23] καὶ ταῖς ἀληθείαις ἐφ᾽ ἡμῖν [Deut. 33:36] παρακαλεῖται καθάπερ διὰ τῆς πρόσωπον ἀντιμαρτυρούσης ᾠδῆς διεσάφησεν Μωυσῆς [Deut. 31:21] λέγων Καὶ ἐπὶ τοῖς δούλοις αὐτοῦ παρακληθήσεται [Deut. 32:36]	⁶"The Lord God is watching over us [cf. LXX Zech. 9:1; Job 34:23] *and in truth has compassion on us* [Deut. 33:36], *as Moses declared in his song that bore witness against the people to their faces* [Deut. 31:21], *when he said, "And he will have compassion on his servants"* [Deut. 32:36].
2nd SON — 9b	σὺ μὲν ἀλάστωρ ἐκ τοῦ παρόντος ἡμᾶς ζῆν ἀπολύεις ὁ δὲ τοῦ κόσμου βασιλεὺς [Pss. 10:16; 145:13] ἀποθανόντας ἡμᾶς ὑπὲρ τῶν αὐτοῦ νόμων εἰς αἰώνιον ἀναβίωσιν ζωῆς ἡμᾶς ἀναστήσει [LXX, Dan. 12:2]	⁹ᵇYou accursed wretch, you dismiss us from this present life, but the King of the universe [Pss. 10:16; 145:13] will raise us up to an everlasting renewal of life [LXX, Dan. 12:2], because we have died for his law.
3rd SON — 11b	ἐξ οὐρανοῦ ταῦτα κέκτημαι καὶ διὰ τοὺς αὐτοῦ νόμους ὑπερορῶ ταῦτα καὶ παρ᾽ αὐτοῦ ταῦτα πάλιν ἐλπίζω κομίσασθαι	¹¹ᵇI got these [his hands] from Heaven, and because of his laws I disdain them, and from him I hope to get them back again.
4th SON — 14b	αἱρετὸν μεταλλάσσοντας ὑπ᾽ ἀνθρώπων τὰς ὑπὸ τοῦ θεοῦ προσδοκᾶν ἐλπίδας πάλιν ἀναστήσεσθαι ὑπ᾽ αὐτοῦ **σοὶ μὲν γὰρ** ἀνάστασις εἰς ζωὴν οὐκ ἔσται [Dan. 12:2; cf. Isa. 14:20-21; 26:14, 19; 66:24]	¹⁴ᵇOne cannot but choose to die at the hands of mortals and to cherish the hope God gives of being raised again by him. **But for you there will be no resurrection to life!** [Dan. 12:2; cf. Isa. 14:20-21; 26:14, 19; 66:24]
5th SON — 16b-17	ἐξουσίαν ἐν ἀνθρώποις ἔχων φθαρτὸς ὧν ὃ θέλεις ποιεῖς μὴ δόκει δὲ τὸ γένος ἡμῶν ὑπὸ τοῦ θεοῦ καταλελεῖφθαι ¹⁷**σὺ δὲ καρτέρει καὶ θεώρει τὸ μεγαλεῖον αὐτοῦ κράτος ὡς σὲ καὶ τὸ σπέρμα σου βασανιεῖ** [Dan. 8:4, 24-25; 11:36]	¹⁶ᵇBecause you have authority among mortals, though you also are mortal, you do what you please. But do not think that God has forsaken our people. ¹⁷**Keep on, and see how his mighty power will torture you and your descendants!** [Dan. 8:4, 24-25; 11:36]

Table 7 continued

	Verse	LXT/LXX	NRSV
6th SON	18c-19	μὴ πλανῶ μάτην ἡμεῖς γὰρ δι' ἑαυτοὺς ταῦτα πάσχομεν ἁμαρτόντες εἰς τὸν ἑαυτῶν θεόν ἄξια θαυμασμοῦ γέγονεν· [19] **σὺ δὲ μὴ νομίσῃς ἀθῷος ἔσεσθαι θεομαχεῖν ἐπιχειρήσας** [Deut. 28:59; Dan 8:24-25]	[18c]*Do not deceive yourself in vain. For we are suffering these things on our own account, because of our sins against our own God. Therefore astounding things have happened.* [19]**But do not think that you will go unpunished for having tried to fight against God!** [Deut. 28:59; Dan. 8:24-25]
MOTHER	22-23	οὐκ οἶδ' ὅπως εἰς τὴν ἐμὴν ἐφάνητε κοιλίαν [Eccl. 8:17; 11:5] οὐδὲ ἐγὼ τὸ πνεῦμα καὶ τὴν ζωὴν [Gen 2:7 (cf. Gen. 6:17; 7:15, 22); cf. Eccl. 12:7; 2 Macc. 7:23; 14:46] ὑμῖν ἐχαρισάμην καὶ τὴν ἑκάστου στοιχείωσιν οὐκ ἐγὼ διερρύθμισα [23]τοιγαροῦν ὁ τοῦ κόσμου κτίστης ὁ πλάσας ἀνθρώπου γένεσιν [Gen. 2:7, 8, 15; LXX, Gen. 5:1] καὶ πάντων ἐξευρὼν γένεσιν [Eccl. 8:17; 11:5] καὶ τὸ πνεῦμα καὶ τὴν ζωὴν [see v. 22] ὑμῖν πάλιν ἀποδίδωσιν [LXX, Isa. 26:12] μετ' ἐλέους [cf. LXX, Isa. 26:20; 54:7] ὡς νῦν ὑπερορᾶτε ἑαυτοὺς διὰ τοὺς αὐτοῦ νόμους	[22]I do not know how you came into being in my womb [Eccl. 8:17; 11:5]. It was not I who gave you life and breath [Gen 2:7 (cf. Gen. 6:17; 7:15, 22); cf. Eccl. 12:7], nor I who set in order the elements within each of you. [23]Therefore the Creator of the world, who shaped the beginning of humankind [Gen. 2:7, 8, 15; LXX, Gen. 5:1] and devised the origin of all things [Eccl. 8:17; 11:5], will in his mercy [cf. LXX, Isa. 26:20; 54:7] give life and breath [see v. 22] back to you again [LXX, Isa. 26:12], since you now forget yourselves for the sake of the laws.
MOTHER	27b-29	Υἱέ, ἐλέησόν με τὴν ἐν γαστρὶ περιενέγκασάν σε μῆνας ἐννέα καὶ θηλάσασάν σε ἔτη τρία καὶ ἐκθρέψασάν σε καὶ ἀγαγοῦσαν εἰς τὴν ἡλικίαν ταύτην καὶ τροφοφορήσασαν [LXX, Deut. 1:31; Lam. 2:22]. [28]ἀξιῶ σε, τέκνον, ἀναβλέψαντα εἰς τὸν οὐρανὸν καὶ τὴν γῆν καὶ τὰ ἐν αὐτοῖς πάντα ἰδόντα [cf. Exod. 40:11; Isa. 40:26] γνῶναι ὅτι οὐκ ἐξ ὄντων ἐποίησεν αὐτὰ ὁ θεός, καὶ τὸ τῶν ἀνθρώπων γένος οὕτω γίνεται. [29]μὴ φοβηθῇς τὸν δήμιον τοῦτον [cf. Isa. 51:13] ἀλλὰ τῶν ἀδελφῶν ἄξιος γενόμενος ἐπίδεξαι τὸν θάνατον ἵνα ἐν τῷ ἐλέει [Isa. 54:8, 10; 56:1; 64:4-11] σὺν τοῖς ἀδελφοῖς σου κομίσωμαί σε	[27b]My son, have pity on me, I carried you nine months in my womb, and nursed you for three years, and have reared you and brought you up to this point in your life, and have taken care of you [LXX, Deut. 1:31; Lam. 2:22]. [28]I beg you, my child, to look at the heaven and the earth and see everything that is in them [cf. Exod. 40:11; Isa. 40:26], and recognize that God did not make them out of things that existed. And in the same way the human race came into being. [29]Do not fear this butcher [cf. Isa. 51:13], but prove worthy of your brothers. Accept death, so that in God's mercy [Isa. 54:8, 10; 56:1; 64:4-11] I may get you back again along with your brothers.

It should not come as a surprise that these speeches contain a strong resurrection hope. It is the first and the second theme which gives a voice to the strong resurrection belief spoken by the heroes. When the second son declares that he would rather be punished limb by limb than break God's law by eating unlawful swine flesh (v. 7), he also claims that this great show of faithfulness will be rewarded by God, who will resurrect the martyrs to an everlasting renewal of life (v. 9). As such, Nickelsburg observes, the resurrection not only "functions as the means by which God will deliver the brothers from the destruction that Antiochus inflict on them,"[25] but also a way for God to vindicate his servants. He adds that the brothers will have their bodies restored at the resurrection "as a remedy for their bodily tortures. [Since] God will heal what Antiochus has hurt; he will bring to life those whom Antiochus has killed. What God created, he will recreate – in spite of the king's attempt to destroy it (7:22-23, 28-29)."[26]

A case could be made that this strong conviction, voiced by the second brother, derives from a literal reading of Deut. 32:39 ("I bring death and I give life; I wound and I heal") since v. 6 has already drawn the readers' attention to the Song of Moses.[27] Goldstein suggests: "The poem there [Deut. 32] teaches that God is always mindful of Israel: Israel's disasters are divine punishment for sin, not signs that God has deserted His people (Deut. 32:15-30); God will take vengeance on the enemy (Deut. 32:35, 41-43), for whom there is no escape (Deut. 32:39), and He will resurrect and restore the maimed martyrs (ibid)."[28]

In addition to Deut. 32:39, there is a clear reference to Dan. 12:2 in the first resurrection speech given by the second brother (v. 9b). Goldstein proposes that the Greek text, εἰς αἰώνιον ἀναβίωσιν ζωῆς ἡμᾶς ἀναστήσει, is redundant and the literal translation is inelegant: "which resurrect us to an eternal revivification of life." However, this redundancy reflects the language of the Greek version of Dan. 12:2 and its content, which states that the righteous "will be resurrected to eternal life":

| Dan. 12:2 | ἀναστήσονται | οἱ μὲν | εἰς | **ζωὴν** αἰώνιον | | |
| 2 Macc. 7:9 | εἰς αἰώνιον | ἀναβίωσιν | | **ζωῆς** ἡμᾶς | ἀναστήσει |

In this speech, the second brother refers to the first of the two resurrections mentioned in Dan. 12:2, adding his interpretation of this text. He

---

25. Nickelsburg, *Resurrection, Immortality, and Eternal Life*, 121.
26. Ibid.
27. This literal reading of Deut. 32:39 is also attested in Rabbinic writings (e.g. *b. Pesaḥ.* 68a; *b. Sanh.* 91b; *Deut. Rab.* 3:15).
28. Goldstein, *2 Maccabees*, 303.

may view "the time of distress such as never has occurred since nations came into being until that time" (Dan. 12:1) as a reference to the persecution experienced in his day, and considers the "wise" who "lead many to righteousness" (Dan. 12:3) as a description of the martyrs suffering during this persecution, which would include his brothers and himself. If this is the case, the second brother may understand the "wise" as those who, according to wisdom literature, "fear God and keeps His commandments" (Eccl. 12:13), those who would rather die than break the law of God. It is the people who would fall within this category that the second brother believes will be rewarded by the "eternal revivification of life" (v. 9b).

The fourth brother may be expanding on this interpretation of Dan. 12:2 when noting that his persecutor, Antiochus IV Epiphanes, the Seleucid king, will not partake in "the resurrection to life" (v. 14b). Although the fourth brother does not state that the king will be resurrected "to shame and eternal contempt" (Dan. 12:2), he does exclude him from the reward held in store for the righteous. Importantly, the fifth, sixth, and the seventh brothers declare that the king's deeds will not go unpunished (vv. 17, 19, 31, 34-35, 36b), warning him that the all-seeing God will judge him (v. 35), torture him and his descendants (v. 17), and punish him for his arrogance (v. 36b) – all pointing forward to a future punishment, although these speeches do not state clearly whether or not it will happen in this present life or at the resurrection of the wicked.[29]

The two resurrection speeches given by the mother of the seven brothers are especially interesting since they both combine a Greek philosophical argument with the reference to both the Creation story and Hebrew Wisdom Literature (see textual references in Table 7), to derive an "extreme form" of the resurrection belief. She supports the belief

29. Regardless of how the brothers interpreted Dan. 12:2, Jason of Cyrene seems to believe that God judged and punished Antiochus in this life. Jason states that God inflicted the king with worms which caused severe pain and anguish. Moreover, his flesh rotted away before he died a dishonorable death in a foreign land (2 Macc. 9:1-12). He concludes: "So the murderer and blasphemer, having endured the more intense suffering, such as he had inflicted on others, came to the end of his life by a most pitiable fate, among the mountains in a strange land" (2 Macc. 9:28, NRSV). Jason's remark that Antiochus "had thought that he could touch the stars of heaven [τῶν οὐρανίων ἄστρων]" (2 Macc. 9:10, NRSV) may allude to Dan. 12:3, ὡσεὶ τὰ ἄστρα τοῦ οὐρανοῦ, "like the stars of heaven," referring to God's righteous, who will awake to eternal life (Dan. 12:2). If this is the case, Jason's remark should be understood as a reference to Antiochus persecution of the righteous. However, Goldstein (*2 Maccabees*, 355) and Kee (*Cambridge Annotated Study Apocrypha*, 168) believe this verse alludes to the prophecy of Isa. 14:12-19; as such, the phrase would refer to Antiochus' great arrogance towards God.

voiced by her third son, that even if the whole body is destroyed by fire they will recover all the members at the time of the resurrection (2 Macc. 7:11b, also voiced by Razis in 14:46). In her comforting words, she seems to support the doctrine of creation *ex nihilo*, that God created the world out of nothing (v. 28),[30] and combines this belief with her experience as a mother, when the embryo grew in her womb (v. 22), noting that in both cases God was able to create something, the material world or a child, out of nothing. If this is the case, she argues, would not God be able to recreate them again on the day of resurrection and give them once more life and breath. Goldstein summarizes her argument:

> The universe came into being after previously not existing, and so does every member of the human race. A dead human being has, indeed, ceased to exist, but he existed previously. Surely it is more conceivable that existence can be restored to what previously existed than that existence should be conferred on what did not exist! Therefore resurrection is *more conceivable* than the creation and than human reproduction![31]

The mother attempts to persuade her youngest son to uphold God's law and accept temporary nonexistence in faith since this would guarantee his resurrection. This is the only way, she argues, she may get him back together with her other six sons (v. 29).

The speeches also contain other possible sources for the resurrection language (see the scriptural references and allusions in Table 7). References and allusions to Isaiah are especially interesting. Goldstein suggests that the mother is echoing Isaiah 26 in 2 Macc. 7:23. This is a text which reveals that God will vindicate his people by punishing their adversaries (Isa. 26:11, 21) and resurrect the righteous at a future time (Isa. 26:19-20), a fitting passage of hope for the mother who witnessed the suffering of her sons. Nickelsburg notices several additional details in the two central martyr passages of 2 Maccabees, the Eleazar story and the Martyrdom of Seven Brothers, which parallels the Servant Songs of Isaiah, especially Isaiah 52–53.[32] This is also an eschatologically fruitful text, alluding to

---

30. For a discussion of the key phrase, οὐκ ἐξ ὄντων, "out of things that existed," in the statement that "God did not make them out of things that existed" (v. 28), see Goldstein, *2 Maccabees*, 307–11; Jonathan Goldstein's two articles: "The Origins of the Doctrine of Creation Ex Nihilo," *JJS* 35 (1984): 127–35, and "Creation Ex Nihilo: Recantations and Restatements," *JJS* 38 (1987): 187–94; and David Winston, "Creation Ex Nihilo Revisited: A Reply to Jonathan Goldstein," *JJS* 37 (1986): 88–91.

31. Goldstein, *2 Maccabees*, 311.

32. The list of parallels is quoted from Nickelsburg, *Resurrection, Immortality, and Eternal Life*, 130–1.

the resurrection of the suffering servant – his future deeds (Isa. 53:10-12), after he had been cut off from the land of the living (Isa. 53:8). Nickelsburg notes the following parallels between 2 Macc. 6:18–7:42 and the Servant Songs of Isaiah:

2 Maccabees 6:18–7:42	The Servant Songs of Isaiah
The Scribe [Eleazar] refuses to be a hypocrite by pretending to eat swine's flesh, while in reality he is eating his own food (6:21-25).	Of the servant, it is said, "…there was no deceit in his mouth" (53:9).
Eleazar's tormentors think that he is out of his mind because he is willing to suffer (6:29).	In Wis. 5:4, in a speech corresponding to Isaiah 53, the ungodly retract their former wrong opinions, among them the idea that the righteous man's life was madness.
The brothers are beaten with scourges (μάστιγες) (7:1), and the king's men tear off the skin of the second brother's head "with the hair" (7:7).	The servant gives his back to the smiters (μάστιγες) and his cheek to those who pluck out (the hair) (Isa. 50:6 MT).
The brothers are disfigured (7:4, 7).	The servant is disfigured (Isa 52:14; 53:2).
The second brother puts out his tongue, saying that he got it from heaven (7:10-11).	The servant says, "The Lord has given me a tongue…" (Isa. 50:4).
The king is astonished at their capacity to suffer (7:12).	Many were astonished at the servant because of his suffering (52:14).

b. Concluding Remarks

2 Maccabees presents a belief in a bodily resurrection in which every limb of the body, even if completely destroyed by fire, will be restored (2 Macc. 7:11b; 14:46). The book also suggests that it is possible to provide a sin offering and prayers on behalf of the dead to expiate for their sins so they will be able to partake in the resurrection of the righteous and receive the splendid reward awaiting them (2 Macc. 12:44-45). It is important to note that the book does not present the dualistic view of body and soul. The book is silent on the condition of humans in the period between their death and their resurrection. It focuses only on the hope of a future resurrection of the righteous.

The resurrection belief in this book derives from an individualistic interpretation of the Deuteronomistic principle (Deut. 28–32) and a literal reading of Deut. 32:39, in which God will reward martyrs who have died to uphold God's law (2 Macc. 7:6, 9, 11, 23, 29, 36) by giving them eternal life (2 Macc. 7:36). This view is also derived from the brothers' interpretation of Dan. 12:1-3, applying this prophecy to their own experience, considering themselves among the "wise" who will be resurrected to eternal life (Dan. 12:2), language that is clearly reflected in the speech of the second brother (2 Macc. 7:9). However, it is not clear whether 2 Maccabees also presents a belief in a second resurrection for the wicked, who will awake to shame and eternal contempt, although there are some allusions to this belief. Additionally, the resurrection belief is supported by the doctrine of creation *ex nihilo* (2 Macc. 7:28), arguing that God will once more be able to recreate the brothers out of nothing on the day of the resurrection. Lastly, it was noted that there were several references and allusions to the book of Isaiah which also presented a resurrection hope (Isa. 26; 52–53). Figure 2 illustrates the death and resurrection concept presented in the book.

Figure 2. Death and Resurrection in 2 Maccabees.

	Life[a]	Death/ Judgment 2 Macc. 7:6, 9, 11, 23, 29, 36	Resurrection of the Righteous[d] 2 Macc. 7:9, 11b, 36; 12:44-45; 14:46	Eternity
GOD				
WORLD	Person[b]		Righteous Person[e]	
GRAVE			Person[c]	

[a] A future resurrection and life eternal is dependent on a person's adherence to God's law/covenant in this life (2 Macc. 7:6, 9, 33, 36).

[b] The text does not present a dualistic view of body and soul.

[c] It is not revealed what happens to the righteous person in the period between death and resurrection. However, the text seems to suggest that it is possible to intercede for the dead (2 Macc. 12:43-45).

[d] 2 Maccabees presents a limited resurrection view, only pertaining to a righteous person who would rather die as a martyr than break God's law/covenant.

[e] The main focus is on the hope of a future resurrection of the righteous and the text states that there will not be any "resurrection to life" (2 Macc. 7:14) for the evil king.

However, it is unclear from the book if God will measure out all the punishment on the wicked in this world or if there will be any additional future punishment for the dead after their a painful death (2 Macc. 7:19, 31, 34-35; 9:5-12, 28).

~ ~ ~

3. Wisdom of Solomon

The Wisdom of Solomon is a pseudepigraphic work[33] originally written in Greek,[34] most likely by a pious Alexandrian Jew.[35] Due to lack of historical references in this book, scholars have not reached a consensus regarding its dating. David Winston believes the book could have been written anywhere between 220 BCE and 100 CE.[36] However, deSilva observes that "the *terminus a quo* is set by the author's use of the Greek translation of Isaiah, Job, and Proverbs, the first of which was probably available by 220 BCE. The *terminus ad quem* is set by the evident use of the work by several New Testament authors."[37] The many thematic parallels between *Wisdom* and Paul's letter to the Romans, which was written no later than 58 CE,[38] have led scholars to argue that Paul was familiar with this book.

---

33. Although King Solomon is not mentioned by name in this book, the anonymous author used Solomon's voice when expanding on the great value of wisdom (Wis. 6–9) and in his personification of wisdom (Wis. 7), by referring to King Solomon's prayer in 1 Kgs 3:3-9 (Wis. 7:7-12; 8:2, 10-11, 21; 9:4-5) and his description of Lady Wisdom in Prov. 8. Solomonic authorship is ruled out due to the book's Greek nature and there is no evidence that there existed a proto-Hebrew version of the book.

34. David Winston, *The Wisdom of Solomon*, AB 43 (Garden City, NY: Doubleday, 1979), 14–18.

35. The following factors support this assumption: use of Greek; use of Greek philosophical rhetoric; similar thoughts to Philo of Alexandria; central role of the Exodus narrative in the third section of the book (Wis. 11–19); anti-Egyptian polemic against their cult practices (Wis. 11:15-16; 15:18–16:4); general anti-Egyptian sentiments (e.g. Wis. 19:13-17); and the special regard given to the Wisdom of Solomon by the Alexandrian Christians (Collins, *Jewish Wisdom in the Hellenistic Age*, 178; deSilva, *Introducing the Apocrypha*, 132; Daniel J. Harrington, *Invitation to the Apocrypha* [Grand Rapids: Eerdmans, 1999], 55; Moyna McGlynn, *Divine Judgement and Divine Benevolence in the Book of Wisdom*, WUNT 2/139 [Tübingen: Mohr Siebeck, 2001], 10). There is also strong evidence for a single authorship due to the literary unity of the book (Collins, *Jewish Wisdom in the Hellenistic Age*, 179–82; Winston, *Wisdom of Solomon*, 9–18).

36. Winston, *Wisdom of Solomon*, 20–5.

37. deSilva, *Introducing the Apocrypha*, 132.

38. Frederick F. Bruce, *The Letter of Paul to the Romans: An Introduction and Commentary*, 2nd ed., TNTC (Leicester: Inter-Varsity; Grand Rapids: Eerdmans,

Accordingly, he argues that *Wisdom* was written no later than the letter to the Romans.[39] Be that as it may, deSilva believes that the most likely period for this literary composition would be during the early phases of the Roman Empire, when they started to dominate Egypt.[40]

The Wisdom of Solomon is a rhetorical work[41] which was most likely addressed to the faithful Jews of Alexandria[42] who were struggling against the pressure of assimilating into the dominant pagan culture. It uses Greek philosophical rhetoric in an attempt to show the superiority of the Jewish wisdom, ethics, and philosophy – the Jewish way of life. The book makes a strong case that Jewish wisdom is superior to Greco-Roman philosophy (Wis. 6-19) in that the righteous Jews, who are persecuted by the wicked, will be vindicated and rewarded by God (3:1-9; 5:15-16) and will, in turn, condemn the wicked (4:16). In the final judgment at the end of days, the

1985), 13–15; James D. G. Dunn, *Romans 1–8*, WBC 38A (Nashville: Nelson, 1988), xliii.

39. For a survey of the various views held regarding the relation between *Wisdom* and Romans, see Jonathan A. Linebaugh, *God, Grace, and Righteousness in Wisdom of Solomon and Paul's Letter to the Romans: Texts in Conversation*, NovTSup 152 (Leiden: Brill, 2013), 13–20.

40. deSilva gives the following support from the text for this dating: (1) the description in Wis. 14:16-20 fits better "the spontaneous, decentralized development of the imperial cult under Augustus" than "the cult of the Ptolemaic kings of Egypt"; (2) 35 of the terms and phrases used in Wisdom do not appear in secular Greek texts until the first century CE (for a list of these words and phrases, see Winston, *Wisdom of Solomon*, 22–3 n. 33); (3) Wis. 6:1-2 seems to fit a Roman Imperial setting and 14:22 may be a critique of the *pax Romana* (deSilva, *Introducing the Apocrypha*, 132–3). Collins concludes: "The account of the persecution of the righteous has the character of a quasi-philosophical argument about the profitability of justice, rather than of a veiled historical commentary, and the apocalyptic scene that it evokes was traditional by the Roman period" (Collins, *Jewish Wisdom in the Hellenistic Age*, 179).

41. Scholars have had difficulties in determining the literary genre used for the whole book. Some have classified it as a *logos protreptickos*, a didactic exhortation (J. M. Reese, *Hellenistic Influence on the Book of Wisdom and Its Consequences*, AnBib 41 [Rome: Pontifical Biblical Institute, 1971], 119–21; Winston, *Wisdom of Solomon*, 18–20) while others as an encomium, a genre of epideictic rhetoric and demonstrative in nature (Collins, *Jewish Wisdom in the Hellenistic Age*, 181–2). The main problem, as pointed out by Collins, is that various genres have been used in the book. He writes: "He [the author] utilizes apocalyptic traditions in the Book of Eschatology [Wis. 1–6:21], draws heavily on philosophical terminology in the praise of Wisdom [Wis. 6:22–10:21], and develops a homiletical exposition of biblical history in chapters 10–19" (ibid., 182).

42. For a discussion on the intended audience, see deSilva, *Introducing the Apocrypha*, 135–7.

unrighteous will have to acknowledge that they were wrong in their ways (3:10-13a; 4:18–5:14).

This composition is heavily influenced by words and concepts from the TaNaKh, assuming that the reader is well versed in the Jewish Scriptures. It draws on passages like the Suffering Servant of Isaiah 52–53; Lady Wisdom of Proverbs 8; Solomon's prayer in 1 Kgs 3:3-9; the anti-idolatry passage of Isaiah 40–55; Psalms – especially the Messianic psalm of Psalm 2; and relevant passages from Genesis, the Exodus/Wilderness narrative, Numbers, and Daniel.[43]

a. Literary Structure

The following section will take a closer look at the textual references and allusions found at the chiastic center of the eschatological segment of the book, especially Wis. 3:1-13a which deals with the question of theodicy and reveals the ultimate destiny of the righteous and the ungodly. Following is a suggested outline of the Wisdom of Solomon showing a three-part structure. It should be noted that Wisdom 6 functions as a bridge between the first section (Wis. 1–5) and the second section of the outline (Wis. 7–10), summarizing and concluding the former and introducing the themes of the latter.[44] The key text for this study, Wis. 3:1-13a, has been highlighted in grey. Wisdom 10 also functions as a bridge chapter, linking the second section (Wis. 6–9) and the third section (Wis. 11–19) of the structure. It begins by expanding on Wis. 9:18, giving examples of people who were saved by wisdom. By the beginning of Wisdom 11, the composition has moved naturally "from speaking about Wisdom's acts in the third person to adopting the form of a confession of God's work in the second person."[45]

---

43. Ibid., 137–40; Harrington, *Invitation to the Apocrypha*, 56. For further study into potential sources for Wisdom, see C. Larcher, *Études sur le livre de la Sagesse* (Paris: Gabalda, 1969), 85–178; P. W. Skehan, *Studies in Israelite Poetry and Wisdom*, CBQMS 1 (Washington, DC: Catholic Biblical Association, 1971); and cross-references in Kee, *Cambridge Annotated Study Apocrypha*, 38–58.

44. deSilva suggests that Wis. 6:1-11 forms an *inclusio* with 1:1-11 by addressing the rulers (see chiastic structure in the outline), while 6:12-25 introduces the themes of the second section. Moreover, 6:9-11 prepares for the speech of King Solomon in the second section, while 6:21 is a deliberate echo of 1:1 and 6:1 and points back to the first section (*Introducing the Apocrypha*, 130).

45. Ibid.

2. Apocryphal/Deuterocanonical Books

I. Book of Eschatology (1:1–6:21)[a]
   A Addressed to rulers, enjoining pursuit of wisdom (1:1-15)

      B Speech of the ungodly (1:16–2:24)
         a. Introduction to the speech of the wicked (1:16–2:1a)
         b. Speech of the wicked: an analysis (2:1b-20)
         c. Conclusion to the speech of the wicked (2:21-24)

         C Contrasts between the just and the impious (3:1–4:20)
         First diptych: The just/the wicked (3:1-12)
                  Second diptych: Sterile woman/the eunuch vs. generation of the wicked (3:13-19)
                  Third diptych: Praise of virtue vs. useless fruit of the wicked (4:1-6)
                  Fourth diptych: Premature death of the just youth vs. the wicked (4:7-20)

      B′ Speech of the ungodly (5:1-23)
         a. Introduction of the scene of judgment (5:1-3)
         b. Speech of the impious – confesses guilt (5:4-13 [14])
         c. Conclusion of the scene of judgment (5:[14]15-23)

   A′ Addressed to rulers, enjoining pursuit of wisdom (6:1-21)
      Kings are exhorted to understand and to learn (6:1-8)
      The positive motives for learning wisdom (6:9-21)

II. Praise of Wisdom (6:1–10:21)[b]
   A. Kings should seek wisdom (6:1-11)
   B. Description of wisdom (6:12-25)
   C. How to obtain wisdom (7:1-22a)
   D. The nature of wisdom (7:22b–8:1)
   E. The search for wisdom with her benefits (8:2-16)
   F. The prayer for wisdom (8:17–9:18)

III. Homiletic Exposition of Biblical History (10:1–19:22)
   A. Role of wisdom in Israel's early history (10:1-21)
   B1. <u>Seven</u> antitheses associated with the Exodus (11:1-14; 16:1–19:22)[c]
      First: Water/thirst (11:1-14)

   C. Theological reflection on God's justice and mercy (11:15–12:27)
      a. Punishment of the wicked (11:15-20)
      b. God is powerful and merciful (11:21–12:2)
      c. Sins of the Canaanites (12:3-11)
      d. Sovereignty and mercy of God (12:12-18)
      e. God's lessons for Israel (12:19-22)
      f. Punishment of the Egyptians (12:23-27)

D. Excursus on idolatry (13:1–15:19)
      a. Nature worship (13:1-9)
      b. Foolishness of idolatry (13:10–14:11)
      c. Origin and Evils of idolatry (14:12-31)
      d. Worship of God vs. idolatry (15:1-19)

   B2. Second: Animals/suffering (16:1-4)
       Third: Plagues – God has power over life and death (16:5-14)
       Fourth: Curse/blessing from heaven (16:15-29)
       Fifth: Darkness/light (17:1–18:4)
       Sixth: Death (18:5-25)
       Seventh: Red Sea (19:1-22)
   E. Concluding observation (19:22)

---

[a] This chiastic structure of the first section is suggested by Michael Kolarcik, *The Ambiguity of Death in the Book of Wisdom 1–6: A Study of Literary Structure and Interpretation*, AnBib 127 (Rome: Pontificio Istituto Biblico, 1991), 62, and is combined with the outline in deSilva, *Introducing the Apocrypha*, 130.

[b] The second and third sections are taken from Harrington, *Invitation to the Apocrypha*, 63–75, with a few modifications.

[c] These seven antitheses are based on the principle stated in Wis. 11:5, "For through the very things by which their enemies were punished, they themselves received benefit in their need" (this principle reiterated in 11:16).

To gain a proper understanding of this crucial passage, it is important to view it in its literary context. As has already be noted, it is located in the middle of the chiastic structure (C) of the first section of the book (see the outline and Table 8), enveloped by two speeches of the ungodly (B-B′), which parallel each other in a chiastic way. Both speeches have an introduction (B-a/B′-a′) and a conclusion reflecting upon the reasoning of the speech (B-c/B′-c′). The first speech reveals the "perception on life" held by the wicked (Wis. 2, B-b) while in the second speech they recognize their flawed thinking and admit that the righteous were indeed right in their ways (Wis. 5, B′-b′) and are truly the children of God (Wis. 2:13, 17-18 vs. 5:5). The core assumption affecting their "perception on life" is the fatalistic view that death is the ultimate end for everyone: "For our allotted time is the passing of a shadow, and there is no return from our death because it is sealed up and no one turns back" (Wis. 2:5, NRSV).

Table 8. The chiastic structure of the Book of Eschatology

A Exhortation to righteousness (1:1-15)				A' Seek Wisdom (6:1-21)		
B-a Introduction (1:16–2:1a)				B'-a' Introduction (5:1-3)		
B-b1	2:1b-5				5:9-13	B'-b1'
	B-b2	2:6-11		5:6-8	B'-b2'	
		B-b3	2:12-20	5:4-5	B'-b3'	
B-c Concluding remark (2:21-24)				B'-c' Concluding remark (5:14-23)		
			C			

It is the central message of the chiastic structure (C) that changes the attitude the wicked have toward the righteous and changes their perception. It reveals that death is not the end of life. As such, the reasoning of the wicked was based merely on present appearance while the reasoning of the righteous was shown to be correct since theirs was based on the hope of a future reality. However, in the composition, this revelation comes too late since it occurs during the final judgment at the end of days. At that point it is too late for the wicked to change their ways to avoid the judgment and to gain the reward given to the righteous. Nevertheless, it is not too late for the reader of the book to change her/her ways or to continue on the path of righteousness.

This is the framing message of the opening and concluding units (A-A') of the chiastic structure addressed to kings and rulers (Wis. 1:1-15 and 6:1-21). The reader is encouraged to seek God and love righteousness (1:1-2; 6:1) so that His wisdom will dwell in them (1:4-5; 6:16). It also reveals that righteousness is associated with immortality (Wis. 1:15) and that every human being will be held accountable for their deeds (1:6-11; 6:1-11). The relationship between wisdom, God, good deeds, and immortality is nicely united in the concluding summary (6:18-20):

> The beginning of **wisdom** is the most sincere desire for **instruction**,
> and concern for instruction is **love of her**,
> and love for her is the keeping of her **laws**,
> and giving heed to her laws is **assurance of immortality**,
> and immortality brings one near to **God**;
> so the desire for wisdom **leads to a kingdom**. (My emphasis added)

Death, on the other hand, was not a part of God's original creative work (Wis. 1:13-14), but entered God's creation due to the deeds of the wicked (1:12) and the envy of the devil (2:24). Accordingly, the question of life and death is based on God's evaluation of a person's character and with which higher-power one is associated (2:24 vs. 3:1). The reward for a righteous life is immortality while death is the outcome of the wicked.[46]

The first six chapters of the Wisdom of Solomon describe an interesting journey for the righteous: the righteous' worldview is questioned by the wicked → they are persecuted and martyred by the wicked → they are vindicated by God → they will judge the wicked → the wicked will have to admit that their worldview was wrong. With this background in mind, this study will turn to the key passage of Wis. 3:1-13a, the turning point of the chiastic structure.

b. Wisdom of Solomon 3:1-13a

The turning point of the chiastic structure reveals that the wicked were wrong in their assumption that death is the ultimate end for everyone and counters: "But the souls of the righteous (δικαίων δὲ ψυχαὶ) are in the hand of God, and no torment will ever touch them" (Wis. 3:1). The contrast could not be made clearer. The wicked did not have any hope for a future (2:1-5), while the righteous considered themselves a child of God (2:13) and hoped for immortality (2:16; 3:4). The wicked believed that since the God of the righteous did not protect "His children" from their torturous hands and let them die (2:17-20), it proved that the righteous were wrong in their claim and hope in immortality. However, the wicked "did not know the secret purpose of God, nor...the wages of holiness, nor...the prize for blameless souls" (2:22). They thought the righteous were dead and that they were right in not believing in life after death. However, the author reveals that the righteous were only seemingly dead. In reality, they were protected by God and would still receive the hoped-for immortality (3:1-4).

Nickelsburg notes that "it is commonly observed that the Wisdom of Solomon teaches immortality of the soul rather than resurrection of the body" and, as such, no bodily resurrection is required for the posthumous judgment since the soul continues to live separately from the body and can be judged by itself.[47] In contrast, Wright argues that 'immortality' and

---

46. For further study into the literary structure of the first section of the Wisdom of Solomon, see Kolarcik, *The Ambiguity of Death in the Book of Wisdom 1–6*, 29–62.

47. Nickelsburg, *Resurrection, Immortality, and Eternal Life*, 113. See, e.g., Marie-Emile Boismard, *Our Victory Over Death: Resurrection?* (Collegeville, MN: Liturgical Press, 1999), 77; Collins, *Jewish Wisdom in the Hellenistic Age*, 182–7; N. Gillman, *The Death of Death: Resurrection and Immortality in Jewish Thought* (Woodstock, VT: Jewish Lights, 1997), 108–12; Lester L. Grabbe, *Wisdom of Solomon* (Sheffield: Sheffield Academic, 1997), 52; William Horbury, "The Wisdom of Solomon," in Baron and Muddiman, eds., *The Oxford Bible Commentary*, 650–6; Larcher, *Études sur le livre de la Sagesse*, 237–327; Robert H. Pfeiffer, *History of New Testament Times*

'resurrection' beliefs are not necessarily mutually exclusive since it all depends on how "immortality" is understood.[48] The word "immortality" by itself "simply means 'a state in which death is not possible'... [resurrection being] one form or type of 'immortality.'" He reasons that a resurrection belief also needs to take into consideration the period between "physical death" and "the physical re-embodiment of resurrection," adding that it would be natural to believe "in an intermediate state in which some kind of personal identity was guaranteed."[49] This is the sense of immortality presented in Wis. 3:1-10.

Wright makes a strong case that "Wisdom 3.1-10 offers a two-stage description of what happens after the death of the 'righteous': a story in which the present existence 'in the hand of God' [3:1-4] is merely the prelude to what is about to happen [in 3:7-10]...a further event which follows upon the state described in verses 1-4" (see Table 9).[50] His case is based on the key phrase, ἡ ἐλπὶς αὐτῶν ἀθανασίας πλήρης, "their hope is full of immortality" (3:4b), which suggests that they have not yet received the hoped for immortality. As mentioned earlier, although "God created us for incorruption, and made us in the image of his own eternity" (2:22-23), immortality is no longer a given and as such is not inherent in a person, but is the reward given to a person by God (1:15; 6:17-20) whom he has tested and deemed just (3:5-6).

with an Introduction to the Apocrypha (New York: Harper, 1949), 336–40; James M. Reese, *Hellenistic Influence on the Book of Wisdom and Its Consequences*, AnBib 41 (Rome: Pontifical Biblical Institute, 1970), 62–71, 109f.; James C. VanderKam, *An Introduction to Early Judaism* (Grand Rapids: Eerdmans, 2001), 125.

48. Wright suggests four types of immortality. First, immortality could refer to a continuous physical life which is uninterrupted by any form of death. Second, immortality could refer to an immortal "soul," which will go on living autonomously after bodily death. Third, immortality could refer to the gift of ongoing life bestowed by God upon a righteous person, something which is "not itself innate in the human make-up, which could then provide the human continuity, across an interim period, between the present bodily life and the future resurrection." Fourth, immortality could be used to describe resurrection itself (Wright, *The Resurrection of the Son of God*, 92).

49. Wright, *The Resurrection of the Son of God*, 164. He notes that there are also other scholars who see the resurrection belief in the Wisdom of Solomon; see, e.g., Maurice Gilbert, "Immortalité? Résurrection? Faut-il choisir?," in *Le Judaïsme à l'aube de l'ère chrétienne: XVIIIe congrès de l'association catholique fançaise pour l'étude de la bible (Lyon, Septembre 1999)* (Paris: Cerf, 1999), 282–7; É. Puech, *La croyance des Esséniens en la vie future: immortalité, résurrection, vie éternelle? Histoire d'une croyance dans le Judaïsme ancien*, 2 vols. (Paris: Cerf, 1993), 92–8, 306. See also the bibliography of Pfeiffer, *History of New Testament Times*, 339 n. 15; Larcher, *Études sur le livre de la Sagesse*, 321–7.

50. Wright, *The Resurrection of the Son of God*, 167.

Table 9. Two phases of life after death

		Verses	LXT/LXX	NRSV
RIGHTEOUS	PHASE 1	1-4	¹δικαίων δὲ ψυχαὶ ἐν χειρὶ θεοῦ καὶ οὐ μὴ ἅψηται αὐτῶν βάσανος ²ἔδοξαν ἐν ὀφθαλμοῖς ἀφρόνων τεθνάναι καὶ ἐλογίσθη κάκωσις ἡ ἔξοδος αὐτῶν ³καὶ ἡ ἀφ' ἡμῶν πορεία σύντριμμα, οἱ δέ εἰσιν ἐν εἰρήνῃ ⁴καὶ γὰρ ἐν ὄψει ἀνθρώπων ἐὰν κολασθῶσιν **ἡ ἐλπὶς αὐτῶν ἀθανασίας πλήρης**	¹**But the souls of the righteous are in the hand of God**, and no torment will ever touch them. ²In the eyes of the foolish they seemed to have died, and their departure was thought to be a disaster [Wis. 4:17; 5:4 | Lk. 9:31], ³and their going from us to be their destruction; but they are at peace. ⁴For though in the sight of others they were punished, **their hope is full of immortality** [Rom. 8:24; 2 Cor. 5:1].
	EXPLANATION	5-6	⁵καὶ ὀλίγα παιδευθέντες μεγάλα εὐεργετηθήσονται ὅτι ὁ θεὸς ἐπείρασεν αὐτοὺς καὶ εὗρεν αὐτοὺς ἀξίους ἑαυτοῦ ⁶ὡς χρυσὸν ἐν χωνευτηρίῳ ἐδοκίμασεν αὐτοὺς καὶ ὡς ὁλοκάρπωμα θυσίας προσεδέξατο αὐτούς	⁵Having been disciplined a little, they will receive great good, because God tested them and found them worthy of himself [Exod. 15:25; | Heb. 12:11]; ⁶like gold in the furnace he tried them, and like a sacrificial burnt offering he accepted them [Prov. 17:3 | 2 Esd. 16:73; | Rom. 12:1; 1 Pet. 1:7].
	PHASE 2	7-9	⁷καὶ ἐν καιρῷ ἐπισκοπῆς αὐτῶν ἀναλάμψουσιν καὶ ὡς σπινθῆρες ἐν καλάμῃ διαδραμοῦνται ⁸κρινοῦσιν ἔθνη καὶ κρατήσουσιν λαῶν καὶ βασιλεύσει αὐτῶν κύριος εἰς τοὺς αἰῶνας ⁹οἱ πεποιθότες ἐπ' αὐτῷ συνήσουσιν ἀλήθειαν καὶ οἱ πιστοὶ ἐν ἀγάπῃ προσμενοῦσιν αὐτῷ ὅτι χάρις καὶ ἔλεος τοῖς ἐκλεκτοῖς αὐτοῦ	⁷**In the time of their visitation they will shine forth** [Dan. 12:3 | Mt. 13:43], and will run like sparks through the stubble [Isa. 5:24; Obad. 18]. ⁸**They will govern nations and rule over peoples, and the Lord will reign over them forever** [Dan. 7:18, 22 | Sir. 4:15; 1QpHab 5,4 1 Cor. 6:2-3]. ⁹Those who trust in him will understand truth, and the faithful will abide with him in love, because grace and mercy are upon his holy ones, and he watches over his elect [Wis. 2:20; 4:15 | Jn 15:10].

WICKED	DESTINY	10-13a	¹⁰Οἱ δὲ ἀσεβεῖς καθὰ ἐλογίσαντο ἕξουσιν ἐπιτιμίαν οἱ ἀμελήσαντες τοῦ δικαίου καὶ τοῦ κυρίου ἀποστάντες ¹¹σοφίαν γὰρ καὶ παιδείαν ὁ ἐξουθενῶν ταλαίπωρος καὶ κενὴ ἡ ἐλπὶς αὐτῶν καὶ οἱ κόποι ἀνόνητοι καὶ ἄχρηστα τὰ ἔργα αὐτῶν ¹²αἱ γυναῖκες αὐτῶν ἄφρονες καὶ πονηρὰ τὰ τέκνα αὐτῶν ἐπικατάρατος ἡ γένεσις αὐτῶν	¹⁰But the ungodly will be punished as their reasoning deserves, those who disregarded the righteous and rebelled against the Lord [Prov. 1:24-31]; ¹¹for those who despise wisdom and instruction are miserable. Their hope is vain, their labors are unprofitable, and their works are useless. ¹²Their wives are foolish, and their children evil [Sir. 41:5]; ¹³ᵃtheir offspring are accursed [Isa. 54:1 | Wis. 12:11].

Wisdom 3:5-6 is introduced by an aorist passive participle (παιδευθέντες), reflecting on the hardship the righteous suffered by the hand of the wicked (2:12-20) while still living in their earthly bodies. The great secret which the wicked did not know (2:22; 4:17) was that their persecution of the righteous functioned as God's testing tool, and that the martyrdom of the righteous was accepted like an atoning sacrifice (3:6).⁵¹ The wicked thought that they had proven the righteous wrong when the righteous died and viewed the destruction as a punishment (3:1-4a), but they had been blinded by their wickedness (2:21). In reality, it was the willingness of the righteous to suffer and die for God's law which made them into children of the Lord, παῖδα κυρίου/υἱὸς θεοῦ/υἱοῖς θεοῦ (2:13, 17-18; 5:5). This is why they are currently resting in their hope for immortality (3:4b).

Wisdom 3:7 introduces the second phase by the phrase, ἐν καιρῷ ἐπισκοπῆς, "in the time of visitation." The noun ἐπισκοπή, "visitation," appears several times throughout the book (Wis. 2:2; 3:13; 4:15; 14:11; 19:15), referring to the day of judgment when God will set things right by condemning the wicked and rewarding the righteous.⁵² Wright remarks that it becomes apparent that this second phase introduces new aspects, something different than what has been described in the first phase (Wis. 3:1-4). From resting in the hope of immortality (v. 4b) they will now shine forth (ἀναλάμψουσιν, future tense)⁵³ – alluding to Dan. 12:3

---

51. An understanding of this concept was also voiced by the seven brothers in 2 Macc. 7.

52. This noun has the same word range in the LXX (e.g. Jer. 6:15; 10:15) and NT (e.g. Lk. 19:44; 1 Pet. 2:12).

53. Wright emphasizes that ἀναλάμπω is a rare word which means "shine forth" (like shining of the sun) but can also have a metaphorical meaning of "'flame up', as

which describes the wise who will shine at the time of the resurrection (ἐκλάμψουσιν) – and will run like sparks through the stubble, a possible reference to the judgment scene in Isa. 5:24 and Obadiah 18. This, according to Wright, prepares the reader for the judgment scene in the remaining part of the passage (Wis. 3:9-13a).

Wisdom 3:7-13a describes the new reality, that the righteous will govern nations and rule over peoples (v. 7a), alluding to the role given to the holy ones of the Most High in Daniel's eschatological vision (Dan. 7:18, 22). The Wisdom of Solomon expands on this reversal of events by noting that "the righteous who have died will condemn the ungodly who are living" (Wis. 4:16), "will stand with great confidence in the presence of those who have oppressed them" (Wis. 5:1), and "will receive a glorious crown and a beautiful diadem from the hand of the Lord" (Wis. 5:15).

The wicked, on the other hand, will acknowledge their mistake (Wis. 5), be judged by God and the righteous (Wis. 3:10-3; 4:16), and are "punished as their reasoning deserves" (Wis. 3:10), suggesting that they, like the righteous, are also going to be proven right in their assumption. However, instead of allying themselves with life-giving righteousness, they made a covenant with death, assuming that:

> there is no remedy when a life comes to its end...[and that the hereafter] shall be as though we had never been, for the breath in our nostrils is smoke, and reason is a spark kindled by the beating of our hearts; when it is extinguished, the body will turn to ashes, and the spirit will dissolve like empty air. Our name will be forgotten in time, and no one will remember our works; our life will pass away like the traces of a cloud, and be scattered like mist that is chased by the rays of the sun and overcome by its heat. For our allotted time is the passing of a shadow, and there is no return from our death, because it is sealed up and no one turns back (Wis. 2:1-5).

Nickelsburg suggests that the chronology of C-B' is not quite clear and that it is therefore difficult to determine whether the wicked will experience a single judgment or a double judgment (like the righteous), the first by God (to determine which category they would fall into – wicked or righteous – suggested by Wis. 3:13, 18; 4:6) and a second by the righteous in the

---

of envy, or 'blaze up' with enthusiasm." Interestingly, in classical Greek, "Plutarch uses it of Brutus' 'reviving,' 'coming to himself'" (*Resurrection of the Son of God*, 169–70). The classical Greek case seems to be most fitting in our context, functioning as a synonym for resurrection at the time of judgment when they, like the "wise" of Daniel, will be vindicated and receive their immortality and kingdom (Wis. 3:8 || Dan. 7:18, 22).

eschatological judgment (suggested by Wis. 5:17-23).[54] This would also require a resurrection of the wicked, but this resurrection is for judgment and damnation. Regardless, after the wicked have been condemned by the righteous at the close of the judgment, "they will become dishonored corpses, and an outrage among the dead forever" (Wis. 4:18).

The author of Wisdom of Solomon seems to have based his eschatological understanding of life after death on a close reading and interpretation of Daniel 7 and 12. Daniel 12:1 refers to a time of great tribulations "such has never has occurred since nations came into being" (CSB), paralleling the great persecution of the righteous suffered by the hand of the wicked (Wis. 2). However, God will protect his people whose names are written in the book (Dan. 12:1) in the same way as he will protect his children (Wis. 3:1). Daniel 12:2 refers to the resurrection to eternal life (for the righteous) and to shame and eternal contempt (for the wicked), paralleling the resurrection of the righteous (Wis. 3:7; 4:16; 5:1) and a possible resurrection of the wicked at the second judgment (Wis. 5:17-23) to become "dishonored corpses and an outrage among the dead forever" (Wis. 4:18). The reference in Dan. 12:3 to the wise who will shine finds its parallel in Wis. 3:7, when the righteous will shine forth – resurrect. At this point, the author of Wisdom interpolates the eschatological judgment scene from Daniel 7 into his composition (Wis. 3:8) to reveal that the righteous will receive God's kingdom (Dan. 7:18, 22 || Wis. 3:8) and suggests that, as rulers, they will also judge the wicked (Wis. 4:16; 5:15-16). The author concludes the passage by focusing on the destiny of the wicked (Wis. 3:10-13a). It should be noted that Wis. 3:5-6, the intermediate period between the righteous death and later bodily resurrection, could have been extrapolated from the concluding words of the book of Daniel, which states, "But as for you [Daniel], go on your way to the end; you will rest [die], then rise [resurrect] to your destiny [of the righteous, the wise] at the end of the day" (Dan. 12:13, CSB), referring to the event of Dan. 12:2-3.

Although Dan. 12:1-3 may not be clear on whether it describes a universal resurrection or a limited resurrection for only some (the wise and the most wicked), it leaves little doubt that all the people who are written in the book will partake in the resurrection of the righteous. The same is the case in the book of Wisdom. An argument could be made that the righteous described in Wisdom 3 are those who suffered martyrdom in Wisdom 2 and that their persecutors are the wicked. However, the message of the book is clear – that whoever loves righteousness (Wis. 1:1-2), pursues wisdom, and observes God's law would gain immortality

---

54. Nickelsburg, *Resurrection, Immortality, and Eternal Life*, 114–15.

(Wis. 1:15; 6:17-20). Death, on the other hand, only entered the world due to the devil's envy (Wis. 2:24) and wicked deeds (Wis. 2 and 5). As such, it would be reasonable to conclude that the resurrection described in Wisdom 3 would at least include all the righteous, regardless of whether they died as a martyr.

It is interesting to note the strong links observed by deSilva between the Servant Song of Isaiah 52–53 and the eschatological section of Wisdom 2–4 (Table 10),[55] since 2 Maccabees contains parallels to the Servant Song (see discussion above). However, deSilva notes the lack of a sacrificial death of the righteous on behalf of the people[56] that was so crucial in understanding the universalistic and individualistic function of martyrdom in 2 Macc. 7:37-38, which profited both the people of Israel and the individual martyr. In Wisdom, the martyrdom only carries an individualistic function, only profiting the martyr (Wis. 3:5-6), guaranteeing their eternal life.

Table 10. Parallels between Isaiah 52–53 and the *Wisdom of Solomon* 2–4

Isaiah 52–53	*Wisdom* 2–4	Theme
53:2	2:12, 16, 18	The righteous is described as a child of God
53:7-9	2:19-20	The righteous suffers heroically
53:4, 11-12 52:13-15	2:2-3 5:1-2	The wicked perceived the death of the righteous as dishonorable
53:6	5:4-6	The wicked confess that they were wrong
54:1	3:13	Undefiled barren woman
56:4-5	3:14–4:15	The righteous eunuch

c. Concluding Remarks

The Wisdom of Solomon presents a belief in a bodily resurrection which also addresses the intermediate period between the death of the righteous and his/her resurrection (Wis. 3:1-4, 7-9). In the book, immortality is attained through wisdom and righteousness (Wis. 6:17-20) and is therefore not innate in a preexistent soul as it is in Platonic immortality. As such, a wicked person will not experience immortality in which he/she will be tormented in Hell; instead, his/her destiny will be as he/she had already assumed – non-existence (Wis. 2; 5). The Wisdom of Solomon, however, does not reveal the nature of existence while the soul is in God's hands (Wis. 3:1), if the soul is conscious or unconscious – merely being stored

---

55. deSilva, *Introducing the Apocrypha*, 138.
56. Ibid.

for safekeeping until the day of resurrection (Wis. 3:7). The text is not very clear either when it comes to chronology – that is, whether the wicked will also experience a dual-judgment which would entitle them to a resurrection, but one resulting in damnation. The references and allusions to the eschatological passages of Daniel 7 and 12 seem to support the latter. Additionally, it also lends scriptural support for the concept of an intermediate period between death and resurrection (Wis. 3:1-4 || Dan. 12:2-3, 13), judgment of the wicked and righteous (Wis. 3:5-6, 13, 18; 4:6; 5:17-23 || Dan. 7:18, 22), and the reward of taking possession of the kingdom (Wis. 5:15-16 || Dan. 7:18, 22). Finally, the Wisdom of Solomon adds that the righteous will judge the wicked (Wis. 4:16). Figure 3 illustrates the death and resurrection concept presented in the book.

Figure 3. Death and Resurrection in Wisdom of Solomon.

	Pre-Existence[a] Wis. 8:19-20	Life[b]	Death/ Judgment Wis. 3:1-4	Resurrection/ Judgment Wis. 2:21-22; 3:7-13, 18; 4:16; 4:20–5:14	Eternity Wis. 2:16-20; 3:7-13; 5:15-16
GOD	Soul		Wis. 3:1-4 Soul[c]		
WORLD		Body Soul		Body Soul	Righteous Wis. 3:7-9; 5:15-16
GRAVE			Body Wis. 3:2		Wicked Wis. 2:16-20; 3:10-13

[a] Wisdom 8:19-20 may suggest a pre-existent soul. However, the text does not reveal much about this phase.

[b] Wisdom 3:5-6 reveals that God "tests" people in the present life to determine whom is "worthy of himself." This would imply a preliminary individualized judgment before the final judgment at the beginning of the eternity.

[c] The text does not reveal what happens to the "Soul" of the wicked since the primary focus of the text is the destiny of the righteous.

~ ~ ~

4. 2 Esdras

2 Esdras, the title used in the English Apocrypha, is an apocalyptic book[57] consisting of three separate compositions which has added to the confusion surrounding the terminology of the books associated with Ezra (see Table 11).[58] The longest section of 2 Esdras (chs. 3–14), also known as *4 Ezra* in the Pseudepigrapha, is the oldest and was probably composed in Hebrew/Aramaic in the late first century by a Palestinian Jew.[59] Written

---

57. John Collins, representing the Apocalypse group of the Society of Biblical Literature, gives the following definition of the apocalyptic genre: "'Apocalypse' is a genre of revelatory literature with a narrative framework, in which a revelation is mediated by an otherworldly being to a human recipient, disclosing a transcendent reality which is both temporal, insofar as it envisages eschatological salvation, and spatial, insofar as it involves another, supernatural world" (John J. Collins, "Introduction: Towards the Morphology of a Genre," *Semeia* 14 [1979]: 9). This genre can be further divided into historical and mystical apocalypse, "between apocalypse which do not have an otherworldly journey and those that do" (13), 2 Esdras would fall into the first category which includes "less than half of the corpus of Jewish apocalypses" (John J. Collins, "The Jewish Apocalypses," *Semeia* 14 [1979]: 23). For a categorization of the Jewish apocalypses, see Table 16. In this table, Collins makes a crucial observation, noting that apocalyptic literature is "clearly envisaging retribution beyond death" (Collins, *The Apocalyptic Imagination*, 6). This is also the case in *4 Ezra*, in which the judgment follows the bodily resurrection.

58. Ezra is often counted among the most important characters in the TaNaKh, second only to Moses, due to the central role he played in rebuilding the Jewish nation after the Babylonian captivity. He has also been given a major role in the final compilation of the TaNaKh (e.g. David Weiss Halivni, *Revelation Restored: Divine Writ and Critical Responses*, Radical Tradition [Boulder, CO: Westview, 1997]). 2 Esdras goes as far as claiming that Ezra restored all the Scriptures which had been lost due to the Babylonian exile: "Make public the twenty-four books that you wrote first [TaNaKh], and let the worthy and the unworthy read them; but keep the seventy that were written last [Apocrypha and Pseudepigrapha], in order to give them to the wise among your people. For in them is the spring of understanding, the fountain of wisdom, and the river of knowledge" (2 Esd. 14:45-47). Several pseudepigraphical works have been attributed to him and many of them are dependent on *4 Ezra* (2 Esd. 3-14): *1 Esdras* and *2 Esdras* (see Table 11), *Greek Apocalypse of Ezra*, *Vision of the Blessed Ezra*, *Apocalypse of Sedrach*, *Questions of Ezra*, and *Revelation of Ezra*. Some of these books will be considered when looking at resurrection passages in the Apocalyptic Literature and Related Works section of the Pseudepigrapha (see Chapter 3).

59. It is generally accepted that the book was originally composed in Hebrew/Aramaic before it was translated into Greek and later Latin and Syriac (there are also Arabic, Ethiopic, and Armenian versions of the book and fragments of a Georgian and Coptic version), although both the Hebrew and the Greek works are now lost

about three decades[60] after the failed Jewish revolt which resulted in the destruction of the Second Temple, the writer addresses the problem of theodicy. He notes that the observable world does not fit with the Jewish world view which adheres to the deuteronomistic principle, God's justice, and Israel's election. Only by viewing the devastating events of his days through apocalyptic eyes, was he able to "reaffirm the observance of the Torah as the path to life and salvation."[61] This monograph, in its discussion, will refer to the Jewish section of this literary composition as *4 Ezra*.

Table 11. Titles given to books associated with Ezra

Date	Hebrew Bible	LXX	Vulgate	English w/ Apocrypha
c. 400 BCE	Ezra–Nehemiah	2 Esdras	1 Esdras	Book of Ezra
			2 Esdras	Book of Nehemiah
2nd cent. BCE		1 Esdras	3 Esdras	1 Esdras
1st–3rd cent. CE		–	4 Esdras	2 Esdras
1 Ezra	Ezra-Nehemiah of the Hebrew Bible			
2 Ezra/5 Ezra	4 Esdras (Vulgate) = 2 Esdras (Eng. Apocrypha) chs. 1–2			
3 Ezra	1 Esdras (LXX) = 3 Esdras (Vulgate) = 1 Esdras (Eng. Apocrypha)			
4 Ezra	4 Esdras (Vulgate) = 2 Esdras (Eng. Apocrypha) chs. 3–14			
5 Ezra/6 Ezra	4 Esdras (Vulgate) = 2 Esdras (Eng. Apocrypha) chs. 15–16			

[a] This table is based on Harold W. Attridge, "Historiography," in *JWSTP*, 158 n. 1.

(John J. Collins, *The Apocalyptic Imagination: An Introduction to Jewish Apocalyptic Literature*, 2nd ed., The Biblical Resource Series [Grand Rapids: Eerdmans, 1998], 195–6; deSilva, *Introducing the Apocrypha*, 329–30; B. M. Metzger, "The Fourth Book of Ezra," *OTP* 1:519–20; Jacob M. Myers, *1 and 2 Esdras*, AB 42 [Garden City, NY: Doubleday, 1974], 115–19; Michael E. Stone, *Fourth Ezra: A Commentary on the Book of Fourth Ezra*, Hermeneia [Minneapolis: Fortress, 1990], 1–9).

60. This is based on the date given in 2 Esd. 3:1, and assumes that the author addressed the theological issues deriving from the destruction of the Second Temple by referring to the destruction of the First Temple, centuries earlier by the Babylonians. If this assumption is correct, "the thirtieth year after the destruction of the city" would place the book at the turn of the second century CE. Myers believes that this date also seems to be supported by the "Eagle Vision" (2 Esd. 11–12), which addresses the events of the Vespasian–Domitian period, 69–96 CE (deSilva, *Introducing the Apocrypha*, 330–2; Metzger, "The Fourth Book of Ezra," 520; Bruce W. Longenecker, *2 Esdras* [Sheffield: Sheffield Academic, 1995], 13–16; Myers, *1 and 2 Esdras*, 129; Stone, *Fourth Ezra*, 9–10).

61. deSilva, *Introducing the Apocrypha*, 323–4.

The prologue and epilogue of 2 Esdras, chs. 1–2 and 15–16, also known as 2 Ezra/5 Ezra and 5 Ezra/6 Ezra (see Table 11), are two Christian texts, originally written in Greek, which were probably added to the Jewish composition in the mid-second century and the mid-third century respectively.[62] The prologue provides a Jewish-Christian response to the cataclysmic events of the second Jewish revolt (the Bar Kochba revolt) in 135 CE – the persecutions of the Jews and the destruction of Jerusalem – by promoting a replacement theology. The Christian writer proposes that God has rejected the Jewish people and replaced them with a new people who are willing to adhere to the covenant (2 Esd. 1:24-27, 33-40; 2:10-14). The epilogue provides a renewed conclusion to the Jewish apocalypse, to update and make the whole composition more relevant for the Christian community.[63] According to deSilva, the appendix was to "encourage the Christians to persevere in their loyalty to God...[making it clear that although] renunciation of God and the Messiah could lead to relief in this life," it would not be an advisable course of action since only the faithful will be delivered on the day of tribulations.[64]

The following outline of 2 Esdras shows the Christian prologue (chs. 1–2), epilogue (chs. 15–16), and the Jewish Ezra apocalypse (chs. 3–14).[65] The Jewish composition consists of seven parts: the first three (parts 1-3) record the dialogue between Ezra and Uriel; the second set of three (parts 4-6) contains three prophetic visions with interpretations; and the final section (part 7) contains a record of God's commission of Ezra and a description of his work as a restorer of Scriptures – a new Moses.[66] The first half of the composition is spurred by Ezra's grave doubts regarding the question of theodicy (similar to the book of Job), since he had lost confidence in God's justice and the value or even the possibility of upholding the law/covenant. In this sense, Ezra focuses on the present and observable reality while Uriel and God, although not addressing Ezra's questions and concerns directly, expose him to a much larger perspective by introducing the eschatological future and help him see the issues from God's perspective.

---

62. Ibid., 347–51; Harrington, *Invitation to the Apocrypha*, 185.
63. Longenecker, *2 Esdras*, 110–20.
64. deSilva, *Introducing the Apocrypha*, 350–1.
65. For a more detailed structure of the book, see Stone, *Fourth Ezra*, 50–1.
66. This seven-part structural pattern is, according to Collins, also to be found in *2 Baruch* and the book of Revelation in the New Testament, both of which are contemporary apocalyptic books (Collins, "Jewish Apocalypse," 33).

The fourth part of the composition (2 Esd. 9:26–10:59), the Mourning Woman vision (the first vision), reveals that Ezra has internalized God's perspective when he tries to comfort the weeping woman, who turns out to be a symbolic representation of Zion (2 Esd. 10:41-50). The key element of Ezra's words of comfort is his strong belief in the resurrection: "For if you acknowledge the decree of God to be just, you will receive your son back in due time, and will be praised among women" (2 Esd. 10:16). This summarizes the divine argument and the greater perspective presented in the book, that God is just, and His covenant is still relevant since there will be a resurrection when all the wrongs will be put right. With this new perspective, Ezra is ready to receive the vision of the second half of the book.

I. Christian Introduction (chs. 1–2)
Introduction (1:1-11)
God's mercies to Israel (1:12-23)
Israel's disobedience and rejection (1:24-40)
God's judgment of Israel (2:1-14)
Exhortation to good work (2:15-32)
Ezra on Mount Horeb (2:33-41)
Ezra sees the Son of God (2:42-48)
II. The Ezra Apocalypse (3-14)
1. First Dialogue (3:1–5:19)
a. Introduction (3:1-3)
b. Before Ezra's address (3:4-36)
c. Dialogue between Uriel and Ezra (4:1-25)
d. Ezra's questions about the future (4:26-52)
e. The signs (5:1-20)
2. Second Dialogue (5:21–6:34)
a. Introduction (5:21-22)
b. Before Ezra's address (5:23-30)
c. Dialogue between Uriel and Ezra (5:31-40)
d. Ezra's question about the future (5:41–6:10)
e. The signs (6:11-34)
3. Third Dialogue (6:35–9:25)
a. Introduction (6:35-37)
b. Ezra's address (6:38-59)
c1. Dialogue between Uriel and Ezra (7:1-25)
God's prediction (7:26-44)
Dialogue between God and Ezra (7:45-74)
Prediction (7:75-115)

c.2. Dialogue between Ezra and Uriel (7:116–8:3)

Ezra's prayers (8:4-36)

    d. Ezra's questions about the future (8:37-62a)
    e. The signs (8:62b–9:25)
4. Mourning Woman Vision (9:26–10:59)
    1. Ezra's address (9:26-37)
    2. Ezra's vision of the mourning woman (9:38–10:28)
    3. Interpretation (10:29-59)
5. Eagle and Lion Vision (10:60–12:51)
    1.
    2. Ezra's dream (11:1–12:3a)
    3. Interpretation (12:3b-51)
6. Man from the Sea Vision (13:1-58)
    1.
    2. Ezra's dream (13:1-13a)
    3. Interpretation (13:13b-58)
7. Ezra the Scribe (14:1-51)
    God's final instruction to Ezra || Moses (14:1-18)
    Ezra's work as a Scribe (14:19-48)

III. Christian Conclusion (15-16)
    Vengeance on the wicked (15:1-27)
    God's judgment of the nations (15:28–16:17)
    Horror of the Last Days (16:18-34)
    God's people must prepare for the end (16:35-50)
    Power and wisdom of God (16:51-67)
    Impending persecution of God's people (16:68-73)
    Promise of Divine deliverance (16:74-78)

Michael Stone proposes that the three symbolic visions (parts 4-6) provide the answers to the questions raised by Ezra in the dialogues of the first half of the book. The visions, he suggests, function in a similar way as the short revelations at the end of each dialogue in that they open "the path to the resolution of the issues raised" in the question. He concludes: "It follows from this, and it is notable, that the questions asked, apparently in the form of learned dialogue, are answered by the revelatory symbolic visions."[67]

---

67. Michael Stone, "Apocalyptic Literature," in *JWSTP* (Philadelphia: Fortress, 1984), 413.

The highlighted sections of the literary structure of 2 Esdras illustrate how prevalent and integrated the resurrection belief (implied and stated) is in the book (see the outline). Table 25 in Appendix A gives a list of the individual resurrection passages and their classifications while the anthology following this list provides their full context. Based on Table 25, it becomes apparent that most of the resurrection statements are clustered in Ezra's third dialogue. Comparing the Christian resurrection passages found in the prologue with those found in the older Jewish composition, it also becomes apparent that the resurrection belief carries a different function in the Christian composition.

As already noted, the Christian prologue presents a supersessionistic interpretation of the cataclysmic events provoked by the failed Bar Kochba revolt. The author considers the crushing and humiliating defeat suffered by the Jews as proof that they were no longer God's special people due to their disobedience (2 Esd. 1:24–2:14, 33). Instead, he argues, the special status (2 Esd. 1:24), glory, and all the promises previously given have now been transferred to the Christians (2 Esd. 1:24; 2:10-13), a new people who will follow God's shepherd (the Messiah; 2 Esd. 2:34, 43, 46-47) and fulfill the law of the Lord (2 Esd. 2:40). In this theological exposition, bodily resurrection is a part of the rewards transferred to the new people of God who will receive glorious garments, be crowned, and receive everlasting habitation in His kingdom, enjoying all the benefits from the Tree of Life (2 Esd. 2:11-12, 18-19, 34-35, 39, 43, 45). As such, this prologue provides a rather basic resurrection concept, showing no interest in the intermediate phase between death and resurrection nor an awareness of a soul that can exist separately from the body. It only reveals that the righteous will not see hell/Gehenna (2 Esd. 2:29), but will, instead, be brought out from their tombs (2 Esd. 2:16) – the hiding places of the earth (2 Esd. 2:31).

In contrast, the Jewish apocalypse gives a detailed description of the state of the dead (Table 12) and a detailed eschatology time-line (Fig. 4), revealing that the bodily resurrection introduces the third era.[68] Segal remarks that *4 Ezra* resembles "nothing so much as a primer about life after death."[69] Figure 5 illustrates the death and resurrection concept presented in *4 Ezra*.

---

68. The first era is the present world and the second era is the period of "primeval silence."
69. Segal, *Life After Death*, 491.

Table 12. The state of the dead (*4 Ezra* 7:81-87, 92-98)

	Wicked	Righteous
1	They have scorned the law of the Most High (81).	They have striven with great effort to overcome the evil thought that was formed with them (92).
2	They cannot now make a good repentance (82).	They see the perplexity in which the souls of the ungodly wander and the punishment that awaits them (93).
3	They shall see the reward laid up for those who have trusted the covenants of the Most High (83).	They see the witness that he who formed them bears concerning them, that throughout their life they kept the law with which they were entrusted (94).
4	They shall consider the torment laid up for themselves in the last days (84).	They understand the rest that they now enjoy, being gathered into their chambers and guarded by angels in profound quiet, and the glory waiting for them in the last days (95).
5	They shall see how the habitations of the others are guarded by angels in profound quiet (85).	They rejoice that they have now escaped what is corruptible and shall inherit what is to come; and besides they see the straits and toil from which they have been delivered, and the spacious liberty that they are to receive and enjoy in immortality (96).
6	They shall see how some of them will cross over into torments (86).	They will see how their faces are to shine like the sun, and how they are to be made like the light of the stars, being incorruptible from then on (97).
7	They shall utterly waste away in confusion and be consumed with shame, and shall wither with fear at seeing the glory of the Most High in whose presence they sinned while they were alive, and in whose presence they are to be judged in the last times (87).	They shall rejoice with boldness, and shall be confident without confusion, and shall be glad without fear, for they press forward to see the face of him whom they served in life and from whom they are to receive their reward when glorified (98).

2. Apocryphal/Deuterocanonical Books

Figure 4. Three-stage Worldview Presented in *4 Ezra*

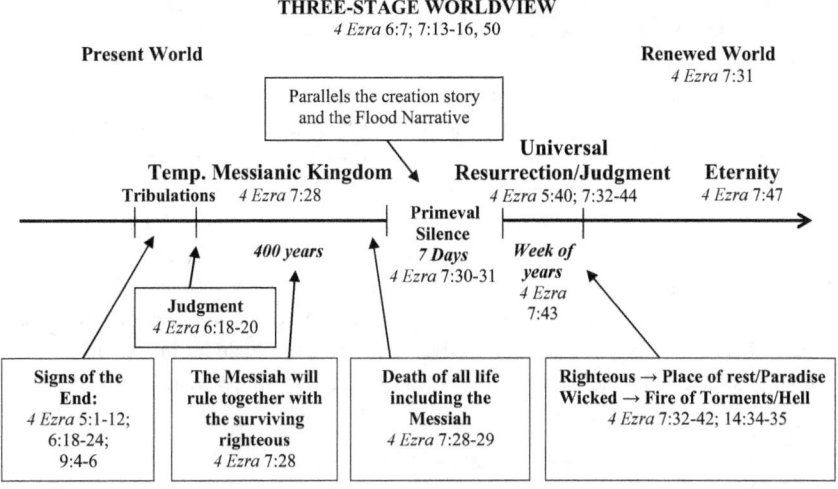

Figure 5. Death and Resurrection in *4 Ezra* (2 Esd. 3–14)

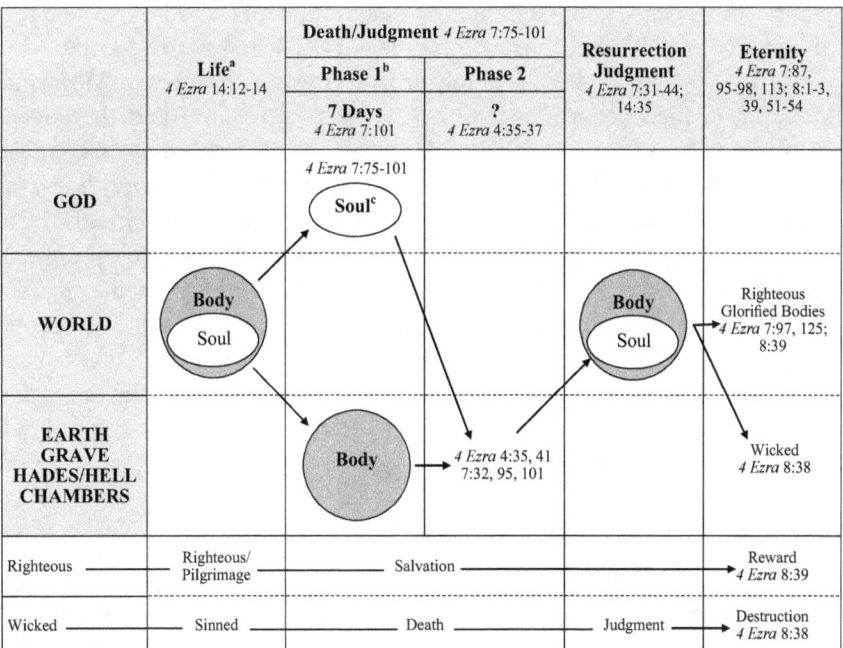

ᵃ *4 Ezra* 7:102-115 states that there will be no intercession for the ungodly in the day of judgment which suggests that this life is the determining factor in deciding a persons' destiny both in the first judgment (the fate of the soul in phase 1 and 2) and in the second universal judgment.

ᵇ *4 Ezra* describes two phases of the state of the dead. During the first phase, which will last for seven days, it will be revealed to the soul what destiny will await the person on the day of resurrection. After these seven days, the soul will enter phase two, and be placed in a holding chamber where it will remain until the day of resurrection when it will once more join with the body.

ᶜ At the time of death, when the soul parts the body, both the righteous and the wicked soul will return to God, suggesting that God has already performed a preliminary judgment of the individual person's life. At that moment, the righteous soul will see with great joy the glory of God and receive rest in seven different ways (*4 Ezra* 7:88-98). The wicked soul, on the other hand, will wander in torment, always grieving and be sad in seven different ways (*4 Ezra* 7:79-87; 9:9, 12).

~ ~ ~

4 Ezra presents a rather detailed description of death and the future resurrection (see Figs. 4 and 5). It makes clear that it is only a person's attitude towards God and His law/covenant which determines that person's destiny in the eschatological judgment (7:102-115). The text also notes that this bodily resurrection is God's first act in the renewed world (7:32-42; 14:34-35), which will follow the temporary Messianic kingdom (which according to 7:28-29 lasts 400 years) and the seven-day-long primeval silence (7:30-31), when all life, including that of the Messiah, has passed away (see Fig. 4). The three-stage worldview as outlined by Ezra requires two judgments of the dead – a limited (7:75-101) and a universal judgment (5:40; 7:32-44).[70] The limited judgment takes place upon a person's death when God determines whether his/her soul should be numbered among the righteous or the wicked. The second and universal judgment, which will last "a week of years," takes place after the resurrection of the renewed world where both the righteous and wicked will receive their destiny, eternal life or eternal destruction (7:87, 95-98, 113; 8:1-3, 39, 51-54).

70. *4 Ezra* also seems to suggest a third judgment – a judgment of the living. This judgment takes place at the end of the tribulations and precedes the temporary Messianic kingdom (*4 Ezra* 6:18-20) during which the Messiah will rule together with the surviving righteous (*4 Ezra* 7:28). If this is the case, this would parallel the apocalypse of Daniel which also presents a judgment scene prior to the Messianic kingdom (Dan. 7:9-10, 26-27).

4 Ezra also presents a dualistic view where, upon death, both the righteous and the wicked soul leaves the body, goes back to God, and enters the first phase which will last seven days. During this phase, the righteous and the wicked souls will be made aware of the destiny awaiting them in the day of resurrection and judgment (*4 Ezra* 7:75-101, see Table 12). At the beginning of the second phase, the soul enters a holding chamber where it will remain until the day of resurrection (4:35-37, 41; 7:32, 95, 101). Importantly, the text suggests that the soul will be conscious during both phases (4:35-37; 7:75-101).[71] At the time of the bodily resurrection, the soul will re-enter the body and resurrect to the judgment of the righteous and the wicked (see Fig. 5). It should be noted that the renewed earth will be a different world order where there will be no more death or corruption (8:53-54). When considering the implicit and explicit resurrection passages in *4 Ezra* (see their classification in Table 25 and in the subsequent anthology, in Appendix A, which places these resurrection statements in their larger context), it should not be surprising that both resurrection and judgment are intimately connected in the eschatological expectations of the book. It is only through the retribution of the wicked and the reward of the righteous that provides a satisfying answer to the problem of theodicy and safeguards God's justice. This is one of the characteristics of apocalyptic literature (see Table 14 and Table 16), and, according to Ezra, resurrection is what makes this universal judgment possible.[72]

---

71. Note the parallel between *4 Ezra* 4:35-37 and Rev. 6:10-11. In both texts, the righteous dead are impatiently asking a question. In *4 Ezra*, they are asking when the New Age will come, when they will receive the harvest of their reward. In Revelation, they are crying out for justice, asking when God will avenge their blood by judging the wicked. In both texts, the righteous are told to wait until their number has been filled. It is also important to point out the differences between these two accounts. The righteous in *4 Ezra* refers to all the righteous dead (universal) and not just the martyred (limited), as is the case in Revelation. The souls of the righteous in *4 Ezra* are calling out from their "chambers" while in Revelation they are calling out from "under the altar." If these contemporary apocalyptic passages are understood literally (which would be the natural reading of 2 Esdras based on the context), they both suggest that the souls of the righteous are conscious while waiting for their justice and reward.

72. Michael E. Stone, *Features of the Eschatology of IV Ezra*, HSS 35 (Atlanta: Scholars Press, 1989), 141–3.

DeSilva observes the formative role the Jewish Scriptures played for the new apocalyptic revelation presented in *4 Ezra*. The most important of these are Genesis (chs. 1–11; 15–17, especially in the first and third complaint-prayer), Job (focuses on the problem of theodicy), and, according to Ezra himself, the book of Daniel (*4 Ezra* 12:11-12).[73] The two explicit resurrection statements alluding to the TaNaKh in *4 Ezra* (see Table 4) allude to Dan. 12:2-3 (*4 Ezra* 7:32; 7:97) and Isa. 26:19 (*4 Ezra* 7:32).

a. *4 Ezra* 7 (2 Esdras 7)

4 Ezra 7:26-44 gives a detailed eschatological chronology revealing that the "two major groupings of associated eschatological ideas"[74] are subsequent eras held together by the "primeval silence." The first major grouping, according to Stone, "centers around the last generation and the increase of evil until its consummation, which is to be followed by the messianic kingdom…[while] the chief elements of the other are resurrection, judgment, reward, and punishment"[75] (see Fig. 4). In this important eschatological passage, Segal sees evidence of exegesis in which Daniel 7 functions as one of the controlling texts, and the resurrection language of *4 Ezra* 7:32, 97, 125 resembles the language of Dan. 12:2-3 and Isa. 26:19 (see the highlighted sections and comments in Table 13).[76]

---

73. deSilva, *Introducing the Apocrypha*, 334–5. The three visions of the second half of *4 Ezra* 11–13 draws and reinterprets Dan. 7–12. deSilva demonstrates Daniel's influence on the vision of the man from the sea (*4 Ezra* 13), noting the following phrases and images: "I looked, and behold" (*4 Ezra* 13:3, 5, 6, 8 || Dan. 7:2, 6, 7, 13); the parallel between the man from the sea and the "Son of Man" image of Dan. 7 (*4 Ezra* 13:3 || Dan. 7:14); "everything under his gaze trembled" (*4 Ezra* 13:3 || Ps. 104:32); "melted like wax" (*4 Ezra* 13:4 || Ps. 97:5; Mic. 1:3-4); "stone broke off without a hand touching it" (*4 Ezra* 13:5-7 || Dan. 2:34-35, 44-45); and destruction of the ungodly by fire (*4 Ezra* 13:10-11 || Ps. 18:8; 97:3; Isa. 11:4; 66:15-16). Harrington could not state it stronger: "the chief biblical source and model is the book of Daniel" (Harrington, *Invitation to the Apocrypha*, 190).

74. Stone, *Fourth Ezra*, 206.

75. Ibid. Almost all the eschatological elements appearing in *4 Ezra* 7 are also mentioned in parallel texts throughout the book (e.g. *4 Ezra* 4:26-31; 5:41-56; 6:25-28; 9:6-12; 11:46; 12:34).

76. Segal, *Life After Death*, 492–3.

Table 13. Parallels between the resurrection passages in
4 Ezra 7 and Daniel/Isaiah

4 Ezra 7:29-35, 97, 125	Daniel/Isaiah
²⁹After those years [400 years]ᵃ <u>my son the Messiah shall die</u>, and all who draw human breath. ³⁰Then the world shall be turned back to primeval silence for seven days, as it was at the first beginnings,ᵇ so that no one shall be left. ³¹After seven days the world that is not yet awake shall be roused, and that which is corruptible shall perish.	Dan. 9:26After those 62 weeksᶜ <u>the Messiah will be cut off</u>ᵈ <u>and will have nothing</u>. The people of the coming prince will destroy the city and the sanctuary. The end will come with a flood, and until the end there will be war; desolations are decreed.
³²<u>The earth</u> shall give up those who are <u>asleep in it</u>, and <u>the dust</u> those who rest there in silence; and <u>the chambers shall give up the souls</u> that have been committed to them.	Dan. 12:2Many of those who <u>sleep in the dust of the earth</u> will awake, some to *eternal life*, and some to shame and *eternal contempt*.
	Isa. 26:14, 19The dead do not live; departed spirits do not rise up. Indeed, you have visited and destroyed them; you have wiped out all memory of them [the wicked]. ¹⁹Your dead will live [the righteous]; their bodies will rise. Awake and sing, you who <u>dwell in the dust</u>! For you will be covered with the morning dew, and <u>the earth</u> will bring out <u>the departed spirits</u> (וְאֶרֶץ רְפָאִים תַּפִּיל).
³³**The Most High shall be revealed on the seat of judgment**, and compassion shall pass away, and patience shall be withdrawn. ³⁴Only judgment shall remain, truth shall stand,ᵉ and faithfulness shall grow strong. ³⁵Recompense shall follow, and the reward shall be manifested; *righteous deeds* shall awake, and *unrighteous deeds* shall not sleep.ᵉ	Dan. 7:9As I kept watching, thrones were set in place, and **the Ancient of Days took His seat**. His clothing was white like snow, and the hair of His head like whitest wool. His throne was flaming fire; its wheels were blazing fire. ¹⁰A river of fire was flowing, coming out from His presence. Thousands upon thousands served Him; ten thousand times ten thousand stood before Him. **The court was convened, and the books were opened**.

⁹⁷The sixth order, when it is shown them [the righteous] _how **their face is to shine like the sun**, and how they are **to be made like the light of the stars**, being **incorruptible from then on**_. ¹²⁵Or that _**the faces of those who practiced self-control shall shine more than the stars**_, but our faces shall be blacker than darkness?	Dan. 12:3 _**Those who are wise will shine like the bright expanse of the heavens**, and those who lead many to righteousness, **like the stars forever and ever**._

ᵃThe 400-year period may be an allusion to the 400 years of oppression in Egypt (Gen. 15:13). In _b. Sanh._ 99a, Rabbi Dosa argues for a Messianic kingdom, lasting 400 years, based on reading Gen. 15:13 in light of Ps. 90:15, noting that the time of rejoicing would equal the time of afflictions. Since the 400-year period is also similar in length to the time of the Judges (1 Kgs 6:1) and the time of the First Temple (mid-tenth century – early sixth century BCE), it may be understood as an era. It may not be a coincidence that the 400-year-long Messianic Kingdom matches the time the "House of David" ruled over the people of Israel (1003 [David]–598 [Jeconiah] BCE = 405 years, although its autonomy came to an end in 605 BCE [Dan. 1:1-2]).

ᵇThe earth is brought back to its pre-creation phase (Gen. 1:2) and readied for a renewed creation similar to the process which took place at the Flood (Gen. 7:21–8:1). Although the eschatological chronology is different in the book of Revelation, the renewed creation is presided by a state of "emptiness" (cf. Gen. 1:2 [τῆς ἀβύσσου] and Rev. 20:1 [τῆς ἀβύσσου]). The seven days of "primeval silence" may be an additional allusion to the creation account, the seven days of the first creation. Interestingly, the first recorded act of God on this newly recreated earth is the resurrection, when the earth and the dust will give up those who sleep in it. This seems to be an allusion to the Eden narrative's account of the creation of humans out of dust (Gen. 2:7) and the curse that they would, upon death, return to dust (Gen. 3:19). It is from this dust that humans were once created, to which they will return upon death, and from which they will once more resurrect.

ᶜ7 weeks + 62 weeks (Dan. 9:25) = 69 weeks out of 70 weeks (Dan. 9:24). The author of 4 Ezra may understand the remaining week to be the "week of years" (_4 Ezra_ 7:43) of the final universal judgment.

ᵈThe LXX (TH) translates the more ambiguous Hebrew word, כָּרֵת ("to cut off") with ἐξολεθρευθήσεται, which specifically states that the Messiah will be completely destroyed or be put to death.

ᵉNickelsburg notes that it is Michael who arises as a witness in the judgment scene in Dan. 12:1. As such, he speculates that "truth" may have been personified as an angelic figure similarly to the case of Dan. 8:12. He also notes that the righteous and the unrighteous deeds function as witnesses in the trial, either for or against the person being judged.

4 Ezra 7:32 shares several elements with Dan. 12:2 (underlined and highlighted gray in Table 13). Both texts refer to the dead as sleeping. Both texts locate the dead in the same location – in the earth and the dust. However, Dan. 12:2 does not present the dualistic view of *4 Ezra* by referring to the souls which are stored in the chambers and will rejoin the body at the moment of resurrection. Interestingly, Isa. 26:19 may allude to this dualistic position.[77] It shares with *4 Ezra* 7:32 and Dan. 12:2 the view that the dead are sleeping by noting that they will awake. It also shares the location of the dead, they dwell in the earth and the dust. Isaiah adds an agricultural image, using as a simile of the resurrection the morning dew which covers the earth and causes the plants to sprout.[78] He concludes his statement regarding the resurrection of the righteous by adding an interesting detail, וְאֶרֶץ רְפָאִים תַּפִּיל, "and the earth will bring out/ give birth to the dead spirits/ghosts of the dead/shades."[79] The noun רְפָאִים carries the meaning "shades" in eight poetic contexts in the TaNaKh (Isa. 14:9; 26:14, 19; Ps. 88:10; Prov. 2:18; 9:18; 21:16; Job 26:5), while the ethnic Rephaim only appear in historical narrative sections (Gen. 14:5; Deut. 2:11; 2:20 [×2]; 3:13; Josh. 15:8; 18:16; 2 Sam. 5:18, 22; 23:13; Isa. 17:5; 1 Chron. 11:15; 14:9). In these eight cases, the noun parallels or is associated with "the dead" (מֵתִים), "death" (מָוֶת), "*Sheol*" (שְׁאוֹל), and "destruction/Abaddon" (אֲבַדּוֹן).[80] It is noteworthy that Isa. 26:19 mentions both the resurrection of the corpses/dead bodies (נְבֵלָתִי יְקוּמוּן)[81] and the bringing forth of the dead spirits (וְאֶרֶץ רְפָאִים תַּפִּיל), which may have influenced the author of *4 Ezra* to promote his dualistic view in which both the body and soul will be resurrected and joined once more to become a living being.[82]

---

77. This dualistic notion does not appear in the LXX, as the spirits (רְפָאִים) are not mentioned in the Greek translation. Instead, the strong resurrection hope is solely concerned with the bodily aspect of the resurrection: "The dead shall rise, and they that are in the tombs shall be raised, and they that are in the earth shall rejoice: for the dew from thee is healing to them: but the land of the ungodly shall perish" (Isa. 26:19, LXE).

78. This simile became important in Early Rabbinic resurrection passages (*y. Ber.* 5:2; *y. Ta'an.* 1:1; *b. Ber.* 33a; *b. Hag.* 12b; *Gen. Rab.* 13:3-6).

79. M. Brown, "רְפָאִים," *NIDOTTE* 3:1173–80; W. White, "רְפָאִים," *TWOT* 2:858–9.

80. Brown, *NIDOTTE* 3:1176.

81. Desmond Alexander notes that this noun is the most common term used for describing a human corpse or animal carcass (D. Alexander, "נְבֵלָה," *NIDOTTE* 3:14).

82. The LXX understands the phrase וְאֶרֶץ רְפָאִים תַּפִּיל as a reference to the wicked (ἀσεβν) as opposed to the spirits (רְפָאִים) of the righteous, translating the phrase as: ἡ δὲ γῆ τῶν ἀσεβῶν πεσεῖται, "but the land of the wicked shall come to an end."

It should also be noted that the judgment follows the resurrection in both *4 Ezra* 7:32 (explicit) and Dan. 12:2 (implicit), although only *4 Ezra* clearly states that this judgment will be universal.[83] Both *4 Ezra* and Daniel divides the resurrected into two groups, people with righteous deeds and people with unrighteous deeds (*4 Ezra* 7:33). The first group will awake to eternal life while the other to eternal contempt (Dan. 12:2). The judgment language of *4 Ezra* is reminiscent of Dan. 7:9-10 (underlined and bolded in Table 13). *4 Ezra* refers to the Most High on the seat of judgment, while Daniel refers to the Ancient of Days who takes his seat and opens the books (cf. *4 Ezra* 6:20 mentions the books will be opened in the firmament as a warning of the coming judgment[84]) in order to convene the judgment.[85]

The punishment and reward given to the wicked and the righteous as a result of the judgment are expanded upon in the second half of *4 Ezra* 7 (see Table 13). The sixth reward foretold to the righteous is directly based on Dan. 12:3 (underlined and italic in Table 12), which promises that they will shine like the sun and be made like the light of the stars (*4 Ezra* 7:97). *4 Ezra* 7:125 takes it even a step further by noting that the faces of the righteous shall shine more than the stars.[86] This may suggest that the righteous will become like angels (cf. Job 38:7)[87] or that the glorified bodies will radiate light as a result of seeing God face to face (*4 Ezra* 7:98). The latter understanding would be similar to the case of Moses, who had to cover his radiant face after he had spoken to the Lord on Mt. Sinai (MT/LXX Exod. 34:29-35). Both understandings are expressed in the New Testament (be like the angels in heaven [Mt. 22:30; Mk 12:25; Lk. 20:36] and radiate light [Mt. 13:43; 1 Cor. 15:35-42]), Pseudepigrapha (e.g. *1 En.* 51:4-5; 104:2; *2 En.* 1:5; *2 Bar.* 51:3, 10;

---

83. Interestingly, Isa. 26 also moves to the judgment theme (vv. 20-21) after the resurrection statement (v. 19).

84. Stone, *Fourth Ezra*, 169–70.

85. This adaptation of judgment language may suggest that the author of *4 Ezra* perceived the judgment scene of Dan. 7 to be the final universal judgment which would preside the eternal reward kept in store for the righteous (*4 Ezra* 7:95-98).

86. This promise is a part of a longer list of rewards promised to the righteous. They include: (1) immortal time; (2) everlasting hope; (3) safe and healthful habitation; (4) the glory of the Most High will defend those who have led a pure life; (5) Paradise shall be revealed; and (6) the face of those who practiced self-control shall shine more than the stars (*4 Ezra* 7:119-125).

87. It may even suggest that the righteous will become greater than the angels, similar to the view presented in *2 Bar.* 49–51; see the discussion in Chapter 3.

Table 14. Judgment scenes in apocalyptic literature

Judgment Scene		Dan. 12	T. Mos. 10	Jub. 23	T. Judah 20, 25	1 En. 104	4 Ezra 7	Rev. 12, 20–22
1. Witness	Good Angel	1	2		20:1-5	1a	34-35	12:7
	Evil Angel	(10:20)	1	29b	20:2			12:7
	His defeat	(11:45)	1	29b	25:3			12:8-9; 20:2-3
2. Book	of Life	1				1b		20:12b
	of Deeds				20:3	7	(6:20)	20:12ac
3. Post-Mortem Judgment	The Good	2	?	31ab	25:4	(103:3-4)	32	20:12-13
	The Evil	2	?			(103:7-8)	32	20:12-13
4. Consequences of Judgment	Vindication	2	9	30ab	25:4-5	2-6	36ac	21:1-7
	Condemnation	2	10	30-31	25:5 (? txt.)		36bd	20:15; 21:8
	Gehenna/See	2	10	30-31			36bd?	
	Exaltation/ Ascension	3?	9		25:5?			20:4-6
	Light Language	3				2, 4	39-42	21:22-25; 22:5
	Stars Angels	3?	9			2	97, 125	

Source: Nickelsburg, *Resurrection, Immortality, and Eternal Life*, 54.

Ps.-Philo 12:1; *LAE Slov.* 18-20.11), and early Rabbinic material (e.g. *b. Ber.* 17a; *Sipre Deut.* 10 [67a]; *Gen. Rab.* 20:12; 23:6).[88] As indicated in Table 14, Nickelsburg lists the main elements appearing in the judgment scene of Daniel 12 (the witnesses, the book, the resurrection, and the consequences of the judgment) and shows how these elements also appear in *4 Ezra*.

It becomes apparent that Ezra's use of Daniel is more than mere exegesis. He is also performing interpretative work, trying to answer the question of theodicy in the aftermath of the destruction of the Temple, the center of Jewish faith.[89] In this attempt, he combined the biblical hope of national restoration, which would introduce the Messianic age, with the apocalyptic hope of an eschatological judgment that would vindicate the righteous by giving them their just reward and punish the wicked for their deeds.[90]

Uriel finally responds to Ezra's grave concern regarding the corrupt nature of humans which was caused by Adam (*4 Ezra* 7:116-118) and which would prevent most people from adhering to God's covenant, thereby preventing them from being saved and receiving the rewards promised the righteous (see Ezra's questions in *4 Ezra* 7:17, 45-48, 62-69, 102-103, 106-111, 116-126). Uriel quotes Moses' words in Deut. 30:19 (*4 Ezra* 7:129) in support of his response. By this he upholds the validity of the Deuteronomistic principle and the two-way theology (Deut. 28–32) by making it clear that each person is able to choose whether he/she would adhere to God's covenant and "love the LORD your God, obey Him, and remain faithful to Him" (Deut. 30:20), thereby choosing life (Deut. 30:11-20). It is important to note that "Uriel" reinterprets Moses' words from promising a prolonged "life in the land the LORD swore to your fathers Abraham, Isaac, and Jacob [i.e. the Land of Canaan/Palestine]" (Deut. 30:20) to an eternal life in the world to come. As such, the future-universal-bodily-resurrection becomes an integral part of the promise that "you and your descendants may live" (Deut. 30:19), and the answer to the question of theodicy discoursed in *4 Ezra*. Bodily resurrection becomes the guarantor and the foundation of God's justice.

---

88. For further study, see Stone, *Fourth Ezra*, 244–5.
89. Segal, *Life After Death*, 494.
90. Collins, *The Apocalyptic Imagination*, 203–4.

5. Conclusion

4 Ezra presents a more detailed death and resurrection view than what is seen in the Wisdom of Solomon, 2 Maccabees (compare Figs. 2, 3 and 5), and Sirach, which only reveals that it will happen in the eschatological age. All four books make it clear that a person's attitude towards God and His law/covenant determines his/her destiny, but only *4 Ezra* and Wisdom of Solomon reveal that there will be an eschatological judgment (*4 Ezra* 7:102-115; Wis. 3:5-6). In contrast to Sirach and 2 Maccabees, both *4 Ezra* and Wisdom of Solomon present a dualistic view where, upon death, the soul leaves the body and goes back to God, although in *4 Ezra* the soul seems to be conscious (*4 Ezra* 4:35-37; 7:75-101 and Wis. 3:1-4). In *4 Ezra*, however, both the wicked and the righteous soul goes back to God as opposed to only the righteous in Wisdom of Solomon. Additionally, *4 Ezra* describes two phases of the state of the dead while Wisdom of Solomon only describes one. The first phase, according to Ezra, will only last seven days (*4 Ezra* 7:101) in which the righteous and the wicked soul will be made aware of the destiny awaiting them in the day of resurrection and judgment (see Table 14). In the second phase, the soul enters a holding chamber where it will remain until the day of resurrection. It should be noted that both *4 Ezra* and the Wisdom of Solomon imply a limited judgment of each individual person upon death, to determine whether they should be numbered among the righteous or the wicked. A second and universal judgment takes place after the resurrection. The resurrection belief presented in both texts is a bodily resurrection in which the soul will re-enter the body and resurrect to the judgment of the righteous and the wicked (*4 Ezra* 7:31-44; 14:35; Wis. 2:21-22; 3:7-13, 18; 4:16, 20-5:14). In contrast, Sirach and 2 Maccabees do not show any interest in the intermediate period between death and resurrection. The destiny for each category of humans is the same – eternal life or eternal destruction (*4 Ezra* 7:87, 95-98, 113; 8:1-3, 39, 51-54; Wis. 2:16-20; 3:7-13; 5:15-16). It is also interesting to note that *4 Ezra*, the Wisdom of Solomon, and 2 Maccabees are all indebted to Daniel 12 for their resurrection and eschatological expectations. It should also be noted that both *4 Ezra* and the Wisdom of Solomon made references and allusion to Daniel 7. In addition to Daniel, *4 Ezra* and 2 Maccabees also refer and allude to Isaiah 26 (2 Macc. 7:23; *4 Ezra* 7:32) and to the Deuteronomistic principle of Deuteronomy 28–32 (2 Macc. 7:6, 9, 11, 23, 29, 36; *4 Ezra* 7:129). Resurrection functions as the answer to the question of theodicy in 2 Maccabees, Wisdom of Solomon, and *4 Ezra*.

Looking at the resurrection passages found in the Apocrypha, it becomes apparent that the earlier books, Sirach and 2 Maccabees, do not show much interest in the minute details regarding this belief, what happens to a person in the period between his/her death and resurrection, and what reward and punishment will befall both the righteous and the wicked. The Wisdom of Solomon and *4 Ezra*, on the other hand, both become much more detail-oriented in their description of the resurrection hope, where *4 Ezra* resembles a primer on the subject. Chapter 3 will look at the resurrection texts found in the Apocalyptic literature of the Pseudepigrapha and the companion volume will consider the remaining literary genres of the Pseudepigrapha to determine whether there is a similar pattern and to determine what texts from the TaNaKh were used, or alluded to, when insinuating or referring to the resurrection belief. Due to the similar nature of the Old Testament Apocryphal and Pseudepigraphical writings, the Summary and Conclusion chapter of the companion volume will provide a combined list of the TaNaKh passages used by these writings.

Part II

OLD TESTAMENT PSEUDEPIGRAPHICAL WRITINGS

The Pseudepigrapha is a "catch-all" category which includes all the books of the Second Temple Period apart from the Apocrypha, Dead Sea Scrolls, Philo, Josephus, New Testament, and Rabbinic material. This monograph follows the broad definition, or rather description, suggested by James H. Charlesworth:

> Those writings 1) that, with the exception of Ahiqar, are Jewish or Christian; 2) that are often attributed to ideal figures in Israel's past; 3) that customarily claim to contain God's word or message; 4) that frequently build upon ideas and narratives present in the Old Testament; 5) and that almost always were composed either during the period 200 B.C. to A.D. 200 or, though late, apparently preserve, albeit in an edited form, Jewish traditions that date from that period.[1]

The term "Pseudepigrapha" comes from the Greek words ψευδής, "false," and ἐπιγραφή, "inscription," referring to books bearing a false inscription. David A. deSilva notes that this term "highlights primarily a literary characteristic of many writings from the Hellenistic and Greco-Roman periods, that is, writings under the assumed name of a great figure from the distant past"; however, he adds that Roman Catholic and Orthodox writers use the term "Apocrypha" when referring to this body of literature while many scholars and Jewish writers often use the term "outside books."[2]

Like "Apocrypha" in the previous chapter, the term "Pseudepigrapha" also has its limitations – the first term "derives from canonical debates and usage; the other from a peculiar literary characteristic."[3] Nickelsburg notes that this term "ignores the pseudonymous nature of some of the

---

1. James H. Charlesworth, "Introduction for the General Reader," *OTP* 1:xxv.
2. deSilva, "Apocrypha and Pseudepigrapha," *DNTB* 58–9.
3. Ibid., 60.

Apocrypha (e.g. Tobit and the Wisdom of Solomon) and some canonical (e.g. Job and Ruth) writings,"[4] and C. T. Fritsch observes that some of the Pseudepigraphical books are better described as anonymous than pseudonymous. Fritsch also states that these books were never included into the Greek and Latin manuscripts of the Bible, so their canonicity was never an issue in mainstream Christianity. However, "many of these works were preserved in the various branches of the oriental churches, and so they came down to us in such languages as Syriac, Ethiopic, Coptic, Georgian, Armenian, Slavonic, etc."[5]

The Old Testament Pseudepigrapha, like the Apocrypha discussed in the previous chapter (see Table 3), also represent several literary genres which fall into the following six categories:

1. Apocalypses;
2. Testaments;
3. Expansion of TaNaKh narratives;
4. Wisdom and philosophical literature;
5. Prayers, psalms, and odes; and
6. Fragments of now-lost Judeo-Hellenistic works.

This monograph only considers the first category, *Apocalyptic Literature*, while the companion volume, *Afterlife and Resurrection Beliefs in the Pseudepigrapha*, considers the remaining five. Table 15 shows the literary genres of the Pseudepigrapha, the date of composition,[6] and the books containing a resurrection belief, either stated or implied (bolded and highlighted) based on the analysis in Appendix A of this monograph and Appendix A in the companion volume. This will help the reader see the extent of this belief in the Pseudepigraphical books. This part of the monograph considers the passages from the apocalyptic literature listed in Table 17 that imply or state a resurrection belief which also refer or allude to the TaNaKh for its foundation of this belief.

---

4. Nickelsburg, *Jewish Literature*, 6.
5. C. T. Fritsch, "Pseudepigrapha," *IDB* 3:963.
6. The suggested dates are primarily based on Charlesworth's two-volume work, *The Old Testament Pseudepigrapha*, and to a lesser degree on Evans, *Ancient Texts for New Testament Studies*.

Table 15. The literary genres of the Pseudepigrapha

Literary Genre	Pseudepigraphical Texts	Date
Apocalyptic Literature and Related Works	**1 Enoch**	3rd cent. BCE–50 CE
	2 Enoch	Late 1st cent. CE
	3 Enoch	5th–6th Century CE
	Sibylline Oracles	2nd cent. BCE–7th cent. CE
	Treatise of Shem	1st cent. BCE
	Apocryphon of Ezekiel	50 BCE–50 CE
	Apocalypse of Zephaniah	100 BCE–70 CE
	Fourth book of Ezra [= 2 Esdras 3–14] (see OT Apocrypha)	Late 1st cent. CE
	Greek Apocalypse of Ezra	2nd–9th cent. CE
	Vision of Ezra	4th–7th cent. CE
	Questions of Ezra	?
	Revelation of Ezra	2nd–9th cent. CE
	Apocalypse of Sedrach	2nd–5th cent. CE
	2 Baruch	Early 2nd cent. CE
	3 Baruch	1st–3rd cent. CE
	Apocalypse of Abraham	1st–2nd cent. CE
	Apocalypse of Adam	1st–4th cent. CE
	Apocalypse of Elijah	1st–4th cent. CE
	Apocalypse of Daniel	9th cent. CE
Testaments (Often with Apocalyptic Sections)	Testament of the 12 Patriarchs	2nd cent. BCE
	Testament of Reuben	
	Testament of Simeon	
	Testament of Levi	
	Testament of Judah	
	Testament of Issachar	
	Testament of Zebulun	
	Testament of Dan	
	Testament of Naphtali	
	Testament of Gad	
	Testament of Asher	
	Testament of Joseph	
	Testament of Benjamin	
	Testament of Job	Early 1st cent. BCE
	Testament of the Three Patriarchs	1st cent. CE
	Testament of Abraham	1st–2nd cent. CE
	Testament of Isaac	1st–2nd cent. CE
	Testament of Jacob	2nd–3rd cent. CE ?
	Testament (Assumption) of Moses	1st cent. CE
	Testament of Solomon	1st–3rd cent. CE
	Testament of Adam	2nd–5th cent. CE

Expansions of the "Old Testament" and Legends	*Letter of Aristeas*	130–70 BCE
	Jubilees	135–105 BCE
	Martyrdom and Ascension of Isaiah [3:13–4:22 = *Testament of Hezekiah*]	2nd cent. BCE
	Joseph and Aseneth	1st cent. BCE–2nd cent. CE
	Life of Adam and Eve	1st cent. BCE–1st cent. CE
	Pseudo-Philo [= *Biblical Antiquities*]	2nd cent. BCE–late 1st cent. CE
	Lives of the Prophets	
	Ladder of Jacob	1st cent. CE
	4 Baruch [= *Omissions of Jeremiah*]	1st cent. CE
	Jannes and Jambres	Late 1st–early 2nd cent. CE
	History of the Rechabites	1st–2nd cent. CE
	Eldad and Modad	1st–4th cent. CE
	History of Joseph	> 2nd cent. CE
		> 400 CE
Wisdom and Philosophical Literature	*Ahiqar*	6th–7th cent. CE
	3 Maccabees	1st cent. CE
	4 Maccabees	1st cent. CE
	Pseudo-Phocylides	1st cent. BCE
	The Sentences of the Syriac Menander	3rd cent. CE
Prayers, Psalms, and Odes	More Psalms of David *Psalm 151* (see OT Apocrypha) *Psalm 152* *Psalm 153* *Psalm 154* *Psalm 155*	3rd cent. BCE–1st cent. CE
	Prayer of Manasseh (see OT Apocrypha)	2nd–1st cent. BCE
	Psalms of Solomon	c. 50 BCE
	Hellenistic Synagogal Prayers	2nd–3rd cent. CE
	Prayer of Joseph	1st cent. CE
	Prayer of Jacob	1st–4th cent. CE
	Odes of Solomon	Late 1st–early 2nd cent. CE

II. *Old Testament Pseudepigraphical Writings* 87

Fragments of Lost Judeo-Hellenistic Work	Philo the Epic Poet	3rd–2nd cent. BCE
	Theodotus	2nd–1st cent. BCE
	Orphica	1st cent. BCE/CE
	Ezekiel the Tragedian	2nd cent. BCE
	Fragments of Pseudo-Greek Poets	3rd–2nd cent. BCE
	Pseudo-Hesiod	
	Pseudo-Pythagoras	
	Pseudo-Aeschylus	
	Pseudo-Sophocles	
	Pseudo-Euripides	
	Pseudo-Philemon	
	Pseudo-Diphilus	
	Pseudo-Menander	
Fragments of Lost Judeo-Hellenistic Work	Aristobulus	2nd cent. BCE
	Demetrius the Chronographer	3rd cent. BCE
	Aristeas the Exegete	Late 2nd–early 1st cent. BCE
	Eupolemus	Late 2nd–early 1st cent. BCE
	Pseudo-Eupolemus	> 1st cent. BCE
	Cleodemus Malchus	> 1st cent. BCE
	Artapanus	3rd–2nd cent. BCE
	Pseudo-Hecataeus	c. 300 BCE

Chapter 3

APOCALYPTIC LITERATURE AND RELATED WORKS

An apocalyptic work is "revelatory literature with a narrative framework" which reveals a transcendent reality.[1] Collins notes that "the main means of revelation are visions and otherworldly journeys, supplemented by discourse or dialogue and occasionally by a heavenly book. The constant element is the presence of an angel who interprets the vision or serves as a guide on the otherworldly journey."[2] Table 16 shows a categorization of some of the Jewish apocalypses listed in Table 15 and divides the literature into two distinctive strands, *Otherworldly Journeys* and *"Historical" Apocalypse*. It should be noted that these two strands are interwoven in the *Apocalypse of Abraham* (chs. 15–32)[3] and *1 Enoch* (the *Apocalypse of Weeks* [91:11-17; 93:1-10] and *Animal Apocalypse* [chs. 83–90] are "historical" apocalypses, while the *Book of the Watchers* [chs. 1–36] and the *Similitudes of Enoch* [chs. 37–71] describes "otherworldly" journeys). Regardless, all fifteen Jewish apocalypses listed in Table 16 "fall within the compass of the definition of the genre"[4] despite the variations between the texts.

It is important to note that all these apocalyptic texts include a judgment scene in which the wicked are destroyed and reveal that the righteous will be rewarded with some form of afterlife. In some texts, this afterlife reward is introduced by a bodily resurrection (see the highlighted sections in Table 16).

The most elaborate and detailed descriptions of the events that will take place following a person's death appear in the apocalyptic literature of the Second Temple period literature, in the books which fall within the first category of Pseudepigraphical books which will be considered in this chapter. Table 17 provides a list of all the relevant resurrection passages. Special emphasis will be placed on the resurrection passages which either refer or allude to the TaNaKh.

1. Collins, "Introduction," 9.
2. Collins, *The Apocalyptic Imagination*, 5.
3. Collins, "Jewish Apocalypses," 36–7.
4. Ibid., 24.

Table 16. Jewish apocalypses

Jewish Apocalypses	Otherworldly Journeys									"Historical" Apocalypse					
	Apoc. Zephaniah	Test. Abraham 10–15	3 Baruch	Test. Levi 2–5	2 Enoch	Similitudes of Enoch	Heavenly Lumin.	1 Enoch 1–36	Apoc. Abraham	2 Baruch	4 Ezra	Jubilees 23	Apoc. of Weeks	Animal Apocalypse	Daniel 7–12
Manner of Revelation															
Vision	×	×	×	×	×	×	×	×	×	×	×		×	×	×
Epiphanies															×
Discourse												×	×		×
Dialogue	×	×	×	×	×	×		×	×	×	×				×
Writing							×					×	×		
Otherworldly mediator	×	×	×	×	×	×	×	×	×	×	×	×	×	×	×
Pseudonymity	×	×	×	×	×	×	×	×	×	×	×	×	×	×	×
Disposition of recipient		×	×	×	×				×	×	×				×
Reaction of recipient			×	×	×	×	×		×	×	×			×	×

Table 16 continued

Jewish Apocalypses	Otherworldly Journeys									"Historical" Apocalypses					
	Apoc. Zephaniah	Test. Abraham 10–15	3 Baruch	Test. Levi 2–5	2 Enoch	Similitudes of Enoch	Heavenly Lumin.	1 Enoch 1–36	Apoc Abraham	2 Baruch	4 Ezra	Jubilees 23	Apoc. of Weeks	Animal Apocalypse	Daniel 7–12
Temporal Axis															
Cosmology					×										
Primordial events			×								×				
Recollection of past								×			×				×
Ex eventu prophecy									×	×	×	×	×		×
Persecution						×					×				×
Other eschatological upheavals		×		×		×	×	×	×	×	×	×		×	×
Judgment/destruction of wicked	×	×	×	×	×	×	×	×	×	×	×	×	×	×	×
Judgment/destruction of world	?				×	×	?	×	×	?			×	×	
Judgment/destruction of otherworldly beings				×	×	×	?	×	×			×		×	×
Cosmic transformation						×				×		?		×	
Resurrection		?	?							×	×	?	?	×	×
Other forms of afterlife	×	×	?	×	×	×	×	×	×		×	×	?	?	×

Table 16 continued

Jewish Apocalypses	Otherworldly Journeys									"Historical" Apocalypse					
	Apoc. Zephaniah	Test. Abraham 10–15	3 Baruch	Test. Levi 2–5	2 Enoch	Similitudes of Enoch	Heavenly Lumin.	1 Enoch 1–36	Apoc Abraham	2 Baruch	4 Ezra	Jubilees 23	Apoc. of Weeks	Animal Apocalypse	Daniel 7–12
Spatial Axis															
Otherworldly regions	x	x		x	x	x	x	x	x	x	x				x
Otherworldly beings	x	x	x	x	x	x	x	x	x	x	x		x	x	x
Paraenesis by Revealer				x	x		x				x				
Concluding Elements															
Instructions to recipient					x		x			x	x	x			x
Narrative Conclusion		x	x		x					x	x			x	x

Source: John J. Collins, *The Apocalyptic Imagination*, 7 and "The Jewish Apocalypses," *Semeia* 14 (1979): 28.

Table 17. Resurrection texts in the apocalypse category of the Pseudepigrapha

	Passage		Notes	Resurrection			Classification		
				Implied	Stated	Ref.	Allude	Phil.	Assume
1 Enoch	Book I (1–36) The Parable of Enoch		**Judgment Texts (Implied Resurrection)** 1:3-9; 5:5-9; 9:2-3; 10:4-6, 11-13, 16-17, 20; 13:6; 14:2-6; 15:7-10; 16:1; 27:2-3	x				x	x
		20:8	Archangel Remiel		x				x
		22	Resurrection of the Soul?		x				x
		25:4-6	The Fragrant tree	x					x
1 Enoch	Book II (37–71) The Book of the Similitudes		**Judgment Texts (Implied Resurrection)** 38; 41:1, 8-9; 45:2-6; 47; 48:7; 50:1; 54:6; 56:8; 58:1-4; 60:6, 24; 61:5, 8	x				x	
			70:4 – Vision of earliest human ancestors						
			70:16 – all the righteous will follow the path of Enoch.						
		40:9	Archangel Phanuel	x					x
		46:3	Son of Man	x					x
		49:3	Sleep ‖ Death	x					x
		51			x				x
		62:13-16	Son of Man		x				x
	Book III (72–82) The Book of Heavenly Luminaries	81:1-4	Judgment	x					x

Table 17 continued

Passage		Notes	Resurrection			Classification		
			Implied	Stated	Ref.	Allude	Phil.	Assume
Book IV (83–90)	84:4	**Judgment Texts (Implied Resurrection)**						
The Dream Visions	89:36-37	Sleep = Death	x					
	90:20-36	Judgment	x			x		x
		New Jerusalem						x
Book V (91–107)	91:8-17	Arise from sleep		x				x
	92:2-5	Arise from sleep		x		x		x
The Two Ways of the Righteous and the Sinner: Including the Apocalypse of Weeks		**The Destiny of the Righteous and the Wicked (94-104): Judgment (Implied Resurrection)**						
		94:9, 11; 95:5-6; 96:2-3, 8; 97:6; 98:6-8, 14; 100:4-5, 10; 102:4-8; 103:1-4; 104:1-7	x				x	x
	108:2-3	Book of Life	x			x		x
	108:8-15	Recompensed	x			x	x	x
		Resplendent						
2 *Enoch*		**Judgment Texts (Implied Resurrection)**						
	J 7:1; J/A 18:7; J/A 19:5; J 39:5/A 39:2; J 42:3, 5, 7; J/A 44:3-5; J/A 48:8-9; J/A 49:2; J/A 50:2, 4-5; J/A 51:3; J/A 52:15; J/A 58:4-6; J 60:4; J 66:6-7		x			x		x
	J 32	Dust to dust		x	x			
	J/A 65:6-11	Judgment	x					x
	J 70:1	Eternal inheritance	x					x
	J/A 70:3	Rest ‖ Death	x					x

Table 17 continued

Passage			Notes	Resurrection		Classification			
				Implied	Stated	Ref.	Allude	Phil.	Assume
3 Enoch	(18:24)		Books of the Dead Books of the Living		×				×
	(28:7; 30:2; 31:2; 33:1)		Every Day is a Judgment	×				×	×
	28:7-10		Third day he will raise us up		×				
	44:7-8		Rest of the Righteous		×				×
Sibylline Oracles	Book 1	355	Lazarus' resurrection		×				×
		378	Announcing the resurrection to the dead		×				×
	Book 2	221-51	Resurrection/Judgment		×	×			
		313-15	Rewards of the Righteous		×				×
	Book 3	66	Satan's work		×				×
		769	Messianic kingdom		×				×
	Book 4	179-92	Resurrection/Judgment		×	×			×
	Book 6	14	Lazarus' resurrection		×				×
	Book 7	144-45	Restoration of the world	×					×
	Book 8	82-83	Resurrection/Judgment		×				×
		170	Eschatological upheaval		×				×
		205-8	Messianic Age		×				×
		226-28	Resurrection/Judgment		×				×
		255	Faith → Eternal life	×					×
		286	Jesus' mission		×				×
		293	Jesus' mission		×				×
		310-14	Jesus' mission		×				×
		413-16	Resurrection/Judgment		×				×
	Frag. 3	41-49	Inheritance of the Righteous	×					×

Table 17 continued

	Passage	Notes	Resurrection			Classification		
			Implied	Stated	Ref.	Allude	Phil.	Assume
Apocryphon of Ezekiel	Frag. 1	Body = Blind Soul = Lame		×	×			
		Judgment parable						
Fourth Book of Ezra	2:16	Exhortation to good work		×				×
	2:22-24	Burial		×				×
	2:31	Sleep ‖ Death		×				×
	4:35-37	Predestined time		×		×		×
	4:42-43	Hades ‖ womb	×					×
	7:31-[44]	Resurrection/Judgment		×		×		×
	7:75-101	The state of the departed before the judgment		×		×		×
	14:36	Resurrection/Judgment	×				×	
Greek Apocalypse of Ezra	2:1; 5:22	The righteous/Patriarchs	×					×
	4:36	Trumpet/Resurrection		×				×
	7:2	Jesus' work		×				×
Questions of Ezra	A. 5	The fate of the righteous and the sinners		×				×
	A. 10	The prophet's question	×					×
	B. 1-14	Resurrection/Judgment		×				×

Table 17 continued

Passage		Notes	Resurrection			Classification		
			Implied	Stated	Ref.	Allude	Phil.	Assume
2 Baruch	11:4	Sleep || Death	x					
	14:12-13	Possesses hope in the future || Resurrection	x					x
	15:7-8	The Righteous	x					x
	21:23-24	Sleep || Death	x					x
	23:5	Appointed number	x					
	24:1-2	Judgment/Resurrection	x			x		x
	30:1-3	The end of time		x				x
	42:7-8	Dust → Resurrection		x		x		x
	49-52	The nature of the resurrection body: The final destiny of the Righteous and the wicked		x	x			x
	57:2	Planned from the beginning		x				
	66:3	Make sure that they are really dead	x					x
	85:3	Sleep || Death	x					x
	85:9	Sleep || Death	x					x
	85:15	Resurrect the righteous	x					x
Apocalypse of Elijah	3:13	Satan cannot resurrect the dead		x				x
	4:24-29	Persecution of the Saints		x		x		x
	4:31	Satan cannot resurrect the dead		x				x
	5:25-39	End-time	x					x

1. *1 Enoch*

1 Enoch is the oldest pseudepigraphical book and is attributed to the Enoch of Gen. 5:24. It is a composite book composed by several anonymous writers between the third century BCE and 50 CE.[5] It was originally written in Hebrew or Aramaic, but the most complete form of the book is the Ethiopic version. Several fragments of this composition were also found among the Dead Sea Scrolls. *1 Enoch* contains five distinct compositions or books, as well as two appendices. Charlesworth suggests the following dating of these sections:[6]

1. *Book of the Watchers* (*1 En.* 1–36)   c. 300–200 BCE
2. *Book of the Parables* (*1 En.* 37–71)   37 BCE–66 CE
3. *Book of Astronomical Writings* (*1 En.* 72–82) prior to 200 BCE
4. *Book of Dream Visions* (*1 En.* 83–90)   about 160 BCE
5. *Book of the Epistle of Enoch* (*1 En.* 91–105) before 100 BCE

Appendices:
Birth of Noah (106–107)   prior to 100 BCE
Another Book of Enoch (108)   not clear; prior to 37 BCE?

Since the second book, the *Book of the Parables* (*1 En.* 37–71), is the only part of *1 Enoch* not found among the Dead Sea Scrolls, most scholars used to advocate a late date for this composition, dating it toward the end of the Second Temple Period.[7] However, Charlesworth argues convincingly that

---

5. See Miryam T. Brand, "*1 Enoch*," in *Outside the Bible: Ancient Jewish Writings Related to Scripture*, ed. Louis H. Feldman, James L. Kugel, and Lawrence H. Schiffman (Philadelphia: Jewish Publication Society of America, 2013), 2:1361–2; James H. Charlesworth, "A Rare Consensus Among Enoch Specialists: The Date of the Earliest Enoch Books," in *The Origins of Enochic Judaism: Proceedings of the First Enoch Seminar, University of Michigan, Sesto Fiorentino, Italy, June 19–23, 2001*, ed. Gabriele Boccaccini (Turin: Zamorani, 2002), 225–34; J. Collins, "Enoch, Book of," *DNTB* 314; and George Nickelsburg, *1 Enoch 1*, Hermeneia (Minneapolis: Fortress, 2001), 7. For a detailed introduction to *1 Enoch*, see Nickelsburg, *1 Enoch 1*, 1–125.

6. James H. Charlesworth, "Preface. The Book of Enoch: Status Quaestionis," in *Parables of Enoch: A Paradigm Shift*, ed. Darrell L. Bock and James H. Charlesworth, JCTS 11 (London: Bloomsbury T&T Clark, 2013), xiv. Also note that several of these books are themselves composites, with possibly different authorship and dating. It is also suggested that fragments of a Book of Noah are scattered throughout *1 Enoch* (*1 En.* 6–11; 54:7–55:2; 60:7-10, 24; 65–69:25; 106–107).

7. For a history of dating, see Darrell L. Bock, "Dating the *Parables of Enoch*: A *Forschungsbericht*," in Bock and Charlesworth, eds., *Parables of Enoch*, 58–113.

just because no fragment from the Dead Sea Scrolls has been identified with this book, one should not conclude a late composition is insignificant as "cumulatively, perhaps we possess only about 10 to 20 percent of the manuscripts that were in the Qumran caves before, or in, June 68 CE." He adds that since this book was probably composed in Galilee, they may not have been aware of it, or the book may not have found much sympathy in the community as its members may not have been "open to the claim that the Messiah is to be identified as the Son of Man; and, indeed, that an archangel revealed that the titles define only Enoch."[8] Based on the internal evidence in the book and archaeological data, a paradigm shift has taken place in modern scholarship regarding its dating, and the emerging consensus is that the cumulative data would suggest dating "to the time of Herod the Great and the Herodians."[9]

Due to the composite nature of *1 Enoch* and its uncertain anonymous authors and dating, this study will consider each distinctive composition by itself, rather than attempting to harmonize the eschatological view presented in the book or outline a development of the resurrection belief found in the five books of *1 Enoch*.

The Book of Watchers (1 Enoch 1–36)

A universal eschatological judgment in which all will be judged (1:7, 9), both angels and humans, both righteous and wicked, is an important theme in the Book of Watchers.[10] This theme is introduced in the first vision of Enoch (chs. 1–5) and is a theme that recurs throughout the book (e.g. 9:2-3, 10; 10:4-6, 11-13, 16-17, 20; 13:6; 15:7-10; 16:1; 19:1; 27:2-3). From the first vision Enoch learns that at the end of time (1:2) God will come down from his dwelling (1:3) to measure out his judgment, destroy of the wicked (1:9; 5:4-6, 7b), and reward the righteous (1:8; 5:7a, 8-10) with light, joy, peace, wisdom, and inheritance of the earth (5:7a, 8).

It is clear that the main concern of these judgment texts is the theodicy, noting that everyone will be held responsible for how they lived according to God's commandments (5:4). It should also be noted that although a resurrection belief (not necessarily a bodily resurrection) is not explicitly stated, these texts presume such a belief since there must be some form

---

8. James H. Charlesworth, "The Date and Provenience of the Parables of Enoch," in Bock and Charlesworth, eds., *Parables of Enoch*, 44–6.

9. Ibid., 56.

10. The universal nature of the judgment is emphasized by the repetition of the word "all" which appears 11 times in the opening vision recorded in *1 En.* 1–5 (5× in *1 En.* 1:7-9 and 6× in *1 En.* 5:6-8).

of resurrection for a person to be held accountable for his/her deeds at the time of the great judgment. As such, there are some important resurrection references in this book which will be considered below.

a. *1 Enoch* 20:8

1 Enoch 20 gives the name and functions of Gods seven[11] archangels who act as angelic guides during Enoch's journey to the outer extremities of the earth as recorded in chs. 21–23. The seventh archangel, Ramiel, oversees those who will be resurrected (v. 8). This angel does not appear again by name in the rest of this book, nor in the other books of *1 Enoch*. However, Nickelsburg makes a case that the unnamed angel speaking to Enoch in *1 En.* 81:1 could be identified as Ramiel.[12] This text will be considered under the subheading "The Book of Heavenly Luminaries."

b. *1 Enoch* 22

The second resurrection passage in the Book of Watchers is *1 Enoch* 22. In this chapter, Raphael, the archangel responsible for the spirits of the deceased (20:3), shows Enoch the place where all the spirits are stored in wait for the great eschatological judgment (22:4). This passage follows the same literary structure as the other visions recorded in chs. 20–36 with the exception of vv. 5-7 (see Table 18), which breaks the pattern.[13]

The reader needs to keep in mind that *1 Enoch* 17–36 describes Enoch's cosmic journey, and as such, the main purpose of ch. 22 is not to give a detailed description of the eschatological events, resurrection, and judgment, but rather a geographical description, showing where the

---

11. The more complete Ethiopian version of the book only gives the name of the first six archangels. However, it could be assumed that the seventh angel, Ramiel, was lost at one point in the translation history, since no other tradition attests to a list of only six archangels. Moreover, he appears in the Greek translation of the text. The seven angels also appear in other passages of *1 Enoch* (81:5; 87:2; 90:21) and in other ancient traditions (e.g. *3 En.* 17–18; Tob. 12:15; *T. Levi* 8:2; Rev. 1:4, 20). However, none of these passages refer to these seven angels as archangels.

12. This identification is based on the following two reasons. First, Ramiel does not appear in the remaining part of the book (21–26) together with the other six archangels. Second, the context of ch. 81 fits well with the function and responsibility of Ramiel. Based on the thematic parallels between *1 En.* 1–36 and 81–82, it might have functioned as a narrative bridge between the first and the last book of *1 Enoch* (see the discussion in Nickelsburg, *1 Enoch*, 334–8).

13. Marie-Theres Wacker, *Weltordnung und Gericht: Studien zu 1 Henoch 22*, FB 45 (Würzburg: Echter, 1982), 101–3.

souls are being stored.[14] Be that as it may, *1 Enoch* 22 is still a rich text regarding these eschatological issues.

Table 18. The literary structure of *1 Enoch* 22

Section	Verse	
1	1a	¹From there I traveled to another place.
2	1b-2a	And he showed me to the west a great and high mountain of hard rock ²And there were four hollow places in it, deep and very smooth. Three of them were dark and one, illuminated; and a fountain of water was in the middle of it.
3a	2b	And I Said, "How smooth are these hollows and altogether deep and dark to view."
3b	3-4	³**Then Raphael answered me**, one of the holy angels who was with me, and said to me, "These hollow places (are intended) that *the spirits (πνεύματα) of the souls (ψυχαί) of the dead* might be gathered into them. For this very (purpose) they were created, (that) here *the souls of all human beings* should be gathered. ⁴**And look, these are the pits for the place of their confinement. Thus they were made until the day (on) which they will be judged, and until the time of the day of the end of the great judgment, that will be exacted from them.**"

	1	5a	⁵There I saw
		5b	*the spirit (πνεύματα) of a dead man* making suit, and his lamentation went up to heaven and cried and made suit
	3a	6	⁶Then I asked Raphael, the watcher and holy one who was with me, and said to him, "This *spirit (πνεύματα)* that makes suit – who is it – that thus his lamentation goes up and makes suit unto heaven?"
	3b	7	⁷**And he [Raphael] answered me** and said, "This is *the spirit (πνεύματα) that went forth from Abel*, whom Cain his brother murdered. And Abel makes accusation against him until his posterity perishes from the face of the earth, and his posterity is obliterated from the posterity of men."

---

14. Nickelsburg, *Resurrection, Immortality, and Eternal Life*, 169.

3. *Apocalyptic Literature and Related Works* 101

3a	8	⁸Then I asked about all the hollow places, why they were separated one from the other.
3b	9-13	⁹**And he [Raphael] answered me and said, "These three were made that** *the spirits* (πνεῦματα) *of the dead* **might be separated.** And this has been separated for *the spirit* (πνεῦματα) *of the righteous*, where the bright fountain of water is. ¹⁰**And this has been created for <*the spirits of the*> sinners, when they die and are buried in the earth, and judgment has not been executed on them in their life.** ¹¹**Here** (ὧδε) **their** *spirits* (πνεῦματα) **are separated for this great torment, until the great day of judgment**, of scourges and tortures of the cursed forever, that there might be a recompense for their spirits. There (ἐκεῖ) will bind them forever. ¹²And this has been separated for *the spirits* (πνεῦματα) *of them that make suit*, who make disclosure about the destruction, when they were murdered in the days of the sinners. ¹³And this was created for *the spirits* (πνεῦματα) *of the people who will not be pious, but sinners, who were godless, and they were companions with the lawless*. And their *spirits* will not be punished on the day of judgment, **nor will they be raised from there.**
4	14	¹⁴Then I blessed the Lord of glory and said, "Blessed is the judgment of righteousness and blessed are you, O Lord of majesty and righteousness, who are Lord of eternity."

This chapter starts with an introductory statement (section 1 in the literary structure) followed by a description of the vision (section 2). This is followed by a dialogue between the guiding angel and Enoch in which Enoch asks for an interpretation of what he just saw (section 3a) and the angel's explanation (section 3b). This chapter concludes with Enoch praising God for his righteous justice (section 4). From this literary structure it becomes clear that sections 3a and 3b in the third part of the structure (vv. 8-13) is a continuation of section 3a and 3b of the first part of the structure (vv. 2b-4).

In Enoch's vision, a person's soul lives on, separately from the body, at the time of death. While the body is buried in the ground (v. 10), the soul of the dead is contained in one of the four "deep and very smooth" (v. 2a) chambers God has made for the souls in "a great and high mountain of hard rock" (v. 2a). A soul's placement is based on the person's behavior during their life. The first chamber is made for the righteous souls while the remaining three chambers were made for the souls of the wicked (see Table 19).

Thus, the vision presents three categories of wicked souls. The second compartment contains the souls of those who did not receive just punishment for all the wickedness they did in their life. The third compartment is more difficult to classify but it seems to contain the souls of the wicked who suffered an unjust death. Although they were wicked, they did not deserve this type of death. The fourth compartment contains a third category of wicked souls. These souls do not seem to experience any suffering following death, nor will they be a part of the eschatological judgment or resurrection (v. 13). Nickelsburg suggests the simplest explanation for why these souls are different from the previously mentioned categories of wicked souls is that "these sinners were judged during their lifetime, and for that reason they need not be recompensed either immediately after death or at the great day of judgment."[15] In other words, they received their just punishment prior to their death (see Table 19).

It is only the righteous souls and the souls of the most wicked, the ones who still need to receive more punishment, that will be resurrected at the time of the eschatological resurrection. The souls in the third and the fourth chamber do not seem to need any more punishment than what they have already received – hence, there is little need to resurrect these souls (v. 13b). This view seems very similar to the view presented in Dan. 12:2-3, which suggests that there will not be a universal resurrection but only a resurrection for the most righteous and the most wicked – although *1 Enoch* 22 implies all righteous souls will be resurrected on the day of judgment.

However, the view that only the souls of the first two chambers will experience resurrection seems to contradict the judgment scene described in the introduction of the book (chs. 1–5), which has a strong emphasis on the universal nature of the eschatological judgment (see above).

---

15. Ibid., 308. Wacker, on the other hand, attempts to limit this category of souls to the wicked generation of Noah's days (Gen. 6:3, 5-7, 11-13, 17) who were destroyed by the Deluge (see the discussion in Wacker, *Weltordnung und Gericht*, 193–5). However, there is insufficient evidence for this limited reading in the vision itself.

Table 19. The four holding compartments for the souls in *1 Enoch* 22

1st Compartment v. 9b	2nd Compartment vv. 10-11	3rd Compartment v. 12	4th Compartment v. 13
Righteous	Wicked		
	Not received just punishment in their life (v. 10)	Suffered an unjust death (v. 12)	Already received their just punishment in their life
Light/Fountain of water (vv. 2b, 9b)	Dark (v. 2b)	Dark (v. 2b)	Dark (v. 2b)
Conscious: Can request justice (e.g. vv. 5-7)	Conscious: Suffers great torment until the day of judgment (v. 11)	Conscious: Seeking vengeance for their murder (v. 12)	Unconscious? Do not seem to suffer any torment
Resurrection	Resurrection	No resurrection mentioned[16]	No need for Resurrection
Receive their reward (*1 En.* 24:2–25:6)	Judgment which will give them their deserved punishment	No judgment mentioned	No judgment needed
	Suffer eternal punishment for their evil deeds (v. 11)		

There could be several reasons for this apparent contradiction. First, it could be due to the composite nature of this book. *1 Enoch* 1–5 may have been written by a different author who may have held a different theological emphasis than the author of *1 Enoch* 22. As previously outlined, *1 Enoch* 22 is a part of Enoch's cosmic journey, where he is shown the geographical location of the souls of the dead, while *1 Enoch* 1–5 has an emphasis on God's theodicy, that everyone will be judged according to their deeds. Second, it could be argued that both *1 Enoch* 1–5 and 22 are in agreement in the sense that all souls/humans receive the reward they deserve. The souls in the third and fourth chambers have already received their deserved justice/punishment, and, as such, have no further need for punishment. The "all" in chs. 1–5 would then be referring

---

16. There may be no need for a resurrection since, through the judgment, the grievance of this person had already been met because his/her murderer receives the just punishment for that deed.

to the souls who still need to be rewarded (righteous souls in chamber one) or punished (wicked souls in chamber two). Third, there is an inconsistency of the number of chambers in ch. 22 (see Table 18, vv. 2a, 9-13).[17] Verse 2a mentions that there are four chambers while v. 9 only mentions three. However, vv. 9b-13 describe the souls in all four chambers. This has led Wacker to see evidence for a literary development of ch. 22 in which the first stage of the development had a mountain, with unspecified numbers of dark caves, where the souls of the dead were kept. The second stage of the development would have introduced the elements of the current text, the four different chambers for the four different categories of souls,[18] and the preliminary judgment of the souls upon the person's death, to determine the appropriate holding chamber. The first stage of this tradition would require a universal resurrection of the souls in order to judge them and give them their appropriate reward or punishment. The second stage of this development would only need the resurrection of the souls held in the first and second chambers since there has already been a preliminary sorting of the souls.[19] Regardless of the explanation of this apparent contradiction, the text does emphasize the justice of God's judgment of the souls of the dead (v. 14).

1) *The Souls Are Conscious*. Reading *1 Enoch* 22 it becomes apparent that the souls in the first three chambers are conscious and the souls' condition in the chamber is a part of their reward or punishment. The only souls who seem to be unconscious are the ones kept in the fourth chamber since these wicked souls have already received all the punishment they deserved (see Table 19). The souls of the righteous in the first chamber are blessed with light and a fountain of water (vv. 2b, 9b). This may be an allusion to the benevolence, described in Ps. 36:9, that God shows to those who seek refuge under his wings: "For with you is the fountain of life; in your light we see light."[20] Both these images are associated with the

---

17. The Ethiopian version is missing the differentiation between the light and the dark chambers in v. 26.

18. Wacker, *Weltordnung*, 122–31, 178–90; see also Nickelsburg, *1 Enoch 1*, 302–3.

19. Segal notes that this sorting is similar to how ancient empires dealt with their war captives – those gathered were divided into groups based on their final destiny (*Life After Death*, 278).

20. This image is similar to the New Jerusalem described in Rev. 22:1-5. However, this describes the final reward for the righteous and not the temporary reward in store for the righteous souls awaiting the resurrection, judgment, and the eternal reward, as is the case in *1 En.* 22.

righteous. The water image with life-giving force (e.g. Jer. 2:13; 17:12), alludes to God's life-giving force itself,[21] while light is often associated with God's presence and life itself (e.g. Pss. 27:1; 49:19; 56:13).[22] Thus, there are two very powerful symbols, life and God's presence, associated with the souls of the righteous who are with God. In a more literal sense, the souls of the righteous are provided water so they will not thirst. This theme is reflected in Jesus' parable of the rich man and Lazarus where the rich man experiences thirst (Lk. 16:24).

The souls of the wicked in the second chamber have a very different experience than the righteous in the first. Instead of dwelling in light, in God's presence, they are in darkness (v. 2b). This already hints at the punishment that is in store for them, where they will not be protected by God's presence.[23] Moreover, these souls have already started their suffering by experiencing great torment (v. 11a) while they are awaiting the great judgment which will bring them the full measure of God's wrath in the abyss, where they will be bound forever (v. 11). Nickelsburg notes: "The transferral [of the wicked souls at the time of judgment] and the distinction between now and then [in v. 13] also indicates that the sinners' present suffering is not to be understood as final and full judgment."[24] He adds: "The contrast between 'here' (ὧδε, *baze*) [v. 11a] and 'there' (ἐκεῖ, *baheya*) suggests that at the judgment they will be transferred to another place of torment, presumably Gehenna."[25]

The souls in the third chamber do not seem to suffer physical pain *per se*, but rather suffer a restless existence while they wait for justice due to their unjustified violent death (v. 12). In some ways, their situation is similar to that suffered by Abel (vv. 5-7), who was murdered by his brother Cain and who also suffered an unjustified violent death (see discussion in the following section) – although Abel's soul is righteous, while the souls

---

21. Jesus plays on this theme in Jn 4:10, 14 by stating that he offers living water and whoever drinks it will have eternal life.

22. Jesus is also referring to himself as the light of the world and claims that whoever follows him will not be in darkness but will have light of life (Jn 8:12). The association of light, God's presence, and the act of salvation is also the emphasis of Jn 1:4-9.

23. This is also a strong image used by Jesus in his parables (e.g. Mt. 8:12; 22:13; 25:30). It is interesting that darkness came over the land when Jesus was dying on the cross, which Jesus understood as an indication that God, his father, had forsaken him (Mt. 27:45-46; Mk 15:33-34).

24. Nickelsburg, *1 Enoch 1*, 308.

25. Nickelsburg, *Resurrection, Immortality, and Eternal Life*, 169.

of the third chamber are wicked. Importantly, the text does not specify whether or not these wicked souls will resurrect. The lack of resurrection may be due to the "rest" they will receive when their murderer is judged at the time of the eschatological judgment, at which time they will have no further grievance.

The souls of the last chamber seem to be unconscious since they have already suffered enough in their life. As such, no further punishment is necessary, hence, no resurrection occurs.

2) *Abel's Suit unto Heaven*. The middle section of the literary structure (see Table 18, vv. 5-7) interprets and elaborates on God's comment to Cain after he had murdered his brother Abel: "What have you done? Listen! Your brother's blood cries out to me from the ground" (Gen. 4:10). John Byron notes that the next narrative, in which the word אָח/ ἀδελφός, *brother* appears, is at the end of the flood narrative (Gen. 9:4-6),[26] in a passage that also contains the word דָם/αἷμα, "blood," and the same subject matter, the killing of a human being – see the highlighted sections of the text. It seems like the author of Gen. 9:5 points back to the Cain and Abel narrative as if to say, "Whoever takes human life is like Cain."[27] Gordon Wenham also notes a close link between Gen. 9:1-7 and Gen. 1:28-29 and considers this link as more than a simple reassertion of the pre-flood food law, but rather, a modification and a reassertion of "the sanctity of human life in light of chapter 4."[28]

Genesis 4:9-10	Genesis 9:4-6
⁹וַיֹּאמֶר יְהוָה אֶל־קַיִן אֵי הֶבֶל אָחִיךָ וַיֹּאמֶר לֹא יָדַעְתִּי הֲשֹׁמֵר אָחִי אָנֹכִי: ¹⁰וַיֹּאמֶר מֶה עָשִׂיתָ קוֹל דְּמֵי אָחִיךָ צֹעֲקִים אֵלַי מִן־הָאֲדָמָה:	⁴אַךְ־בָּשָׂר בְּנַפְשׁוֹ דָמוֹ לֹא תֹאכֵלוּ: ⁵וְאַךְ אֶת־דִּמְכֶם לְנַפְשֹׁתֵיכֶם אֶדְרֹשׁ מִיַּד כָּל־חַיָּה אֶדְרְשֶׁנּוּ וּמִיַּד הָאָדָם מִיַּד אִישׁ אָחִיו אֶדְרֹשׁ אֶת־נֶפֶשׁ הָאָדָם: ⁶שֹׁפֵךְ דַּם הָאָדָם בָּאָדָם דָּמוֹ יִשָּׁפֵךְ כִּי בְּצֶלֶם אֱלֹהִים עָשָׂה אֶת־הָאָדָם:

---

26. J. Byron, *Cain and Abel in Text and Tradition: Jewish and Christian Interpretation of the First Sibling Rivalry*, TBN 14 (Leiden: Brill, 2011), 188.

27. U. Cassuto, *A Commentary on the Book of Genesis. Part 2, From Noah to Abraham* (Jerusalem: Magnes, 1949), 127.

28. G. Wenham, *Genesis 1–15*, WBC 1 (Waco, TX: Word Books, 1987), 192.

⁹καὶ εἶπεν ὁ θεὸς πρὸς Καιν ποῦ ἐστιν Αβελ ὁ ἀδελφός σου ὁ δὲ εἶπεν οὐ γινώσκω μὴ φύλαξ τοῦ ἀδελφοῦ μού εἰμι ἐγώ ¹⁰καὶ εἶπεν ὁ θεὸς Τί ἐποίησας φωνὴ αἵματος τοῦ ἀδελφοῦ σου βοᾷ πρός με ἐκ τῆς γῆς	⁴πλὴν κρέας ἐν αἵματι ψυχῆς οὐ φάγεσθε ⁵καὶ γὰρ τὸ ὑμέτερον αἷμα τῶν ψυχῶν ὑμῶν ἐκζητήσω ἐκ χειρὸς πάντων τῶν θηρίων ἐκζητήσω αὐτὸ καὶ ἐκ χειρὸς ἀνθρώπου ἀδελφοῦ ἐκζητήσω τὴν ψυχὴν τοῦ ἀνθρώπου ⁶ὁ ἐκχέων αἷμα ἀνθρώπου ἀντὶ τοῦ αἵματος αὐτοῦ ἐκχυθήσεται, ὅτι ἐν εἰκόνι θεοῦ ἐποίησα τὸν ἄνθρωπον
⁹ Then the LORD said to Cain, "Where is your brother Abel?" "I don't know," he replied. "Am I my brother's guardian?" ¹⁰ Then He said, "What have you done? Your brother's blood cries out to Me from the ground!	⁴ However, you must not eat meat with its lifeblood in it. ⁵ I will require the life of every animal and every man for your life and your blood. I will require the life of each man's brother for a man's life. ⁶Whoever sheds man's blood, his blood will be shed by man, for God made man in His image.

In Gen. 4:10, Abel's blood has been personified and cries out to God for justice. A case could be made that the author of *1 Enoch* 22 understood this personification literally, especially in light of Gen. 9:4 which sees a connection between דָּם/αἷμα, "blood," and נֶפֶשׁ/ψυχή,[29] "life." Given these two closely connected texts, the ancient interpreter may have understood these texts to suggest that "something" survives a person's death and that "something" is conscious and, in the case of Abel, demands justice from God due to the great injustice committed against him. Moreover, the interpreter may have identified the נֶפֶשׁ/ψυχή, "life," of Gen. 9:4 with נְשָׁמָה/πνοή or רוּחַ/πνεῦμα,[30] "breath," which is the word used in the creation story when God "formed man of the dust of the ground (עָפָר מִן־הָאֲדָמָה) and breathed into his nostrils the breath of life (נִשְׁמַת חַיִּים) and man became a living being (לְנֶפֶשׁ חַיָּה)" (Gen. 2:7). In Eccl. 12:7,

---

29. Later Greek thinking, ψυχη, held "three areas of meaning; (a) psychē in the sense of the impersonal basis of life, life itself; (b) the inward part of man; (c) and independent soul, in contrast to the body" (C. Brown, "ψυχη," *NIDNTT*, 3:677). The third meaning (c) is the one used in *1 En.* 22.

30. E. Kamlah notes that πνεῦμα, due to Hellenistic influence, was understood in Judaism as "a vital force divinely breathed into man and forming a distinct part of his being; it was not distinguished from the 'soul' as far as terminology was concerned, but was contrasted rather with the body: the body is of the earth, the spirit stems from heaven" (E. Kamlah, "πνεῦμα," *NIDNTT*, 3:692).

the writer describes death as the reversal of the creation act and uses רוּחַ/πνεῦμα, "breath," for spirit instead: "Then the dust will return to the Earth as it was, and the spirit (רוּחַ/πνεῦμα) will return to God." Thus, the "something" is the spirit/soul that God placed in the body to make a living person and this "something" leaves the body at the point of death. This is how *1 Enoch* 22 can suggest that Abel's voice/soul will be heard until the final judgment when Cain and his seed will receive all the punishment they are due. Byron adds that this notion could also be supported by the present tense of the verbs describing Abel's blood crying out, suggesting that the blood would never go silent.[31] Thus, Abel's cry for vengeance would be ongoing.

Byron also observes that Abel's blood in Gen. 4:9 is in the plural form, דְּמֵי, "bloods." This indicates that the blood is not only the blood of Abel but would also include the blood of all his descendants who were never born.[32] This would explain Abel's demand that Cain's descendants need to be erased too, based on the *lex talionis* principle. Thus, Cain became the arch-type of the wicked while Abel serves as an arch-type of any innocent person who has been murdered.[33]

It is easy to see how this interpretation of Gen. 4:9-10 fits nicely into the context of *1 Enoch* 22, where it almost functions as the exegetical foundation of the chapter. If the "essence" of the person survives death, where is it going? *1 Enoch* 22 reveals that there are holding chambers for these "souls." If Abel's soul is demanding justice, it must be conscious in the period it is in the chamber, as is expanded upon in *1 Enoch* 22. Since Cain did not suffer the deserved punishment for his murderous act at the time of this heinous deed due to God's "protection" (Gen. 4:15), Abel still has an "open case" against Cain, hence, why his voice is still heard, and Cain still has a punishment in store for him in the last judgment (*1 En.* 22:7). Since Cain functions as a type of all murderers and is the father of the "evil seed" (v. 7), *1 Enoch* 22 finds support for the destiny of the souls in the second chamber (the wicked souls who did not receive all their punishment in this life). If Abel's "soul" can demand justice for his unjust death, it would be reasonable to assume that even the wicked souls

---

31. Byron, *Cain and Abel*, 190.

32. Ibid. This is also the interpretation given to Gen. 4:10 in rabbinic traditions: "Whoever destroys a soul, it is considered as if he destroyed an entire world. And whoever saves a life, it is considered as if he saved an entire world" (*y. Sanh.* 4:1 [22a]; cf. *b. Sanh.* 37a).

33. For further reading, see the chapter, "The Blood of Righteous Abel," in Byron, *Cain and Abel*, 167–205.

could have such a demand (souls in the third chamber) if they suffered a similar fate. This is supported by the law in Gen. 9:5-6 which does not differentiate between righteous and wicked but presents a universal law protecting everyone.

3) *Bodily or Spiritual Resurrection.* The *Book of Watchers* does not explicitly address the nature of the eschatological resurrection – whether it will be a bodily or just a resurrection of the soul. In *1 En.* 22:11b and 13b, Raphael seems to indicate that it will only be a resurrection of the spirit for the wicked, rather than body and soul, and it is the soul which will receive the punishment. Chapter 22 does not reveal what will happen to the righteous souls on the day of judgment, however, *1 En.* 20:8 reveals that the archangel Ramiel is in charge of those who resurrect. Nickelsburg suggests that Ramiel may be identified with the angel Jeremiel in *4 Ezra* 4:35-37, who is associated with the souls of the righteous who await the resurrection.[34] *1 Enoch* 5:7-10 and 25:1-7 reveal the destiny intended for the righteous, after the resurrection and the great judgment. The righteous will be rewarded with "light, joy, and peace, and they shall inherit the earth" (5:7). The righteous will also be able to touch the fragrant fruit tree and eat of its fruit for life (25:4-5). Moreover, the fragrance from this place of reward shall penetrate their bones (25:6). Collectively this suggests that the resurrection in store for the righteous will be a bodily one. Although, Elledge notes *1 Enoch* 25 does not describe this eschatological life as everlastting but, rather, as antediluvian – similar in length to those described in Genesis 5–9 that were very long, but did have an end point.[35] This unique feature seems to contradict *1 Enoch* 22, which suggests the wicked souls will exist past the eschatological Day of Judgment (*1 En.* 22:13) and be bound and plagued forever (*1 En.* 22:11). Thus, the net effect of the view presented in the *Book of Watchers* is that while the wicked soul will exist forever, the lives of the resurrected righteous will not. Figure 6 illustrates the death and resurrection concept in the *Book of Watchers*.

---

34. Nickelsburg, *Resurrection, Immortality, and Eternal Life*, 170.
35. Elledge, *Resurrection of the Dead in Early Judaism*, 143. It could be argued this long, but limited eschatological life for the righteous feature is influenced by the description of the New Earth by Isaiah (Isa. 65:17-25). In this passage, Isaiah seems to suggest there will still be death as he writes: "No more shall there be in it an infant that lives but a few days, or an old person who does not live out a lifetime; for one who dies at a hundred years will be considered a youth, and one who falls short of a hundred will be considered accursed" (Isa. 65:20, NRSV).

Figure 6. Death and Resurrection in the *Book of Watchers*.

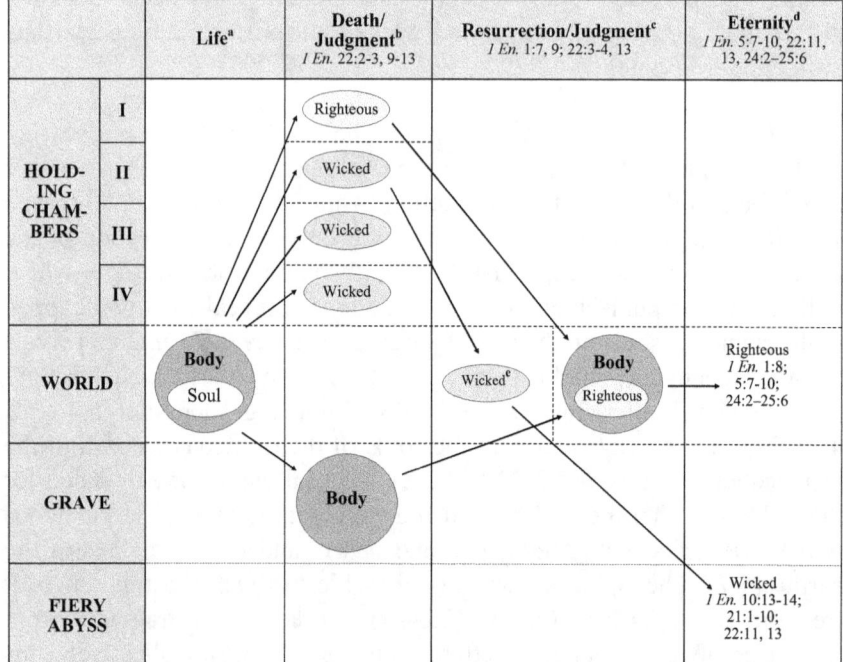

ᵃ *1 Enoch* 22 states that the soul of the dead person will be kept in one of four holding chambers while waiting for the eschatological judgment. This suggests that this life is the determining factor deciding a person's destiny both in the first judgment (sorting of souls into the four chambers) and in the final eschatological judgment.

ᵇ *1 Enoch* 22:2a mentions that there will be four distinct holding chambers for the souls, one for the righteous and three for the wicked (22:2, 9-13). The reward and punishment experienced by the souls in this phase of existence is a foretaste of what they have in store for them on the day of judgment and should be considered a part of their reward or sentence (22:9-13).

ᶜ Only the righteous and the wicked who did not receive the punishment they deserved while living will be resurrected in order to receive further punishment in the fiery abyss.

ᵈ *1 Enoch* 25:6 seems to suggest the eschatological life of the resurrected righteous will not be everlasting, but rather, is antediluvian. However, the *Book of Watchers* seems to suggest an eternity for the wicked souls.

ᵉ *1 Enoch* 22:11 is not clear where the souls in the second chamber will end up in the final judgment. It all depends on what the phrase "There he will bind them forever" refers to. Is it the original chamber or a secondary place? Nickelsburg suggests that v. 11 may be a reference to "the fiery abyss," the place where all the rebellious angels are cast as a part of their punishment (*1 Enoch 1*, 308).

~ ~ ~

The Book of Parables (*1 Enoch* 37–71)

The *Book of Parables* is the second and the longest section of *1 Enoch*. Most scholars consider these parables to be the latest addition to the *1 Enoch* collection. Nickelsburg and VanderKam date them "between the latter part of Herod's reign and the early decades of the first century C.E., with some preference for the earlier part of this time span."[36] Charlesworth notes that the consensus view has come to date the chapters "to the time of Herod the Great and the Herodians."[37] The introduction, ch. 37, introduces Enoch by providing his genealogy (v. 1) and notes that there are three "things" that he would like to reveal "to those who dwell upon the earth" (v. 5). These three "things" are revealed through the three parables, which is the main content of this book. The first, regards the coming judgment of the wicked (chs. 38–44). The second, the lot of the sinners (chs. 45–57). The third, the destiny of the righteous and the elect ones (chs. 58–69).

The eschatological judgment is the dominant theme[38] and, as such, permeates the book.[39] Nickelsburg and VanderKam note that each parable "begins with an oracular introduction and then features scenes that take place in heaven," these heavenly scenes "focus on the developing drama of the judgment over which the chosen one [Son of Man] will preside"[40] Since the book seems to call for an eschatological judgment of both the righteous and the wicked, the judgment would require a resurrection of all who have lived. As such, the judgment texts of this book imply a resurrection belief. Although there are many hints of a resurrection belief,[41] there are only two clear resurrection texts in this book, *1 Enoch* 51 and 61.

---

36. George W. E. Nickelsburg and James C. VanderKam, *1 Enoch 2: A Commentary on the Book of 1 Enoch, Chapters 37–82*, Hermeneia (Minneapolis: Fortress, 2012), 63. For further discussion on the dating of the book, see ibid., 58–63.

37. Charlesworth, "The Date and Provenience of the Parables of Enoch," 56; see also Bock, "Dating the Parables of Enoch," 112.

38. Nickelsburg and VanderKam, *1 Enoch 2*, 49.

39. The judgment is mentioned throughout the book; see Table 17 for a list of some of these texts.

40. Nickelsburg and VanderKam, *1 Enoch 2*, 19.

41. *1 Enoch* 40:9 gives the name of four archangels, the fourth being Phanuel, who is "set over all actions or repentance unto the hope of those who would inherit eternal life." Although resurrection is not mentioned in this text, it is certainly implied by the "hope" held by the righteous who will "inherit eternal life."

1 Enoch 49:3 also hints at a future resurrection by referring to the dead righteous as "those who have fallen asleep." Referring to death as sleep suggests that death is a temporary condition, just like sleep. If you are sleeping, it is expected that you will awake at some point. This figurative language is also used in Dan. 12:2 when

a. *1 Enoch* 51.

The first resurrection passage can be divided into three subsections, introduced by the phrase "in those days" (highlighted in gray), a term associated with the judgment (see Table 20).[42] Based on this structure, resurrection is considered a part of the eschatological judgment, which is presided over by the Chosen One (v. 2) who is "the second-most-dominating figure in the Parable."[43] It is he who functions as God's agent, who has been given the authority to sit upon God's throne, and who reveals the God-given secrets of wisdom (v. 3). At the conclusion of this judgment, all the righteous, whom the Son of Man has found among the resurrected, will dwell on the transformed earth (vv. 4-5) while the wicked will receive their punishment (50:4-5; 52–54).

Although the main focus is on the role and function of God's Chosen One (bolded in the text), the text still reveals some interesting details regarding the resurrection of the dead. From the second subsection (vv. 5a-3), it becomes apparent that both the righteous and the wicked will partake in this resurrection, since the Chosen One will "choose the righteous and holy from among them" (v. 2a). The "them" is a reference to all those who were resurrected, meaning that he chooses the righteous from this group, the un-chosen members presumably are the wicked. Thus, it seems the author of this parable expects a double resurrection, if not a universal resurrection and judgment. This fits nicely with the introduction to the Book of Watchers, which states unequivocally that "there will be judgment on all" (*1 En.* 1:7; see the discussion above).

The first subsection regards the nature of the resurrection and makes it clear to the reader that it will be a bodily resurrection. Nickelsburg and VanderKam note that "the three lines of the tristich stand in complementary and almost synonymous parallelism to one another" (see the boxed words in Table 20) and adds that the three words, entrusted–entrusted–owes, for the dead who will be resurrected "derives from the world of finance"[44] (see the underlined words in Table 20). This vocabulary emphasizes the temporalness of death and God's ownership of all the people. The text considers the dead bodies (and souls?) as great treasures which were only placed in the earth or in *Sheol* (v. 1a-b) for safekeeping awaiting the

---

describing death and resurrection and is well attested in the New Testament (Mt. 27:52; Jn 11:11; Acts 7:60; 13:36; 1 Cor. 7:39; 11:30; 15:6, 18, 20, 51; 1 Thess. 4:13–15; 2 Pet. 3:4).

42. Nickelsburg and VanderKam, *1 Enoch 2*, 13.
43. Ibid., 42.
44. Ibid., 183–4.

eschatological judgment ("in those day"), or as a great debt which needs to be repaid in full by the destruction (v. 1c) whenever God decides to collect what belongs to him.

Table 20. Literary structure of *1 Enoch* 51

Resurrection	⁵¹:¹ In those days, the earth will give back what has been entrusted to it,
	    and Sheol will give back what has been entrusted to it,
	    and destruction will restore what it owes.

Judgment
 	
(Presided over by the Son of Man)
	⁵ᵃ For in those days, my **Chosen One [Son of Man]** will arise,
	² and choose the righteous and holy from among them,
	    for the day on which they will be saved has drawn near.
	³ And the **Chosen One [Son of Man]**, in those days, will sit upon my throne,
	    and all the secretes of wisdom will go forth from the counsel of **his** mouth,
	    for the Lord of Spirits [God] has given (them) to **him** and glorified **him**.

The Earth to Come
 	
(The Righteous will live on a transformed earth)
	⁴ In those days the mountain will leap like rams,
	    and the hills will skip like lambs satisfied with milk;
	    and the faces of all the angels in heaven will be radiant with joy,
	⁵ᵇ and the earth will rejoice,
	    and the righteous will dwell on it,
	    and the chosen will go upon it.

How the tristich relates to each other is a matter of interpretation. If earth–*Sheol*–destruction are considered as synonyms, they would all refer to the earth where the body was buried, with no reference to the soul/ spirit of the person which was the main concern of *1 Enoch* 22, in the first book of *1 Enoch*. However, if Earth, *Sheol* and Destruction are viewed as complementing each other by referring to two different places, earth and *Sheol*, it would imply that the body would be returned from the earth and the Spirit from *Sheol* (e.g. *1 En.* 102:5) on the day of resurrection. Thus, the soul/spirit would reunite with the body before the judgment takes place. "Destruction" could either be read as a synonym of *Sheol*, where the soul/spirit dwells, or as literal destruction or decaying which takes place after a person has died. In either case, the earth, *Sheol*, and destruction all have to give back what belongs to God. These three phrases parallel *4 Ezra* 7:32 (see the section on *4 Ezra* in the previous chapter) and *Pseudo-Philo* 3:16, which will be discussed later.

The last subsection of the text reveals the reward that will be experienced by the chosen on the transformed earth,[45] those who the Son of Man found righteous (vv. 4-5b), using the words from Ps. 114:4. This psalm describes God's deliverance of his people from the land of Egypt, a fitting analogy to the ultimate salvation (v. 2) God's people will experience when the kings, the mighty, and the sinners will be made powerless as a result of the eschatological judgment. Thus, the righteous will be liberated from their suffering and abuse and be rewarded, much like the slaves were liberated from their slave masters in Egypt and were made into the people of God with whom he dwelt.

Nickelsburg and VanderKam observe several shared elements between *1 Enoch* 51 and Dan. 12:1-3 but present them in a different order:[46]

Daniel 12	***1 Enoch* 51**
Michael arises (v. 1a)	Chosen One arises (v. 5a)
Time of trouble (v. 1b)	Presumed from previous context
Your people will be saved (v. 1cα)	Righteous and holy will be saved (v. 2)
The book (v. 1cβ)	– (but see 47:5)
Resurrection (v. 2a)	Resurrection (v. 1)
Long life in Jerusalem (v. 2β)	Life on renewed earth (v. 5b-d)
Condemnation of wicked (v. 2γ)	Condemnation of sinners (v. 3b)
Everlasting life in Jerusalem	Righteous will dwell on the earth
Righteous will shine like the stars (v. 3)	Angels are radiant (v. 4c)

It is the activity of Michael (he will raise up) that introduces the judgment scene (Dan. 12:1) in which the resurrection is a key element (Dan. 12:2), while in *1 Enoch* 51 the judgment follows the resurrection event in which the Chosen One will arise. This reordering of the author *of 1 Enoch* 51 may be to emphasize that it is not the Chosen One who will resurrect the dead, but rather, that God has only placed him in charge of the judgment.

b. *1 Enoch* 61:1-5 and 62:12-16

The second resurrection passage, *1 En.* 61:1-5, begins with the same phrase, "in those days," as the first passage (*1 En.* 51), thus appearing in the same context, the eschatological judgment. This resurrection statement is also mentioned before God "seated the Chosen One up on the throne of glory and he will judge all the works of the holy ones" (v. 8). It follows a

---

45. Nickelsburg and VanderKam, *1 Enoch 2*, 40.
46. Ibid., 186.

similar literary pattern as *1 Enoch* 22 by giving the new setting (v. 1a – "in those days"), followed by a vision shown (v. 1), Enoch's question to the guiding angel (v. 2a), and the angels' explanation of the vision (vv. 2b-5), see Table 21.

Table 21. The literary structure of *1 Enoch* 61:1-5

Setting	1a And I saw in those days,
Vision	1b Long cords were given to those angels, and they took for themselves wings and flew and went towards the North
Question	2a And I asked the angel, "Why did these take the cords and go?"
Explanation	2b And he said me, "They went so that they may measure." 3 And the angel who went with me said to me, "These will bring the measurements of the righteous, and the ropes of the righteous to the righteous; so that they may rely on the name of the Lord of Spirits forever and ever. 4 And the chosen will begin to dwell with the chosen; and these are the measurements that will be given to faith, and they will strengthen righteousness. 5 And these measurements will reveal all the secrets of the depths of the earth, and those who were destroyed by the desert, and those who were devoured by beasts, and those who were devoured by the fish of the sea; so that they may return and rely on the day of the Chosen One, for no one will be destroyed in the presence of the Lord of Spirits, and no one is able to be destroyed."

The vision shows angels bringing measuring cords with them (vv. 1, 2b) to measure the place which has been prepared for the righteous in the North (v. 1; cf. *1 En.* 32:1-3; 70:3; 77:3; Zech. 2). It is only after their return that they reveal these measurements to the righteous. This revelation, according to the angel, gives great hope and strengthens the faith of the righteous (v. 4).[47] Nickelsburg and VanderKam note "the point here seems to be that, by bringing to the righteous the measurements of the place of their future habitation, the angels provide the righteous with

---

47. This would be similar to the encouraging words given by Jesus to his followers in Jn 14:1-4 to calm their troubled hearts. He is assuring them that God is already preparing a place for them in his house and they can be confident there will be more than enough space.

the 'ropes' or the moorings that stabilize them, or enables them to rely (lit. 'to lean'), through faith, on the name of the Lord of Spirits."[48] This will ensure their steadfastness and give them the strength to remain righteous so that they can receive their reward at the resurrection.

Since this is the backdrop of the resurrection passage, it should not be too surprising that it only concerns itself with the resurrection of the righteous (v. 5).[49] According to the angel, the measurement, the great promise regarding the future dwelling place of the righteous, is also given to the righteous dead (v. 5a), to those who have been destroyed by the desert (v. 5b), devoured by beasts (v. 5c), or devoured by the fish of the sea (v. 5d). Nickelsburg and VanderKam state that these modes of death, by focusing on those who died outside "the limits of human habitation," the desert and the sea (v. 5b, d), or by the beasts or fish (v. 5c, d) inhabiting those areas, are still included in the resurrection hope.[50] In other words, regardless of how and where you died, if you are righteous, you will be resurrected in order to receive your reward.[51] This is the good news which the angels would share with those who are currently dwelling in the depths of the earth, perhaps referring to the souls of the righteous residing in *Sheol* (v. 5a).

The second half of the resurrection promise (v. 5e-g) reinforces the all-inclusive nature of the resurrection of the righteous, noting that "no one will be destroyed in the presence" of God (v. 5f) and "no one is able to be destroyed" (v. 5g). Thus, death is not the final destination but a temporary condition while waiting for the eschatological judgment presided over by the Chosen One (61:8-9). The righteous will then be rewarded with a bodily existence that will never end (62:13-15). The resurrection language of *1 En.* 62:15a, referring to the garment of glory (eschatological bodies), sounds similar to Paul's depiction of the resurrection in 1 Cor. 15:40-45. Nickelsburg and VanderKam observe that the language used in v. 15a is traditional and parallels Isa. 52:1-2 "with its double reference to rising from the dust and putting on new garments of strength" adding that "the

---

48. Nickelsburg and VanderKam, *1 Enoch 2*, 244.

49. It is implied in the following chapters that the wicked are also resurrected and reveals the judgment and punishment given to them (chs. 62–63).

50. Nickelsburg and VanderKam, *1 Enoch 2*, 245. This hope sounds familiar to the faith demonstrated by the widow in 2 Macc. 7, who encouraged her seven sons to hold onto the resurrection hope even if their bodies would be completely destroyed, since the creator God would still be able to recreate them on the day of judgment (see the discussion in section "2 Maccabees 7" above).

51. This issue is also addressed by Rabbi Eleazar and Rabbi Abba ben Memel in *b. Ketub.* 111a, and by Rabbi Simai in *Gen. Rab.* 94.

language of 62:15 may refer to the assumption of new bodies both by the living, whose degradation could be described as laying in the dust (cf. Isa. 52:2), and by the dead, whose bodies have been committed to the earth."[52] The last verse refers to the garments of glory as the garments of life (v. 16a) which will never wear out (v. 16b), since they will dwell with God forever (v. 16c).

c. Concluding Remarks

The main difference between these two resurrection passages is the function held by the resurrection. In *1 Enoch* 51, the resurrection takes place in order for the judgment to take place. However, in *1 Enoch* 61, the resurrection is a part of the judgment, since the righteous will receive their reward. This is probably the reason why the resurrection of the wicked is specifically mentioned in the second passage.

The difference in emphasis between the resurrection passages in the *Book of Watchers* and the *Book of Parables* should also be noted. In *1 Enoch* 22, the main focus is where the souls will be stored while waiting for the eschatological judgment, while the actual resurrection itself is only implied as a part of the judgment scene. In *1 Enoch* 51 and 61, the resurrection is the key event for the commencement of the judgment (ch. 51) or is a part of the judgment (ch. 61). The details of the phase between death and resurrection seems less important. The resurrection passage in the first book has more of a geographical function while the passage in the second book has more of a theological function.

The Book of Astronomical Writings (1 Enoch 72–82)

The third book contained in *1 Enoch* is mainly concerned with astronomical data. It was originally written in Aramaic, attested by the copies found among the Dead Sea Scrolls (4Q208-211), and was later translated into Greek. Based on the Aramaic script of the oldest fragments, this composition is dated to about 200 BCE.[53] Due to the content of this book, it only contains one possible allusion to the resurrection as a part of a reference to a future judgment. In *1 En.* 81:1-4, the angel Uriel shows Enoch all the heavenly tablets (v. 1), one of which contains the actions of all people who will be living on earth for all the generations of the world (v. 2). At the end of Enoch's study of these books, he states "blessed is the one who dies righteous and good; regarding him no book

---

52. Nickelsburg and VanderKam, *1 Enoch 2*, 267–8.
53. VanderKam, *An Introduction to Early Judaism*, 89.

of wickedness has been written and no day of judgment will be found" (v. 4). This alludes to a future resurrection due to the expected judgment where everyone will be kept responsible for their deeds written in the book. Apart from revealing a possible resurrection view, this text provides little information regarding that possible resurrection belief.

The Book of Dream Visions (1 Enoch 83–90)

The fourth book of *1 Enoch* dates to the time of the Maccabees, this dating being based on the content of the two dream visions contained in the book. However, some of the material in these dreams may be dated earlier.[54] These visions were originally written in Aramaic, which is attested by the fragments found among the Dead Sea Scrolls (4QEn-c-f). The first vision (chs. 83–84) reveals the coming judgment of the flood while the much larger second vision, the animal apocalypse (chs. 85–90), gives an allegorical description of the world's history starting with Adam and ending with the eschatological judgment. Nickelsburg notes that Noah's flood functions as a type in these two dream visions for the eschatological judgment.[55]

There are three passages which may allude to a future resurrection. The first, *1 En.* 84:4-6, mentions the great day of judgment which is paralleled with the judgment of the flood story. Enoch's request and supplication (vv. 5-6) asks God to differentiate between the sinful humanity and the righteous humanity, by keeping a remnant, much like Noah and his family, who survived the judgment and became like "seed-bearing plants forever" (v. 6).

The second allusion to a resurrection belief is the use of the word "sleep" as an allegory for "death" (89:36-38). In the dream vision, regarding the Exodus to the death of Moses, the vision refers to the death of Moses as the sheep who had become a man falling asleep (v. 38). As has already been noted, the term "sleep" emphasizes the temporary nature of death, that a person will once more awake in the great day of judgment.

The last text of interest is *1 En.* 90:20-37 which describes the eschatological judgment and the new age. In this passage, God summons certain wicked individuals who will be judged and "thrown into that fiery abyss" to be burned (vv. 26-27). These individuals belong to three separate groups of people: the first group to be judged are the first fallen

---

54. Nickelsburg, *1 Enoch 1*, 8. Nickelsburg adds that most of the content of the first dream vision is reworked material and "modified to fit the present context" (346, 361).

55. Ibid., 347.

stars/angels (vv. 21, 23); the second group refers to the seventy shepherds whom God had placed in charge of his sheep but who had killed more than he had permitted (vv. 22, 25); and the last group refers to the blinded sheep (vv. 26-27). The identity of these blinded sheep is not clear. They may refer to the wicked who have survived until the day of judgment or they could be referring to all the wicked who have lived since the time of the golden calf, the later alternative requiring a resurrection.

The description of the new age includes a new temple which will be greater than the old and will be able to house all God's righteous sheep (v. 28). Verse 33 draws the attention to *1 En.* 89:75, stating that all "those who had been destroyed and dispersed" have returned to the new "house." Nickelsburg suggests this pairing points to Ezekiel 34 and 37, the latter using "the metaphor of death and resurrection" when describing the dispersion and the future return. Thus, "the return of those who have been 'destroyed' suggests a literal resurrection of the dead, which is sometimes described as a return of the dispersion."[56] The dream vision concludes by noting that the new age will be filled with peace (v. 34) and all the sheep, the wild beasts, and all the birds of heaven (v. 37) were changed and became white cattle (v. 38). In other words, the new age will include both Jews and Gentiles, indicating a return to "created unity" and transforming them "into primordial righteousness and perfection."[57]

The Book of the Epistle of Enoch and Other Writings (*1 Enoch* 91–105)

The last book of *1 Enoch* is a collection of many small literary units which have been skillfully combined into "a unified work with direction and generic shape."[58] Chapter 91, in which Enoch gives his final instruction to his son and the rest of his family (91:1), functions as a bridge chapter. It follows Enoch's instructions to his son Methuselah by recounting the *Dream Visions* (83–90) and the *Apocalypse of Weeks* which focuses on the judgment theme (92–93), followed by six lengthy discourses (94:6–104:8), all dealing with the two-way theology and the problem of theodicy. The last chapters of the book contain a narrative regarding the *Birth of Noah* (106–107) and some additional Enoch material (108). John Collins considers the dating of this collection of works to be "the same as the other early Enoch books, [dated to] the early second century B.C."[59]

56. Ibid., 405–6.
57. Ibid., 407.
58. Ibid., 420.
59. Collins, "Enoch, Book of," *DNTB* 316.

Due to the judgment theme and the great interest shown in the question of theodicy, it is not surprising that there are several references to the resurrection hope in this book.

a. *1 Enoch* 91:8-17

The first passage of interest opens with the phrase "in those days," and describes the total destruction of evil in the judgment of fire where they (the wicked) will be destroyed in fierce eternal judgment (vv. 8-9). At the end of this judgment scene, the text turns its attention towards the righteous, who "will arise from his sleep" (v. 10a). Nickelsburg and VanderKam note that vv. 10-17 are textually problematic in their current location and were probably "displaced from their original location after 93:10."[60] They suggest the resurrection reference in v. 10 was added to create a transition between v. 9 and the misplaced section (vv. 11-17).[61] Regardless of its role, v. 9 does contain evidence of a resurrection hope for the righteous, who will be given wisdom upon their resurrection. This verse uses the same metaphor, sleep for death, as other texts of *1 Enoch*, emphasizing the temporary nature of death suffered by the righteous. The last statement of this narrative bridge ends with the warning that those who "walk in the path of violence" will "perish forever" (v. 19), suggesting that those who walk in the path of the righteous will experience a different outcome.[62]

b. *1 Enoch* 92:2-5

It is not clear if this text uses the terminology "arise from sleep" (v. 3a) as a metaphor for the resurrection or as a metaphor for awakening in a spiritual sense. The latter interpretation seems more likely since the comment that the righteous will arise in order to walk in the path of righteousness would seem strange if this passage was referring to the righteous in the world to come.

c. *1 Enoch* 102:4–104:8

In Enoch's sixth and last discourse, "the announcement of the coming judgment reaches its climax."[63] In this section, the author contrasts the

---

60. George W. E. Nickelsburg and James C. VanderKam, *1 Enoch: A New Translation* (Minneapolis: Fortress, 2004), 138.

61. See the discussion on "The Original Order of Chapter 91–93," in Nickelsburg, *1 Enoch 1*, 414–15.

62. This observation is also made in *1 En.* 98:13-14, which suggests the wicked lack any hope of life (v. 14b), and thus, implies the righteous will.

63. Nickelsburg, *Resurrection, Immortality and Eternal Life*, 143.

views held by the wicked and the righteous, both dead and alive, regarding the judgment and the resurrection. The author quotes and summarizes the views held by these groups before addressing and refuting them (see Table 22 for the literary structure of the sixth discourse, based on Nickelsburg's structure[64]).

Table 22. The literary structure of *1 Enoch* 102:4–104:8

I	Addressed to the righteous dead	102:4–103:4
	a. Exhortation to the righteous	102:4-5
	b. Quotes the speech of the sinners	102:6-11
	c. Author's answer to this	103:1-4
II	Addressed to the dead sinners	103:5-8
	a. Address	103:5ab
	b. Quotes the speech of sinners	103:5c-6
	c. Author's answer to this	103:7-8
III	Addressed to the living righteous	103:9–104:6
	a. Address	103:9a
	b. Quotes the righteous	103:9b-15
	c. Author's answer to this	104:1-6
IV	Addressed to the living sinners	104:7-8
	a. Address	104:7a
	b. Quotes the sinners	104:7b
	c. Author's answer to this	104:7c-8

1) *The First Section*. The first section of this literary structure is addressed to the righteous dead (102:4–103:4). The author tells the righteous souls to be hopeful since they have died in righteousness ensuring (that although they were not rewarded for their piety during their bodily life) their death is not the end of the matter (102:4-5). They will receive justice although the sinners may claim that everyone will receive the same destiny, *Sheol*, regardless of behavior in the bodily life,[65] and that there is no reward for a righteous life (102:6b-11b).[66]

The author, however, refutes this sentiment (103:1-4) by noting that God has indeed prepared "Good things and joy and honor for them" and "much good will be given you [them] on the place of your [their] labors"

64. Ibid., 144.
65. This is reminiscent of the observation made in Eccl. 7:15 that everything is vanity, since the just are perishing while the wicked prosper.
66. This observation brings to light two unsettling possibilities. Either God does not care how people live their lives and, thus, does not reward or punish people, or the righteous are really the wicked and the wicked are really the righteous. These are the troubling questions contemplated by the righteous souls.

(103:3). In fact, their future reward will surpass the pleasure experienced in this life by the sinners (103:3c). All this, according to the author, will be possible due to the eschatological resurrection of "the souls of the pious" who will never perish but spend eternity with God (103:4). Because of this, the souls of the righteous dead should not fear (102:4; 103:4).

The great news for the righteous souls is that their reward is still in store for them; God has not forgotten them (103:3a states everything has been written down). It is important to remember that the first section only addresses resurrection of the soul, excluding the body (103:3a [ψυχαι], 4a [πνεύματα]).

2) *The Second Section.* The second section addresses the dead sinners (103:5-8) who took great pleasure in the fact that they got away with their sinful lives without suffering any consequences (see the repetition of the phrase, "in their life," in v. 6b and v. 6d). They view only the present world as the place for reward or punishment.

However, the author makes it clear that there will be a day of reckoning. The souls/spirits of the wicked will be brought to *Sheol*, like the souls/spirits of the righteous, but their experience of *Sheol* will be quite different. The souls of the righteous are experiencing grief while the souls of the wicked will experience great anguish (103:7b). Their existence will be "in darkness and in a trap and in a burning flame" (103:8a). Moreover, their spirit/souls will participate in the eschatological judgment (103:8b). Thus, they will have no peace while in *Sheol* (103:8c). This section continues its focus on the soul/spirit, referring to their existence in *Sheol* and to their future judgment (vv. 7-8 using ψυχαί in both cases).

3) *The Third Section.* The third section addresses the living righteous (103:9–104:6), who are experiencing the curses rather than the promised covenant blessings of Deuteronomy 28. The righteous seem to agree with the observation held by the wicked, that the theology of the two scenarios are flawed or non-factual (103:9-15). The author refutes this sentiment since the angels of heaven remember them and their names are written down (104:1). Moreover, their oppressors will be held responsible (104:3d), so they do not have to fear the great judgment which will hold the sinners accountable for their actions (104:5). Thus, the sinners will be dealt with in the future so the righteous are told "do not be companions with them" (104:6b). Instead, the righteous will shine like "the lights of heaven" (104:2b), "the portals of heaven will be open" for them (104:2c),

and they "will have great joy like the angels of heaven" (104:4b). Rather than being companions with the sinners, the righteous will dwell with the hosts of heaven (104:6d). Although this section does not address the topic of resurrection, it does reveal that the living will be brought to heaven and become like lights (stars) or angels, alluding to Dan. 12:3.

4) *The Fourth Section*. The last section addresses the living sinners, warning them that all of their sins are written down (104:7c). They may think there are no consequences for their sinful behavior, but at the day of judgment they will receive their full eternal punishment (104:5d).

5) *Concluding Remarks*. These four sections share many similarities with Dan. 12:1-3: both texts address the day of judgment (Dan. 12:1; *1 En.* 103:8; 104:5); both texts refer to books with names which will be used to measure out the judgment (Dan. 12:1; *1 En.* 104:7-8); both texts mention the resurrection (Dan. 12:2; *1 En.* 103:4a) and the permanence of the rewards and punishments (Dan. 12:2-3; *1 En.* 103:4c, 8b); and finally, both texts mention the righteous, or wise, will shine like stars (Dan. 12:3; *1 En.* 104:2b), suggesting the righteous will become like angels.

There are also some significant differences between these two texts. First, in Daniel the dead sleep in the dust of the earth (אַדְמַת־עָפָר) while in *1 En.* 102:4–103:8 the souls of the dead dwell in *Sheol*. Second, Dan. 12:2a describes a limited resurrection of some of the righteous and some of the wicked (Dan. 12:2a) while *1 En.* 102:4–103:8 seems to suggest that only the righteous will be resurrected from *Sheol* while the wicked souls will remain in what has now become "Hell," but the text really is unclear. Third, Dan. 12:2 describes a bodily resurrection while *1 En.* 103:3-4 describes only the resurrection of the soul. Fourth, Dan. 12:1-3 gives no indication that a soul/spirit can live independently from the body while *1 En.* 102:4–104:8 says the soul/spirit lives on after death and is what will be judged and will receive the reward or punishment. Fifth, Dan. 12:1-3 suggests that there will be a limited judgment for only those who have been resurrected while *1 En.* 102:4–104:8 claims that everyone will be judged. Sixth, in Dan. 12:1-3 there is no indication that the dead are conscious while in *1 En.* 102:4–104:8 the souls/spirits seem to have an awareness while in *Sheol*. Figure 7 illustrates the death and resurrection concept in the sixth discourse of the *Book of the Epistle of Enoch* (102:4–104:8).

Figure 7. Death and Resurrection in the *Book of the Epistle of Enoch*.

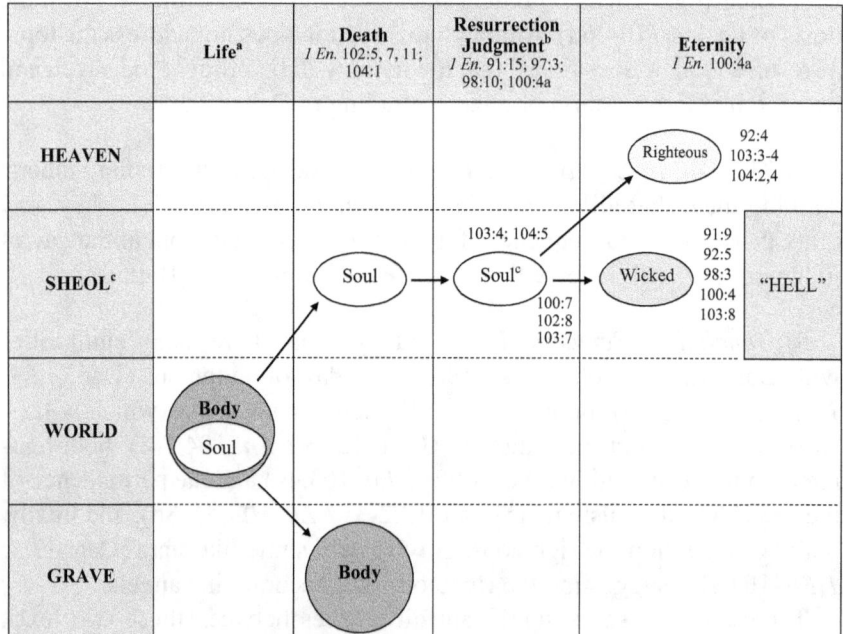

[a] The destiny of the righteous and the wicked is determined by their deeds while they are alive in this life. This two-way theology is prevalent in the book (e.g. *1 En.* 94:1-5 which sets the tone for the major part of the book), noting this world will be a testimony against the sinners since all their deeds are written down day by day until the day of judgment (*1 En.* 95:3; 96:4; 97:4,6; 98:6-8; 104:8). The sinners will be recompensed according to their deeds (*1 En.* 100:7), as such, the righteous will judge the living sinners (*1 En.* 98:12).

[b] While the righteous souls will experience the eschatological resurrection to receive their longed for reward, the wicked souls seem to remain Sheol to continue their punishment. At this point, after the resurrection, Sheol seems more like Dante's Inferno than the Sheol of the TaNaKh. The wicked spirits will be in a fiery furnace (*1 En.* 98:3b), burning (*1 En.* 102:1) and cursed forever without peace (*1 En.* 102:3). The book seems to show no interest in a bodily resurrection of the righteous. It only focuses on their souls which will shine like the luminaries of heaven (*1 En.* 104:2b) and experience great joy like the angels of heaven (1 *En.* 104:4b). Thus, their heavenly existence will be different than while on earth – the soul will no longer dwell in an earthy body but will dwell in something similar to the angels.

[c] This book does not mention specific chambers for the dead souls like *1 Enoch* 22, it only mentions Sheol as the destiny of the dead souls – righteous and wicked. However, Sheol will be experienced differently by the righteous and the wicked souls. The souls of the righteous will descend into Sheol with grief (*1 En.* 102:5) due to the problem of theodicy. The wicked souls, while in Sheol, will experience great distress,

darkness, snare, and flaming fire (*1 En.* 103:7-8). The text is not clear if the righteous souls will also be conscious while in Sheol or if they will merely rest peacefully (*1 En.* 91:10).

~ ~ ~

d. *1 Enoch* 108

The last resurrection passage of *1 Enoch* appears in an addendum to the book. Although it is a later edition to the larger work and may have been written during the first century CE, elements of this addendum reflect much older material.[67] Nickelsburg observes that this chapter "is actually a summarizing and interpretive conclusion to the corpus."[68] It reveals what will happen to the sinners (vv. 2-6) and the righteous (vv. 10-12) as the result of the eschatological judgment, their ruling being based on what has been written in the heavenly records (vv. 7-10a, 15b). The author concludes that it will be a transparent judgment since both the righteous and the wicked will see what happened to the other group (vv. 14-15); thus, the righteous are vindicated and the wicked are punished in "Hell."

In this chapter, the author makes clear that the current life determines whose name will be written in the book of life (vv. 1b, 7-10), and only those who have their name written in that book will have their spirit resurrected (v. 11), transformed (into shining lights, v. 12a), manifested (shining like stars, v. 12), and exalted (heavenly enthronement, v. 12b) by this vindication.

As in *1 Enoch* 102–104, no mention is made of a resurrection of the souls of the wicked. The text only states that they will suffer in *Sheol*, describing it almost as if it is "Hell" (108:5-6). Thus, the wicked souls may be in no need for a resurrection since they are already experiencing "Hellfire." Regarding the living sinners, they will be punished on the day of judgment and will join the wicked souls in "Hell" (v. 2). From this it seems that the judgment will be universal – everyone will receive judgment according to what is written in the book, but only the righteous dead will be resurrected and will join the righteous living in heaven.[69]

Regarding the nature of this resurrection, at first glance it appears that a resurrection of the spirit only, but a careful reading of the text seems to

---

67. Nickelsburg, *1 Enoch 1*, 554.
68. Ibid., 552.
69. Verse 11c may suggest that there are some righteous who were properly compensated for their piety in this world (in their body) and would therefore not require any further reward. This would be in line with Dan. 12:2. However, the many categories of righteous listed in the book of life and books of records (vv. 3, 7, 10) seems to suggest a universal reward for the righteous, including the righteous dead.

suggest a physical reality of the righteous in heaven, more like a bodily experience. The saved will sit on the throne of their honor (v. 12b) and they will shine like the righteous in Dan. 12:3. This may suggest that they will receive "new" bodies which radiate light in contrast to the old ones who were buried in the earth.[70]

e. Concluding Remarks

The five books of *1 Enoch* present various views on the resurrection belief. All the books view the eschatological judgment as the solution to the problem of theodicy, and the resurrection belief is what makes the judgment possible. Without it, a person could not be held responsible for his/her behavior and God would not be able to hand out His blessings and curses. Several of these resurrection passages share similar language and concepts with the book of Daniel, especially with the resurrection statement in Daniel 12. Genesis 4:9-10 functions as the foundation of the resurrection concept in *1 Enoch* 22.

Considering the resurrection views illustrated in Figures 6 and 7, it becomes clear that each book has a different emphasis. The first book shows a greater emphasis or interest in the "extra-terrestrial" geography, exploring the place where all the souls will be held in wait for the eschatological judgment. The fifth book, on the other hand, focuses on the theological problem of the two-way theology. It also becomes clear that the place prepared for the righteous influences the nature of the resurrection belief. If the righteous are to dwell on a renewed earth, a bodily resurrection becomes necessary. If a heavenly dwelling is proposed, a "spiritual" body, like that of the angels, seems to be the answer. Regardless of where the righteous go upon their resurrection, the wicked will spend their eternity in the fiery abyss or "Hell."

2. 2 Enoch

2 Enoch has only survived in two Old Slavonic recensions (one short [A] and one longer [J]), both translated from Greek, but may have had a Semitic origin.[71] Craig Evans suggests a late first-century CE date for the

---

70. This would be similar to the idea presented in the discussion on the nature of the resurrected body by Paul in 1 Cor. 15:35-57. The resurrected bodies are here described as glorified, incorruptible, radiant, and spiritual.

71. F. I. Andersen, "2 (Slavonic Apocalypse of) Enoch," *OTP* 1:94; Michael E. Stone, "Apocalypse Literature," in *Jewish Writings of the Second Temple Period*, ed. Michael E. Stone, CRINT 2 (Assen: Van Gorcum; Philadelphia: Fortress, 1984), 406–7.

composition, possibly authored by an Egyptian Jew.[72] The composition expands on Gen. 5:21-32, from Enoch to the flood, and adds a great amount of apocalyptic material. It has three major sections: Enoch's heavenly journey (1–34), his revelation and instructions to his children (35–68), and ends with the antediluvian priesthood (69–73).[73] Andersen notes the eschatological predictions in the book, which, in addition to the flood, reveal the fate of humans after their death, both the good and the bad. This revelation was, according to the author, shown to Enoch on his guided tour of the seven heavens,[74] which included Paradise and the place of punishment (second [7–10], third [8–10] and fifth heaven [18]).[75]

The many judgment texts in *2 Enoch* also allude to an eschatological resurrection (see Table 17 for a list of these texts). *2 Enoch* 65:6-11 serves as a great example, noting that "each person will go to the Lord's great judgment" (v. 6), implying also the dead will also be judged. All the righteous who survive this judgment will then be gathered in the "great age" to spend all eternity in Paradise, where they will have great light (v. 9) and shine forth like the sun (v. 11). The resurrection hope is also alluded to in *2 En.* J70:1, which reveals Methusalam's hope "in an eternal inheritance," and 70:3 compares his death to rest, the same metaphor used in *1 Enoch*. However, there is only one clear resurrection text in *2 Enoch* and it will be explored in the following section.

a. *2 Enoch* J32

2 Enoch J32 is found at the end of the author's interpretation and expansion on the creation story which began in *2 En.* J24:2b. As a consequence of Adam and Eve's transgression in Paradise, just hours after their creation, God cursed "mankind's evil fruit-bearing" so the "fruit of doing good is sweet and exertion" (J31:7-9),[76] and adds an interesting exegetical, or rather a Midrashic, reading of Gen. 3:19b, the last phrase of the "curse" spoken to Adam.[77]

---

72. Evans, *Ancient Texts for New Testament Studies*, 30.

73. There is also an appendix to the book, *2 Enoch in Merilo Pravednoe*, which is a thirteenth-century composition containing material taken from *2 Enoch*.

74. The longer recension (J) lists an additional three heavens, bringing the total to ten.

75. Andersen, "*2 (Slavonic Apocalypse of) Enoch*," 91.

76. The author attempts to lessen the impact of the curses in Gen. 3:14-19 by limiting them to human actions rather than a curse on the humans in general, the earth, or any other creature (*2 En.* J31:7).

77. This interpretation is also attested in *Gen. Rab.* 20:10.

2 Enoch J32:1	Genesis 3:19 (CSB)
	You will eat bread by the sweat of your brow until you return to the ground,
You are earth,	since you were taken from it.
and into the earth once again you will return out of which I took you.	For you are dust, and you will return to dust.
And I will not destroy you, but I will send you away to what I took you from.	
Then I can take you once again at my second coming.	

The author perceives a resurrection hope in the biblical texts, noting that death will not ultimately destroy a person. Although a body will return to earth at the point of death, the person will once more be recreated from this earth at the second coming. The connection between a bodily resurrection belief and the creation account was already observed in the mother's encouraging words to her seven sons in 2 Macc. 7:23 (see the discussion regarding 2 Macc. 7 in the previous chapter of this study). This thought is also expressed in *Targum Pseudo-Jonathan*, one of the Aramaic translations of the Hebrew Scripture,[78] presenting the resurrection as a part of the eschatological judgment in which everyone will be judged, as opposed to the more general reference to the second coming in *2 En.* J32:1.[79]

Genesis 3:19

PJT	WTT
בליעות כף ידך תיכול מזונא	בְּזֵעַת אַפֶּיךָ תֹּאכַל לֶחֶם
עד דתיהדור לעפרא	עַד שׁוּבְךָ אֶל־הָאֲדָמָה
דמינא איתבראת	כִּי מִמֶּנָּה לֻקָּחְתָּ
ארום עפרא אנת ולעפרא תתוב	כִּי־עָפָר אַתָּה וְאֶל־עָפָר תָּשׁוּב:
ומן עפרא אנת עתיד למיקום	
למיתן דינא וחושבנא על כל מה דעבדת	
ביום דינא רבא:	

78. *Targum Pseudo-Jonathan* tends to paraphrase the biblical text, adding midrashim which is not found in other Targumim (Martin McNamara, *Targum and Testament Revisited: Aramaic Paraphrases of the Hebrew Bible*, 2nd ed. [Grand Rapids: Eerdmans, 2010], 264). The earlier *Targum of Onqelos* gives a literal translation of the Hebrew text and therefore does not share the interpretative expansion of Gen. 3:19b given by *Pseudo-Jonathan* and *2 Enoch*.

79. Andersen argues that the phrase "second coming" does not necessarily suggest the expansion to be a Christian interpolation. He observes "the idea is [already] present in *Jub.* 1:26, where God descends at the end of the world, and lives with his purified children for eternity" ("*2 [Slavonic Apocalypse] Enoch*," 155 n. 32c).

By the labor of your hands you shall eat food until you turn again to the dust from which you were created: for dust you are, and unto dust you shall return; for from the dust it is to be that you are to arise, to render judgment and reckoning for all that you have done, in the day of the great judgment.	You will eat bread by the sweat of your brow until you return to the ground, since you were taken from it. For you are dust, and you will return to dust.

Comparing *Targum Pseudo-Jonathan* with *2 En.* J32:1 expansion, J32:1 places special emphasis on the belief that death will not be able to destroy the person, perhaps as an attempt to neutralize the great certainty of death God warned Adam he would suffer as a consequence of eating of the forbidden fruit: בְּיוֹם אֲכָלְךָ מִמֶּנּוּ מוֹת תָּמוּת, "on the day you eat of it [the fruit] you will certainly die" (Gen. 2:17).

b. Concluding Remarks

2 Enoch does not address what happens to the soul in the intermediate period, between physical death and the physical re-embodiment at the time of resurrection based on the interpretation of Gen. 3:19. *2 Enoch* J23:5 implies not only the pre-existence of the souls[80] but also their predestination (cf. J49:2; J53:2), noting: "All the souls of men, whatever of them are not yet born, and their places, prepared for eternity. For all the souls are prepared for eternity, before the composition of the earth."

The author of *2 Enoch* also states that the spirits will not perish (*2 En.* 58:6). However, it is not revealed where the souls will be stored or whether or not they are conscious.[81] At the time of the resurrection, everyone will be judged according to deeds while alive (*2 En.* 62:3 makes clear that there is no repentance after death). The righteous will receive their eternal inheritance in Paradise, located in the third Heaven (*2 En.* 8:1–9:1;

---

80. This belief seems to be more clearly stated in Wis. 8:19-20 and is also present in the writings of Philo, Josephus, and among the Rabbis of the Amoraic Period (see Winston, *Wisdom of Solomon*, 25–32, 198).

81. The condemned angels, those who joined the rebellion against God (*2 En.* 7:3), who are imprisoned in the Second Heaven, and are tormented unceasingly while waiting for the eschatological judgment (*2 En.* J7:1), belong to a different category than the humans.

42:3-14; 44),[82] receiving glorious bodies (*2 En.* 22:8) and becoming like the angels (*2 En.* 22:10; 66:7). This is the same image presented in Dan. 12:3, where the righteous will become like stars. The wicked, on the other hand, will receive their eternal reward in "Hell" (*2 En.* 10:1-6; 40:12-13; 41:2; 42:1), located in the fifth heaven. There they will experience all kinds of torture and torment, in cruel darkness and lightless gloom with black fire blazing up perpetually with a river of fire (*2 En.* 10:1-2). Figure 8 illustrates the death and resurrection concept in *2 Enoch*.

Figure 8. Death and Resurrection in *2 Enoch*.

	Pre-Creation[a] *2 En.* J49:2	Life[b] *2 En.* 2:2; 9:1; 10:4; 19:5	Death[c] *2 En.* 58:6; J62:2-3	Resurrection/ Judgment *2 En.* J32:1; 39:5; 42:7; J65:6	Eternity *2 En.* 9:1; 10:6; 50:2; 61:2; J63:4; 66:7
GOD?	Soul				
Paradise **3rd Heaven**					Righteous *2 En.* 8:1-9:1; 42:3-14; 44; 66:7
"Hell" **5th Heaven**				*2 En.* 22:8	Wicked *2 En.* 10:1-6; 40:12-13; 41:2; 42:1
WORLD		Body Soul		Body Soul	
GRAVE			Body Soul		

[a] *2 Enoch* J49:2 suggests that souls are pre-existent. However, the text reveals little regarding this phase.

[b] This life determines the future destiny—eternity in Paradise or eternity in "Hell."

[c] *2 Enoch* does not reveal where the soul goes during the in-between period, but it does state that it will reunite with the body at the time of resurrection.

~ ~ ~

82. *2 Enoch* 8:5 reveals that the third Heaven, the location of Paradise, is located between the corruptible and incorruptible. Thus, Paradise is not located on the present earth (corruptible) nor in God's abode (incorruptible), which according to *2 Enoch* is located in the seventh through to the tenth heaven (*2 En.* 20–22). Paul also gives an explicit reference to the third heaven as the place where he was taught by God in Paradise (2 Cor. 12:2-4).

3. *3 Enoch*

3 Enoch, according to the introduction, was written by Rabbi Ishmael, the High Priest (*3 En.* 1:1; 2:3), who died in 132 CE, the year the Bar Kokhba revolt started. Although *3 Enoch* has been attributed to Ishmael, most scholars believe it was written over a longer time-period, the oldest section reflecting traditions from the time of the Maccabees, while the final redaction would be dated to the fifth or sixth century CE.[83] It was originally written in Hebrew and is a part of Jewish mystical tradition, *Hekhalot* literature.[84] Collins notes that "while this book is considerably later than *1 Enoch* and *2 Enoch*, it may, in a sense, be considered the culmination of the tradition about Enoch's ascent to heaven."[85] The book records Ishmael's Heavenly journey (*3 En.* 1–2), where he meets the exalted Enoch who is called Metatron (*3 En.* 3–16),[86] and is shown the heavenly household (*3 En.* 17–40), and the wonders of Heaven (*3 En.* 41–48).[87]

The universal judgment and resurrection themes are also important in *3 Enoch*. However, unlike *1 and 2 Enoch*, this book shows no interest in the eschatological judgment, nor sees any need for an eschatological resurrection. Instead, it presents an individual judgment at the point of death which includes a resurrection of the soul in order for it to be judged before God's throne. The two resurrection passages in *3 Enoch* will be considered in the following sections.

a. *3 Enoch* 28:7-10

The first resurrection passage appears at the end of the judgment scene found in *3 Enoch* 28. In this passage, God sits on his throne of judgment every day (*3 En.* 28:7) to reward or punish the souls of those who have just died (cf. *3 En.* 28:10; 31:2; 44:3). The language used to describe this judgment (*3 En.* 28:7) seems to be taken from Dan. 7:9-10 – see the highlighted sections of the text. Both texts mention "the throne of judgment," the books needed for the judgment to take place, the heavenly host and the judge.

---

83. P. Alexander, "*3 (Hebrew Apocalypse of) Enoch*," *OTP* 1:299.
84. Collins, "Enoch, Books of," 317.
85. Ibid.
86. In *3 Enoch*, Metatron is the lesser YHWH (*3 En.* 12:5; 48C:7; 48D:1 [90]), God's vice-regent (*3 En.* 10:3-6), and sits on a throne next to God's presiding over the court (*3 En.* 16:1). This angel shares many similarities with the archangel Michael and with Jesus Christ of the New Testament.
87. Evans, *Ancient Texts for New Testament*, 31.

Daniel 7:9-10	3 Enoch 28:7[88]
⁹חָזֵה הֲוֵית עַד דִּי כָרְסָוָן רְמִיו וְעַתִּיק יוֹמִין יְתִב לְבוּשֵׁהּ ׀ כִּתְלַג חִוָּר וּשְׂעַר רֵאשֵׁהּ כַּעֲמַר נְקֵא כָּרְסְיֵהּ שְׁבִיבִין דִּי־נוּר גַּלְגִּלּוֹהִי נוּר דָּלִק: ¹⁰נְהַר דִּי־נוּר נָגֵד וְנָפֵק מִן־קֳדָמוֹהִי אֶלֶף אַלְפִים יְשַׁמְּשׁוּנֵּהּ וְרִבּוֹ רִבְבָן קָדָמוֹהִי יְקוּמוּן דִּינָא יְתִב וְסִפְרִין פְּתִיחוּ:	⁷ ובכל יום ויום כשה[ק]ב״ה יושב על כסא הדין ודין את העולם כולו <u>וספרי חיים וספרי מתים פתוחים לפניו</u>. *כל בני עליונים עומדים לפניו באימה ובירא ובפחד וברעדה.* באותה שעה ה[ק]ב״ה יושב על כסא הדין בדין. לבושו לבן כמו שלג ושער ראשו כמו צמר נקי ומעולה כולו כאור נגה וכולו מלא צדקה בשריון
⁹"As I kept watching, **thrones were set in place, and the Ancient of Days took His seat**. His clothing was white like snow, and the hair of His head like whitest wool. His throne was flaming fire; its wheels were blazing fire. ¹⁰ A river of fire was flowing, coming out from His presence. *Thousands upon thousands served Him; ten thousand times ten thousand stood before Him.* **The court was convened**, *and* <u>the books were opened</u>.	⁷And every day, as the Holy One, blessed be He, is sitting upon the Throne of Judgment and judges the whole world, <u>and the Books of the Living and the Books of the Dead are opened before Him</u>, *then all the children of heaven are standing before him in fear, dread, awe and trembling.* At that time, (when) **the Holy One, blessed is He, is sitting upon the Throne of Judgment to execute judgment**, his garment is white as snow, the hair on his head as pure wool and the whole of his cloak is like the shining light. And he is covered with righteousness all over as with a coat of mail.

Moreover, the concept of the court officers, עירין, "watchers," and קדישין, "holy ones," in *3 En.* 28:8-9 is probably taken from Daniel 4, which refers to celestial beings descending from heaven to carry out God's judgment on King Nebuchadnezzar (Dan. 4:13, 17, 23). This is the only passage in the TaNaKh where these two words appear together, also in the context of divine judgment.

---

88. Unless otherwise stated, the Hebrew text and the English translation of *3 Enoch* is taken from Hugo Odeberg, *3 Enoch or the Hebrew Book of Enoch: Edited and Translated for the First Time with Introduction, Commentary & Critical Notes*, Library of Biblical Studies (New York: Ktav, 1973).

The main difference between these two passages is when the judgment will take place. While the judgment scene in Dan. 7:9-10 is a unique eschatological event, taking place after the "time and times and half a time" period (Dan. 7:25), and introduces the Messianic era (Dan. 7:13-14, 27), the judgment scene in *3 Enoch* 28 suggests that the author understood this judgment as a daily occurrence (ובכל ויום יום, "and every day"). Regardless of this difference, the outcome of both judgment scenes are in the favor of the saints (Dan. 7:27) and the righteous (*3 En.* 28:10).

It is in the author's concluding remark on the judgment scene (v. 10) where he explains the meaning of the names of the court officers (עירין, "watchers," and קדישין, "holy ones") that the resurrection is mentioned.

Why are they called 'Irin and Qaddishin? By reason that they sanctify the body and the spirit with lashes of fire on the third day of the judgment, as it is written (**Hos. vi. 2**): "**After two days will he revive us**: on the third **he will raise us up**, and we shall live before him."	ולמה נקרא שמן עירין וקדישין. על שם שמקדישין את הגוף ואת הנשמה בפלסאות של אש ביום הג׳ של דין שנאמ׳ ((**הושע ב׳ ו׳**)) יחיינו מיומים הג׳ יקימנו ונחיה לפניו:

Their names reflect their function as being in charge of the sanctifying process of both the body (הגוף) and the soul (הנשמה) with the help of purifying fire, during the three-day-long judgment process everyone will experience upon death. The author quotes Hos. 6:2 in support of this "judgment of the grave" phase, which will culminate in the resurrection, the reviving (חיה) and raising up (קום) of the person to life (חיה) before God. The only difference between Hos. 6:2 and the quote in *3 Enoch* 28 is the abbreviation of "the third day," בַּיּוֹם הַשְּׁלִישִׁי in Hosea and הג׳ in *3 Enoch*.[89]

This resurrection text discloses little regarding the nature of the resurrection apart from revealing that it will take place after a three-day purification process and involves both the dead person's body and soul. It also seems to suggest the resurrection to be universal and the said purification process will enable everyone to come before God, whether the person was righteous or wicked during his/her life. This understanding is supported by the judgment scene in *3 Enoch* 44, which reveals that the wicked and the intermediate souls will be brought down from the presence (מלפני) of God and the *Šekinah* in Heaven, as they are receiving

---

89. *Gen. Rab.* 56:1-2 is also commenting on the three-day period in Hos. 6:2 in light of the resurrection belief.

their sentences (v. 3), eternal fire in Gehinnom,[90] or a limited purification process in *Sheol* before they will join the righteous souls for all eternity in Heaven. This passage also supports the body and soul aspect of the resurrection suggested in *3 En.* 28:10. According to *3 En.* 43:2 and 44:5-6, the resurrected souls will have bodies. However, these bodies seem to be different from the earthly ones (see Table 23). *3 Enoch* 15:1 lends further support to this belief since Enoch's earthly body was transformed when he was taken to heaven.[91]

Table 23. The bodily forms of the soul

15:1	Righteous	Forthwith my flesh was changed into flames, my sinews into flaming fire, my bones into coals of burning juniper, the light of my eye-lids into splendor of lightnings, my eye-balls into fire-brands, the hair of my head into hot flames, all my limbs into wings of burning fire and the whole of my body into glowing fire.
43:2		And he lifted me up to his side, took me by his hand lifted me up near the Throne of Glory by the place of the *Shekina*; and he revealed the Throne of Glory to me, and he showed me the spirits that have been created and had returned: and they were flying above to Throne of Glory before the Holy One, blessed be He.
44:5	Intermediate	And behold the appearance of their faces (and, lo, it was) as the appearance of children of men, and their bodies like eagles. And not only that but (furthermore) the color of the countenance of the intermediate was like pale grey on account of their deeds, for there are stains upon them until they have become cleaned from their iniquity in the fire.
44:6	Wicked	And the color of the wicked was like the bottom of a pot on account of the wickedness of their doings.

90. The text does not clearly state how long the wicked will be tortured in the fire of Gehinnom, but it would be reasonable to assume it will last for all eternity. Like *2 Enoch*, *3 Enoch* also implies that the soul (נְשָׁמָה) pre-exists (cf. *2 En.* J49:2; *3 En.* 43:1, 3), but *3 Enoch* adds a few more details and places a strong emphasis on the immortal nature of the soul. Thus, all souls will survive death, the righteous with God and the wicked in Gehinnom (*3 En.* 43–44). The "intermediate souls," those who are neither righteous enough for Heaven or wicked enough for Gehinnom, will be purified in *Sheol* until they are fit to join the righteous souls in Heaven (*3 En.* 44:2-3a, 5b).

91. The theme of a celestial body is also hinted at in the fragment 15B:5 when Moses was taken to heaven to receive God's law, expanding on Exod. 34, noting that "light shines from the skin of your [Moses'] face from one end of the world to the other" (*OTP* 1:304).

b. *3 Enoch* 44:7a

In the second clear resurrection reference, Rabbi Ishmael is shown the souls of the patriarchs and the righteous (*3 En.* 44:7a) who bring petitions before God on behalf of God's people, to intervene and redeem His people and reveal His kingdom on earth (v. 7b):

And I saw the spirits of the Patriarchs and *Abraham*, *Isaac*, *Jacob* and the rest of *the righteous* **whom they have brought up out of their graves and who have ascended to the Heaven**. And they were praying before the Holy One, blessed be He, saying in their prayer: "Lord of the Universe!"	וראיתי נשמתן של אבות העולם <u>אברהם יצחק ויעקב</u> ושאר <u>הצדיקים</u> **שמעמידים אותם מקבריהם ועולים לרקיע** ומתפללין לפני ה[ק]״בה ואומר׳ בתפלה רש״ע.

This passage does not add any new details regarding the resurrection, but it does support the reading given to the first resurrection text (*3 En.* 28:10) and the judgment scene in *3 Enoch* 43–44, that the righteous will spend eternity in Heaven upon the completion of the three-day judgment of the grave.

c. Concluding Remarks

3 Enoch presents a rather developed picture of the events that will take place upon the death of a person. The person will undergo a three-day cleansing process which will enable him/her to stand before God's throne, before he/she is resurrected and brought to Heaven in order to receive his/her eternal sentence based on their behavior before the point of death, which is supported by the author's interpretation of Daniel 7. Based on this outcome, they will either remain in Heaven, spend eternity in Gehinnom, or be purified in *Sheol* before being able to join the righteous in Heaven. Thus, *3 Enoch* lacks both an eschatological judgment and resurrection due to the individual purification process, resurrection, and judgment experienced by each person upon death. The person receives his/her punishment and reward immediately following their sentencing. Hosea 6:2 served as an important resurrection text. Figure 9 illustrates the death and resurrection concept in *3 Enoch*.

Figure 9. Death and Resurrection in *3 Enoch*.

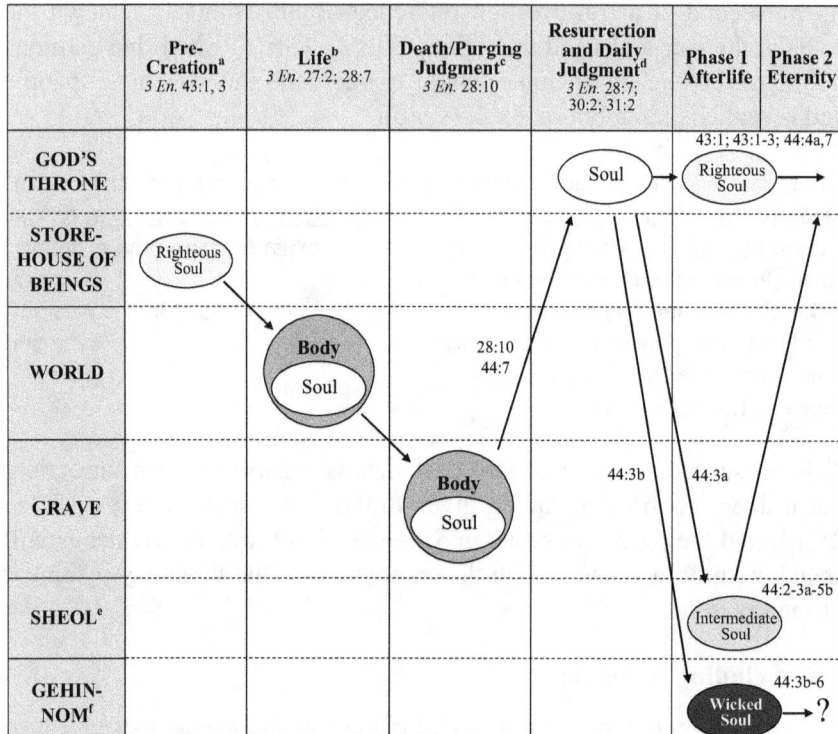

[a] *3 Enoch* 43:1, 3 implies that the souls pre-exist. These "unborn" spirits are kept in the Heavenly storehouse until they are "created" or "born," when they are given a body. During this stage, *3 Enoch* suggests they are righteous. Thus, it is the earthly phase that will determine their ultimate destination, if a soul will return to God's throne or receive eternal punishment in Gehinnom.

[b] This life determines the future destiny of the soul. Based on all the heavenly records, each individual soul receives its reward in Heaven or proper punishment in Sheol or Gehinnom.

[c] *3 Enoch* 28:10 seems to suggest a three-day purgatory phase upon death as a part of the "judgment of the grave." It is not clear from the text if this is a pre-judgment phase or a part of the final judgment of the individual dead. *3 Enoch* 44:3 may indicate the former, since the "intermediate" and the wicked souls are brought down from God's presence and not from the grave. During this phase, the Watchers are sanctifying the body and the soul with "lashes of fire on the third day of judgment," to prepare the soul to stand before God's presence in Heaven, implying a universal, but also an individual, resurrection.

[d] *3 Enoch* does not present an eschatological resurrection and judgment, instead, God sits on the throne of judgment every day, interpreting Dan. 7:10 as a daily occurrence. Each day, God judges every single matter that comes before him pertaining to

the world's affairs (*3 En.* 28:8-9; 30:2) and passes judgment on those who have just died (28:10; 31:2; 44:3). Based on this judgment of the souls, they are divided into three categories: the righteous, the wicked, and the in-betweens. The resurrected souls will receive "spiritual bodies" with human form. The righteous souls will have bodies like eagles (*3 En.* 44:5a, i.e. like angels, cf. *3 En.* 2:1; 24:11; 26:3), the intermediate souls will be gray (or greenish) since they are tainted by sins (44:5b), and the wicked will be black as "the bottom of a pot" due to their wickedness (44:6).

e The "Intermediate Souls" are purified from sin in Sheol (Phase 1). As a soul becomes pure, it joins the "righteous" souls in heaven (Phase 2).

f Gehinnom is the final destination place where the wicked souls are brought after the individual resurrection and judgment before God's throne (*3 En.* 44:3b). In this place, the wicked will be punished with fire, with rods of burning coal (*3 En.* 44:3b-6). *3 Enoch* does not specify how long this punishment will last, but it would be reasonable to assume that it would last for all eternity since the emphasis of this book is on the immortal nature of the soul.

~ ~ ~

4. Sibylline Oracles

The *Sibylline Oracles* is a collection of Jewish and Christian *vaticinium ex eventu* oracles ranging in date from the second century BCE to the seventh century CE (see Table 24 for their provenance). It is important to keep in mind that these oracles were collected over a 700-year time-period, and that although some of these oracles were of Jewish origin, they were later incorporated into a Christian composition or received a Christian redaction.

Table 24. The provenance of the *Sibylline Oracles*

Oracle	Date of Composition	Religious Affiliation	Place of Origin
Prologue	after 6th cent. CE	Most likely Christian	Unknown
1-2	Turn of the era	Jewish	Asia Minor
	2nd cent. CE	Christian redaction	
3	after mid-2nd cent. BCE but before 70 CE	Jewish	Egypt
4	after Alexander but before 80 CE	Jewish	Syria
5	after 70 CE but before 132 CE	Jewish	Egypt
6	before c. 300 CE	Christian	Syria
7	2nd cent. CE	Christian	Syria
8	before 180 CE	Jewish	Most likely Near East
	before 240–320 CE	Christian redaction	
11-14	after the turn of the era but before 7th cent. CE	Jewish/Pagan?	Egypt

These oracles are pseudepigraphical texts attributed to the legendary Sibyls of the antiquity,[92] depicted as an aged pagan woman who gave ecstatic prophecies. The earliest references to the Sibyl are from the fifth and fourth century BCE, but numerous Sibyls appeared in the following centuries.[93] Collins notes: "the most famous collection of *Sibylline Oracles* in antiquity was the official one at Rome," which was lost in 83 BCE, when the temple of Jupiter burned down.[94]

The prologue of the composition explains the importance of the oracles and why he, the author, decided to collect them. He explains that *Sibyl* is a Latin word meaning "prophetess" and that Sibyls "have lived in various times and places and are ten in number" (line 30). He adds: "In manifold ways they tell of certain past history, and equally, foretell future events, and, to speak simply, they can profit those who read them in no small way" (line 27).

With the exception of *Oracles* 11–13, the work is saturated with eschatological material. John Collins observes that "the eschatology of the Jewish oracles is political in nature," focusing on the future messianic kingdom, while the Christian oracles show "extensive interest in the fate of the individual after death."[95] He notes:

> Belief in a resurrection is attested in the Jewish *Sibylline Oracles* 4 but only very tersely. There is some doubt as to how much of the judgment scene in *Sibylline Oracles* 2 is Jewish or Christian. However, the developed interest in the suffering of the condemned is most prominently displayed in *Sibylline Oracles* 2, which is largely Christian, the Christian *Sibylline Oracles* 7, and the Christian parts of Sibylline 8. *Sibylline Oracles* 2 is especially characterized by its detailed interest in the fiery sufferings of the damned. Even in the Christian books, however, the paradise of the resurrected saints is an earthly one, depicted in terms of a transformation of the earth.[96]

This work will not try to harmonize all the resurrection texts appearing in this collection but will consider them within the context of each book. It will also pay close attention to the religious background of the various resurrection texts, whether they are Jewish or Christian. Moreover, this work will only focus on the passages that refer or allude to the TaNaKh.

---

92. Evans, *Ancient Texts for the New Testament Studies*, 31.
93. J. J. Collins, "The *Sibylline Oracles*," in Stone, ed., *Jewish Writings of the Second Temple Period*, 358.
94. Ibid.
95. J. J. Collins, "*Sibylline Oracles*," OTP 1:323.
96. Ibid.

a. Book 1

The first book of Sibyl is a Jewish oracle with a large Christian redaction. It gives an overview of the world history (1.1-4) and was probably divided into ten periods. However, the last three periods are now lost due to the large Christian addition. The first five periods of the book bring the reader from the Creation (1.5-64) down to the destruction of the earth at the Flood Narrative (1.282), the primeval history of Genesis 1–11. The last five periods of the world history start with the golden period after the Flood (1.283) down to the second destruction of the world, this time by fire, which is expanded upon in *Book 2* (the eighth and ninth period is missing in the current composition). Both sets of five periods seem to follow the same pattern as Daniel 2, four declining ages followed by judgment/destruction. The resurrection passage appears in the large Christian addition at the end of the book (1.324-400; see the highlighted section of the text in Appendix A, 1.349, 355, 378). Reading this addition, it becomes apparent that the author has integrated key events from Jesus' life and included references from the TaNaKh, to create an oracle which would find its fulfillment in the New Testament Jesus, who even carries the numerical value of 888 (1.326-329)[97] as the promised Messiah (see the textual references added to the text in Appendix A). The Christian author has not attempted to find any support from the TaNaKh regarding this belief, only stating it was a part of Jesus' gospel message to the righteous when warning about the eschatological judgment (1.349), adding that Jesus, upon his death, even went down to the house of Hades to announce the resurrection hope to the already dead (1.377-378).[98] This passage also alludes to Jesus' resurrection miracles during his ministry (1.355) and to the resurrection of Jesus himself after three days in Hades (1.379). All these resurrection references take the belief for granted.

---

97. This is an example of Gematria by which a numerical value is given to a word based on the letters of that word – in this case, the number 888. This number most likely refers to Jesus since that is the value of the Greek letters of Ἰησοῦ, and it also fits the other two criteria given in the text: "bearing four vowels, and the consonants in him are two" (1.326). This is similar to the book of Revelation which gives the numerical value of 666 to the beast/power/person who opposes God and His people (Rev. 13:18).

98. This is referring to Peter's statement that Jesus, upon his death, "went and made a proclamation to the spirits (πνεύμασιν) in prison," who had died in their disobedience "in the days of Noah" (1 Pet. 3:19-20).

b. Book 2

The second book of the *Sibylline Oracles* focuses on the events taking place during the last period of world history (2.15) and the eschatological crises leading up to the last judgment (2.32-347). Collins suggests that many Christian redactions to the original Jewish composition took place, considering numerous passages as certainly Christian (2.45-55, 177-183, 190-192, 238-251, 254, 311-312).[99]

Before the eschatological judgment takes place, Sibyl reveals the signs of the end (2.154-173), the eschatological role of the Hebrews (2.174-186), and the coming of Elijah (2.187-195) followed by the complete destruction of the whole creation by fire (2.196-213). This eschatological destruction will even include the "implacable Hades and the Heavenly vault" (2.199-200) so that "all will melt into one and separate into clear air" (2.212-213). After this total destruction, the universal judgment will take place (2.217-219) which will decide whether a person "acted lawlessly or righteously" during their lifetime (2.93-94). This universal judgment would demand a universal resurrection.

1) *Sibylline Oracles 2.221-251*. The resurrection passage begins by noting the central role God holds in the resurrection process since He will give "souls and breath and voice to the dead" (2.221-222), which, according to Gen. 2:7, are the crucial divine elements required to create life. The opening statement is followed by a detailed description of the resurrection process itself, taken from Ezek. 37:1-10 (see the highlighted sections), concluding that the universal resurrection will happen in a single day (2.226).

Ezekiel 37:1-10 (CSB)	Sibylline Oracles 2.221-226
[1] The hand of the LORD was on me, and He brought me out by His Spirit and set me down in the middle of the valley; it was full of bones. [2] He led me all around them. There were a great many of them on the surface of the valley, and they were very dry. [3] Then He said to me, "Son of man, can these bones live?" I replied, "Lord GOD, only You know." [4] He said to me, "Prophesy concerning these bones and say to them: Dry bones, hear the word of the LORD!	

99. Collins, *"Sibylline Oracles," OTP* 1:330.

⁵ This is what the Lord GOD says to these bones: I will cause breath to enter you, and you will live. ⁶ I will put tendons on you, make flesh grow on you, and cover you with skin. I will put breath in you so that you come to life. Then you will know that I am the LORD." ⁷ So I prophesied as I had been commanded.	Then the heavenly one will give souls and breath and voice to the dead
While I was prophesying, there was a noise, a rattling sound, and the bones came together, bone to bone. ⁸ As I looked, tendons appeared on them, flesh grew, and skin covered them, but there was no breath in them.	and bones fastened with all kinds of joinings… flesh and sinews and veins and skin about the flesh, and the former hairs.
⁹ He said to me, "Prophesy to the breath, prophesy, son of man. Say to it: This is what the Lord GOD says: Breath, come from the four winds and breathe into these slain so that they may live!" ¹⁰ So I prophesied as He commanded me; the breath entered them, and they came to life and stood on their feet, a vast army.	Bodies of humans, made solid in heavenly manner, breathing and set in motion, will be raised on a single day.

Comparing these two texts, it becomes clear Sibyl had Ezek. 37:1-10 in mind when describing the resurrection. Both texts view God as the source of life and the instigator of the resurrection process. The subject of both texts is death (loss of breath) and resurrection (regaining breath), illustrated by the dry bones which will once more come alive. The resurrection process, described in both texts, is a reversal of the decaying process which starts at the time of death,[100] although Sibyl has added a few more steps to the process. There is, however, a major difference between these two accounts. The Ezekiel prophecy was given to the people of Israel, who found themselves in exile after the destruction of their nation, to give

---

100. The proposed dying process is as follows: at the moment God's breath departs the body, the person is dead. Not long after a person dies, the body starts decaying, first the skin, then the flesh, followed by the tendons which holds the bones together. In the end, the body has turned into a pile of bones. The resurrection process described in the two resurrection texts follows the dying process in reverse order.

them hope of a future resurrection of that nation. Sibyl interpreted this prophecy universally, as a reference to the eschatological resurrection – a necessary element of the eschatological judgment. Elledge argues, regarding the same interpretation of Ezekiel 37 found in 4Q385 frg.2, "if our author is reading Ezekiel 37 as a prophecy about the resurrection, then he [she] likely understood the resurrection as a physical reconstitution of the same body that had been lost in death."[101]

It may be of some importance that the text describes souls and breath in a more general sense (2.221) and that Book 2 does not show any interest in the fate of the soul upon the death of a person, specifying that the soul is an integral part of a person which lives on separately from the body upon death in wait for the resurrection, when it once more can join its recreated body. However, it could be argued that the mournful forms in Hades (2.230), the souls of men from the murky dark (2.217), and the heavenly vault (2.200) are the places of the wicked and the righteous souls who are awaiting the resurrection. Regardless, the main emphasis of the resurrection statement is the universal nature of the resurrection. In the Christian addition to this Oracle (2.238-250), Moses will be present at the eschatological judgment, after he has put on flesh (2.245-246), perhaps suggesting that he had a non-bodily existence before the time of judgment. The Oracle also mentions the presence of the patriarchs (Abraham, Isaac, and Jacob), some of the great prophets (Joshua, Daniel, Elijah, Habakkuk, and Jonah), and the martyrs killed by the Hebrews (2.246-248), insinuating that they went to Heaven upon their death and came down with Christ and His angels to be present at the judgment.

The universal nature of the resurrection is made clear in the verses following the opening resurrection statement (2.227-237). Sibyl reveals that Uriel, the great angel, will lead all the mournful forms he has broken out of Hades to judgment. These forms would include "those of ancient phantoms, Titans and the Giants and such as the Flood destroyed"

---

101. C. D. Elledge, "Resurrection of the Dead: Exploring Our Earliest Evidence Today," in Charlesworth et al., eds, *Resurrection: The Origin and Future of a Biblical Doctrine*, 35. This text was also considered as a "proof-text" in the Rabbinical discussion on the resurrection belief (*b. Sanh.* 92b; see also *Song Rab.* 7:15), although Rabbi Judah considered it a parable. Rabbi Eliezer understood it literally and speculated with Rabbi Samuel, and Jeremiah ben Abba regarding who these people Ezekiel resurrected were and what they did upon their resurrection. The Rabbinic discussion on what bone(s) is/are needed to be resurrected may also be influenced by *the valley of the bone* narrative in Ezekiel. They concluded that a person will be resurrected from the nut of the spinal column (e.g. *Gen. Rab.* 28:3; *Lev. Rab.* 18:1; *Eccl. Rab.* 12:5).

(2.231-232), "those whom the wave of the sea destroyed in the oceans" (2.233), "those whom wild beasts and serpents and birds devoured" (2.234), and "those whom the flesh-devouring fire destroyed by flame" (2.236). In other words, none will escape God's judgment. The Oracle goes on to describe the judgment by the blazing river of fire which all have to pass through, the righteous will be saved while the wicked will be destroyed for all ages (2.252-255). The text describes the punishment the wicked will experience in the burning fire (2.283-310) through which they are repaying "threefold what evil deed they committed burning in much fire. They will all gnash their teeth, wasting away with thirst and raging violence" (2.303-306). Sybil also describes the reward given to the righteous (2.313-338) who will live on a recreated earth.

Curiously, Sibyl notes that the righteous will be able to ask God to save the wicked "from the raging fire and deathless gnashing" (2.332). God will grant the righteous' wishes by releasing the wicked "from the undying fire" (2.334) and give them eternal life "with the immortals in the Elysian plain" (2.337). This limit to the punishment of the wicked is refuted by the manuscripts belonging to the ψ sources, which makes a point of refuting it by remarking that the fire "which tortures the condemned will never cease."[102]

2) *Concluding Remarks*. In contrast to the resurrection reference found in the Jewish Oracles of Book 2, which was supported by Ezek. 37:1-10, the Christian resurrection reference (2.239) does not show any attempt to support it. Instead, the Oracle takes it for granted as an integral part of the eschatological judgment. The last Christian addition to the Book 2 (2.311-312) seems to be aware of the seven-day period in which the souls are shown their eschatological destiny, Phase 1 of the state of the dead, in 2 Esd. 7:101 (see Fig. 5), but unlike *4 Ezra* 7:102-115 which makes clear that there will be no intercession for the ungodly in the day of judgment, 2.311-312 states that this seven-day period is given to the souls "for repentance through the intercession of the holy virgin."

c. Book 3

There are only two brief resurrection references in Book 3 of the *Sibylline Oracles*. The first reference appears in a section (3.1-96) most scholars would dissociate from the rest of the book.[103] *Sibylline Oracles* 3.63-74

---

102. Collins, "*Sibylline Oracles*," *OTP* 1:353 n. c3.
103. Ibid., 359.

reveals that one of the deceiving powers of Beliar is his ability to raise up the dead.[104] This resurrection should not be confused with the eschatological resurrection which is linked with the eschatological judgment.

The second resurrection passage (3.767-776) does address the eschatological resurrection; however, the text does not reveal any details except that God had promised the pious "to open the earth and the world and the gates of the blessed and all joys and immortal intellect and eternal cheer" (3.769-771).

d. Book 4

Book 4 contains oracles pertaining to the Hellenistic era and was probably updated towards the end of the first century CE since the Oracle about the rise of Rome (4.102-51) seems out of place and must have been added to an earlier version of the Oracle. The Oracle divides the history into ten generations and adds that these generations will be ruled by four different kingdoms (Assyrians will rule for six generations [4.49-53], the Medes for two generations [4.54-64], the Persians for one generation [4.65-87], and the last generation by the fourth kingdom, the Macedonians [4.88-101]).[105] The Roman kingdom, which is a fifth kingdom, breaks this pattern, supporting the notion that the section is a later addition to the Oracle. The resurrection passage appears in the conclusion of the expanded composition (4.179-192) at the end of the tenth generation, as a part of the eschatological judgment (4.40-47, 183-192). However, Collins believes this conclusion was probably the conclusion of the original Oracle too,[106] thus dating this resurrection passage to the Macedonian period.

As in 2.196-213, the resurrection and judgment will take place after God has destroyed the whole earth by fire. He "will destroy the whole race of men and all cities and rivers at once, and the sea. He will destroy

---

104. The *Apoc. Elij.* 3:12-13 and 4:31 argues that resurrection is the very act the son of lawlessness cannot perform: "He [the son of lawlessness] will do the works which the Christ did, except for raising the dead alone. In this you will know that he is the son of lawlessness, because he is unable to give life."

105. This twofold division of history also appears in the book of Daniel, although it is not intertwined like in this Oracle. In two of the visions, the world history is divided into four kingdoms by a vision of a statue made of four metals: gold-silver-bronze-iron (Dan. 2), and four animals, lion-bear-leopard-beast (Dan. 7). In contrast to this four-kingdom pattern, the vision in Dan. 9 divides the history into 70 prophetic weeks of years ($7 \times 70 = 490$ years), which could also be presented as ten jubilee cycles.

106. Collins, "*Sibylline Oracles,*" OTP 1:381.

everything by fire, and it will be smoking dust" (4.176-178). When everything has turned into "dusty ashes" (4.179), God will quench the fire and resurrect all the people just as they were before (4.182). Like 2.221-226, also 4.181 uses the imagery of Ezek. 37:1-10 with the same emphasis on God as the initiator, although this is a much more abbreviated reference: "God himself will again fashion the bones and ashes of men and he will raise them up mortals again as they were before" (4.181-182).

While there is a strong emphasis on the bodily resurrection in this text, it remains silent regarding the spirit/soul of the person.[107] Those whom God deems pious in the eschatological judgment will be rewarded with a pleasant life on a fertile earth (4.45-46, 187) while the impious will be punished in the fire of Gehenna (4.43-44, 184-186).

e. Book 6

The sixth book of the *Sibylline Oracle* is a short hymn to Christ. Thus, there is no reference to the eschatological resurrection nor the judgment. However, this Christian hymn does state that Jesus will resurrect from the dead.

f. Book 7

The seventh book of the *Sibylline Oracle*, although Christian in origin, has a similar eschatology to that of the Jewish Oracles of Book 2 and 4; however, it lacks the organizational structure featured so prominently in Book 2 and 4 (the ten generations of world history of Books 1 and 2 and the four-kingdoms-ten-generations structure of Book 4). The large eschatological section of the book does not seem to follow a chronological order either (7.118-151); like Books 2 and 4, it reveals that the earth will be completely consumed by fire (7.119-123). At this point, Book 7 shifts to the destiny of the wicked who will "burn in spirit by their perishing flesh for the years of ages forever," learning through dire torture "that it is not possible to deceive the law of God" (7.126-129). The resurrection passage (7.144-145) does not add any new elements to the belief compared with Books 2 and 4 – it will happen after the fire has been quenched and a recreated world appears (7.140-144), in which the resurrected righteous can live (7.144-151) and be provided for by God, just as He did for the Israelites when He gave them manna in

---

107. The only reference found in the book regarding the soul/spirit of the person gives no information except that God will give the pious "spirit and life and favor at once" (4.46, 189-190).

the wilderness (7.148-149; cf. Exod. 16). Curiously, the eschatological judgment element is lacking in this book, although it is implied since the two categories of people, the wretched and the pure-minded people (7.124-129 and 144-145), who are punished and blessed, would require a judgment procedure by God to determine the category to which a person belonged. Moreover, this book does not state clearly that the wicked are a part of the eschatological resurrection, although this could be assumed, since the wicked would need to be resurrected after the all-consuming fire (7.120-121) if they are to receive their eternal punishment (7.126-131).

g. Book 8

The resurrection passages in the eighth book of the *Sibylline Oracles* (see Table 17) appear both in the first (8.1-126) and the second (8.217-500) half of the book. The first half is considered by most scholars to be of Jewish origin,[108] while the second half is clearly a Christian composition.[109] In the first resurrection passage (8.81-99), Rome's oracle of woes is compared with that of the wicked who will be judged by "the universal ruler himself" (8.82). Describing the ultimate destiny of the Roman Empire (8.96-99),[110] the oracle alludes to Job 1:21a and Genesis 3:19b, possibly following the resurrection reading seen in *Targum Pseudo-Jonathan*:[111]

---

108. This is due to the lack of the Christological theme which is so prominently featured in the second half of the book, the strong anti-Roman sentiment, and great animosity shown towards Hadrian.

109. Collins, "*Sibylline Oracles*," *OTP* 1:415–17.

110. Collins notes the Oracle's emphasis on the equalizing function of Hades (8.107-121) is an allusion to the description of *Sheol* in Job 3:17-19 (ibid., 417).

111. Applying the judgment and resurrection language normally used when describing the eschatological judgment of the wicked, to the Roman Empire, seems, at first, surprising. However, Dan. 7 does not only describe the eschatological judgment and the vindication of the righteous, but also the downfall of the little horn, the political/religious entity which "was making war against the saints" (Dan. 7:21). Due to this judgment, this power or beast will be slain, its body destroyed, and given to the burning fire (Dan. 7:11), as alluded to in *Sib. Or.* 8.104-106, where everyone will be able to "hear a mournful great bellowing from Hades and gnashing of teeth as you [Rome] strike your breast with your hand." It becomes clear that the Oracle understood the persecuting power of Dan. 7 to be the Roman Empire.

Gen. 3:19 (MT)	Gen. 3:19 (PJT)	Job 1:21	Sib. Or. 8.96-99
You will eat bread by the sweat of your brow **until you return to the ground, since you were taken from it**. For you are dust, and you will return to dust.	By the labor of your hands you shall eat food **until you turn again to the dust from which you was created**: for dust you are, and unto dust you shall return; for from the dust it is to be that you are to arise, to render judgment and reckoning for all that you have done, in the day of the great judgment.	<u>Naked</u> I came from my mother's womb, and <u>naked</u> **I will leave this life**. The LORD gives, and the LORD takes away. Praise the name of Yahweh.	You did not perceive whence you came, <u>naked</u> and unworthy to the light of the sun, so that **you might go again** <u>naked</u> **to the same place** and later come to judgment because you judged unjustly…

This resurrection passage does not reveal much about the resurrection itself, only that it will be a bodily one which will take place as a part of the eschatological and universal judgment.[112]

The second and the third resurrection texts appear at the beginning (8.169-170) and towards the end (8.205-208) of the eschatological upheavals section concluding the first half of the book (8.169-216). While the second reference only associates the eschatological resurrection with the reign of the "holy prince" who will "gain control of the scepters of the

---

[112]. It should also be noted that the Oracle alludes to the woes pronounced by Micah when describing the moral condition of Judah in his own days, prior to the Assyrian captivity (722 BCE). Craig L. Blomberg proposes that this text was later understood eschatologically by the *Targum*, as a description of the larger society at the time of the eschatological judgment (using the future tense): "For *in that time* son shall spurn father, a daughter shall quarrel with her mother, a daughter-in-law *shall treat* her mother-in-law *with contempt*; a man's own household shall be his enemies" (cf. Mic. 7:6; *Sib. Or.* 8.84). He adds that applying this text to the day of the Messiah also appears in later rabbinic literature (e.g. *b. Sanh.* 97a; cf. *m. Sotah* 9:15; *b. Sotah* 49b; *Midr. Song* 2:13); see Craig L. Blomberg, "Matthew," in *Commentary on the New Testament Use of the Old Testament*, ed. G. K. Beale and D. A. Carson (Grand Rapids: Baker Academic, 2007), 36.

whole world for all ages" (8.169-170),[113] the third reference reveals some additional details.[114] Describing the eschatological resurrection event, it alludes to Isa. 35:4-7 which concerns the future judgment and salvation of God. Although this text does not address the resurrection hope directly, it could be argued that it is implied in the eschatological judgment. The Oracle may also have been alluding to Isa. 29:18-19, which pertains to the future world renewal, individually and spiritually, when describing the eschatological changes that will take place following the eschatological resurrection and judgment.[115]

113. This description may be alluding to the Son of Man in Daniel 7, who will be given "the dominion and glory and a kingdom, that all people, nations, and languages should serve Him" (v. 13). In *Sib. Or.* 8.169-170, however, the context seems to suggest the holy prince to be a reference to God himself, the Most High (8.171).

114. Collins observes that some scholars consider this eschatological section Christian. This conclusion is based on the parallels between the eschatological reign of the woman in vv. 194-216 and Revelation 17–18, 21, and the assumed dependency of vv. 205-208 on Mt. 11:5 or on the Christian oracle in 1.353-355. However, the eschatological woman could "well be modeled on the oracle about Cleopatra" (3.75-92) while the details in vv. 205-208 could have derived directly from the book of Isaiah, see discussion below (Collins, "*Sibylline Oracles*," *OTP* 1:415–16). Thus, it is not clear if this section had a Jewish (with a possibly Christian interpolation in v. 196-197) or a Christian origin.

115. This is also the same language used by Jesus in Mt. 11:5, when John the Baptist asked his disciples to ask Jesus if he was the promised Messiah. He told John's disciples to report what they had seen using the eschatological language of Isaiah, describing the coming judgment and Messianic age. Interestingly, Jesus' answer also includes the resurrection aspect, though not the eschatological kind referred to in *Sib. Or.* 8.205, but rather to his many miracles which resurrected the dead to a mortal life (category 14; p. 14 n. 33). It seems Jesus did understand his mission in light of the eschatological act of salvation and judgment associated with the year-of-jubilee in Isa. 61:1.

Sib. Or. 8.205-212	Mt. 11:4-5
There will be a resurrection of the dead and most swift racing of the **lame**, and the **deaf** will hear, and the **blind** will see, those who cannot speak will speak, and life and wealth will be common to all. The earth will equally belong to all, not divided by the walls or fences, and will then bear more abundant fruits. It will give fountains of sweet wine and white milk and honey . . .	[4]Jesus replied to them, "Go and report to John what you hear and see: [5]the **blind** see, the **lame** walk, those with skin diseases are healed, the **deaf** hear, the dead are raised, and the poor are told the good news [Isa. 61:1]

Sib. Or. 8.205-212	Isa. 29:18-19	Isa. 35:4-7
There will be a resurrection of the dead and **most swift racing of the lame**, and *the deaf will hear*, and *the blind will see, those who cannot speak will speak*, and life and wealth will be common to all. The earth will equally belong to all, not divided by the walls or fences, and **will then bear more abundant fruits. It will give fountains of sweet wine and white milk and honey...**	29:18On that day *the deaf will hear* the words of a document, and out of a deep darkness the eyes of *the blind will see*. 19The humble will have joy after joy in the LORD, and the poor people will rejoice in the Holy One of Israel.	35:4Be strong; do not fear! Here is your God; vengeance is coming. God's retribution is coming; He will save you." 5Then *the eyes of the blind will be opened*, and *the ears of the deaf unstopped*. 6Then **the lame will leap like a deer**, and *the tongue of the mute will sing for joy*, for water will gush in the wilderness, and streams in the desert; 7the parched ground will become a pool of water, and the thirsty land springs of water. In the haunt of jackals, in their lairs, there will be grass, reeds, and papyrus.

The eschatological resurrection texts in the first half of the book do not show much interest in the afterlife, but they do present a physical resurrection to judgment which will result in a life for the righteous on a newly created world and a punishment in Hades for the wicked.

The second half of the book (8.217-500) begins with an acrostic poem on the judgment with several resurrection references (8.217-250). The poem summarizes Jesus' role as the eschatological judge, savior, and king, noting that he will judge all flesh, both the faithful and the faithless (8.218-223, 242), who will resurrect the dead by breaking the gates of Hades (8.226-228) and by the trumpet blast (8.239-242), who will punish the wicked by a torturous fire forever (8.228-231), and he will rule as king with his iron shepherd's rod (8.218, 248).

The second poem (8.251-336) focuses on Jesus' earthly aspect by summarizing the key aspects of the gospel story (first coming) rather than the eschatological aspect of his Messianic mission (second coming), and states that resurrection hope and the eternal life is pending on believing in Jesus (8.255). The poem highlights Jesus' miracles of resurrecting the dead and curing the sick (8.286), noting that he willingly died so he could speak to the dead in Hades (8.293, 310-311), and resurrected on the third day as the "first of the resurrection" (8.313-314).

The last resurrection reference appears in God's speech against idolatry towards the end of the book (8.359-428). In this speech God makes clear that there are only two paths (8.399-400), one that leads to life (the way of the righteous) and one that leads to death and eternal fire (the way of the wicked). At the end of time, God will raise the dead, both the righteous and the wicked (8.413-416), and judge each person by fire. Those who behaved ethically toward people in need (those who were hungry, thirsty, and naked) will receive "immortal fruits," eternal light, and unfading life (8.404-411), while the lawless souls will suffer in the eternal fire (8.401) since, according to 8.350-358, they did not repent from their sins when they had the chance during the "seven days of ages for repentance."

h. Fragment 3[116]

Fragment 3 of the Sibylline corpus reveals an implied resurrection text in its speech against idolatry. The Oracle emphasizes God as the creator and the only one deserving worship. In fact, according to the text, only by becoming sober and "com[ing] to a prudent mind and know[ing] God the king" (41-42) and honor Him (46) will a person "inherit life, dwelling in the luxuriant garden of Paradise for the time of eternity, feasting on sweet bread from starry heave" (47-49), otherwise, he/she will be "burned with torches all day, throughout eternity" (44).

5. *Apocryphon of Ezekiel*

Josephus notes that Ezekiel wrote "and left behind him in writing two books" (*Ant.* 10.5.1 [79]), the second of which may have been *Apocryphon of Ezekiel*. Evans notes that "the *Apocalypse of Ezekiel* was probably written in either Hebrew or Greek between 50 BCE and 50 CE."[117] Only five fragments of this composition have survived, *Fragment 1* being the longest. It is this fragment that is most interest for this study since it addresses the eschatological resurrection and judgment with the aid of the parable of the lame and the blind keepers. Unlike the other

---

116. Collins notes that *fragment 3* was "probably part of the lost book 2 and belongs with *Sibylline Oracles* 3.1-45" ("*Sibylline Oracles*," *OTP* 1:469).

117. Evans, *Ancient Texts for New Testament Study*, 32. For further study into the background of these fragments, see James R. Mueller and S. E. Robinson, "*Apocryphon of Ezekiel*," *OTP* 1:487–90.

fragments, it has been preserved both in Greek and Hebrew versions. The Greek version attributes the parable to the *Apocryphon of Ezekiel* (see introduction of fragment, τοῦ Ἰεζεκιὴλ τοῦ προφήτου ἐν τῷ ἰδίῳ ἀποκρύφῳ) and is preserved in *Against Heresies* (64.70, 5-17) written by Epiphanius,[118] bishop of Salamis (Cyprus), thus in a Christian composition. The Hebrew versions of the parable, however, appear in several Rabbinical texts and are attributed to either Rabbi Judah haNasi (c. 200 CE)[119] or Rabbi Ishmael (c. 130 CE),[120] although one version is without attribution.[121] By comparing the various Hebrew versions of the parable, James R. Mueller concludes that *Lev. Rab.* 4:5 probably "preserves the more original form of the story," although it is difficult to determine if the *Apocryphon* had a Jewish or Christian origin.[122]

a. Fragment 1

The parable about the lame and the blind men who together caused mischief in the garden of the king and later were judged together as one person, serves the same purpose in both the Christian and the Jewish texts. The parable illustrates why it is necessary for an eschatological bodily resurrection, and why the reward or punishment cannot only be given to the soul. Since both the body (σῶμα/גוף) and soul (ψυχὴ/נשמה) were together when a person behaved wickedly, it is necessary for both the body and soul to be once more together when the same person will be judged for his/her wicked deeds. However, the Christian and the Jewish version of the parable is used to explain two different perceived resurrection texts from the TaNaKh.

---

118. He was born in Judea c. 310–320 CE and died in 403 CE and is best known for his collection of the many heresies leading up to his time period.
119. See *b. Sanh.* 91ab and *Mekilta of Rabbi Simeon ben Yochai* on Exod. 15:1.
120. See *Lev. Rab.* 4:5 and *Mekilta of Rabbi Ishmael* on Exod. 15:1.
121. See *Midr. Tanhuma* on Lev. 4:1.
122. James R. Mueller, *The Five Fragments of the Apocryphon of Ezekiel: A Critical Study*, JSPSup 5 (Sheffield: Sheffield Academic, 1994), 99. Appendix A shows the parallel Greek and Hebrew (*Lev. Rab.* 4:5) versions of the parable in English. Comparing the two versions, it becomes apparent that while there are many similarities between the versions, there are also some significant differences. See Mueller's discussion of the many similarities, differences, and additions to this parable (ibid., 78–100).

Epiphanius, in his attack on Origen's position regarding a resurrection of a spiritual body as supposed to a physical body,[123] quotes Isa. 26:19 from the Septuagint and said parable from the prophet Ezekiel to refute what he considered to be Origen's heresy, and prove it has to be a resurrection of a physical body.

The *Apocryphon of Ezekiel*	Isaiah 26:19-21 (BGT and LXE)
Ἀναστήσονται γὰρ οἱ νεκροὶ ἐγερθήσονται οἱ ἐν τοῖς μνημείοις φησὶν ὁ προφήτης.	[19]ἀναστήσονται οἱ νεκροί καὶ ἐγερθήσονται οἱ ἐν τοῖς μνημείοις καὶ εὐφρανθήσονται οἱ ἐν τῇ γῇ· ἡ γὰρ δρόσος ἡ παρὰ σοῦ ἴαμα αὐτοῖς ἐστιν ἡ δὲ γῆ τῶν ἀσεβῶν πεσεῖται [20]βάδιζε λαός μου εἴσελθε εἰς τὰ ταμιεῖά σου ἀπόκλεισον τὴν θύραν σου ἀποκρύβηθι μικρὸν ὅσον ὅσον ἕως ἂν παρέλθῃ ἡ ὀργὴ κυρίου [21]ἰδοὺ γὰρ κύριος ἀπὸ τοῦ ἁγίου ἐπάγει τὴν ὀργὴν ἐπὶ τοὺς ἐνοικοῦντας ἐπὶ τῆς γῆς καὶ ἀνακαλύψει ἡ γῆ τὸ αἷμα αὐτῆς καὶ οὐ κατακαλύψει τοὺς ἀνῃρημένους
"For **the dead will be raised and those in the tombs will be lifted up**," speaks the prophet.	[1]**The dead shall rise, and they that are in the tombs shall be raised**, and they that are in the earth shall rejoice: for the dew from thee is healing to them: but the land of the ungodly shall perish. [20]Go, my people, enter into thy closets, shut thy door, hide thyself for a little season, until the anger of the Lord have passed away. [21]For, behold, the Lord is bringing wrath from *his* holy place upon the dwellers on the earth: the earth also shall disclose her blood, and shall not cover her slain.

It is reasonable to assume Isa. 26:19-21 was not quoted or even referred to in conjunction with the parable in its original setting of the *Apocryphon of Ezekiel*, since the reference appears in the introduction written by Epiphanius, and the rabbinic versions of the parable refer to Ps. 50:4 as the proof-text.[124] Regardless, Epiphanius understood Isa. 26:19 to speak

---

123. Ibid., 80–1.

124. Although the rabbinic version of the parable does not refer to Isa. 26:19, this biblical text was still considered by some rabbis as a resurrection text, as is evident by the discussion regarding what biblical texts support the resurrection belief in *b. Sanh.* 90b.

of a physical bodily resurrection and may also have viewed vv. 20-21 as a reference to the eschatological judgment which would punish the wicked, much like the broader context of the parable in which both the lame and the blind men were held responsible for the wickedness they committed together at the king's judgment.

In all but one of the Rabbinic versions of the parable (Mashal),[125] Ps. 50:4 appears in the explanation of the parable (Nimshal). This judgment psalm is used as a proof-text showing that in the same way the blind and the lame men had to be judged together, since they committed the wicked deed together as one person, so must the spirit and the body be reunited before they can be judged together and receive their sentence, punishment or reward.

Psalm 50:1-6 CSB	b. Sanhedrin 91b
¹מִזְמוֹר לְאָסָף אֵל אֱלֹהִים יְהוָה דִּבֶּר וַיִּקְרָא־אָרֶץ מִמִּזְרַח־שֶׁמֶשׁ עַד־מְבֹאוֹ: ²מִצִּיּוֹן מִכְלַל־יֹפִי אֱלֹהִים הוֹפִיעַ: ³יָבֹא אֱלֹהֵינוּ וְאַל־יֶחֱרַשׁ אֵשׁ־לְפָנָיו תֹּאכֵל וּסְבִיבָיו נִשְׂעֲרָה מְאֹד: ⁴יִקְרָא אֶל־הַשָּׁמַיִם מֵעָל **וְאֶל־הָאָרֶץ לָדִין עַמּוֹ**: ⁵אִסְפוּ־לִי חֲסִידָי כֹּרְתֵי בְרִיתִי עֲלֵי־זָבַח: ⁶וַיַּגִּידוּ שָׁמַיִם צִדְקוֹ כִּי־אֱלֹהִים שֹׁפֵט הוּא סֶלָה:	אף הקדוש ברוך הוא מביא *נשמה* וזורקה **בגוף** ודן אותם כאחד שנאמר יקרא אל השמים מעל **ואל הארץ לדין עמו** יקרא אל השמים מעל זו *נשמה* **ואל הארץ לדין עמי** זה *הגוף*
¹ *A psalm of Asaph.* Yahweh, the god of gods speaks; He summons the earth from east to west. ² From Zion, the perfection of beauty, God appears in radiance. ³ Our God is coming; He will not be silent! Devouring fire precedes Him, and a storm rages around Him. ⁴ On high, **He summons heaven and earth in order to judge His people**. ⁵ "Gather My faithful ones to Me, those who made a covenant with Me by sacrifice." ⁶ The heavens proclaim His righteousness, for God is the Judge. *Selah*	So the Holy One, blessed be he, brings *the spirit* and placing (it) in *the body*, he also judges them as one. For it is said, '**He will call to the heavens from above and the earth to judge his people**.' 'He will call to the heaven from above' – this is *the spirit*. '**And the earth to judge his people**' – this is *the body*.

125. The exception is the greatly abbreviated version of the parable found in *Mekilta of Rabbi Ishmael* on Exod. 15:1, which assumes the audience is already familiar with the unabridged version of the parable which concludes with an interpretation of Ps. 50:4.

The Rabbis interpreted the reference to "heaven" (v. 4a) as a reference to the place where the soul went upon death[126] while considering the "earth" (v. 4b) as the final resting place of the body at the time of burial. Thus, on the day of judgment, God would call both to heaven and to the earth, so the soul and the body of the deceased can once more be unified in order for the unified person to be judged in the eschatological judgment.

b. Concluding Remarks

The parable of the lame and the blind man appearing in Fragment 1 of the *Apocryphon of Ezekiel* serves the same general purpose both in the Christian and the Rabbinic texts. It was used to illustrate the need for the body and spirit to once more reunite at the time of the resurrection in order to be judged as one unit. Thus, the parable speaks against the Platonic or Gnostic notion (cosmological dualism) that the soul, "the spiritual," is pure while the body, "the physical or material," should be viewed as impure, the source of evil which had imprisoned the soul.[127] They cannot be evaluated separately since they both act together. Moreover, the parable also makes it clear that everyone will be held responsible for their deeds. It was also noted that each of the religious traditions explained this parable by quoting the TaNaKh to prove the view presented by the parable, the Christian version used Isa. 26:19 while the rabbinic versions used Ps. 50:4. Both the Christian and the Rabbinic use of the parable seems to suggest a bodily and earthly existence following the resurrection. However, Fragment 1 does not expand on the final destiny of the righteous and the wicked.

Furthermore, the parable does not reveal much regarding the period between death and resurrection, except, according to the rabbinic versions, that the souls of the people of God (עמו) will dwell in heaven until they

---

126. According to *b. Sanh.* 91a, following death, the soul flies in the air like a bird. This metaphoric image of a "bird-soul" appears in several rabbinical sources as noted by V. Aptowitzer ("Die Seele als Vogel: Ein Beitrag zu den Anschauungen der Agada," *MGWJ* 69 [1925]: 150–68) and was a well-known image in the ancient Near East. For a detailed discussion, see Steiner's chapter, "From Dream-Souls to Bird-Souls," in *Disembodied Souls*, 55–67.

127. The body without the spirit is, in the rabbinic versions, like "a silent stone in the grave" (argued by Antoninus, the Emperor of the Roman Empire, or the body itself in *b. Sanh.* 91a and *Mek. of R. Simeon ben Yochai* on Exod. 15.1) or like "a piece of pottery thrown upon a dung-heap" (*Lev. Rab.* 4.5). The evaluation of the soul and body as pure and impure respectively is noted by Rabbi in *Mek. of R. Ishmael* on Exod. 15.1. Both the simile and the ethical evaluation of the soul and body are missing in the Christian version.

will be reunited with their earthly bodies at the time of the eschatological judgment.[128] The whereabouts of the wicked souls are of no interest. The Christian text, on the other hand, does not show any interest in the location of the souls. Instead, it seems to focus on the resurrection and judgment of the wicked, those who were not invited to the king's feast, a possible allusion to the "great feast" of Mt. 22:2,[129] or those who were drafted into the king's service.

It is unclear whether this parable in its original context of the *Apocryphon of Ezekiel* presented a universal resurrection and judgment view. Be that as it may, the two faith traditions used this parable to focus on different aspects of the eschatological resurrection and judgment. This becomes clear when considering the context of the biblical texts used by each faith group when explaining the parable – Isa. 26:19-21, quoted in the Christian version, focuses on the judgment of the wicked, while Ps. 50:1-6, quoted in the Rabbinic versions, focuses on the resurrection of the righteous.[130]

6. *Apocalypse of Zephaniah*

The *Apocalypse of Zephaniah* was most likely composed "in Greek sometime between 100 BCE and 70 CE,"[131] by a Jewish author living in the Greek-speaking diaspora, possibly in Egypt. Carl Schmidt suggests the present text, which was partly preserved in two manuscripts by the Coptic Christians, only account for a quarter of the original composition.[132] Although fragmentary in its current form, the text consists of several self-contained scenes and episodes which suggests some type of overall structure. The longest surviving manuscript, the eight-page long

---

128. The rabbinic texts using this parable, however, are not clear whether or not the souls are conscious when separated from the body.

129. Mueller notes the words used by Epiphanius are almost the exact words used in Mt. 22:2, but they appear in a different order (Mueller, *The Five Fragments of the Apocryphon of Ezekiel*, 84).

130. A case could be made that some of the differences between the Christian and the Rabbinic versions of the parable may be due to the proof-text used by each faith community to support a bodily resurrection belief. Unfortunately, there is no way of knowing if the original context of the parable in *Apocryphon of Ezekiel*, associated the parable with a biblical proof-text.

131. Evans, *Ancient Texts for New Testament Studies*, 33.

132. Carl Schmidt, cited by O. S. Wintermute, "*Apocalypse of Zephaniah*: A New Translation and Introduction," *OTP* 1:497. For a detailed introduction to this literary work, see ibid., 1:497–506.

Akhmimic manuscript, gives a travelogue of Zephaniah's guided journey through the heavenly spheres which included the place of the righteous and the wicked souls, contains seven episodes (*Apoc. Zeph.* 1–8), and concludes with four trumpet scenes (*Apoc. Zeph.* 9–12).[133]

In its current form, there are two basic themes appearing in the manuscript. The first, the importance and the call for repentance (*Apoc. Zeph.* B6; 7:8) which will bring God's compassion upon the tormented souls (2:8-9; 10:10-14; 11:2-6). The second and most important, the universal nature of God's judgment in the form of the trial of Hades (*Apoc. Zeph.* 7–8) and a future (perhaps eschatological) judgment of the unrepented souls who are being punished in Hades until that time (*Apoc. Zeph.* 10:11).

The trial of Hades takes place after the soul has been brought down to Hades, at the point of death, and is based on the records kept by the accuser (bad deeds) and God (the good deeds). The lack of reference to an eschatological resurrection in this apocalypse may be due to the trial of Hades and final destiny of the righteous, the heavenly city (*Apoc. Zeph.* 2:7; 5:1-6; 9:4-5), thus ruling out the necessity of a future judgment of the righteous and the need for an earthly body. However, the righteous souls will be clothed in angelic garments (8:3), while even the wicked souls will have a physical form (10:4-9, 12-14). Although resurrection is not specifically mentioned – it is implied when the soul passes the trial and is able to escape Hades and "cross over the crossing place" (7:9; 8:1) in order to enter the heavenly realm possessing a celestial body (8:3). The resurrection is also hinted at as a possibility for unrighteous souls if they are repenting from their sins (10:10-11). The text is also clear that the Patriarchs (Abraham, Isaac, and Jacob) but also Enoch, Elijah, and David[134] are already in Heaven (9:4), suggesting that at least the patriarchs and King David must have resurrected.

This apocalypse does not attempt to prove the afterlife belief which includes a resurrection of the righteous or repentant, by referring or alluding to the TaNaKh – it is only assumed. Figure 10 illustrates the death and resurrection concept in the *Apocalypse of Zephaniah*.

---

133. Ibid., 1:498–99.

134. The TaNaKh suggests that Enoch (Gen. 5:24) and Elijah (2 Kgs 2:11-12) did not die like everyone else but instead ascended to Heaven. This explains the great body of tradition regarding these two characters developed during the Second Temple Period. The author of this apocalypse may also have included David in the list since Ps. 16:10 (LXX 15:10) notes that David's soul will not be abandoned in Hades (ὅτι οὐκ ἐγκαταλείψεις τὴν ψυχήν μου εἰς ᾅδην).

Figure 10. Death and Resurrection in the *Apocalypse of Zephaniah*.

	Life[a] *Apoc. Zeph.* 3:2-9; 7:1-11	Death and Afterlife			Judgment[e] *Apoc. Zeph.* 10:11; 12:5-8	Eternity[f] *Apoc. Zeph.* 4:7
		Phase 1[b] *Apoc. Zeph.* 4:7	Phase 2[c] *Apoc. Zeph.* 7:1-11	Phase 3[d] *Apoc. Zeph.* 8:1–9:5; 10:1–11:6		
HEAVENLY CITY				Righteous Soul	-------- →	
THE AIR		Soul 4:7				
WORLD	Body Soul		B4; 8:1–9:5		10:10-14	
GRAVE		Body				
HADES			Soul	Wicked Soul	-------- → 4:7	

[a] This life determines the future destiny of the soul and is based on the records of sins (*Apoc. Zeph.* 3:2-4, 8-9; 7:1-9) and good deeds (3:5-7; 7:10-11) recorded by the angels of the Accuser and of God.

[b] In the first phase of the afterlife, the soul of an ungodly person "spends three days going around… in the air before" the soul is brought down to Hades by an "ugly" angel representing the Accuser (*Apoc. Zeph.* 4:7). It could be assumed that this would also be the case for the soul of a godly person, however, it would probably be escorted by a "good looking" angel who represents God.

[c] In the second phase of the afterlife, the soul is judged or "weighted in the balance" (*Apoc. Zeph.* 8:5) in Hades based on the records of the deeds of the soul kept by the Accuser and by God (7:1–8:5). *Apocalypse of Zephaniah* 7:8 seems to suggest the possibility for mercy, as demonstrated by Zephaniah who, on his journey of the soul, begs the Lord Almighty to wipe out the records held by the Accuser.

[d] In the third phase of the afterlife, the soul receives its reward or punishment. If judged righteous and pure, a soul will escape Hades, put on an angelic garment and join the other righteous in the Heavenly City (*Apoc. Zeph.* 8:1–9:5). A soul judged wicked and impure will remain in Hades and be severely punished (10:1-9). However, the *Apocalypse of Zephaniah* 10:10-14 suggests a sinful soul can repent and escape the deserved punishment up to the point "when the Lord will judge." *Apocalypse*

of Zephaniah 1:4-6 notes that the Patriarchs and all the righteous (in heaven and on earth) prays to "the Lord Almighty daily on behalf of these who are in all these torments."

ᵉ Apocalypse of Zephaniah, in its current form, only hints at a future eschatological judgment (*Apoc. Zeph.* 10:11; 12:5-8), but it would be reasonable to assume that the last four missing pages of the apocalypse would give more details since the last chapter of the surviving manuscript presents the fourth trumpet blast (12:1) which heralds the coming wrath of God.

ᶠ Whatever happens on the day of the eschatological judgment, the righteous will spend eternity in the Heavenly City (*Apoc. Zeph.* 2:7) while the wicked will be punished in Hades for all eternity (4:7).

~ ~ ~

7. Other Ezra Texts

In addition to 2 Esdras, which was considered in Chapter 2, there are four other texts that are pseudepigraphically attributed to Ezra of the TaNaKh. They are the *Greek Apocalypse of Ezra* (150–850 CE), *Vision of Ezra* (350–600 CE), *Questions of Ezra* (date unknown) and *Revelation of Ezra* (X > 9th cent. CE), all of which have a Christian provenance.[135]

Apart from the strictly astrological book of *Revelation of Ezra*, these works all deal with God's justice and what will happen to the righteous and the wicked upon death. According to these books, the souls of the righteous will be rewarded in heaven (*Gk. Apoc. Ezra* 1:12; 5:20-22; *Vis. Ezra* 63-66; *Ques. Ezra* A3, 6, 10, 14-15, 20; B2, 6), while the wicked will be punished in Tartarus (*Gk. Apoc. Ezra* 4:5-24; 5:2-6, 23-28; *Vis. Ezra* 1-2, 8-55) or in the eternal fire (*Ques. Ezra* A3, 10, 14-15; B2, 6-14). The *Greek Apocalypse of Ezra* and *Questions of Ezra* both allude (*Gk. Apoc. Ezra* 2:1; 5:22; *Ques. Ezra* A10) or mention (*Gk. Apoc. Ezra* 4:36; 7:2; *Ques. Ezra* A5; B3, 11-14) the resurrection belief (see the highlighted passages in Appendix A), although they do not quote or allude to the TaNaKh in support of this belief. Figures 11-13 illustrate the death and resurrection concept in these books.

---

135. On the dating and providence of these books, see Evans, *Ancient Texts for New Testament Studies*, 34–5; D. Fiensy, "Revelation of Ezra," *OTP* 1:601–2; James R. Mueller and G. Robbins, "*Vision of Ezra*," *OTP* 1:583; M. Stone, "*Greek Apocalypse of Ezra*," *OTP* 1:563; idem, "*Questions of Ezra*," *OTP* 1:592; J. E. Wright, "Esdras, Books of," *DNTB* 339–40.

Figure 11. Death and Resurrection in the *Greek Apocalypse of Ezra*.

	Life[a] Gk. Apoc. Ezra 1:14	Death and Judgment[b] Gk. Apoc. Ezra 6:3-4, 5-15; 7:3	Final Judgment Resurrection[c] Gk. Apoc. Ezra 1:23; 2:26; 4:36-43	Eternity[d] Gk. Apoc. Ezra 5:20-28
HEAVEN PARADISE		6:3, 17, 21 Righteous Soul		Reward (a crown) 1:12-15 5:20-22 6:17, 21
WORLD	Body / Soul		Body / Soul	Rise up uncorrupted 4:36 A different or new body?
EARTH		Body		
BOWEL OF HADES[e] GEHENNA TARTARUS		Implied 4:7-36 5:1-6 Wicked Soul		Punishment 1:24 5:23-28

[a] This life determines the destiny of the person upon death, reward in Heaven (*Gk. Apoc. Ezra* 1:12-14) or eternal punishment (1:24).

[b] Death is viewed as the reversal of the creation process as described in Gen. 3:19b, the soul (of the righteous Christian) departs for Heaven while the body departs for the earth (cf. *Gk. Apoc. Ezra* 6:3-4, 17) to be consumed by worms (*Gk. Apoc. Ezra* 6:24). This text implies a preliminary judgment upon death, to decide where the "soul" should go – back to God in Heaven or down to Hades to be punished while waiting for the eschatological resurrection and judgment (4:36). It should be noted that the prayers given by the righteous on behalf of the wicked may alleviate some of their suffering (5:10). The text seems to suggest that there will be two periods of judgment of the wicked, the first starts at the point of death and lasts until the day of resurrection while the second period will be eternal, starting at the end of the eschatological judgment.

[c] Although the righteous will include both key characters from the TaNaKh [Enoch, Elijah, Moses and Patriarchs] and the New Testament [Peter, Paul and Luke], it also includes all the righteous, the text notes that Jesus went down to Hades to summon up His elect ones, which included Adam (*Gr. Apoc. Ezra* 7:20), after His death. This may suggest that the author differentiated between the righteous Christians (e.g. 1:6; 2:7; 5:1, 21-22) and the righteous of the TaNaKh (e.g. 5:21-22; 7:20), indicating that the first group receives their reward upon death, while the latter group will have to wait for their reward until the day of the eschatological judgment, when they would be raised up uncorrupted (*Gk. Apoc. Ezra* 4:36). If this is an allusion to Paul's words

in 1 Cor. 15:52, this would include both the righteous and the wicked. Interestingly, this could also explain how the wicked will be able to be punished for all eternity, since they will have incorruptible bodies. The text is not clear whether or not the uncorrupted body will be the same or different from the one held before death. The earth will be destroyed by fire at the conclusion of the eschatological judgment (*Gk. Apoc. Ezra* 4:37-39, 43).

[d] The text suggests that the reward and punishment will be of an eternal nature (*Gk. Apoc. Ezra* 1:24; 5:20-28).

[e] It is difficult to determine what the author of the book has in mind when referring to the "Bowel of Hades" (*Gk. Apoc. Ezra* 6:26). Michael Stone speculates that it may be "compared with the 'hollow places' in which the souls reside according to *1 En.* 22," although he notes that these two texts use a different Greek word (Stone, "Greek Apocalypse of Ezra," *OTP* 1:578).

~ ~ ~

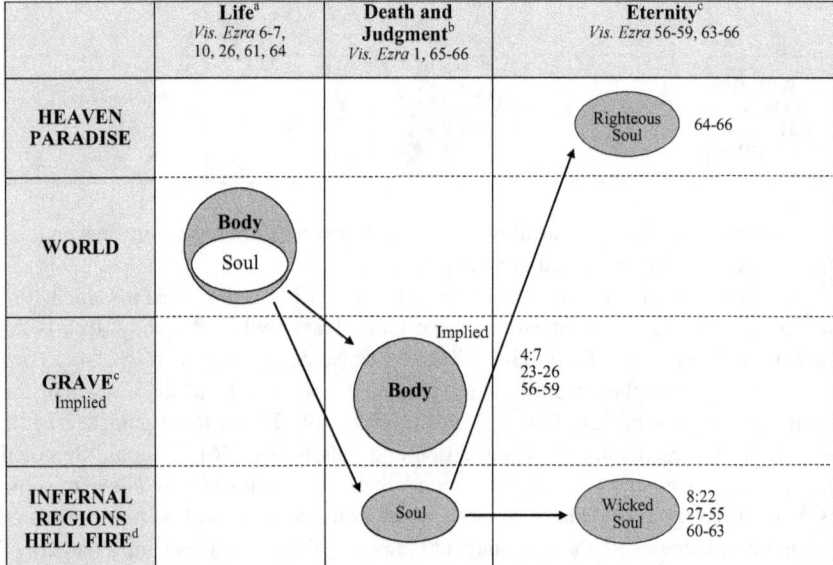

Figure 12. Death and "Resurrection" in the *Vision of Ezra*.

[a] The destiny of a person is determined by their deeds in this life. The righteous are those who "gave alms generously, clothed the naked, and desired a good desire" (*Vis. Ezra* 6-7), who "daily were making better confession before God and the holy priests, freely bringing alms (and) resisting sin" (*Vis. Ezra* 25-26), and who "rest on account of confession, penitence, and largesse in almsgiving" (*Vis. Ezra* 64) – they will receive their reward in the heavenly Paradise. The wicked, on the other hand, who denied the Lord, will suffer punishment in the infernal regions (*Vis. Ezra* 8-22, 27-55, 60-63).

[b] The punishment of the wicked begins upon the person's death when both the righteous and the wicked are brought down to the infernal regions. The wicked will

be unable to escape the punishment in the Hell fire, while the righteous will be able to pass through the infernal regions unscathed on their way to their Heavenly reward of eternal rest in Paradise (*Vis. Ezra* 64-65). The text does not present a clear dualistic view of body and soul, in fact, *Vision of Ezra* 53 gives the only reference to the human soul in this book. In addition, the personal afterlife view seems very "bodily," almost as if the person passed from life into death in a physical and literal sense (this figure illustrates this by showing the *soul* in the same shade of grey at the *body*).

[c] This text shows no interest in the earthly body upon death, instead, it shows a very literal and physical depiction of the human existence in the afterlife. Thus, the separation of body and soul is only implied in the text.

[d] The wicked souls will be punished in the Hell fire for all eternity. Although the soul left the earthly body in the grave, it is still described as being physical since the various forms of torture to be experienced would require a "body" (*Vis. Ezra* 8-22, 27-55).

~ ~ ~

Figure 13. Death and "Resurrection" in the *Questions of Ezra*.

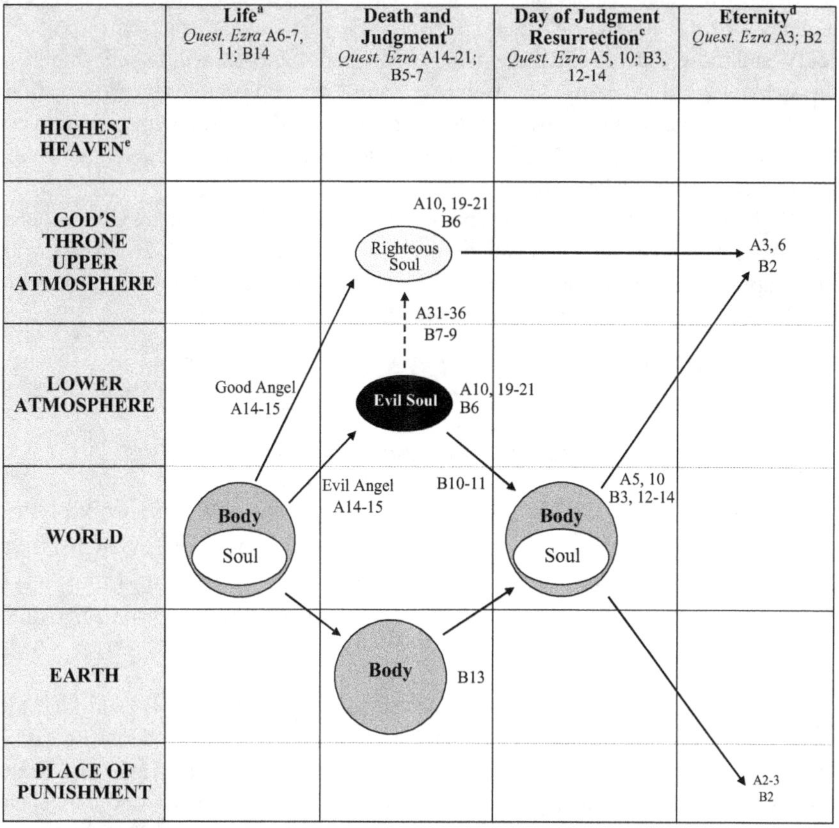

ᵃ This life determines the destiny of the person upon death – honor or punishment (*Quest. Ezra* A6-7, 11; B14).

ᵇ At the point of death, a good angel comes to collect the soul of the righteous and an evil angel the soul of the evil (*Quest. Ezra* A14-15). The good or evil angel starts the journey with the soul through the seven steps of the divinity in which the fifth step functions as the divider between the lower and upper atmosphere, since each soul will be investigated – "if he is just, he shines, and if he is a sinner, he is darkened" (*Quest. Ezra* A20). The righteous souls are able to complete the journey by passing on to the seventh step into the upper atmosphere where it will be honored and will worship God while the sinners are imprisoned by the demons and punished by Satan in the lower atmosphere (*Quest. Ezra* A10, 19-21; B6). However, by offering prayers and fasting for 40 days for the dead and by giving alms to the poor, a relative or a friend of the dead can help a soul move from the lower to the upper atmosphere before the day of judgment (*Quest. Ezra* A31; B7-9).

ᶜ In the eschatological judgment, the entrapped souls in the lower atmosphere will be released from Satan's punishment to reunite with their body in order to be judged by the coming Christ during the eschatological judgment (*Quest. Ezra* B11-14) in which He will "judge (those on) the earth, that is the righteous and the wicked, and requites each for his deeds" (*Quest. Ezra* B14). This suggests that only the "evil souls" and those who are still alive, both wicked and righteous, will be judged during the eschatological judgment, the "righteous souls" have no need for the resurrection.

ᵈ The righteous will be crowned (*Quest. Ezra* A6) and honored with great joy and eternal light (*Quest. Ezra* A3; B2) while the wicked are tortured with eternal fire for all eternity in outer darkness (*Quest. Ezra* A2-3; B2).

ᵉ God's throne is the closest any human can come to God and stay alive (*Quest. Ezra* A21) due to His fiery and wondrous divinity (*Quest. Ezra* A22-26). Apart from the seraphim and the Cherubim guardians of God (*Quest. Ezra* A27-30), not even the angels have seen God's face (*Quest. Ezra* A22-26).

~ ~ ~

8. *Apocalypse of Sedrach*

The *Apocalypse of Sedrach*[136] (second–fifth cent. CE) is probably of Jewish origin (the apocalyptic section) but was later adopted by a Christian community who added the sermon of love (*Apoc. Sedr.* 1) and may have replaced references to Michael with ones to Jesus.[137] In this book, Sedrach

---

136. Some scholars would also associate this book with Ezra, arguing that the name Sedrach is a corruption of the name Ezra, adding that the Sedrach of this apocalypse does not resemble the Sedrach of the book of Daniel. There also seem to be similarities between Ezra's debate with God in the Ezra books and the debate recorded in *Apocalypse of Sedrach* (Wright, "Esdras, Books of," *DNTB* 339–40).

137. S. Agourides, "*Apocalypse of Sedrach*," *OTP* 1:606–7.

questions God's justice in punishing humans and argues that He should show mercy towards those who repent. This book presents a sharp distinction between soul (10:1-4) and body (11:1-9, 12-13). The soul enters a person while still in the womb (9:1), it spreads out to all the parts of the body (9:2), and is removed through the mouth at the time of death with great difficulty (9:3). Upon death, a person's soul "ascends where the Lord calls" it, while the "wretched body goes away for judgment" (11:11). The righteous soul, like Sedrach, is brought to Paradise/Third Heaven (2:5; 9:1; 16:6), God's Kingdom (15:5), or the "bosom of Abraham" (14:5) to "be with the just ones in a place of refreshment and rest" (16:3). The soul of the wicked, however, will "see the place of punishment" (4:1; 14:9; 16:3). Thus, there would be no need for an eschatological and universal judgment. However, there is one clear resurrection statement in the Christian sermon on love which states that the "Son of God" came down, thus "death was trampled down, Hades was made captive, Adam was recalled (from death), and through love one flock was made thereafter of angels and men" (1:21). Christ also tells Sedrach, "Paradise has been opened to you, and after dying you will live" (12:1), implying that death is not the end, but the beginning. The parting of the soul from the body at the point of death is described as a kind of resurrection of the soul. Be that as it may, there are no references or allusions to the TaNaKh regarding the resurrection belief.

9. *2 Baruch*

2 Baruch, also known as the *Syriac Apocalypse of Baruch*, was originally "composed in Hebrew or Aramaic, translated in to Greek and ultimately translated from Greek into Syriac,"[138] as noted in the heading of the book. This book was written sometime after the cataclysmic events of the Roman destruction of the Second Temple in 70 CE,[139] although the narrative setting is the Babylonian destruction of the First Temple in

---

138. J. E. Wright, "Baruch, Books of," *DNTB* 149. See also A. Klijn, "2 *(Syriac Apocalypse of) Baruch*," *OTP* 1:616.

139. Based on the internal evidence in the book (e.g. *2 Bar.* 32:2-4; 61:7; 68:5), Klijn ("2 *[Syriac Apocalypse of] Baruch*," 616–17) notes that most scholars date the book to the beginning of the second century CE, since *2 Bar.* 61:7 is quoted in *Gos. Barn.* 11:9 (*Barnabas* may have been written in 117 or 132 CE) and *2 Baruch* may be dependent on *4 Ezra* (late first century CE), although it should not be ruled out that both *4 Ezra* and *2 Baruch* may be relying on a common source or tradition. If the latter, scholars still assume that *2 Baruch* is later since the theology seems to be more

587/6 BCE. In both cases, there was a need for encouraging messages to the people. In the same way as Jeremiah and Baruch gave encouraging words to the Jewish people who experienced this catastrophe, both in the land of Israel but also to those already living in the Babylonian and Assyrian diaspora, encouraging messages were given once more by the words of "Baruch" to the Jews experiencing the second destruction of the Temple.[140]

The universal eschatological resurrection hope, judgment and reward/ punishment of the righteous and the wicked, and references to the "World to come" proliferate the book. According to *2 Baruch*, the eschatological resurrection will take place after "a period of national exaltation" by the Messiah and will introduce a second phase of the salvation process (*2 Bar.* 29; 44:8-12; 73–74).[141] The "Apocalypse of the Clouds" (*2 Bar.* 53–74) divides the present history into twelve alternating good and evil time-periods[142] which culminates with *the Messianic era* (*2 Bar.* 28–29).[143] Collins observes that this Messianic period will be limited (*2 Bar.* 40:3) and thus only provides "a temporal fulfillment of national eschatology before the resurrection and final judgment," introducing the "world to

---

developed than that of *4 Ezra*. Regardless, the author probably made use of earlier sources, predating the destruction of the Second Temple. Be that as it may, *2 Baruch* would have been written during the same time-period as the *Book of Revelation*.

140. J. Edward Wright, "The Social Setting of the Syriac *Apocalypse of Baruch*," *JSP* 16 (1997): 81–96.

141. Collins, "Jewish Apocalypse," 35.

142. These alternate periods describe the history from the beginning of God's creation until the end, "(the times) which are known by deceit and by truth" (*2 Bar.* 56:2), they are: (1) Black – begins at the Fall (56:5-16); (2) **Bright** – starts with Abraham and his generation (57:1-3); (3) Black – describes the slavery in Egypt (58:1-2); (4) **Bright** – introduced by Moses who received revelations from God (59:1-12); (5) Black – the time of the judges (60:1-2); (6) **Bright** – the united kingdom of David and Solomon and the building of the Temple (61:1-8); (7) Black – introduced by Jeroboam which rebelled and led to the exile of the northern tribes (62:1-8); (8) **Bright** – the reforms of King Hezekiah (63:1-11); (9) Black – the wicked reign of Manasseh (64:1–65:2); (10) **Bright** – the reforms of King Josiah (66:1-8); (11) Black – destruction of Jerusalem by the Babylonians (67:1-9); and (12) **Bright** – the rebuilding of Jerusalem (68:1-8).

143. The Messiah appears at the end of the twelve calamities described in *2 Bar.* 26–27. These tribulations take place during the additional and final Dark-**Bright** cycle of apocalyptic vision. The final dark period (69:1–71:2) will be more evil than all the previous periods but it will be followed by the final bright period (72:1–74:4) which is the time of the Messiah, God's servant, who will bring national exaltation to the nation of Israel (*2 Bar.* 28–29).

come," which will be the second and final stage of the salvation process (*2 Bar.* 30).[144] The eschatological time-line of *2 Baruch* (Fig. 14) is similar to that of *4 Ezra* (Figure 4) in the sense that the Messianic era will take place before the universal resurrection/judgment and the eternal reward for the righteous. However, there are also some important differences. Notably, unlike the three-stage worldview of *4 Ezra*, with its seven-day long period of "primeval silence," *2 Baruch* presents a two-stage-worldview which transitions from the present world to the world to come through the transformation of the righteous following the resurrection. In both eschatological time-lines, the resurrection and judgment functions as the beginning of the new age, which is also the case in the book of Revelation (Rev. 20:4-6).[145]

Figure 14. The Two-Stage Worldview Presented in *2 Baruch*.

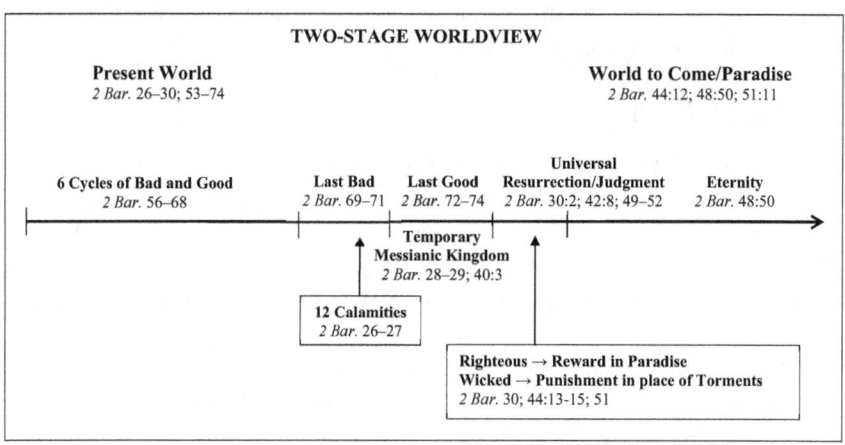

Unlike *4 Ezra*, which reveals that the Messianic Kingdom will last for 400 years, no such information is given in *2 Baruch*. It only notes that the Messianic period is the final "bright" period leading up to the "world to come." Similarly, *2 Baruch* does not reveal the final destiny of the Messiah at the end of his period of reign, which is death in the case

---

144. Collins, "Jewish Apocalypses," 35.

145. The resurrection view presented in Revelation is unique in the sense the eschatological resurrection and judgment takes place in two phases, separated by a millennium (Rev. 20:6). The first resurrection involves the righteous and their reward, while the second resurrection at the end of the millennium only regards the wicked and their eternal punishment. According to Rev. 21–22, the righteous will return to a newly re-created world at the end of the millennium in order to live the rest of the eternity there, together with God in the New Jerusalem.

of *4 Ezra* 7:28-29. The book of Revelation does not present a Messianic Kingdom before the eschatological resurrection/judgment.

2 Baruch does not state clearly the location of the "world to come" or Paradise (e.g. *2 Bar.* 48:50), whether it will be otherworldly (*2 Bar.* 51:3, 11) or on a renewed earth (*2 Bar.* 32:6; 44:13; 57:2) as is the case in *4 Ezra*. The book of Revelation, however, presents a two stage view, in which the righteous will spend a millennium with God in heaven (Rev. 20:4-6) before God and the righteous will return to a renewed earth (Rev. 21:1, 4), bringing the New Jerusalem with them (Rev. 21:2, 9-27; 22:1-5), and dwell there for all eternity (Rev. 22:5).

Apart from the many allusions to the eschatological resurrection appearing in *2 Baruch*,[146] the following three references are explicit: *2 Bar.* 30:2; 42:8; 49–50, the last of which gives the most detailed description. However, this study will also consider *2 Baruch* 14:10-14 since it strongly implies the universal resurrection and appears in a context with strong links to biblical wisdom literature.

a. *2 Baruch* 14:10-14

Daewoong Kim observes "*2 Baruch* deliberately uses the biblical sapiential tradition and closely connects it with the apocalyptical tradition in the book of Daniel."[147] In *2 Baruch* 14, Kim sees "Job's theological skepticism" expressed in "Baruch's five-fold rhetorical questions that contain a polyphonic voice (*2 Bar.* 14:8-9)."[148] Both the book of Job and

---

146. Describing death as sleep suggests a belief in a resurrection. Thus, like the resurrection, a person sleeping will wake up from their sleep and become conscious once more (*2 Bar.* 11:4; 21:24; 30:1; 85:3, 9). *2 Baruch* contains several references to the hope the righteous have regarding a future after their death (*2 Bar.* 14:12-13; 30:1; 57:2; 78:6), the reward that is in store for them (*2 Bar.* 14:13; 15:7-8; 21:12-13; 30:1-2; 44:11-13; 48:6, 50; 51:8-9, 11; 52:6-7; 57:2; 59:2; 76:2; 84:6; 85:15), and the punishment kept in store for the wicked (*2 Bar.* 14:14; 21:12-13; 30:3-5; 36:11; 44:15; 51:6, 16; 52:1-5; 54:14, 21-22; 59:2; 85:15). There are also several statements regarding a universal eschatological judgment in which everyone will be judged, both the living and the dead (*2 Bar.* 5:2-3; 21:8; 24:1-2; 48:2, 27, 39; 51:1; 57:2; 82:2; 83:2, 7; 85:9). Lastly, *2 Baruch* makes it clear that the world to come is created for the righteous: "And with regard to the righteous ones, those whom you said the world has come on their account, yes, also that which is coming is on their account. For this world is to them a struggle and an effort with much trouble. And that accordingly which will come, a crown with great glory" (*2 Bar.* 15:7-8). See the highlighted passages from *2 Baruch* in Appendix A.

147. Daewoong Kim, "Wisdom and Apocalyptic in *2 Baruch*," *Henoch* 33 (2011): 250.

148. Ibid., 254.

2 Baruch 14 address the issue of theodicy and question the orthodox view, presented in Deuteronomy (Deut. 28–30) and emphasized in Proverbs (e.g. 9:9-10, 27; 14:27; 19:23), that the righteous will receive blessings while the wicked will be punished. Like Job, the righteous who experienced the destruction and were massacred by the hand of the Babylonians (i.e. Romans) suffered unjustly (Job 1–2; 32:1-2; *2 Bar.* 14:3-7). Both books recognize the limitations of human wisdom, and *2 Baruch* contrasts this limitation with God's ultimate wisdom by the use of the five-fold rhetorical questions which echoes the book of Job:

Who can understand your judgment? (*2 Bar.* 14:8a)	Would you really challenge My justice? (Job 40:8a)
Who can explore the depth of your way? (*2 Bar.* 14:8b)	But God understands the way to wisdom, and He knows its location. (Job 28:23)
Who can discern the majesty of your path? (*2 Bar.* 14:9a)	
Who can discern your incomprehensible counsel? (*2 Bar.* 14:9b)	Who is this who obscures My counsel with ignorant words? (Job 38:2)
Who of those who are born has ever discovered the beginning and the end of your wisdom? (*2 Bar.* 14:9c)	

The author of *2 Baruch* acknowledges that God's wisdom cannot be challenged and would seem to agree with God's answer when He finally speaks to Job (Job 38:1–42:6). It should be noted that God never answers Job's questions (Job 7:11-21). Instead, God makes it clear that only He is truly wise, thus, Job should place his trust in Him, because only the wise knows the best course of action in every situation. Interestingly, Job's comment that "My days are swifter than a weaver's shuttle and are spent without hope. Oh, remember that my life is a breath [רוּחַ]!" (Job 7:6-7a) is also expressed by Baruch, who states: "For we all have been made like breath. For as breath ascends without human control and vanishes, so it is with the nature of men, who do not know what will happen to them in the end" (*2 Bar.* 14:10-11).

These sentiments are shared by Qohelet, who also observes the limitations of wisdom and concludes that everything is *hevel*, nothingness.[149] He writes that both humans and animals will die and return to dust from

---

149. The word *hevel* appears throughout the book (Eccl. 1:2, 14; 2:1, 11, 15, 17, 19, 21, 23, 26; 3:19; 4:4, 7-8, 16; 5:7, 9; 6:2, 9, 11; 7:6; 8:10, 14; 11:8, 10; 12:8) and is a major theme of the book, emphasizing the limitation of all human endeavor, noting that only God's gifts have true value.

where they came, adding "Who knows if the spirit (רוּחַ) of people rises upward and the spirit (רוּחַ) of animals goes downward to the earth?" (Eccl. 3:19-21). Moreover, Qohelet also laments the perversion of justice in which the righteous perish while the wicked prosper (Eccl. 7:15; 8:12-14). Like Job, Qohelet does not reach a satisfactory solution to the problem of theodicy but concludes that a person should remember God (Eccl. 12:1, 6), adding that, although everything is *hevel*, one should still fear God and keep his commandments since every work will be brought into judgment (Eccl. 12:13-14). This last statement could be an allusion to a future resurrection.

In contrast to Job and Qohelet, *2 Baruch* solves the problem of theodicy by introducing the resurrection hope. He states:

> [12]For the righteous wait rightly for the end and without fear depart from this life, because they possess with you the power of the deeds that are kept in reservoir. [13]For this reason, also, they leave this world [or: age] behind without fear, and trusting with gladness they are waiting to receive the world [or: age] that you have promised them. (*2 Bar.* 14:12-13)

The righteous have nothing to fear since God remembers their righteous deeds which are stored in the heavenly treasuries, a concept which is well attested in both the New Testament and in Early Rabbinic Judaism.[150]

Regardless of the destiny of the righteous and the wicked in this world, God reveals to Baruch that the wicked will receive their just punishment since he/she broke the Law and was thus aware of his/her transgressions (*2 Bar.* 15:1-7). God emphasizes the world to come is made for the righteous who will be crowned with great glory (*2 Bar.* 15:7-8).

b. *2 Baruch* 30:1-5

The first explicit resurrection text appears in *2 Bar.* 30:1-5, which reveals this resurrection to be universal, involving both the righteous and the wicked, and it will take place at the end of the Messianic age (v. 1a).[151] At

---

150. On several occasions, Jesus encourages the people to consider the big perspective and plan for the world to come by collecting treasures in Heaven instead of on Earth (Mt. 6:19-21; Lk. 11:33-34). During the Second Temple Period, almsgiving became the means for collecting heavenly treasures (e.g. Sir. 29:9-13; Tob. 4:8-11; Mt. 19:21; Mk 10:21, 30; Josephus, *Ant.* 20.17-96; *t. Pe'ah.* 4:18). For further reading, see Joseph Frankovic, "Treasures in Heaven," released 18 February 2008, http://www.jerusalemperspective.com/4661.

151. Although the main emphasis of this resurrection text is the soul of the righteous, only referring to "all who sleep in the hope of him will rise," it could

that time, the treasuries will be opened and the souls will be released, the souls of the righteous will enjoy themselves and not be sad (v. 2) since "they know that the time has come of which it is said that it is the end of times" (v. 3). However, the souls of the wicked will see the joy of the righteous and "waste away" since they "know that their torment has come and that their perditions have arrived" (vv. 4-5). There are no allusions nor references to the TaNaKh in this resurrection text.

c. *2 Baruch* 42:7-8

The second explicit resurrection statement appears in *2 Bar.* 42:8, following the *Apocalypse of the Forest, the Vine, the Fountain, and the Cedar* (*2 Bar.* 36–40), in God's expansion on the apostates and the believers (*2 Bar.* 41–43:3). Like *2 Baruch* 30, this second resurrection statement also appears at the end of the Messianic age (*2 Bar.* 40:3); however, this passage is closely related to the apocalyptic vision of Dan. 2:31-45 and Dan. 7:2-28.

Similar to Daniel 2, the apocalyptic vision in *2 Baruch* 36–37 is also divided into four kingdoms followed by the Messianic age. The first kingdom in both visions is the Babylonian kingdom, the power which destroyed Zion (Dan. 2:37-38; 7:4-5; *2 Bar.* 39:2), which will be followed by two other kingdoms (Persia and Greece). The fourth kingdom (Dan. 2:40; 7:7-8, 11, 19-26; *2 Bar.* 39:5-6) is presented as "harsher and more evil than those which were before it" (*2 Bar.* 39:5; cf. Dan. 2:40; 7:7, 19, 23), and this kingdom "will reign a multitude of times" (a possible reference to the "time, times, half a time" period of the little horn) and "it will rule the times and exalt itself" (*2 Bar.* 39:5-6; cf. Dan. 7:25). Although neither Daniel nor *2 Baruch* names this fourth kingdom, it could be assumed that the author of *2 Baruch* considered this fourth kingdom to represent the Roman Empire which destroyed Zion in the year 70 CE.

In both Daniel and *2 Baruch*, this fourth kingdom will be destroyed by the Messiah, who will establish his kingdom (*2 Bar.* 39:7; Dan. 2:44; 7:14, 27) and will convict the last evil ruler (*2 Bar.* 40:1-2), a possible allusion to the little horn of Dan. 7:8, 11, 24-25, thus protecting the "rest of my [God's] people who will be found in the place that I have chosen" (*2 Bar.* 40:2; cf. Dan. 7:27). Both Daniel and *2 Baruch* note that the dominion of

---

also be assumed that the wicked souls were kept in treasuries and will therefore also resurrect. This is supported by the concluding verses of this text which reveal the reaction and the ultimate destiny of the souls of the wicked. Thus, since both the righteous and the wicked souls are included in this resurrection text, this eschatological resurrection is universal.

God's Anointed will "last forever" (*2 Bar.* 40:3; Dan. 2:44-45; 7:14, 27). Unlike Daniel's version, the Messianic kingdom in *2 Baruch* seems to be of limited time: the dominion of God's Anointed "will last forever until the world of corruption has ended and until the times which have been mentioned before have been fulfilled" (*2 Bar.* 40:3).

Both Daniel and Baruch ask for more details regarding certain parts of the visions – Daniel regarding the reign of the little horn (Dan. 7:19-20), and Baruch regarding the time of the corruption (*2 Bar.* 41:1-6). In both expansions, the vision presents two groups of people, God's Saints, who keep His Law and who will receive all the good promises (*2 Bar.* 42:2; Dan. 7:22), and the wicked, who have rejected the Law and "mingled themselves with the seed of the mingled nations" (*2 Bar.* 42:4) or have associated themselves with the "little horn" (Dan. 7:21). Unlike Daniel 2 and 7, *2 Bar.* 42:7-8 concludes the Messianic age with an universal resurrection, stating: "For corruption will take away those who belong to it, and life those who belong to it. And dust will be called, and told, 'Give back that which does not belong to you and rise up all that you have kept until its own time.'" The two-stage salvation process in *2 Baruch* may be an interpretation of the Son of Man passage in Dan. 7:9-14 and the Michael text in Dan. 12:1, which could be read as a reference to a limited Messianic reign before the eschatological resurrection described in Dan. 12:2-3, 13. Be that as it may, the third explicit and most extensive resurrection text in *2 Baruch* is also the text most closely connected with the resurrection text in Daniel 12.

d. *2 Baruch* 49–51

The third explicit resurrection text follows a section revealing what will happen to the wicked (*2 Bar.* 48:26-47), and it is introduced by the transitional statement:

> [48]Now, then, let us leave the wicked and inquire about the righteous. [49]I will recount their blessedness and will not be silent to proclaim their glory, which is preserved for them. [50]For surely, just as in a little time in this world [or: age] that passes by, in which you live, you have endured much labor, so in that world [or: age] that has no end you will receive a great light. (*2 Bar.* 48:48-50)

The context of the third resurrection passage presents two groups of people: the wicked, who "knew when he [/she] acted unrighteously, and they did not know my Law because of their pride" (*2 Bar.* 48:40); and the righteous, who adhere to God's Law and keep His statutes (*2 Bar.* 48:22). From this, the ultimate destiny of a person is based on which group he/

she belongs to since God's "judgment asks for its own, and my [God's] Law demands its right" and "there is nothing that will be destroyed unless it acted wickedly" (*2 Bar.* 48:27-29).

Baruch's main concern regarding this universal eschatological resurrection is the nature of the resurrected body, particularly whether the resurrected dead will be able to be recognized. He asks God:

> ²Indeed, in what shape will those live who live in your day? Or how will the splendor of those persist who [will be] after them? ³Will they indeed then take this form of the present, and will they put on these members of chains, those that are now [steeped] in evils and through which evils are wrought? Or will you perhaps change these, those that are in the world, as also the world [or: age] [itself]? (*2 Bar.* 49:2-3).

This question is not only raised in the New Testament,[152] but was also of interest in Early Rabbinic Judaism – as attested by the interpretation made by Resh Lakish (*b. Sanh.* 91b; *Gen. Rab.* 95:1), Rava (*b. Sanh.* 91b; *Gen. Rab.* 102:2, also known as Abba ben Joseph bar Hama), and Hanina bar Hama (*Eccl. Rab.* 1:6-7), who all made a case that the dead would resurrect with the same body and condition they were in when they died before God "heals" them. Resh Lakish derived his opinion by interpreting Isa. 35:6 and Jer. 31:8 in light of each other, while Raba and R. Hanina argued their case from Deut. 32:39.

God provides a similar answer to Baruch's question. However, in contrast to the Rabbis, He also provides the reason for why He would not change anything in the form of the resurrected body:

> ²For surely the earth will then return the dead, which it now receives to preserve them, while not changing anything in their form. But as it has received them, so it returns them, and as I have handed them over to it, so too it will restore them. ³<u>For then it will be necessary to show to the living that the dead are living again and that those have come [back] who had been</u>

---

152. In 1 Cor. 15:35, Paul is asked: How are the dead raised? What kind of body will they have when they come? Using the analogy of a seed which only grows or "resurrects" after it has been buried or "died" in the ground, Paul makes the case that the resurrected body (seedling) is different than the buried body (seed), although the seedling comes from the seed. The resurrected body of the righteous is incorruptible, glorious, powerful, and spiritual and is ready for an eternal life, while the current body is corruptible and will therefore die (1 Cor. 15:42-44). Paul also makes it clear that the righteous who are not dead when God returns will also be changed and transformed so they too can partake in the heavenly Paradise (1 Cor. 15:51-54). It should be noted that unlike *2 Bar.* 50:2-4, Paul is only concerned with the future of the righteous.

gone. ⁴And when those who know [each other] now will have recognized each other, **then judgment will be strong,** and those [things] that were formerly spoken of will come. (*2 Bar.* 50:2-4, my emphasis added)

The lack of an initial bodily transformation upon resurrection plays an important function in the eschatological judgment. It is crucial for both the righteous and the wicked living to recognize the resurrected to presumably solve the question of theodicy, since everyone will witness the righteous and the wicked dead receive their just reward or deserved punishment. Both the living and the resurrected dead will see with their own eyes that God's judgment is universal – that the wicked dead did not get away with their wickedness, and the righteous dead will still receive their reward for adhering to God's Law.

It is only after this initial recognition and realization by the righteous and the wicked that the first bodily transformation will take place as a part of the universal judgment process. Both the righteous and the wicked will be transformed to expose their true character for everyone to see. The righteous will be glorified and the shape of their face will be changed into "the light of their beauty" (*2 Bar.* 51:3), "into the splendor of angels" (*2 Bar.* 51:5), and they will be "like the angels and be equal to the stars" (*2 Bar.* 51:10a).[153] They will even be able to "change into any shape which they wished, from beauty to loveliness, and from light to the splendor of glory" (*2 Bar.* 51:10b). The wicked, upon seeing the transformation of the righteous, will also be transformed; however, their "shape will be made more evil" (*2 Bar.* 51:2) and made "into startling vision and horrible shapes; and they will waste away even more" (*2 Bar.* 51:5). At the conclusion of the judgment, the righteous will enter Paradise, the world to come (*2 Bar.* 51:3, 8-14; 52:7), while the wicked will be sent to the place of Torment (*2 Bar.* 51:6, 16; 52:1-5).[154]

---

153. This idea may derive from the description given of Moses when coming down from the mountain, after spending 40 days with God and receiving the two tablets of the covenant from him. According to Exod. 35:29-30, "the skin of his face shone" or was radiating light.

154. The analogy of a seed which only grows or "resurrects" after it has been buried or "died" in the ground is also used in Early Rabbinic Judaism to support and illustrate a resurrection belief (*b. Ketub.* 111b; *b. Sanh.* 90b; *Eccl. Rab.* 1:6-7; 3:11; cf. *Gen. Rab.* 28:3; *Lev. Rab.* 18:1; *Eccl. Rab.* 12:5). Interestingly, Jesus also uses this analogy when referring to his own death and the result of his sacrifice which will bring life to all who believe in him (Jn 12:23-26). For further reading regarding Paul's discussion on the nature of the resurrected body, see David Hodgens, "Our Resurrection Body: An Exegesis of 1 Corinthians 15:42-49," *MJT* 17, no. 2 (2001): 65–91.

Liv Ingeborg Lied suggests the importance of the recognition motif as a part of the great reversal. It is only through the transformation process of the righteous and the wicked that the wicked will be able to identify the righteous and realize their true position. Their roles have been reversed. The wicked were exalted over the righteous in the corruptible world, but in the incorruptible world, it is the righteous who are exalted and will transform from earthly bodies to take on angelic bodies. Accordingly, they can possess Paradise while the wicked will diminish and receive the consequences of their decisions in the place of torment. Thus, it becomes clear to the wicked that it is the righteous who finally triumphed.[155] Ingeborg Lied considers this as a second punishment for the wicked, stating: "It is not enough that the wicked are made aware of their transgressions and punished by the Judge in 48:40, it is just as crucial that they see their opponents excel (51:5-6)."[156]

While in Paradise, the righteous seem to experience a second transformation. From being like or equal to the angels (*2 Bar.* 51:10), they will become greater than the angels (*2 Bar.* 51:12).[157] This double

---

155. Liv Ingeborg Lied, "Recognizing the Righteous Remnant? Resurrection, Recognition and Eschatological Reversals in *2 Baruch* 47–52," in *Metamorphoses: Resurrection, Body and Transformative Practices in Early Christianity*, ed. Turid Karlsen Seim and Jorunn Økland (Berlin: de Gruyter, 2009), 328.

156. Ibid., 329.

157. This theme of the hierarchical structure of the heavenly world and the ranking of humans within this structure also appears in the books of *The Life of Adam and Eve*, which ranks humans above the angels before the fall and below the angels as the result of sin, after the fall. Several traditions developed concerning the ranking of the angels and speculation of how humans would fit into this structure. According to some traditions, a person who follows his good inclination (יצר הטוב) is considered to be ranked higher than the angels while, if following the evil (יצר הרע), he is likened to an animal (*Gen. Rab.* 14:3-4; 48:11). Other traditions consider the angels to always be ranked above humans. For further study, see Gary A. Anderson, "The Exaltation of Adam and the Fall of Satan," in *Literature on Adam and Eve*, ed. Gary A. Anderson and Michael E. Stone (Leiden: Brill, 2000), 83–110, and, in the same volume, Michael E. Stone, "The Fall of Satan and Adam's Penitence," 43–56; David Flusser, *Judaism and the Origins of Christianity* (Jerusalem: Magnes, 1988), 246–79; and Efraim E. Urbach, *The Sages: Their Concepts and Beliefs*, 2nd ed. (Cambridge, MA: Harvard University Press, 1979), 150–9.

The elevated creation ranking of humans is based on an interpretation of the statement that human beings were created in God's image and likeness (Gen. 1:26-27), hence why the angels were to worship Adam, and the MT version of Ps. 8:5-6 (ET, 4-5) which states that humans were created a little lower than God and were crowned

transformation theme seems to go beyond the transformation scene of the righteous/wise described in Dan. 12:3 – "Those who are wise will shine like the bright expanse of the heavens (רָקִיעַ), and those who lead many to righteousness, like the stars forever and ever." It could be argued that *2 Baruch* understood רָקִיעַ, "God's heavenly expand," named שָׁמַיִם, "heaven/sky," in Gen. 1:8, as a reference to Paradise, thus implying that there is a need for a transformation before entering the realm of Paradise. Thus, if there is a need for a transformation, it implies that the righteous must have resurrected in an untransformed shape, perhaps resurrecting with the same shape they had before they died. However, *2 Baruch* takes this interpretation a step further and argues that if the righteous were to experience a transformation this would also hold true for the wicked – not to prepare them for entry into Paradise (*2 Bar.* 51:3), but for their place of torment (*2 Bar.* 51:6). In contrast to a more limited resurrection event in Dan. 12:2, which seems to only concern the most wise and the most wicked,[158] *2 Baruch* seems to present a universal resurrection which concerns all the righteous and all the wicked, both dead and alive. A judgment scene is only assumed in these two passages to determine who will be resurrected and who should be rewarded or punished. However, the judgment scenes appearing in *2 Baruch* and Daniel are closely related:

with glory and honor: וַתְּחַסְּרֵהוּ מְּעַט מֵאֱלֹהִים וְכָבוֹד וְהָדָר תְּעַטְּרֵהוּ (Jan A. Sigvartsen, "The Hierarchical Structures Found in the Books *The Life of Adam and Eve*," forthcoming).

This theme is also alluded to in Jesus' response regarding resurrection of the spouse and the longevity of the marriage vow, noting that since humans will be like the angels, there will be no marriage in Heaven (Mt. 22:24-30; Lk. 20:34-36). Paul alludes to this ranking in 1 Cor. 6:1-3, noting that the righteous will judge the angels, suggesting a heightened position. Hebrews 2:7-9 presents Jesus as accepting a rank lower than the angels temporarily, in order to die a substitutionary death on behalf of humankind, implying Jesus returned to his original ranking upon completion of His mission. Thus, it could be argued, righteous humans who have accepted Jesus' sacrifice and have been reborn into a life in Him will, like Jesus, upon resurrection, be exalted above the angels.

158. Daniel 12:2 uses limiting, and not universal vocabulary, when describing the resurrected as many (רַבִּים) instead of "all" (כֹּל). He is also referring to each category of resurrected as "these" (אֵלֶּה). Thus, the writer gives the impression that not every single person who has lived will be resurrected – many will resurrect, some for life and others for reproach, and assumingly, some not at all.

2 Bar. 24:1-2	Dan. 7:10, 22
¹For, see, days are coming and **books will be opened** in which are written the sins of all who have sinned, and furthermore also the reservoirs in which the <u>righteousness is gathered of all who have been found righteous in creation</u>. ²At that time, you and the many who are with you will see the long-suffering of the Most High that is throughout all generations, who has been long-suffering for the sake of all who are born, both sinners and righteous.	A river of fire was flowing, coming out from His presence. Thousands upon thousands served Him; ten thousand times ten thousand stood before Him. The court was convened, and the **books were opened**…until the Ancient of Days arrived and a <u>judgment was given in favor of the holy ones of the Most High</u>, for the time had come, and the holy ones took possession of the kingdom.

The purpose of both judgment scenes is to vindicate the righteous and punish the wicked, based on detailed records of both sins and good deeds, which are kept in the books to guarantee God's theodicy.

e. Concluding Remarks

2 Baruch uses the language from the wisdom tradition and presents the resurrection belief as the solution to the problem of theodicy stated in Job and Qohelet. The wisdom element was combined with Daniel's apocalyptic perspective in the second and third explicit resurrection statements (*2 Bar.* 47:7-8; 49–51), dividing humans into two groups – the righteous who follow God's Law and are thus wise, and the wicked who lack God's wisdom and are acting unrighteously due to their pride (*2 Bar.* 48:40). The resurrection belief in this book is mainly based on an interpretation, reworking, and expansion on Daniel 2, 7 and 12. *2 Baruch* shows the necessity of the recognition element as a part of the judgment which is followed by a double transformation for the righteous and a single transformation for the wicked. The righteous will become equal to the angels in the first transformation and greater than the angels in the second. This transformation is crucial since it will prepare the righteous for an eternal life in the world to come. Figure 15 illustrates the resurrection concept in *2 Baruch*.

Figure 15. Death and Resurrection in *2 Baruch*.

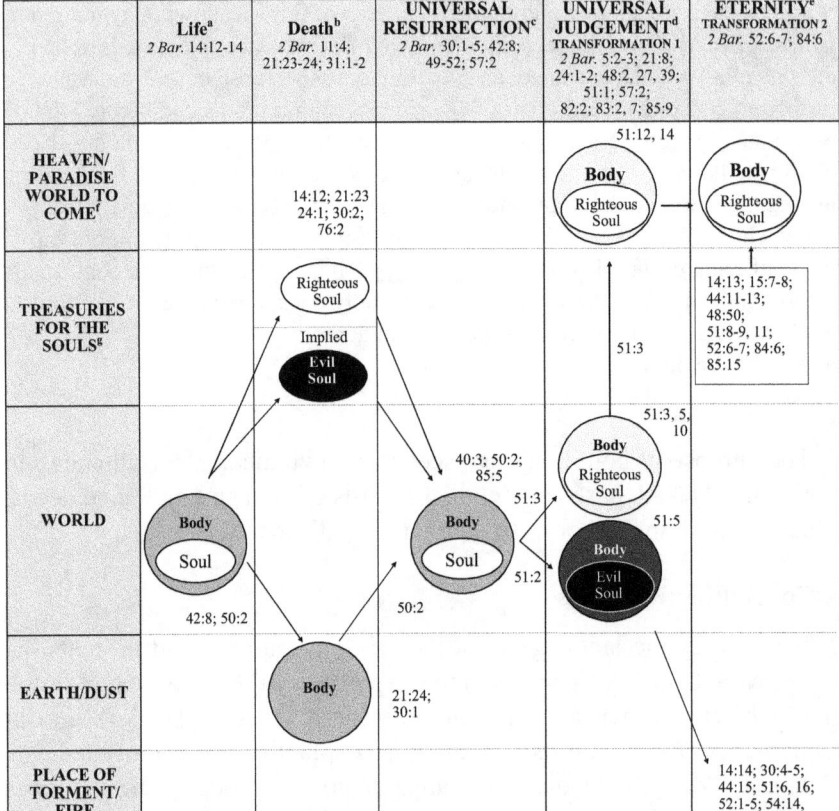

[a] The current life determines the future destiny of a person. If a person lives according to the Law (*2 Bar.* 78:7), that person will be a part of the world to come (*2 Bar.* 30:1-2; 32:1; 38:1; 48:22; 51:3-4, 7; 54:15), if not, he/she will be punished by fire in the place of Torment (*2 Bar.* 30:4-5; 51:6; 52:3).

[b] Upon death, the body is deposited in the earth/dust (*2 Bar.* 42:8; 50:2) and the soul is stored in the treasuries (*2 Bar.* 14:12; 21:23; 24:1; 30:2; 76:2). Death is labeled sleep since there will be an eschatological universal resurrection (*2 Bar.* 11:4; 21:24; 30:1; 36:11; 85:3, 9).

[c] The eschatological resurrection will be universal and the souls of the dead will once more join their former body - the body from the earth and the soul from the treasuries. Both the righteous and the wicked will be resurrected with the same body/form as when they died, so everyone will be able to be recognized.

[d] The eschatological judgment will be universal, and everyone will be judged based on the sins recorded in the books (*2 Bar.* 24:1; 82:2; 83:2) and the good works which are preserved in the treasuries (*2 Bar.* 14:2). During the judgment process, both the righteous and the wicked will experience a transformation which will expose their

true character. The righteous will be glorified and the shape of their faces will be changed into "the light of their beauty" (*2 Bar.* 51:3), "into the splendor of angels" (*2 Bar.* 51:5) and they will be "like the angels and be equal to the stars" (*2 Bar.* 51:10). The wicked, upon seeing the transformation of the righteous, will also be transformed. Their "shapes will be made more evil" (*2 Bar.* 51:2), "into startling vision and horrible shapes; and they will waste away even more" (*2 Bar.* 51:5). At the conclusion of the judgment, the righteous will enter Paradise, the world to come, while the wicked will be sent to the place of torment.

^e The righteous seems to experience a second transformation while in Paradise. From being like and equal to the angels, and having the ability to "change into any shape which they wished" (*2 Bar.* 51:10), they will become greater than the angels (*2 Bar.* 51:12).

^f The location of the "world to come," Paradise, is not clearly stated in the book, whether or not it will be outer worldly. There are a few references suggesting that Paradise will be on a renewed earth (*2 Bar.* 32:6; 44:12; 57:2).

^g *2 Baruch* does not reveal much regarding the treasuries for the souls except that the souls will dwell there until the day of resurrection. Although *2 Baruch* 30:2 only mentions the treasuries of the righteous souls, it could be assumed there would also be treasuries for the wicked souls.

~ ~ ~

10. *Apocalypse of Elijah*

The *Apocalypse of Elijah* is an eschatological work written sometime between the first and fourth century CE. There are two versions of this apocalypse, one in Coptic (C) and one in Hebrew (H), both presenting a resurrection view. Most scholars consider the Coptic version to be of Christian origin, originally written in Greek towards the end of the third century CE in Alexandria and probably developed in three stages.[159] However, this version is most likely a composite text, in which the Jewish stratum "seems to predate the destruction of the Jewish quarter in Alexandria in A.D. 117."[160] The Hebrew version also shows "evidence of a complex reediting of earlier material."[161] Moses Buttenwieser believes the author lived in Palestine during the Perso-Roman wars (540–562/604–628 CE), but derived most of his material from an older and larger apocalypse written about 261 CE.[162] The relationship between the Coptic and

159. Orval S. Wintermute, "Elijah, Apocalypse of," *ABD* 2:467–8.
160. Orval S. Wintermute, "*Apocalypse of Elijah*," *OTP* 1:730.
161. Wintermute, "Elijah, Apocalypse of," 2:467.
162. Moses Buttenwieser, *Die hebräische Elias-Apokalypse, Part 1: Und ihre Stellung in der apokalyptischen Litteratur des rabbinischen Schrifttums und der Kirche* (1897; repr., Whitefish, MT: Kessinger Publishing, 2010), 68–79; and idem,

the Hebrew versions of the apocalypse is not clear, although they share certain details that are significantly different. Wintermute suggests that the section regarding the Antichrist in these two versions may indicate a common ancestor. He suggests this ancestor "would have been an episode within a *Jewish Apocalypse of Elijah* composed before 100 C.E."[163] and may also have included details regarding the punishment of the wicked. The following section will consider these two traditions separately.

a. *Apocalypse of Elijah* (C)

This apocalypse reveals details "concerning the kings of Assyria and the dissolution of the heaven and the earth and the things beneath the earth" (2:1). The coming of the Antichrist and his reign (3:1-18) takes place in the fourth year of the righteous king who sided with the Persians (2:47–3:1) and ruled in a Messianic-like way for three and a half years (2:52).[164] During the reign of the Antichrist, in which the righteous will suffer and die as martyrs (4:1–5:1) then be resurrected (4:5, 15, 27),[165]

"Apocalyptic Literature, Neo-Hebraic," *Jewish Encyclopedia*, http://www.jewishencyclopedia.com/articles/1643-apocalyptic-literature- neo-hebraic; and Wintermute, "Elijah, Apocalypse of," 2:467.

163. Wintermute, "Elijah, Apocalypse of," 2:468.

164. Influenced by the *Oracle of the Potter* (see C. C. McCown, "Egyptian Apocalyptic Literature," *HTR* 8 [1925]: 397–400, and L. Koenen, "Die Prophezeiungen des Töpfers," *ZPE* 2 [1968]: 178–209), a third-century BCE Egyptian text concerning the future of Egypt, reveals the future rulership of a righteous king who will overthrow the Greek dominion (see Wintermute, "*Apocalypse of Elijah*," 723–4). Based on this tradition combined with motifs from Jewish and Christian apocalyptic texts, the *Apocalypse of Elijah* presents a native Egyptian from Heliopolis who will ally himself with the Persians and kill the Assyrian kings. He will cleanse the land of the wicked and rebuild the temple of the saints, so that even the righteous will say "The Lord sent us a righteous king so that the land will not become a desert" (2:51).

His three-and-a-half-year rule of peace (2:52) may either be an allusion to Dan. 7:25 (although this passage refers to the rulership of the little horn) or to Dan. 9:27. The latter passage seems to suggest that following the three and a half prophetic day period (or three and a half literal years) of Messianic rulership, "And the abomination of desolation will be on a wing of the temple until the decreed destruction is poured out on the desolator" (Dan. 9:27b). Interestingly, the author of the *Apocalypse of Elijah* introduces the son of lawlessness, the Antichrist, following the righteous king, and notes that this evil power will rule until the eschatological judgment, when he will be executed by Elijah and Enoch (5:32).

165. In the martyrdom text regarding Elijah and Enoch, the composition describes their "spiritual body of Heavenly realms" and their earthly bodies which they will possess while on earth (4:16-19; 5:32). Upon their resurrection, after the Antichrist

the righteous will be removed from this earth (5:2-6), natural disasters will take place due to the removal of the righteous, the Antichrist will pursue the righteous (5:7-21), and the earth will be destroyed (5:22-24). These events will be followed by God's universal judgment in favor of the righteous, punishment for the wicked, and execution of the Antichrist (5:25-35), concluding with the millennial kingdom (5:36-39).

The work of the Antichrist closely parallels that of Christ since he will be able to walk on water, cause the lame to walk, the deaf to hear, the dumb to speak, and the blind to see; he will even cleanse the lepers, heal the sick, and cast out demons (3:8-10; cf. Mk 6:48; Mt. 11:5). According to the *Apocalypse of Elijah*, the *son of lawlessness* will be able to do every work which the Christ did, "except for raising the dead" since he will have "no power to give life" (3:12-13; 4:31). This is how the righteous will be able to know that he is not the true Christ.

The *Apocalypse of Elijah* reveals that the righteous, those who are sealed with God's name on their forehead and his seal on their right hand (1:9), will receive thrones and crowns in heaven (1:8) and walk with the angels up to the city of God (1:10), while the sinners will be shamed and the thrones of death will seize them and rule over them (1:11). When the righteous die, their spirit and their soul will return to God while their body will turn into rock to protect it from being eaten by wild animals (4:25-26). On the last day of the great judgment, the righteous will be resurrected and receive their reward. There will be one reward for those who died as martyrs and a different reward for those who fled into the wilderness to escape martyrdom. The first group of righteous will be "in the kingdom of the Christ as those who have endured because the Lord said, 'I will grant to them that they sit on my right hand.' They will receive favor over others, and they will triumph over the son of lawlessness. And they will witness the dissolution of heaven and earth. They will receive the thrones of glory and the crowns" (4:27-29). The second group of righteous will also receive their reward, but "they will be raised up and receive a place of rest" (4:27a).

The final chapter of the apocalypse reveals the removal of the righteous before the natural disasters, destruction of the earth, and the eschatological judgment. During the persecution of the righteous by the hand of the Antichrist, God will pity the righteous and send his angels to gather them into his kingdom, where they will be given full access to the tree

killed them, they will once more shine, a possible allusion to Dan. 12:3. This description may serve as an example for what will happen to all the righteous – in order for them to take possession of God's kingdom, they will also have to take on a shining spiritual body.

of life and will be given white garments to wear (5:6). In the eschatological judgment, the righteous dead will be resurrected (the text does not mention a resurrection of the wicked) and they "will see the sinners and those who persecuted them and those who handed them over to death in their torments" while the wicked "will see the place of the righteous" (5:28-29).[166] Upon the final destruction of the Antichrist, the righteous will dwell on a newly created earth with Christ for a thousand years.[167]

b. *Apocalypse of Elijah* (H)

In the Hebrew version of the *Apocalypse of Elijah*, Michael, the great prince of Israel (Dan. 12:1), reveals "the eschaton and what was scheduled to transpire and the End of Days at the end of the four empires (and) the things which would take place during the reign of the fourth ruler," placing the apocalypse within the eschatological framework of Daniel 2 and 7. The Antichrist is identified with the "little horn" of Daniel and the text describes his physical features and evil acts; it adds that he "shall encroach upon 'the holy beautiful mountain' (Dan. 11:45) and burn it," showing his intent of destroying God's people. Following a list of important eschatological events, which includes the war of Gog and Magog against Jerusalem which will bring in "the final day,"[168] the apocalypse ends with the five visions of Elijah (see the full text in Appendix A):

---

166. This is similar to the recognition and transformation theme in *2 Bar.* 51, which was a part of the punishment and reward of the wicked and the righteous during the eschatological judgment. There also seems to be a contradiction between 1:10 and 4:24-26. In the first account, the righteous seem to be led to the heavenly city upon death while in the second they will "sleep" in wait for the judgment, their spirits and souls returning to God until they will once more unite with their bodies. If 1:10 is understood as a reference to the journey of the righteous soul upon death to its holding place, the heavenly city, where it will rest until the day of judgment and resurrection, the discrepancy disappears. Regardless, the apocalypse does not seem interested in what happens to the souls of the wicked.

167. This view is similar to Revelation in the sense that the premillennial resurrection only concerns the righteous (Rev. 20:6). It differs in a major way in that the millennium will take place on a newly created earth (5:37) as opposed to in heaven (Rev. 20–21). The scenario in Revelation also differs in the sense that the recreation takes place at the end of the millennium instead of the beginning, as is the case in *Apocalypse of Elijah*.

168. All the wicked will go to war and surround Jerusalem, but God and his Messiah will wage war on them and defeat them. The righteous of Israel will "spend seven years burning their weaponry" and seven months burying their corpses (Ezek. 39:9, 12). This vision shares some similarities with Rev. 20:8-9, which describes the war effort of the wicked against the New Jerusalem at the end of the millennium.

1. Description of the resurrection.
2. Description of the punishment of the wicked and the reward for the righteous.
3. Description of the three patriarchs together with all the righteous ones in the Garden.
4. Description of the New Jerusalem descending from Heaven.
5. Description of the dwelling quarters of the righteous.

It is not clear from this apocalypse if both the righteous and the wicked will take part in the eschatological resurrection since the current text only mentions the resurrected will "render praise to God" as He is the sole deity.[169] However, the text does mention that in the Western region of the world, the souls undergo a painful judgment, each one in accordance with its deeds. Again, it is not clear if this torment only regards the wicked souls, or if it also functions as a purifying process for the righteous souls, preparing them for the resurrection. Be that as it may, the apocalypse depicts the resurrection process as the reversal of death, in which the dust of the dead is reshaped and "made like (the forms they had) when they were formerly alive."[170] This resurrection act is supported in the apocalypse by quoting Deut. 32:39 – "See now that I alone am He; there is no God but Me. I bring death and I give life; I wound, and I heal. No one can rescue anyone from My hand" – a text also used by the Rabbis to support said view (*b. Pesaḥ.* 68a; *b. Sanh.* 91b; *Deut. Rab.* 3:15; *Eccl. Rab.* 1:6), and by quoting Ezek. 37:8, which concerns the resurrection scene of the valley of the bones. In Elijah's resurrection vision, God's angels play an active role. They are the ones who open the tombs, inject the dead righteous "with their 'animating breaths'" so they will revive, and help the newly resurrected with standing on their feet. After their role in the resurrection, the angels turn their attention to the wicked, who merit punishment, and place them into a large hollow place, all while being observed by the righteous who will see the downfall of the wicked as promised by the prophet Isaiah (Isa. 66:24).

---

169. A case could be made that both the righteous and the wicked are included in this resurrection since both groups will have to acknowledge God's power. It is given that the righteous will offer God praise, but the wicked, who did not recognize God, would have to accept His uniqueness after they have been resurrected to receive their punishment.

170. That the righteous will resume their appearance from before they died sounds similar to *Apoc. El.* [C] 5:28-29 and *2 Bar.* 51.

The second vision of Elijah reveals the punishment of the wicked who will suffer in the fire and brimstone which God sends from heaven according to Ps. 11:6. In this vision, God finds it necessary to ensure the righteous do not hear the suffering of the wicked so the righteous will not beg for mercy on their behalf. Thus, the wicked will be forgotten and it "will be as if they never were."

In the third vision, Elijah is shown the patriarchs and the righteous dwelling in the Garden with the great tree which was prepared for them standing in its midst, a possible allusion to the Tree of Life (Gen. 2:9; Rev. 22:2, 14, 19) which will once more be made available for God's people. The final two visions in the Hebrew version describe the New Jerusalem and the houses which have been prepared for the righteous.

c. Concluding Remarks

The resurrection belief appears in both the Coptic and the Hebrew version of the *Apocalypse of Elijah* and follows the appearance of the Antichrist. Neither text states clearly whether this resurrection will be universal and would include both the righteous and the wicked, although the Hebrew version seems to suggest this. In both versions the punishment of the wicked functions as a part of the vindication of the righteous. The New Earth motif follows the resurrection and judgment in both versions. The Coptic version, however, insinuates that there will be two groups of righteous who will receive different rewards. Those who suffered a martyr's death will be a part of the kingdom of Christ, sit on His right hand, receive the thrones of glory, and crowns. Those who did not die for their faith will just be given a place of rest. The Hebrew version has no such differentiation between the righteous. Although the Coptic version used the Daniel material, it did not attempt to provide "proof texts" for the resurrection belief as in the case of the Hebrew version. The Hebrew version seems to be more in line with Early Rabbinic texts which also show interest in providing biblical "proof texts" in support of the various aspects of their resurrection beliefs.

Chapter 4

CONCLUDING OBSERVATIONS

This chapter provides a brief concluding remark based on the literary work discussed in this monograph. A complete summary and conclusion based on all the afterlife and resurrection passages appearing in the Apocrypha and the Pseudepigrapha is found in the companion volume, *Afterlife and Resurrection Beliefs in the Pseudepigrapha*. Comparing the resurrection passages appearing in the Apocrypha and the apocalyptic literature, it becomes clear they present very diverse views. Each literary work containing a "life-after-death" view seems to present a unique perspective, even compositions presenting scant details regarding the events following death and eschatological time. This monograph identified twelve distinct and complete views (from death to eternity) regarding life-after-death with varying degrees of complexity. These views are found in: *2 Maccabees* (Fig. 2); *Wisdom of Solomon* (Fig. 3); *4 Ezra* (Fig. 5); the *Book of Watchers* (Fig. 6); the *Book of the Epistle of Enoch* (Fig. 7); *2 Enoch* (Fig. 8); *3 Enoch* (Fig. 9); the *Apocalypse of Zephaniah* (Fig. 10); the *Greek Apocalypse of Ezra* (Fig. 11); the *Vision of Ezra* (Fig. 12); the *Question of Ezra* (Fig. 13); *2 Baruch* (Fig.15). The companion volume to this monograph adds an additional six distinct and complete views, bringing the combined number to eighteen.

There are several elements causing these diverse resurrection views. Among them is the understanding of human anthropology – whether or not a person has a soul that can exist apart from the body following death. There is also a question of the nature of this soul, if it is mortal or immortal, and what happens to it when it separates from the body. An important element is what will be the state of this disembodied soul, if it will be conscious or unconscious, if the righteous and the wicked soul will face a different fortune following the death of the body. There is also the question of whether the soul will return to a physical body at one point in the future. Regarding the eschatological resurrection, the views appearing in the Apocrypha and the apocalyptic literature also differ in their scope, ranging from a universal resurrection to a more limited one. There is also the question of what this resurrected body will look like. Will it be similar or different to how it appeared at death? A closely related question regards the number and function(s) of the judgments and the final destiny of the righteous and the wicked. These questions are discussed in the summary and conclusion of the companion volume.

This monograph has noted the many references and allusions to the TaNaKh in the resurrection passages found in the Apocrypha and apocalyptic literature of the Pseudepigrapha. A careful reading of these texts reveals that the most distinct views of life after death, regardless of their complexity, are often supported by several key passages from the books that later became a part of the TaNaKh or shared motifs with these books. For ease of comparison, the companion volume provides a list of the TaNaKh passages referred or alluded to in the context of the resurrection statements surveyed from the Apocrypha and the Pseudepigrapha, in this monograph and its companion volume, with a special interest in the eighteen distinct and complete afterlife views appearing in this body of literature.

Some of the ramifications of the findings discussed in this monograph and its companion volume are also discussed in the summary and the concluding chapter of the companion volume – again, for ease of comparison.

Appendix A

CLASSIFICATION AND ANTHOLOGY OF RESURRECTION TEXTS

Appendix A gives a survey of the resurrection passages compiled from the Apocrypha and the apocalyptic and related works section of Charlesworth's two-volume Pseudepigrapha. For a survey of the resurrection passages compiled from the other sections of the Pseudepigrapha, see Appendix A in the companion volume. For a survey of the resurrection passages from the Dead Sea Scrolls, Josephus, New Testament, and Early Rabbinic Period, see Appendix B.

Table 25, Classification of the Resurrection Texts in the Apocrypha, and Table 26, Classification of the Resurrection Texts in the Apocalyptic Literature and Related Works, are followed by an anthology of the resurrection passages listed in the Table. This is to show the larger context of the resurrection statement and provide the general reader convenient access to these resurrection texts which are discussed in this monograph.[1] Chapters two and three of this monograph examine the passages listed in the tables of this Appendix which are either referring or alluding to texts from the TaNaKh in support of a resurrection belief.

The following list shows the different categories used when analyzing and classifying these resurrection texts and provides a short explanation of each category. Since the books appearing in the Apocrypha and the Apocalyptic section of the Pseudepigrapha were composed, edited and even redacted during a period ranging several centuries (second century

---

1. The relevant passages for the anthologies are collected from: *Revised Standard Version* (RSV)/*New Revised Standard Version* (NRSV); James H. Charlesworth, ed., *The Old Testament Pseudepigrapha*, 2 vols. (New York: Doubleday, 1983–85); George W. E. Nickelsburg and James C. VanderKam, *1 Enoch: The Hermeneia Translation* (Minneapolis: Fortress, 2012); John C. Reeves, *Trajectories in Near Eastern Apocalyptic: A Postrabbinic Jewish Apocalypse Reader* (Atlanta: Society of Biblical Literature, 2005); Michael E. Stone and Matthias Henze, *4 Ezra and 2 Baruch: Translations, Introductions, and Notes* (Minneapolis: Fortress, 2013).

BCE [*1 Enoch*] – ninth century CE [*Greek Apocalypse of Ezra*]) it becomes helpful to include a suggested dating for each book in these two Tables for a proper evaluation of the resurrection passage since it may also shed some light on the developmental stages of the resurrection belief.[22] Appendix B provides similar table of categories to show the relevant categories when classifying and evaluating resurrections texts found in the Dead Sea Scrolls, Josephus, New Testament, Jewish Liturgy texts, and in early rabbinic literature.

Category		Explanation
Date		Date the book was written.
Passage		Passage reference.
Notes		Author's notes.
Resurrection	Implied	A resurrection belief is implied in the passage.
	Stated	A resurrection belief is stated clearly in the passage.
Classification	Reference	The resurrection passage refers to a resurrection text in the TaNaKh.
	Allusion	The resurrection passage alludes to a resurrection text in the TaNaKh.
	Philosophical	Resurrection passage uses a philosophical argument as a proof for a resurrection belief.
	Assumed	Since the resurrection belief is assumed, no attempt is made to prove biblically or philosophically that there will be a resurrection.

The relevant sections referring directly or indirectly to a resurrection belief have been highlighted in gray for emphasis in the anthologies. The reader will also notice that these anthologies have placed these resurrection statements in the larger context, a decision made to better understand the underlying reasoning behind each statement. Additionally, references and allusions to the TaNaKh, Apocrypha, Pseudepigrapha, Dead Sea Scrolls, Rabbinic Literature, and the New Testament, most of

2. The suggested dates given for the literary works belonging to the Apocrypha are mainly based on David A. deSilva, *Introducing the Apocrypha: Message, Context, and Significance* (Grand Rapids: Baker Academic, 2002) and to a lesser degree on Craig A. Evans, *Ancient Texts for New Testament Studies: A Guide to the Background Literature* (Peabody, MA: Hendrickson, 2005). The works belonging to the Pseudepigrapha are mostly based on Charlesworth's two-volume work, *The Old Testament Pseudepigrapha* and to a lesser degree on Craig A. Evans, Ancient Texts for New Testament Studies. Additionally, the dating of each literary work is considered in chapter two and three when discussing the resurrection passages appearing in these literary works.

these references appears in the margin and in the footnotes of Charles'[3] and Charlesworth's collections of Pseudepigraphical writings, are placed [in brackets] in the resurrection passage. References and allusions to the TaNaKh, alluding or directly supporting a resurrection belief have also been **bolded** for emphasis. It should be noted that many of these references are cross-references referring to synonymous or related thoughts found in the larger body of Second Temple Period texts and as such, does not necessarily reflect or suggest a dependency between the passage and the given reference. Obvious Christian interpolation in an original Jewish text has been <u>underlined</u> in the anthology.

---

3. Charles, ed., *The Apocrypha and Pseudepigrapha of the Old Testament in English*.

Resurrection Texts in the Apocryphal Writings

Table 25. Classification of the Resurrection Texts in the Apocrypha

Date	Passage		Notes	Resurrection			Classification		
				Imp.	Stat.	Ref.	Allude	Phil.	Assum.
2nd cent. BCE	Ecclesiasticus (Sirach)	2:9c; (7:17b); 16:22c; 19:19	These passages in the longer GII recension hints to a resurrection hope	x					x
		46:19-20	Sleep = Death						x
		48:11b	Ben Sira's grandson may have added this resurrection hope	x					x
1st cent. BCE	2 Maccabees	6:26	No one will escape the hands of God	x					x
		7	The Martyrdom of the seven brothers		x	x	x	x	
		12:43-45	Made atonement for the dead. Paul uses this argument in 1 Cor. 15:29		x			x	x
		14:37-46	Death of Razis		x	x			x
1st cent. BCE	Wisdom of Solomon	3:1-13a	Body/Soul They will shine forth	x					x
		4:16–5:16	The triumph of the righteous and the final judgment	x			x		x
2ns cent. CE	2 Esdras/ 5 Ezra	2:10-47	Exhortation to good work; Proper burial practice; Replacement theology; Resurrection/Reward of the Kingdom; Sleep ∥ Death		x				x

Table 25 continued

A. Classification and Anthology of Resurrection Texts

Date	Passage	Notes	Resurrection			Classification		
			Imp.	Stat.	Ref.	Allude	Phil.	Assum.
1st cent. CE	*2 Esdras/ 4 Ezra*							
	4:7-11	Exits of Hades – Entrances of Paradise	×					
	4:33-43	Predestined time; Hades ‖ womb; Souls in the chambers of Hades are impatient; The number needs to be filled	×				×	×
	5:38-40	Only God knows his judgment and the goal of his love	×					×
	7:10-16	Two worlds, this world is the test	×					×
	7:26-51	Body + Soul = Resurrection; Universal resurrection (Individuals/nations); Detailed eschatology		×		×		×
	7:66-105	The state of the departed before the judgment		×		×		×
	7:112-115	Universal judgment	×					
	7:117-131	Future promises given to the righteous	×					
	8:1-3	Two worlds. "Many have been created, but only a few shall be saved"	×					×
	8:12-19	Ezra questions God's judgment/justice	×					
	8:37-40	The final destiny of the two ways	×					×
	8:46-54	The final destiny of the righteous	×					
	9:7-13	The wicked will acknowledge God's justice	×					×
	10:10, 15-17	"If you acknowledge the decree of God to be just, you will receive your son back"	×					
	14:34-35	Resurrection/Judgment	×					×

Sirach (Ecclesiasticus)

Sirach 2:7-11

⁷You who fear the Lord, wait for his mercy;
   do not stray, or else you may fall [Ps. 37:7-9].
⁸You who fear the Lord, trust in him,
   and you reward will not be lost [Sir. 51:30].
⁹You who fear the Lord, hope for good things,
   for lasting joy and mercy
   [For his reward is an everlasting gift with joy].
¹⁰Consider the generation of old and see:
   has anyone trusted in the Lord and been disappointed?
Or has anyone persevered in the fear of the Lord [of him] and been forsaken?
   Or has anyone called upon him and been neglected? [Pss. 37:25; 145:18 | 1 Macc. 2:61]
¹¹For the Lord is compassionate and merciful;
   he forgives sins and saves in time of distress [Ps. 86:15 | Sir. 51:12].

Sirach 7:15-17

¹⁵Do not hate hard labor
   or farm work, which was created by the Most High [Gen. 3:19, 23].
¹⁶Do not enroll in the ranks of sinners;
   remember that retribution does not delay.
¹⁷Humble yourself to the utmost,
   for the punishment of the ungodly is fire and worms [Isa. 66:24 | Jdt. 16:17; Sir. 18:21 | Mk 9:48]
   [Heb: for the expectation of mortals is worms]

Sirach 12:4-7

⁴Give to the devout, but do not help the sinner [Tob. 4:17 | Mt. 5:43-48].
⁵ Do good to the humble, but do not give to the ungodly;
Hold back their bread, and do not give it to them,
   for by means of it they might subdue you;
   then you will receive twice as much evil
   for all the good you have done to them.
⁶For the Most High also hates sinners
   and will inflict punishment on the ungodly [Ps. 11:5-6]
   [and he is keeping them for the day of their punishment].
⁷Give to the one who is good, but do not help the sinner.

Sirach 16:17-23

¹⁷Do not say, "I am hidden from the Lord,
   and who from on high has me in mind? [Ps. 138:7]
Among so many people I am unknown,
   for what am I in a boundless creation?

¹⁸Lo, heaven and the highest heaven,
   the abyss and the earth, treble at his visitation! [1 Kgs 8:27; Mic. 1:3-4 | 2 Pet. 3:7, 10]
¹⁹The very mountains and the foundations of the earth
   quiver and quake when he looks upon them [Isa. 24:18; Pss. 18:7; 104:32].
²⁰But no human mind can grasp this,
   and who can comprehend his ways? [Rom. 11:33]
²¹Like a tempest that no one can see,
   so most of his works are concealed [Ps. 97:2; Prov. 25:2 | Sir. 43:32]
   [Heb/Syr: If I sin, no eye can see me, and if I am disloyal all in secret, who is to know?].
²²Who is to announce his acts of justice?
   Or who can await them? For his decree [Heb: the decree; Gr: the covenant] is far off"
   [and a scrutiny for all comes at the end].
²³Such are the thoughts of one devoid of understanding;
   a senseless and misguided person thinks foolishly.

Sirach 19:13-19
¹³Question a friend; perhaps he did not do it;
   or if he did, so that he may not do it again [Lev. 19:17].
¹⁴Question a neighbor; perhaps he did not say it;
   or if he said it, so that he may not repeat it.
¹⁵Question a friend, for often it is slander;
   so do not believe everything you hear.
¹⁶A person may make a slip without intending it.
   Who has not sinned with his tongue? [Sir. 14:1]
¹⁷Question your neighbor before you threaten him;
   and let the law of the Most High take its course [and do not be angry] [Lev. 19:17].
[¹⁸The fear of the Lord is the beginning of acceptance,
   and wisdom obtains his love.
¹⁹The knowledge of the Lord's commandments is life-giving discipline,
   and those who do what is pleasing to him enjoy the fruits of the tree of immortality.]

Sirach 46:11-20
¹¹The judges also, with their respective names,
   whose hearts did not fall into idolatry and who did not turn away from the Lord –
   may their memory be blessed! [Judg. 2:17 | Sir. 45:1; 1 Macc. 3:7]
¹²**May their bones send forth new life from where they lie,**
   and may the names of those who have been honored
   live again in their children! [Sir. 49:10]

[13]Samuel was beloved by his Lord;
   a prophet of the Lord, he established the kingdom
   and anointed rules over his people [1 Sam. 10:1 | Acts 13:20].
[14]By the law of the Lord he judged the congregation,
   and the Lord watched over Jacob.
[15]By his faithfulness he was proved to be prophet,
   and by his words he became known as a trustworthy seer [1 Sam. 3:19, 20].
[16]He called upon the Lord, the Mighty One,
   when his enemies pressed him on every side,
   and he offered in sacrifice a suckling lamb [1 Sam. 7:7-10; Ps. 99:6].
[17]Then the Lord thundered from heaven,
   and made his voice heard with a mighty sound;
[18]he subdued the leaders of the enemy
   and all the rulers of the Philistines.
[19]**Before the time of his eternal sleep**,
   Samuel bore witness before the Lord and his anointed:
"No property, not so much as a pair of shoes,
   have I taken from anyone!"
   And no one accused him. [1 Sam. 12:3]
[20]**Even after he had fallen asleep**, he prophesied
   and made known to the king his death, and lifted up his voice from the ground
   in prophecy, to blot out the wickedness of the people. [1 Sam. 28:16-19 | Sir. 48:13]

Sirach 48:1-11

[1]Then Elijah arose, a prophet like fire,
   and his word burned like a torch [Mal. 4:5].
[2]He brought a famine upon them,
   and by his zeal he made them few in number.
[3]By the word of the Lord he shut up the heavens,
   and also three times brought down fire [1 Kgs 17:1; 18:38; 2 Kgs 1:10, 12].
[4]How glorious you were, Elijah, in your wondrous deeds!
   Whose glory is equal to yours?
[5]You raised a corpse from death [1 Kgs 17:21-22],
   And from Hades, by the word of the Most High.
[6]You sent kings down to destruction,
   and famous men, from their sickbeds [2 Kgs 1:2-4, 6, 16-17; 2 Chron. 21:12-15].
[7]You heard rebuke at Sinai,
   and judgements of vengeance at Horeb [1 Kgs 19:8-18].
[8]You anointed kings to inflict retribution [1 Kgs 19:15-17; 2 Kgs 8:12-15; 9:1-10],
   and prophets to succeed you [1 Kgs 19:15, 16].
[9]You were taken up by a whirlwind of fire,
   in a chariot with horses of fire [2 Kgs 2:1, 11; 6:17].

¹⁰At the appointed time, it is written, you are destined
   to calm the wrath of God before it breaks out in fury,
to turn the hearts of parents to their children [Mal. 4:5-6 | Sir. 36:13 | Lk. 1:17],
   and to restore the tribes of Jacob.
¹¹**Happy are those who saw you**
   and were adorned, [and have died]
   For we also shall surely live.

2 Maccabees

2 Maccabees 6:21-30

²¹Those who were in charge of that unlawful sacrifice took the man aside because of their long acquaintance with him, and privately urged him to bring meat of his own providing, proper for him to use, and to pretend that he was eating the flesh of the sacrificial meal that had been commanded by the king [1 Macc. 1:47; 2 Macc. 6:7], ²²so that by doing this he might be saved from the death, and be treated kindly on account of his old friendship with them [1 Macc. 2:18]. ²³But making a high resolve, worthy of his years and the dignity of his old age and the gray hairs that he had reached with distinction and his excellent life even from childhood, and moreover according to the holy God-given law, he declared himself quickly, **telling them to send him to Hades** [Prov. 16:31; 20:29 | *4 Macc.* 5:7].

²⁴"Such pretense is not worthy of our time of life," he said, "for many of the young might suppose that Eleazar in his ninetieth year had gone over to an alien religion [2 Macc. 4:13], ²⁵and through my pretense, for the sake of living a brief moment longer, they would be led astray because of me, while I defile and disgrace my old age. ²⁶Even if for the present I would avoid the punishment of mortals, **yet whether I live or die I shall not escape the hands of the Almighty** [2 Esd. 7:56 | Mt. 10:28; Lk. 12:4-5; Heb. 10:31]. ²⁷Therefore, by bravely giving up my life now, I will show myself worthy of my old age ²⁸and leave to the young a noble example of how to die a good death willingly and nobly for the revered and holy laws [2 Macc. 6:31]." When he had said this, he went at once to the rack. ²⁹Those who a little before had acted toward him with goodwill now changed to ill will, because the words he had uttered were in their opinion sheer madness [Wis. 5:4]. ³⁰When he was about to die under the blows, he groaned aloud and said: "It is clear to the Lord in his holy knowledge that, though I might have been saved from death, I am enduring terrible sufferings in my body under this beating, but in my soul I am glad to suffer these things because I fear him [*4 Macc.* 6:27 | Heb. 11:35-36]."

2 Maccabees 7

¹It happened also that seven brothers and their mother were arrested and were being compelled by the king, under torture with whips and thongs, to partake of unlawful swine's flesh [2 Macc. 6:18]. ²One of them, acting as their spokesman, said, "What do you intend to ask and learn from us? For we are ready to die rather than transgress the laws of our ancestors [2 Macc. 4:48; 6:19]." ³The king fell into a rage, and gave orders to have pans and caldrons heated [2 Macc. 7:39]. ⁴These were heated

immediately, and he commanded that the tongue of their spokesman be cut out and that they scalp him and cut off his hands and feet, while the rest of the brothers and the mother looked on. ⁵When he was utterly helpless, the king ordered them to take him to the fire, still breathing, and to fry him in a pan. The smoke from the pan spread widely, but the brothers and their mother encouraged one another to die nobly, saying, ⁶ **"The Lord God is watching over us and in truth has compassion on us, as Moses declared in his song that bore witness against the people to their faces, when he said, 'And he will have compassion on his servants'"** [Deut. 31:21, 26, 30; 32:36; Ps. 135:14]. ⁷After the first brother had died in this way, they brought forward the second for their sport. They tore off the skin of his head with the hair, and asked him, "Will you eat rather than have your body punished limb by limb? [Heb. 11:36]" ⁸He replied in the language of his ancestors and said to them, "No." Therefore he in turn underwent tortures as the first brother had done [2 Macc. 7:21, 27; 12:37; 15:29]. ⁹And when he was at his last breath, he said, "You accursed wretch, you dismiss us from this present life, **but the King of the universe will raise us up to an everlasting renewal of life, because we have died for his laws [Dan. 12:2** | 2 Esd. 14:35; 2 Macc. 7:14, 23, 36]." ¹⁰After him, the third was the victim of their sport. When it was demanded, he quickly put out his tongue and courageously stretched forth his hands, ¹¹and said nobly, **"I got these from Heaven, and because of his laws I disdain them, and from him I hope to get them back again."** ¹²As a result the king himself and those with him were astonished at the young man's spirit, for he regarded his sufferings as nothing. ¹³After he too had died, they maltreated and tortured the fourth in the same way. ¹⁴When he was near death, he said, **"One cannot but choose to die at the hands of mortals and to cherish the hope God gives of being raised again by him. But for you there will be no resurrection to life!"** [Dan. **12:2** | 2 Esd. 14:35; 2 Macc. 7:23, 26]" ¹⁵Next they brought forward the fifth and maltreated him. ¹⁶But he looked at the king, and said, "Because you have authority among mortals, though you also are mortal, you do what you please. But do not think that God has forsaken our people. ¹⁷Keep on, and see how his mighty power will torture you and your descendants! [2 Macc. 9:5, 6, 9]" ¹⁸After him they brought forward the sixth. And when he was about to die, he said, "Do not deceive yourself in vain. For we are suffering these things on our own account, because of our sins against our own God. Therefore astounding things have happened [2 Macc. 6:12-17; 7:32, 33, 38]. ¹⁹But do not think that you will go unpunished for having tried to fight against God! [2 Macc. 9:5, 6, 9 | Acts 5:39]" ²⁰The mother was especially admirable and worthy of honorable memory. Although she saw her seven sons perish within a single day, **she bore it with good courage because of her hope in the Lord**. ²¹She encouraged each of them in the language of their ancestors. Filled with a noble spirit, she reinforced her woman's reasoning with a man's courage, and said to them [2 Macc. 7:8, 27; 12:37; 15:29], ²²**"I do not know how you came into being in my womb. It was not I who gave you life and breath, nor I who set in order the elements within each of you [Ps. 139:13-16; Eccl. 11:5]**. ²³**Therefore the Creator of the world, who shaped the beginning of humankind and devised the origin of all things, will in his mercy give life and breath back to you again, since you now forget yourselves for the sake of his laws." [2 Macc. 1:24; 6:16; 7:9, 33] [24]Antiochus felt that he was being treated with contempt, and he was suspicious of her reproachful tone. The youngest brother being still alive, Antiochus not only appealed to him in words, but promised with oaths that he would make him rich and enviable if he would turn from the ways of his ancestors, and that he would take him for his Friend and entrust him with public affairs [1 Macc. 2:18]. [25]Since the young man would not listen to him at all, the king called the mother to him and urged her to advise the youth to save himself. [26]After much urging on his part, she undertook to persuade her son. [27]But, leaning close to him, she spoke in their native language as follows, deriding the cruel tyrant: "My son, have pity on me. I carried you nine months in my womb, and nursed you for three years, and have reared you and brought you up to this point in your life, and have taken care of you [2 Macc. 7:8, 21; 12:37; 15:29]. [28]I beg you, my child, to look at the heaven and the earth and see everything that is in them, and recognize that **God did not make them out of things that existed. And in the same way the human race came into being [Gen. 1; 2:7 | Rom. 4:17; Heb. 11:3]**. [29]Do not fear this butcher, but prove worthy of your brothers. **Accept death, so that in God's mercy I may get you back again along with your brothers"** [2 Macc. 7:9; 14:29; 2 Esd. 10:16]. [30]While she was still speaking, the young man said, "What are you waiting for? I will not obey the king's command, but I obey the command of the law that was given to our ancestors through Moses. [31]But you, who have contrived all sorts of evil against the Hebrews, will certainly not escape the hands of God [2 Macc. 7:17; 15:37]. [32]For we are suffering because of our own sins [2 Macc. 7:18]. [33]And if our living Lord is angry for a little while, to rebuke and discipline us, he will again be reconciled with his own servants [2 Macc. 5:17, 20; 6:16: 7:23]. [34]But you, unholy wretch, you most defiled of all mortals, do not be elated in vain and puffed up by uncertain hopes, when you raise your hand against the children of heaven [2 Macc. 5:17, 21]. [35]You have not yet escaped the judgment of the almighty, all-seeing God. [36]**For our brothers after enduring a brief suffering have drunk of ever-flowing life, under God's covenant;** but you, by the judgment of God, will receive just punishment for your arrogance [2 Macc. 9:5-8 | 2 Cor. 4:17]. [37]I, like my brothers, give up body and life for the laws of our ancestors, appealing to God to show mercy soon to our nation and by trials and plagues to make you confess that he alone is God [2 Macc. 9:12-17], [38]and through me and my brothers to bring to an end the wrath of the Almighty that has justly fallen on our whole nation" [2 Macc. 7:18]. [39]The king fell into a rage, and handled him worse than the others, being exasperated at his scorn [2 Macc. 7:3]. [40]**So he died in his integrity, putting his whole trust in the Lord.** [41]Last of all, the mother died, after her sons. [42]Let this be enough, then, about the eating of sacrifices and the extreme tortures [*4 Macc.* 17:1].

2 Maccabees 12:43-45
[43]He [Judas Maccabeus] also took up a collection, man by man, to the amount of two thousand drachmas of silver, and sent it to Jerusalem to provide for a sin offering. In doing this he acted very well and honorably, **taking account of the resurrection** [Lev. 4:2-35 | 2 Macc. 4:19]. [44]**For if he were not expecting that those who had fallen would rise again, it would have been superfluous and foolish to pray for**

the dead. ⁴⁵But if he was looking to the splendid reward that is laid up for those who fall asleep in godliness, it was a holy and pious thought. Therefore he made atonement for the dead, so that they might be delivered from their sin [2 Macc. 12:43].

2 Maccabees 14:37-46

³⁷A certain Razis, one of the elders of Jerusalem, was denounced to Nicanor as a man who loved his compatriots and was very well thought of and for his goodwill was called father of the Jews. ³⁸In former times, when there was no mingling with the Gentiles, he had been accused of Judaism, and he had most zealously risked body and life for Judaism [2 Macc. 6:6; 14:3]. ³⁹Nicanor, wishing to exhibit the enmity that he had for the Jews, sent more than five hundred soldiers to arrest him; ⁴⁰for he thought that by arresting him he would do them an injury. ⁴¹When the troops were about to capture the tower and were forcing the door of the courtyard, they ordered that fire be brought and the doors burned. Being surrounded, Razis fell upon his own sword, ⁴²preferring to die nobly rather than to fall into the hands of sinners and suffer outrages unworthy of his noble birth. ⁴³But in the heat of the struggle he did not hit exactly, and the crowd was now rushing in through the doors. He courageously ran up on the wall, and bravely threw himself down into the crowd. ⁴⁴But as they quickly drew back, a space opened and he fell in the middle of the empty space. ⁴⁵Still alive and aflame with anger, he rose, and though his blood gushed forth and his wounds were severe he ran through the crowd; and standing upon a steep rock, ⁴⁶with his blood now completely drained from him, **he tore out his entrails, took them in both hands and hurled them at the crowd, calling upon the Lord of life and spirit to give them back to him again**. This was the manner of his death.

Wisdom of Solomon

Wisdom of Solomon 3:1-13a
¹**But the souls of the righteous are in the hand of God,**
    and no torment will ever touch them.
²In the eyes of the foolish they seemed to have died,
    and their departure was thought to be a disaster [Wis. 4:17; 5:4 | Lk. 9:31],
³and their going from us to be their destruction;
    but they are at peace.
⁴For though in the sight of others they were punished,
    their hope is full of immortality [Rom. 8:24; 2 Cor. 5:1].
⁵Having been disciplined a little, they will receive great good,
    because God tested them and found them worthy of himself [Exod. 15:25 | Heb. 12:11];
⁶like gold in the furnace he tried them,
    and like a sacrificial burnt offering he accepted them [Prov. 17:3 | 2 Esd. 16:73 | Rom. 12:1; 1 Pet. 1:7].
⁷**In the time of their visitation they will shine forth** [Dan. 12:3 | Mt. 13:43],
    and will run like sparks through the stubble [Isa. 5:24; Obad. 18].

⁸**They will govern nations and rule over peoples,**
   and the Lord will reign over them forever [Dan. 7:18, 22 | 1 Cor. 6:2-3].
⁹Those who trust in him will understand truth,
   and the faithful will abide with him in love,
   because grace and mercy are upon his holy ones,
   and he watches over his elect [Wis. 2:20; 4:15 | Jn 15:10].
¹⁰But the ungodly will be punished as their reasoning deserves,
   those who disregarded the righteous and rebelled against the Lord [Prov. 1:24-31];
¹¹for those who despise wisdom and instruction are miserable.
   Their hope is vain, their labors are unprofitable,
   and their works are useless.
¹²Their wives are foolish, and their children evil [Sir. 41:5];
¹³their offspring are accursed [Isa. 54:1 | Wis. 12:11].

Wisdom of Solomon 4:16–5:16
¹⁶**The righteous who have died will condemn the ungodly who are living,**
and youth that is quickly perfected [ended] will condemn the prolonged old age of the unrighteous [Isa. 65:20 | Mt. 12:41-42]
¹⁷For they will see the end of the wise,
   and will not understand what the Lord purposed for them,
   and for what he kept them safe [Wis. 3:2].
¹⁸The unrighteous [they] will see, and will have contempt for them,
   but the Lord will laugh them to scorn.
   After this they will become dishonored corpses,
   and an outrage among the dead forever [Isa. 14:19; Pss. 2:4; 37:13];
¹⁹because he will dash them speechless to the ground,
   and shake them for the foundation;
   they will be left utterly dry and barren,
   and they will suffer anguish,
   and the memory of them will perish [Ps. 9:6].

²⁰They will come with dread when their sins are reckoned up,
   and their lawless deeds will convict them to their face [Jer. 2:19].
⁵:¹**Then the righteous will stand with great confidence**
   in the presence of those who have oppressed them
   and those who make light of their labors [Lk. 21:36].
²**When the unrighteous [they] see them, they will be shaken with dreadful fear,**
   and they will be amazed at the unexpected salvation of the righteous [2 Esd. 9:9 | Lk. 13:28].
³They will speak to one another in repentance,
   and in anguish or spirit they will groan, and say [2 Esd. 16:19 | Rom. 8:35],
⁴"These are persons whom we once held in derision
   and made a byword of reproach – fools that we were!
   We thought that their lives were madness

and that their end was without honor [Jer. 24:9; Ps. 69:11 | Wis. 3:2; 4:17 | Acts 26:24].

⁵Why have they been numbered among the children of God?
>And why is their lot among the saints?

⁶So it was we who strayed from the way of truth,
>and the light of righteousness did not shine on us,
>and the sun did not rise upon us [Prov. 2:31 | Jn 3:19; 12:35].

⁷We took our fill of the paths of lawlessness and destruction,
>and we journeyed through trackless deserts,
>but the way of the Lord we have not known [Ps. 107:40; Job 12:24].

⁸What has our arrogance profited us?
>And what good has our boasted wealth brought us?

⁹All those things have vanished like a shadow,
>and like a rumor that passes by [Wis. 2:5];

¹⁰like a ship that sails through the billowy water,
>and when it has passed no trace can be found,
>no track of its keel in the waves [Job 9:26];

¹¹or as, when a bird flies through the air,
>no evidence of its passage is found;
>the light air lashed by the beat of its pinions
>and pierced by the force of its rushing flight,
>it traversed by the movement of its wings,
>and afterward no sign of its coming is found there [Prov. 30:19; Job 9:26];

¹²or as, when an arrow is shot at a target,
>the air, thus divided, comes together at once,
>so that no one knows its pathway [Wis. 5:21].

¹³So we also, as soon as we were born ceased to be,
>and we had no sign of virtue to show,
>but were consumed in our wickedness."

¹⁴Because the hope of the ungodly is like thistledown [dust] carried by the wind,
>and like a light frost [spider's web] driven away by a storm;
>it is dispersed like smoke before the wind,
>and it passes like the remembrance of a guest who stays but a day [Ps. 68:2; Job 21:18 | Jas 1:10-11].

¹⁵**But the righteous live forever,**
>**and their reward is with the Lord;**
>**the Most High take care of them** [Gen. 15:1 | Rev. 22:12].

¹⁶**Therefore they will receive a glorious crown**
>**and a beautiful diadem from the hand of the Lord,**
>**because with his right hand he will cover them,**
>**and with his arm he will shield them** [Isa. 28:5; 62:3 | Wis. 19:8 | 1 Pet. 5:4].

2 Esdras

2 Esdras 2:10-47 (5 Ezra 2:10-47)

¹⁰Thus says the Lord to Ezra: "Tell my people that I will give them the kingdom of Jerusalem, which I was going to give to Israel. ¹¹Moreover, I will take back to myself their glory, **and will give to these others the everlasting habitations, which I had prepared for Israel.** ¹²**The tree of life shall give them fragrant perfume, and they shall neither toil nor become weary** [Prov. 3:18 | 2 Esd. 8:52 | Rev. 22:14]. ¹³Go and you will receive; pray that your days may be few, that they may be shortened. The kingdom is already prepared for you; be on the watch! [Mt. 24:22; 25:34] ¹⁴Call, O call heaven and earth to witness: I set aside evil and created good; for I am the Living One, says the Lord.

¹⁵"Mother, embrace your children; bring them up with gladness, as does a dove; strengthen their feet, because I have chosen you, says the Lord [**Deut. 7:6; Isa. 60:8** | 2 Esd. 2:25, 30]. ¹⁶**And I will raise up the dead from their places, and bring them out from their tombs, because I recognize my name in them** [Ezek. 37:12-13 | Jn 5:28-29]. ¹⁷Do not fear, mother of children, for I have chosen you, says the Lord. ¹⁸I will send you help, my servants Isaiah and Jeremiah [Mt. 16:14; Rev. 22:2]. According to their counsel I have consecrated and prepared for you twelve trees loaded with various fruits, ¹⁹and the same number of springs flowing with milk and honey [**Exod. 3:8**], and seven mighty mountains on which roses and lilies grow; by these I will fill your children with joy. ²⁰"Guard the rights of the widow, secure justice for the ward, give to the needy, defend the orphan, clothe the naked [**Isa. 1:17; 58:7** | Mt. 25:36], ²¹care for the injured and the weak, do not ridicule the lame, protect the maimed, and let the blind have a vision of my splendor. ²²Protect the old and the young within your walls; ²³**When you find any who are dead, commit them to the grave and mark it, and I will give you the first place in my resurrection** [Tob. 1:17-18 | Mt. 19:28]. ²⁴**Pause and be quiet, my people, because your rest will come** [Exod. 14:14; Isa. 30:15]. ²⁵Good nurse, nourish your children; strengthen their feet. ²⁶Not one of the servants whom I have given you will perish, for I will require them form among your number. ²⁷Do not be anxious, for when the day of tribulation and anguish comes, others shall weep and be sorrowful, but you shall rejoice and have abundance [Jn 16:20, 22]. ²⁸The nations shall envy you, but they shall not be able to do anything against you, says the Lord [**Isa. 54:17**]. ²⁹My power will protect you, so that your children may not see hell [Gehenna].

³⁰Rejoice, O mother, with your children, because I will deliver you, says the Lord [2 Esd. 2:2, 15, 17]. ³¹**Remember your children that sleep, because I will bring them out of the hiding places of the earth, and will show mercy to them**; for I am merciful, says the Lord Almighty. ³²Embrace your children until I come, and proclaim mercy to them; because my springs run over, and my grace will not fail."

³³I, Ezra, received a command from the Lord on Mount Horeb to go to Israel [**Exod. 3:1; Deut. 4:10, 15** | Sir. 48:7]. When I came to them they rejected me and refused the Lord's commandment. ³⁴Therefore I say to you, O nations that hear and understand, "Wait for your shepherd; he will give you everlasting rest, because he who will come at the end of the age is close at hand [Mt. 11:2, 9; Jn 10:11; Heb. 10:37]. ³⁵**Be ready for the rewards of the kingdom, because perpetual light will shine on you forevermore** [Isa. 60:19-20 | Rev. 21:23]. ³⁶Flee from the shadow of this age, receive the joy of your glory [**1 Chron. 29:15** | 2 Esd. 2:39]; I publicly call on my savior to witness. ³⁷Receive what the Lord has entrusted to you and be joyful, giving thanks to him who has called you to the celestial kingdoms [1 Thess. 2:12; 1 Pet. 5:10]. ³⁸Rise, stand erect and see the number of those who have been sealed at the feast of the Lord [2 Esd. 6:5 | Rev. 7:4]. ³⁹**Those who have departed from the shadow of this age have received glorious garments from the Lord** [**Isa. 61:10** | 2 Esd. 2:36]. ⁴⁰Take again your full number, O Zion, and close the list of your people who are clothed in white, who have fulfilled the law of the Lord [**Isa. 61:10** | Rev. 3:5; 7:13-14]. ⁴¹The number of your children, whom you desired, is now complete; implore the Lord's authority that your people, who have been called from the beginning, may be made holy [2 Esd. 4:36; 9:8 | Eph. 1:4; Rev. 6:11]."

⁴²I, Ezra, saw on Mount Zion a great multitude that I could not number, and they all were praising the Lord with songs [Rev. 7:9; 14:1]. ⁴³In their midst was a young man of great stature, taller than any of the others, and on the head of each of them **he placed a crown**, but he was more exalted than they [2 Esd. 2:46 | Rev. 2:10; 4:4]. And I was held spellbound. ⁴⁴Then I asked and angel, "Who are these, my lord?" [Rev. 7:13-14] ⁴⁵He answered and said to me, **"These are they who have put off mortal clothing and have put on the immortal, and have confessed the name of God. Now they are being crowned, and receive palms** [1 Cor. 15:53-54; Rev. 2:10; 4:4; 7:9]." ⁴⁶Then I said to the angel, "Who is that young man who is placing crowns on them and putting palms in their hands?" ⁴⁷He answered and said to me, "He is the Son of God, whom they confessed in the world [Mt. 10:32; Lk. 12:8; Rev. 3:5]." So I began to praise those who had stood valiantly for the name of the Lord.

2 Esdras 4:7-11 (*4 Ezra* 4:7-11)

⁷And he said to me, "If I had asked you, 'How many dwellings are in the heart of the sea, or how many streams are at the source of the deep, or how many streams are above the firmament [**Job 38:16**], **or which are the exits of Hades, or which are the entrances of paradise?'** [*Lat.* lacks the last part; 2 Esd. 7:36, 123; 8:52] ⁸perhaps you would have said to me, 'I never went down into the deep, nor as yet into Hades, neither did I ever ascend into heaven [Rom. 10:6-7].' ⁹But now I have asked you only about fire and wind and the day – things that you have experienced and from which you cannot be separated, and you have given me no answer about them [**Eccl. 11:5** | Wis. 9:16 | Jn 3:12]." ¹⁰He said to me, "You cannot understand the things with which you have grown up; ¹¹how then can your mind comprehend the way of the Most High? And how can one who is already worn out by the corrupt world understand incorruption? [**Ezek. 1:28; 3:23** | 2 Esd. 4:2]"

2 Esdras 4:33-43 (*4 Ezra* 4:33-43)

³³Then I answered and said, "How long? When will these things be? Why are our years few and evil?" [2 Esd. 5:56; 6:11; 8:42; 12:7] ³⁴He answered me and said, "Do not be in a greater hurry than the Most High. You, indeed, are in a hurry for yourself, but the Highest is in a hurry on behalf of many [2 Esd. 5:44; 6:34 | Heb. 10:37; 2 Pet. 3:9]. ³⁵**Did not the souls of the righteous in their chambers ask about these matters, saying, 'How long are we to remain here? And when will the harvest of our reward come?'** [2 Esd. 4:41; 5:9, 37; 7:32 | Rev. 6:9-10] ³⁶And the archangel **Jeremiel** *[According to 1 En. 20:1-8, he is the 7th Archangel who is responsible for the resurrection]* answered and said, 'When the number of those like yourselves is completed; for he has weighed the age in the balance [2 Esd. 2:41; 5:43 | 1 Thess. 4:16; Rev. 6:11], ³⁷and measured the times by measure, and numbered the times by number; **and he will not move or arouse them until that measure is fulfilled** [Wis. 11:20].'"

³⁸Then I answered and said, "But, O sovereign Lord, all of us also are full of ungodliness [2 Esd. 7:17]. ³⁹It is perhaps on account of us that the time of threshing is delayed for the righteous – on account of the sins of those who inhabit the earth." ⁴⁰He answered me and said, "Go and ask a pregnant women whether, when her nine months have been competed, her womb can keep the fetus within her any longer."
⁴¹And I said, "No, lord, it cannot."
He said to me, "**In Hades the chambers of the souls are like the womb** [2 Esd 4:35; 5:9, 37; 7:32]. ⁴²For just as a woman who is in labor makes haste to escape the pangs of birth, **so also do these places hasten to give back those thinks that were committed to them from the beginning**. ⁴³Then the things that you desire to see will be disclosed to you."

2 Esdras 5:38-40 (*4 Ezra* 5:38-40)

³⁸I said, "O sovereign Lord, who is able to know these things except him whose dwelling is not with mortals? [**Dan. 2:11** | 2 Esd. 4:38; 5:23] ³⁹As for me, I am without wisdom, and how can I speak concerning the things that you have asked me? [**Jer. 1:6**]"
⁴⁰He said to me, "Just as you cannot do one of the things that were mentioned, so you cannot discover my judgment, **or the goal of the love that I have promised to my people** [Eph. 3:19]."

2 Esdras 7:10-16 (4 Ezra 7:10-16)

¹⁰I said, "That is right, lord." He said to me, "So also is Israel's portion. ¹¹For I made the world for their sake, and when Adam transgressed my statues, what had been made was judged [2 Esd. 3:7; 6:55]. ¹²And so the entrances of this world were made narrow and sorrowful and toilsome; they are few and evil, full of dangers and involved in great hardships [**Job 5:7; 14:1** | 2 Esd. 4:33]. ¹³But the entrance of the greater world are broad and safe, and yield the fruit of immortality [**Gen. 2:9**]. ¹⁴**Therefore unless the living pass through the difficult and futile experiences, they can never receive those things that have been reserved for them** [Mt. 7:14]. ¹⁵**Now therefore why are you disturbed, seeing that you are to perish? Why are

you moved, seeing that you are mortal? ¹⁶Why have you not considered in your mind what is to come, rather than what is now present?"

2 Esdras 7:26-51 (*4 Ezra* 7:26-51)

²⁶"For indeed the time will come, when the signs that I have foretold to you will come to pass, that the city that now is not seen shall appear, and the land that now is hidden shall be disclosed [2 Esd. 4:52 | Rev. 21:2]. ²⁷Everyone who has been delivered from the evils that I have foretold shall see my wonders [2 Esd. 6:25]. ²⁸For my son the Messiah shall be revealed with those who are with him, and those who remain shall rejoice four hundred years [2 Esd. 13:32, 37, 52; 14:9]. ²⁹After those years my son the Messiah shall die [**Dan. 9:26**], and all who draw human breath. ³⁰Then the world shall be turned back to primeval silence for seven days, as it was at the first beginnings, so that no one shall be left [2 Esd. 6:39]. ³¹After seven days the world that is not yet awake shall be roused, and that which is corruptible shall perish. **³²The earth shall give up those who are asleep in it, and the dust those who rest there in silence [Isa. 26:19; Dan. 12:2 | Jn 5:28-29]; and the chambers shall give up the souls that have been committed to them.** ³³The Most High shall be revealed on the seat of judgment [**Dan. 7:9-10** | Mt. 25:31; Lk. 13:25], and compassion shall pass away, and patience shall be withdrawn. ³⁴Only judgment shall remain, truth shall stand, and faithfulness shall grow strong [2 Esd. 6:28]. ³⁵Recompense shall follow, and the reward shall be manifested; righteous deeds shall awake, and unrighteous deeds shall not sleep [**Eccl. 12:14** | 2 Esd. 13:56 | Mt. 16:27]. **³⁶The pit of torment shall appear, and opposite it shall be the place of rest; and the furnace of hell shall be disclosed, and opposite it the paradise of delight** [2 Esd. 4:7; 6:2; 7:38 | Lk. 16:23f; Rev. 9:2; 20:14-15]. **³⁷Then the Most High will say to the nations that have been raised from the dead,** 'Look now, and understand whom you have denied, whom you have not served, whose commandments you have despised. ³⁸Look on this side and on that; here are delight and rest, and there are fire and torments [2 Esd. 7:36].' Thus he will speak to them on the day of judgment – ³⁹a day that has no sun or moon or stars [2 Esd. 7:42], ⁴⁰or cloud or thunder or lightning, or wind or water or air, or darkness or evening or morning, ⁴¹or summer or spring or heat or winter or frost or cold, or hail or rain or dew, ⁴²or moon or night, or dawn or shining or brightness or light, but only the splendor of the glory of the Most High [**Isa. 60:19-20** | Rev. 22:5], by which all shall see what has been destined. ⁴³It will last as though for a week of years. ⁴⁴This is my judgment and its prescribed order; and to you alone I have shown these things [2 Esd. 6:33; 7:104; 13:53, 56]."

⁴⁵I answered and said, "O sovereign Lord, I said then and I say now: Blessed are those who are alive and keep your commandments! [**Pss. 1:1-2; 119:2**] ⁴⁶But what of those for whom I prayed? For who among the living is there that has not sinned, or who is there among mortals that has not transgressed your covenant? [2 Esd. 8:17, 35] **⁴⁷And now I see that the world to come will bring delight to few, but torments to many** [2 Esd. 8:1; 9:15]. ⁴⁸For an evil heart has grown up in us, which has alienated us from God, and has brought us into corruption and the ways of death, and has

shown us the paths of perdition and removed us far from life – and that not merely for a few but for almost all who have been created [2 Esd. 3:20-22; 4:30-31; 7:92]." ⁴⁹He answered me and said, "Listen to me, Ezra, and I will instruct you, and will admonish you once more. ⁵⁰For this reason the Most High has made not one world but two [2 Esd. 8:1]. ⁵¹Inasmuch as you have side that the righteous are not many but few, hear the explanation for this.

2 Esdras 7:66-105 (*4 Ezra* 7:66-105)

⁶⁶It is much better with them [wild animals] than with us: **for they do not look for a judgment and they do not know of any torment or salvation promised after death.** ⁶⁷What does it profit us that we shall be preserved alive but cruelly tormented? ⁶⁸For all who have been born are entangled in iniquities, and are full of sins and burdened with transgressions. ⁶⁹**And if after death we were not to come into judgment, perhaps it would have been better for us** [2 Esd. 7:117]."

⁷⁰He answered them me and said, "When the Most High made the world and Adam and all who have come from him, he first prepared the judgment and the things that pertain to the judgment [Mt. 20:23; 25:34, 41; Mk 10:40]. ⁷¹But now, understand from your own words – for you have said that the mind grows with us [2 Esd. 7:64]. ⁷²For this reason, therefore, those who live on earth shall be tormented, because though they had understanding, they committed iniquity; and through they received the commandments, they did not keep them; and though they obtained the law, they dealt unfaithfully with what they received [2 Esd. 7:21-24]. ⁷³What then, will they have to say in the judgment, or how will they answer in the last times? ⁷⁴How long the Mist High has been patient with those who inhabit the world? – and not for their sake, but because of the times that he has foreordained [Rom. 2:4; 2 Pet. 3:9]."

⁷⁵I answered and said, "If I have found favor in your sight, O Lord, show this also to your servant: **whether after death, as soon as everyone of us yields up the soul, we shall be kept in rest until those times come when you will renew the creation, or whether we shall be tormented at once?** [**Isa. 65:17** | Mt. 19:28; Acts 3:21; Rev. 21:1, 5]" ⁷⁶He answered me and said, "I will show you that also, but do not include yourself with those who have shown scorn, or number yourself among those who are tormented. ⁷⁷For you have a treasure of works stored up with the Most High, but it will not be shown to you until the last times [Tob. 4:9 | Mt. 6:20; Lk. 12:33]. ⁷⁸**Now concerning death, the teaching is**: When the decisive decree has gone out from the Most High that a person shall die, as the spirit leaves the body to return again to him who gave it, first of all it adores the glory of the Most High [**Eccl. 12:7** | 2 Esd. 7:91]. ⁷⁹If it is one of those who have shown scorn and have not kept the way of the Most High, who have despised his law and hated those who fear God – ⁸⁰such spirits shall not enter into habitations, but shall immediately wander about in torments, always grieving and sad, in seven ways [2 Esd. 7:85, 95, 101]. ⁸¹The **first** way, because they have scorned the law of the Most High. ⁸²The **second** way, because they cannot now make a good repentance so that they may live. ⁸³The **third** way, they shall see the reward laid up for those who have trusted the covenant of the Most High [Wis. 5:2 | Lk. 16:23]. ⁸⁴The **fourth** way, they shall consider the torment laid up for themselves

in the last days. ⁸⁵The **fifth** way, they shall see how the habitations of the others are guarded by angels in profound quiet [2 Esd. 7:80, 95, 101]. ⁸⁶The **sixth** way, they shall see how some of them will cross over into torments. ⁸⁷The **seventh** way, which is worse than all the ways that have been mentioned, because they shall utterly waste away in confusion and be consumed with shame, and shall wither with fear at seeing the glory of the Most High in whose presence they sinned while they were alive, and **in whose presence they are to be judged in the last time.**

⁸⁸"Now this is the order of those who have kept the ways of the Most High, when they shall be separated from their mortal body. ⁸⁹During the time that they lived in it, they laboriously served the Most High, and withstood danger every hour so that they might keep the law of the Lawgiver perfectly [1 Cor. 15:30; Jas 4:12]. ⁹⁰Therefore this is the teaching concerning them: ⁹¹First of all, they shall see with great joy the glory of him who receives them, for they shall have rest in seven orders [2 Esd. 7:78]. ⁹²The **first** order, because they have striven with great effort to overcome the evil thought that was formed with them, so that it might not lead them astray from life into death [2 Esd. 7:48]. ⁹³The **second** order, because they see the perplexity in which the souls of the ungodly wander and the punishment that awaits them [Rev. 14:10]. ⁹⁴The **third** order, they see the witness that he who formed them bears concerning them, that throughout their life they kept the law with which they were entrusted [Mt. 10:32; Lk. 12:8; Rev. 3:5]. ⁹⁵The **fourth** order, **they understand the rest that they now enjoy, being gathered into their chambers and guarded by angels in profound quiet, and the glory waiting for them in the last days** [2 Esd. 4:35; 7:32, 80, 85, 101]. ⁹⁶The **fifth** order, they rejoiced that they have now escaped what is corruptible and **shall inherit what is to come**; and besides they see the straits and toil form which they have been delivered, and **the spacious liberty that they are to receive and enjoy in immortality** [Rom. 7:24; 8:18; 1 Cor. 15:53-54]. ⁹⁷The **sixth** order, when it is shown them **how their face is to shine like the sun, and how they are to be made like the light of the stars [Dan. 12:3** | 2 Esd. 7:125 | Mt. 13:43], **being incorruptible from then on.** ⁹⁸The **seventh** order, which is greater than all that have been mentioned, because they shall rejoice with boldness, and shall be confident without confusion, and shall be glad without fear, for the press forward to see the face of him [Mt. 5:8; 1 Jn 3:2; Rev. 22:4] whom they served in life **and from whom they are to receive their reward when glorified** [1 Cor. 3:14; Rev. 22:12]. ⁹⁹This is the order of the souls of the righteous, as henceforth is announced; and the previously mentioned are the ways of torment that those who would not give heed shall suffer hereafter."

¹⁰⁰Then I answered and said, "Will time therefore be given to the soul, after they have been separated from the bodies, to see what you have described to me?"

¹⁰¹He said to me, "They shall have freedom for seven days, so that during these seven days they may see the things of which you have been told, and afterwards **they shall be gathered in their habitations** [2 Esd. 7:80, 85, 95]."

¹⁰²I answered and said, "**If I have found favor in your sight, show further to me, your servant, whether on the day of judgment the righteous will be able to intercede for the ungodly or to entreat the Most High for them** [2 Esd. 4:44]

— ¹⁰³fathers for sons or sons for parents, brothers for brothers, relatives for their kindred, or friends for those who are most dear."
¹⁰⁴He answered me and said, "Since you have found favor in my sight, I will show you this also. The day of judgment is decisive and displays to all the seal of truth [**Joel 3:14** | 2 Esd. 7:44]. Just as now a father does not send his son, or a son his father, or a master his servant, or friend his dearest friend, to be ill or sleep or eat or be healed in his place, ¹⁰⁵**so no one shall ever pray for another on that day, neither shall anyone lay a burden on another; for then all shall bear their own righteousness and unrighteousness [Ezek. 18:20** | Gal. 6:7-8]."

2 Esdras 7:112-115 (*4 Ezra* 7:112-115)
¹¹²He answered me and said, "This present world is not the end; the full glory does not remain in it; therefore those who were strong prayed for the weak. ¹¹³**But the day of judgment will be the end of this age and the beginning of the immortal age to come, in which corruption has passed away** [2 Esd. 6:27-28 | 1 Cor. 15:53-54], ¹¹⁴sinful indulgence has come to an end, unbelief has been cut off, and righteousness has increased and truth has appeared [2 Esd. 7:34]. ¹¹⁵Therefore no one will then be able to have mercy on someone who has been condemned in the judgment, or to harm someone who is victorious [2 Esd. 7:128 | Rev. 3:5]."

2 Esdras 7:117-131 (*4 Ezra* 7:117-131)
¹¹⁷For what good is it to all that they live in sorrow now [**Jer. 20:18; Job 3; Eccl. 2:22-23**] and **expect punishment after death**? [2 Esd. 4:12; 7:69] ¹¹⁸O Adam, what have you done? For through it was you who sinned, the fall was not yours alone, but ours also who are your descendants [2 Esd. 3:21; 4:30; 7:11 | Rom. 5:18]. ¹¹⁹For what good is it to us, if an immortal time has been promised to us, but we have done deeds that bring death? ¹²⁰And what good is it that an everlasting hope has been promised to us, but we have miserably failed? ¹²¹Or the safe and healthful habitations have been reserved for us, but we have lived wickedly? ¹²²Or that the glory of the Most High will defend those who have led a pure life, but we have walked in the most wicked ways? ¹²³Or that a paradise shall be revealed, whose fruit remains unspoiled and in which are abundance and healing [2 Esd. 4:7 | Rev. 2:7; 22:2], but we shall not enter it ¹²⁴because we have lived in perverse ways? ¹²⁵Or that the faces of those who practiced self-control shall shine more than the stars [**Lam. 4:8** | 2 Esd. 7:97 | Mt. 13:43], but our faces shall be blacker than darkness? ¹²⁶**For while we lived and committed iniquity we did not consider what we should suffer after death**."
¹²⁷He answered and said, "This is the significance of the contest that all who are born on earth shall wage [Eph. 6:10-17; 1 Tim. 6:12]: ¹²⁸**if they are defeated they shall suffer what you have said, but if they are victorious they shall receive what I have said.** ¹²⁹For this is the way of which Moses, while he was alive, spoke to the people, saying, '**Choose life for yourself, so that you may live!**' [**Deut. 30:19**] ¹³⁰But they did not believe him or the prophets after him, or even myself who have spoken to them [2 Esd. 1:32]. ¹³¹Therefore there shall not be grief at their destruction, so much as joy over those to whom salvation is assured [2 Esd. 7:60-61 | Lk. 15:7, 10]."

2 Esdras 8:1-3 (*4 Ezra* 8:1-3)

¹He answered me and said, "**The Most High made this world for the sake of many, but the world to come for the sake of only a few** [2 Esd. 7:47; 8:3, 55; 9:15 | Mt. 7:14; Lk. 13:24]. ²But I tell you a parable, Ezra. Just as, when you ask the earth, it will tell you that it provides a large amount of clay from which earthenware is made, but only a little dust from which gold comes, so is the course of the present world [2 Esd. 7:54; 10:9]. ³**Many have been created, but only a few shall be saved** [2 Esd. 8:1]."

2 Esdras 8:12-19 (*4 Ezra* 8:12-19)

¹²You have nurtured it in your righteousness, and instructed it in you law, and reproved it in your wisdom. ¹³**You put it to death as your creation, and make it live as your work** [Rom. 8:11, 13; Col. 3:5]. ¹⁴If then you will suddenly and quickly destroy what with so great labor was fashioned by your command, to what purpose was it made [**Job 10:8**]? ¹⁵And now I will speak out: About all humankind you know best; but I will speak about your people, for whom I am grieved, ¹⁶and about your inheritance, for whom I lament, and about Israel, for whom I am sad, and about the seed of Jacob, for whom I am troubled. ¹⁷Therefore I will pray before you for myself and for them, for I see the failings of us who inhabit the earth [2 Esd. 7:46]; ¹⁸and now also **I have heard of the swiftness of the judgment that is to come** [Mal. 3:5 | 2 Esd. 8:61 | Jas 5:9; Rev. 22:12]. ¹⁹Therfore hear my voice and understand my words, and I will speak before you [2 Esd. 6:26; 14:9, 36-48]."

2 Esdras 8:37-40 (*4 Ezra* 8:37-40)

³⁷He answered me and said, "Some things you have spoken rightly, and it will turn out according to your words. ³⁸For indeed I will not concern myself about the fashioning of those who have <u>sinned</u>, **or about their <u>death</u>, their <u>judgment</u>, or their <u>destruction</u>** [Gen. 6:5 | 2 Esd. 7:61; 9:12]; ³⁹but I will rejoice over the creation of <u>the righteous</u>, over their <u>pilgrimage</u> also, **and their salvation, and their receiving their reward** [2 Esd. 7:60; 13:56]. ⁴⁰As I have spoken, therefore, so it shall be.

2 Esdras 8:46-54 (*4 Ezra* 8:46-54)

⁴⁶He answered me and said: "Things that are present are for those who live now, and things that are future are for those who will live hereafter. ⁴⁷For you come far short of being able to love my creation more than I love it. But you have often compared yourself to the unrighteous. Never do so! ⁴⁸But even in this respect you will be praiseworthy before the Most High, ⁴⁹because you have humbled yourself, as is becoming for you, and have not considered yourself to be among the righteous. **You will receive the greatest glory**, ⁵⁰for many miseries will affect those who inhabit the world in the last times [2 Esd. 8:63; 10:59; 12:23-24 | 2 Tim. 3:2], because they have walked in great pride. ⁵¹But think of your own case, and inquire concerning the glory of those who are like yourself [2 Esd. 4:36; 8:62], ⁵²because **it is for you that paradise is opened, the tree of life is planted, the age to come is prepared, plenty is provided, a city is built, rest is appointed, goodness is established and wisdom perfected beforehand** [2 Esd. 2:12; 7:26; 10:27 | Heb. 11:16; Rev. 22:14].

⁵³**The root of evil is sealed up from you, illness is banished from you, and death is hidden; Hades has fled and corruption has been forgotten** [2 Esd. 2:38 | Rev. 20:14]; ⁵⁴**sorrows have passed away, and in the end the treasure of immortality is made manifest** [Rev. 21:4].

2 Esdras 9:7-13 (*4 Ezra* 9:7-13)
⁷It shall be that all who will be saved and will be able to escape on account of their works, or on account of the faith by which they have believed [2 Esd. 8:33; 13:23 | Rom. 3:28], ⁸will survive the dangers that have been predicted, and will see my salvation in my land and within my borders, which I have sanctified for myself form the beginning [2 Esd. 6:25; 12:34; 13:48]. ⁹Then those who have now abused my ways shall be amazed, and those who have rejected them with contempt shall live in torments [Wis. 5:2]. ¹⁰For as many as did not acknowledge me in their lifetime, though they received my benefits [Lk. 16:25], ¹¹and as many as scorned my law while they still had freedom, and did not understand but despised it while an opportunity of repentance was still open to them [2 Esd. 8:56 | Heb. 12:17], ¹²**these must in torment acknowledge it after death** [2 Esd. 8:38]. ¹³Therefore, do not continue to be curious about how the ungodly will be punished; but inquire how the righteous will be saved, those to whom the age belongs and for whose sake the age was made [1 Cor. 3:22]."

2 Esdras 10:10, 15-17 (*4 Ezra* 10:10, 15-17)
¹⁰From the beginning all have been born of her [Zion], and others will come; and, lo, almost all go to perdition, and a multitude of them will come to doom [Wis. 7:1; 2 Esd. 9:15].

¹⁵Now, therefore, keep your sorrow to yourself, and bear bravely the troubles that have come upon you. ¹⁶**For if you acknowledge the decree of God to be just** [1 Sam. 3:18; Ps. 145:17], **you will receive your son back in due time, and will be praised among women.** ¹⁷Therefore go into the town to your husband."

2 Esdras 14:34-35 (*4 Ezra* 14:34-35)
³⁴**If you, then, will rule over your minds and discipline your hearts, you shall be kept alive, and after death you shall obtain mercy.** ³⁵**For after death the judgment will come, when we shall live again; and then the names of the name of the righteous shall become manifest, and the deeds of the ungodly shall be disclosed** [Eccl. 12:14; Dan. 12:1-2 | Wis. 5:15]. ³⁶But let no one come to me now, and let no one seek me for forty days [2 Esd. 14:23, 45]."

Resurrection Texts in the Apocalyptic Literature and Related Works

Table 26. Classification of the resurrection texts in the apocalyptic literature and related works

Date	Passage		Notes	Resurrection			Classification		
				Implied	Stated	Ref.	Allude	Phil.	Assume
2nd cent. BCE–1st cent. CE	*1 Enoch*	Book I (1-36)	**Judgment Texts (Implied Resurrection)**	x					x
		The Parable of Enoch	1:3-9; 5:5-9; 9:2-3; 10:4-6, 11-13, 16-17, 20; 13:6; 14:2-6; 15:7-10; 16:1; 27:2-3					x	
			20:8 Archangel Remiel		x				x
			22 Resurrection of the Soul?		x				x
			25:4-6 The Fragrant tree	x					x
		Book II (37-71)	**Judgment Texts (Implied Resurrection)**	x					
		The Book of the Similitudes	38; 41:1, 8-9; 45:2-6; 47; 48:7; 50:1; 54:6; 56:8; 58:1-4; 60:6, 24; 61:5, 8					x	
			70:4 – Vision of earliest human ancestors						
			70:16 – all the righteous will follow the path of Enoch.						
			40:9 Archangel Phanuel	x					x
			46:3 Son of Man	x					x
			49:3 Sleep ‖ Death	x					x
			51		x				x
			62:13-16 Son of Man		x				x

Table 26 continued

Date	Passage	Notes	Resurrection			Classification		
			Implied	Stated	Ref.	Allude	Phil.	Assume
	Book III (72-82) The Book of Heavenly Luminaries							
	81:1-4	Judgment	x					x
	Book IV (83-90)	**Judgment Texts (Implied Resurrection)**						
	84:4							
	The Dream Visions							
	89:36-37	Sleep = Death	x					x
	90:20-36	Judgment New Jerusalem	x			x		x
	Book V (91-107)							
	91:8-17	Arise from sleep		x				x
	92:2-5	Arise from sleep		x		x		x
	The Two Ways of the Righteous and the Sinner: Including the Apocalypse of Weeks	**The Destiny of the Righteous and the Wicked (94-104): Judgment (Implied Resurrection)** 94:9, 11; 95:5-6; 96:2-3, 8; 97:6; 98:6-8, 14; 100:4-5, 10; 102:4-8; 103:1-4; 104:1-7	x				x	x
	108:2-3	Book of Life	x			x		x
	108:8-15	Recompensed Resplendent	x			x	x	x

Table 26 continued

Date	Passage	Notes	Resurrection			Classification		
			Implied	Stated	Ref.	Allude	Phil.	Assume
Late 1st cent. CE	2 *Enoch*	**Judgment Texts (Implied Resurrection)**						
	J 7:1; J/A 18:7; J/A 19:5; J 39:5/A 39:2; J 42:3, 5, 7; J/A 44:3-5; J/A 48:8-9; J/A 49:2; J/A 50:2, 4-5; J/A 51:3; J/A 52:15; J/A 58:4-6; J 60:4; J 66:6-7		x				x	x
	J 32	Dust to dust		x	x			x
	J/A 65:6-11	Judgment	x					x
	J 70:1	Eternal inheritance	x					x
	J/A 70:3	Rest ∥ Death	x					x
5th to 6th cent. CE	3 *Enoch*							
	(18:24)	Books of the Dead Books of the Living	x	x				
	(28:7; 30:2; 31:2; 33:1)	Every Day is a Judgment	x				x	
	28:7-10	Third day he will raise us up		x				
	44:7-8	Rest of the Righteous		x				x

A. *Classification and Anthology of Resurrection Texts*   211

Table 26 continued

Date	Passage		Notes	Resurrection			Classification		
				Implied	Stated	Ref.	Allude	Phil.	Assume
2nd cent. BCE–7th cent. CE	*Sibylline Oracles*	Book 1	355	Lazarus' resurrection						x
			378	Announcing the resurrection to the dead		x				x
		Book 2	221-251	Resurrection/Judgment			x			x
			313-315	Rewards of the Righteous		x				x
		Book 3	66	Satan's work		x				x
			769	Messianic kingdom		x				x
		Book 4	179-192	Resurrection/Judgment		x	x			x
		Book 6	14	Lazarus' resurrection		x				x
		Book 7	144-145	Restoration of the world	x					x
		Book 8	82-83	Resurrection/Judgment		x				x
			170	Eschatological upheaval		x				x
			205-208	Messianic Age		x				x
			226-228	Resurrection/Judgment		x				x
			255	Faith → Eternal life	x					x
			286	Jesus' mission		x				x
			293	Jesus' mission		x				x
			310-314	Jesus' mission		x				x
			413-416	Resurrection/Judgment		x				x
		Frag. 3	41-49	Inheritance of the Righteous	x					x
1st cent. BCE–1st cent. CE	*Apocryphon of Ezekiel*	Frag. 1		Body = Blind Soul = Lame		x	x			
				Judgment parable						

Table 26 continued

Date		Passage	Notes	Resurrection		Classification			
				Implied	Stated	Ref.	Allude	Phil.	Assume
Late 1st cent.	Fourth Book of Ezra	2:16	Exhortation to good work						×
		2:22-24	Burial		×				×
		2:31	Sleep ‖ Death		×				×
		4:35-37	Predestined time		×		×		×
		4:42-43	Hades ‖ womb	×					×
		7:31-[44]	Resurrection/Judgment		×		×		×
		7:75-101	The state of the departed before the judgment		×		×		×
		14:36	Resurrection/Judgment	×				×	×
2nd to 9th cent. CE	Greek Apocalypse of Ezra	2:1; 5:22	The righteous/Patriarchs	×					×
		4:36	Trumpet/Resurrection		×				×
		7:2	Jesus' work		×				×
Date unknown	Questions of Ezra	A. 5	The fate of the righteous and the sinners		×				×
		A. 10	The prophet's question	×					×
		B. 1-14	Resurrection/Judgment		×				×

Table 26 continued

Date		Passage	Notes	Resurrection		Classification			
				Implied	Stated	Ref.	Allude	Phil.	Assume
Early 2nd cent. CE	2 Baruch	11:4	Sleep ‖ Death	x					x
		14:12-13	Possesses hope in the future ‖ Resurrection	x					x
		15:7-8	The Righteous	x					x
		21:23-24	Sleep ‖ Death	x					x
		23:5	Appointed number	x					
		24:1-2	Judgment/Resurrection	x			x		x
		30:1-3	The end of time		x				x
		42:7-8	Dust → Resurrection		x		x		x
		49–52	The nature of the resurrection body: The final destiny of the Righteous and the wicked		x	x			
		57:2	Planned from the beginning		x				x
		66:3	Make sure that they are really dead	x					x
		85:3	Sleep ‖ Death	x					x
		85:9	Sleep ‖ Death	x					x
		85:15	Resurrect the righteous	x					x
1st to 4th cent. CE	Apocalypse of Elijah	3:13	Satan cannot resurrect the dead		x				x
		4:24-29	Persecution of the Saints		x		x		x
		4:31	Satan cannot resurrect the dead		x				x
		5:25-39	End-time	x					x

Resurrection Texts in the Apocalyptic Literature and Related Works

1 Enoch

1 Enoch 1:3-9   Hermeneia, 19–21

³And concerning the chosen I speak now, and concerning them I take up my discourse. The Theophany "The Great Holy One will come forth from his dwelling, ⁴and the eternal God will tread from thence upon Mount Sinai. He will appear with his army, he will appear with his mighty host from the heaven of heavens. ⁵All the watchers will fear and <quake>, and those who are hiding in all the ends of the earth will sing. All the ends of the earth will be shaken, and trembling and great fear will seize them (the watchers) unto the ends of the earth. ⁶The high mountains will be shaken and fall and break apart, and the high hills will be made low and melt like wax before the fire. ⁷**The earth will be wholly rent asunder, and everything on the earth will perish, and there will be judgment on all. ⁸With the righteous he will make peace, and over the chosen there will be protection, and upon them will be mercy. They will all be God's, and he will grant them his good pleasure. He will bless (them) all, and he will help (them) all. Light will shine upon them, and he will make peace with them.** ⁹Look, he comes with the myriads of his holy ones, to execute judgment on all, and to destroy all the wicked, and to convict all humanity for all the wicked deeds that they have done, and the proud and hard words that wicked sinners spoke against him.

1 Enoch 5:5-10   Hermeneia, 22–3

⁵"Then you will curse your days, and the years of your life will perish, and the years of your destruction will increase in an eternal curse; and there will be no mercy or peace for you! ⁶Then you will leave your names as an eternal curse for all the righteous, and by you all who curse will curse, and all the sinners and wicked will swear by you. But all the <chosen>will rejoice; and for them there will be forgiveness of sins and all mercy and peace and clemency. For them there will be salvation, a good light, and they will inherit the earth. But for all you sinners there will be no salvation, but on all of you a curse will abide. ⁷**For the chosen there will be light and joy and peace, and they will inherit the earth**. But for you wicked there will be a curse. ⁸Then wisdom will be given to all the chosen; and they will all live, and they will sin no more through godlessness or pride. In the enlightened man there will be light, and in the wise man, understanding. And they will transgress no more, nor will they sin all the days of their life, ⁹nor will they die in the heat of <God's> wrath. But the number of the days of their life they will complete, and their life will grow in peace, and the years of their joy will increase in rejoicing and eternal peace all the days of their life."

1 Enoch **20:1-8**   Hermeneia, 40–1

These are the names of the holy angels who watch. ²**Uriel**, one of the holy angels, who is in charge of the world and Tartarus. ³**Raphael**, one of the holy angels, who is in charge of the spirits of men. ⁴**Reuel**, one of the holy angels, who takes vengeance on the world of the luminaries. ⁵**Michael**, one of the holy angels, who has been put in charge of the good ones of the people. ⁶**Sariel**, one of the holy angels, who is in charge of the spirits who sin against the spirit. ⁷**Gabriel**, one of the holy angels, who is in charge of paradise and the serpents and the cherubim. ⁸**Remiel, one of the holy angels, whom God has put in charge of them that rise.** The names of the seven archangels.

1 Enoch **22**   Hermeneia, 42–3
The Mountain of the Dead
¹From there I traveled to another place. And he showed me to the west a great and high mountain of hard rock. ²And there were four hollow places in it, deep and very smooth. Three of them were dark and one, illuminated; and a fountain of water was in the middle of it. And I said, "How smooth are these hollows and altogether deep and dark to view." ³Then Raphael answered me, one of the holy angels who was with me, and said to me, "These hollow places (are intended) that the spirits of the souls of the dead might be gathered into them. For this very (purpose) they were created, (that) here the souls of all human beings should be gathered. ⁴**And look, these are the pits for the place of their confinement. Thus they were made until the day (on) which they will be judged, and until the time of the day of the end of the great judgment that will be exacted from them.**" ⁵There I saw the spirit of a dead man making suit, and his lamentation went up to heaven and cried and made suit. ⁶Then I asked Raphael, the watcher and holy one who was with me, and said to him, "This spirit that makes suit—whose is it—that thus his lamentation goes up and makes suit unto heaven?" ⁷And he answered me and said, "This is the spirit that went forth from Abel, whom Cain his brother murdered. And Abel makes accusation against him until his posterity perishes from the face of the earth [Gen. 4:10], and his posterity is obliterated from the posterity of men." ⁸Then I asked about all the hollow places, why they were separated one from the other. ⁹And he answered me and said, **"These three were made that the spirits of the dead might be separated. And this has been separated for the spirits of the righteous, where the bright fountain of water is.** ¹⁰**And this has been created for <the spirits of the> sinners, when they die and are buried in the earth, and judgment has not been executed on them in their life.** ¹¹**Here their spirits are separated for this great torment, until the great day of judgment**, of scourges and tortures of the cursed forever, that there might be a recompense for their spirits. There he will bind them forever. ¹²And this has been separated for the spirits of them that make suit, who make disclosure about the destruction, when they were murdered in the days of the sinners. ¹³And this was created for the spirits of the people who will not be pious, but sinners, who were

godless, and they were companions with the lawless. **And their spirits will not be punished on the day of judgment, nor will they be raised from there.**" [14]Then I blessed the Lord of glory and said, "Blessed is the **judgment of righteousness** and blessed are you, O Lord of majesty and righteousness, who are Lord of eternity."

1 Enoch 25:3-7   Hermeneia, 45

[3]And he answered me and said, "This high mountain that you saw, whose peak is like the throne of God, is the seat where the Great Holy One, the Lord of glory, the King of eternity, will sit, when he descends to visit the earth in goodness. [4]**And (as for) this fragrant tree, no flesh has the right to touch it until the great judgment, in which there will be vengeance on all and a consummation forever. Then it will be given to the righteous and the pious,** [5]and its fruit will be food for the chosen [Ezek. 47:12]. And it will be transplanted to the holy place, by the house of God, the King of eternity.
[6]**Then they will rejoice greatly and be glad,
and they will enter into the sanctuary.
Its fragrances \<will be\> in their bones,
and they will live a long life on the earth,
such as your fathers lived also in their days,
and torments and plagues and suffering will not touch them.**"
[7]Then I blessed the God of glory, the King of eternity, who has prepared such things for people (who are) righteous, and has created them and promised to give (them) to them.

1 Enoch 40:9-10   Hermeneia, 55

[9]And he said to me, "The first one, \<who\> is merciful and long-suffering, (is) **Michael**. The second one, who (is) in charge of every sickness and every wound of the sons of men, is **Raphael**. The third one, who (is) in charge of every power, is **Gabriel**. The fourth one, **who (is) in charge of the repentance to hope of those who inherit everlasting life, his name (is) Phanuel**." [10]These are the four angels of the Lord of Spirits; and the four voices I heard in those days.

1 Enoch 49   Hermeneia, 63–4

[1]For wisdom has been poured out like water, and glory will not fail in his presence forever and ever. [2]For he is mighty in all the secrets of righteousness; and unrighteousness will vanish like a shadow, and will have no place to stand. For the Chosen One has taken his stand in the presence of the Lord of Spirits; and his glory is forever and ever, and his might, to all generations. [3]And in him dwell the spirit of wisdom and the spirit of insight, and the spirit of instruction and might, **and the spirit of those who have fallen asleep in righteousness**. [4]And he will judge the things that are secret, and a lying word none will be able to speak in his presence; For he is the Chosen One in the presence of the Lord of Spirits according to his good pleasure.

1 Enoch 51　　　　　　　　　　　　　　　　　　　　　　　　Hermeneia, 65
Resurrection, Judgment, Life on a Renewed Earth
¹In those days, the earth will give back what has been entrusted to it,
and Sheol will give back what has been entrusted to it,
and destruction will restore what it owes.
⁵ªFor in those days, my Chosen One will arise
²and choose the righteous and holy from among them,
for the day on which they will be saved has drawn near.

³And the Chosen One, in those days, will sit upon my throne,
and all the secrets of wisdom **will go forth** from the counsel of his mouth,
for the Lord of Spirits has given (them) to him and glorified him.

⁴In those days the mountains will leap like rams,
and the hills will skip like lambs satisfied with milk;
and the faces of all the angels in heaven will be radiant with joy,

⁵ᵇand the earth will rejoice,
and the righteous will dwell on it,
and the chosen will go upon it.

1 Enoch 61:1-5　　　　　　　　　　　　　　　　　　　　　Hermeneia, 77–8
The Angels Prepare to Gather the Righteous
¹And I saw in those days, long cords were given to those angels, and they took for themselves wings and flew and went toward the North. ²And I asked the angel, "Why did these take the cords and go?" And he said to me, "They went so that they may measure." ³And the angel who went with me said to me, "These will bring the measurements of the righteous, and the ropes of the righteous to the righteous; so that they may rely on the name of the Lord of Spirits forever and ever. ⁴And the chosen will begin to dwell with the chosen; and these are the measurements that will be given to faith, and they will strengthen righteousness. ⁵And these measurements will reveal all the secrets of the depths of the earth, and those who were destroyed by the desert, and those who were devoured by beasts, and those who were devoured by the fish of the sea; **so that they may return and rely on the day of the Chosen One**, for no one will be destroyed in the presence of the Lord of Spirits, and no one is able to be destroyed."

1 Enoch 62:12-16　　　　　　　　　　　　　　　　　　　　Hermeneia, 81–2
¹²And they will be a spectacle for the righteous and for his chosen ones; and they will rejoice over them, because the wrath of the Lord of Spirits rests upon them, and his sword is drunk with them [Isa. 34:6]. The Salvation of the Righteous and Chosen ¹³**And the righteous and the chosen will be saved on that day**; and the faces of the sinners and the unrighteous they will henceforth not see. ¹⁴And the Lord of Spirits will abide over them, and with that Son of Man they will eat, **and they will lie down and rise up forever and ever.** ¹⁵And the righteous and chosen will have arisen

from the earth, and have ceased to cast down their faces, and have put on the garment of glory. ¹⁶And this will be your garment, the garment of life from the Lord of Spirits; and your garments will not wear out, and your glory will not fade in the presence of the Lord of Spirits.

1 Enoch 81:1-4 — Hermeneia, 111

¹He said to me: "Enoch, look at these heavenly tablets, read what is written on them, and understand each and every item." ²I looked at everything on the heavenly tablets, read everything that was written, and understood everything. I read the book, all the actions of people and of all humans who will be on the earth for the generations of the world. ³From that time forward I blessed the great Lord, the king of glory forever, as he had made every work of the world. I praised the Lord because of his patience; I blessed (him) on account of humanity. ⁴Afterwards I said:

**"Blessed is the one who dies righteous and good;
regarding him no book of wickedness has been written
and no day of judgment will be found."**

1 Enoch 90:20-36 — Hermeneia, 133–5

The Judgment and the New Age
The Judgment

²⁰And I saw until a throne was constructed in the pleasant land and the Lord of the sheep sat upon it, and he took all the sealed books and opened those books before the Lord of the sheep. ²¹And the Lord summoned those first seven white men, and he commanded them to bring before him beginning with the first star that had preceded those stars whose organs were like the organs of horses, and they brought all of them before him. ²²And he said to the man who had been writing before him—who was one of those seven white ones—he said to him, 'Bring those seventy shepherds to whom I delivered the sheep and who took and killed more than I commanded them.' ²³And look, I saw all of them bound, and they all stood before him. ²⁴And judgment was exacted first on the stars, and they were judged and found to be sinners. And they went to the place of judgment, and they threw them into an abyss; and it was full of fire, and it was burning and was full of pillars of fire. ²⁵And those seventy shepherds were judged and found to be sinners, and they were thrown into that fiery abyss. ²⁶And I saw at that time that an abyss like it was opened in the middle of the earth, which was full of fire. And they brought those blinded sheep, and they were all judged and found to be sinners. And they were thrown into that fiery abyss, and they burned. And that abyss was to the south of that house. ²⁷And I saw those sheep burning and their bones burning.

A New Beginning

²⁸And I stood up to see, until that old house was folded up—and they removed all the pillars, and all the beams and ornaments of that house were folded up with it—and they removed it and put it in a place to the south of the land. ²⁹And I saw until the Lord of the sheep brought a new house, larger and higher than that first one, and he

erected it on the site of the first one that had been rolled up. And all its pillars were new, and its beams were new, and its ornaments were new and larger than (those of) the first one, the old one that he had removed. **And all the sheep were within it.**
³⁰And I saw all the sheep that remained. And all the animals on the earth and all the birds of heaven were falling down and worshiping those sheep and making petition to them and obeying them in every thing. ³¹After that, those three who were clothed in white and who had taken hold of me by my hand, who had previously brought me up (with the hand of that ram also taking hold of me), set me down among those sheep before the judgment took place. ³²And all those sheep were white, and their wool was thick and pure. ³³**And all that had been destroyed and dispersed <by> all the wild beasts and all the birds of heaven were gathered in that house. And the Lord of the sheep rejoiced greatly because they were all good and had returned to that house.** ³⁴And I saw until they laid down that sword that had been given to the sheep; they brought it back to his house and sealed it up in the presence of the Lord. And all the sheep were enclosed in that house, but it did not contain them. ³⁵And the eyes of all were opened, and they saw good things; and there was none among them that did not see. ³⁶And I saw how that house was large and broad and very full.

1 Enoch 91:8-19   Hermeneia, 137

⁸And in those days, violence will be cut off from its roots,
as well as the roots of iniquity, together with deceit,
and they will be destroyed from under heaven.

⁹And all the idols of the nations will be given up,
and the tower(s) will be burned with fire.
They will be removed from all the earth,

and they will be thrown into the fiery judgment,
and they will be destroyed in fierce, everlasting judgment.

¹⁰{**And the righteous will arise from his sleep,**
and wisdom will arise and be given to them.}

11–17   . . . .

¹⁸And now I tell you, my children,
and I show you the paths of righteousness and the paths of violence,
and I shall show you them again, that you may know what is coming.

¹⁹And now hear me, my children,
and walk in the paths of righteousness,
and do not walk in the paths of violence;
for they will perish forever
– all who walk in the paths of iniquity."

1 Enoch 92:2-5   Hermeneia, 138–9

²Let not your spirit be troubled because of the times;
for the Great Holy One has appointed days for everything.

³**The righteous one will arise from sleep** [cf. Isa. 26:19; Dan. 12:2];
he will arise and walk in the paths of righteousness,
and all his path and his journey (will be) in piety and everlasting mercy.

⁴And (God) will be merciful to the righteous one, and to him he will give everlasting truth;
and (to him) he will give authority, and he will judge in piety and in righteousness;
and he will walk in everlasting light.

⁵Sin will be destroyed in darkness forever;
and it will not be seen from that day forever.

1 Enoch 98:13-14   Hermeneia, 150

¹³Woe to you who rejoice over the troubles of the righteous;
your grave will not be dug.
¹⁴Woe to you who annul the words of the righteous;
you will have no hope of salvation.

1 Enoch 102:3c-8   Hermeneia, 156–7

³ᶜAnd you, sinners, will be cursed forever; you will have no peace. ⁴**Fear not, souls of the righteous; take courage, you pious who have died.** ⁵And do not grieve because your souls have descended into Sheol with grief, and your body of flesh did not fare in your life according to your piety, because the days that you lived were days of sinners and curses on the earth. ⁶When you die, then the sinners say about you, "The pious have died according to fate, and what have they gained from their deeds? ⁷Look, then, how they die in grief and darkness, and what advantage do they have over us? ⁸Henceforth let them arise and be saved, and they shall forever see <the light>. But, look, they have died, and henceforth (and) forever they will not see the light.

1 Enoch 103:1-4   Hermeneia, 158

¹And now I swear to you, the righteous, by the glory of the Great One, and by his splendid kingship and his majesty I swear to you ²that I know this mystery. For I have read the tablets of heaven, and I have seen the writing of what must be, and I know the things that are written in them and inscribed concerning you— ³that good things and joy and honor have been prepared and written down for the souls of the pious who have died; and much good will be given to you in the place of your labors, **and your lot will exceed the lot of the living.** ⁴**The souls of the pious who have died will come to life, and they will rejoice and be glad; and their spirits will not perish, nor their memory from the presence of the Great One for all the generations of eternity.** Therefore, do not fear their reproaches.

1 Enoch 104:1-7   Hermeneia, 160–1

¹I swear to you that the angels in heaven **make mention of you** for good before the glory of the Great One, and your names are written before the glory of the Great One, ²**Take courage**, then; for formerly you were worn out by evils and tribulations, but now you will **shine like the luminaries of heaven**; you will shine and appear, and the portals of heaven will be opened for you. ³Your cry will be heard, and the judgment for which you cry will also appear to you. For from the rulers inquiry will be made concerning your tribulation, and from all who helped them who oppressed you and devoured you, (inquiry will be made) regarding your evils. ⁴**Take courage** and do not abandon your hope, for you will have great joy like the angels of heaven. ⁵And what will you have to do? **You will not have to hide on the day of the great judgment**, and you will not be found as the sinners, and the great judgment will be (far) from you for all the generations of eternity. ⁶Fear not, O righteous, when you see the sinners growing strong and prospering, and do not be their companions; but stay far from all their iniquities, for you will be companions of the host of heaven. A Refutation of the Sinners Who Are Alive ⁷Do not say, O sinners, "None of our sins will be searched out and written down." All your sins are being written down day by day.

1 Enoch 108:2-3   Hermeneia, 167

²You who have observed (it [the law]) and are waiting in these days until the evildoers are brought to an end and the power of the sinners is brought to an end— ³you wait until sin passes away. **For their names will be erased from the book of life and from the books of the holy ones** [cf. Pss. 69:28; 139:16], and their descendants will perish forever; their spirits will be slaughtered, and they will cry out and groan in a desolate, unseen place, and in fire they will burn, for there is no earth there.

1 Enoch 108:8-15   Hermeneia, 168–9

⁸those who love God, and do not love gold and silver and all the good things that are in the world; but gave their bodies to torment; ⁹and those who from the time they existed did not desire the food that is in the world, but considered themselves as a breath that passes away; and to this they kept. The Lord tested them much, and their spirits were found pure, so that they might bless his name. ¹⁰And all their blessings I have recounted in the books. **And he has recompensed them for their lives**, for these were found to have loved heaven more than their life that is in the world. Although they were trampled down by evil men and heard reproach and insult from them and were abused, yet they blessed me. ¹¹**And now I will summon the spirits of the pious** (who are) from the generation of light; and I will transform those who <have descended into> darkness, who in their bodies were not recompensed with the honor appropriate to their faithfulness. ¹²Indeed, I will bring forth in shining light those who loved my holy name, and I will seat each one on the throne of his honor, ¹³and they will shine for times without number. For righteous is the judgment of God, and to the faithful he shows faithfulness, because they abide in the paths of truth. ¹⁴**And the righteous, as they shine**, will see those who were born in darkness cast

into darkness; ¹⁵and the sinners will cry out and see them shining; and they, for their part, will depart to where the days and times are written for them.

2 Enoch

2 Enoch J32   OTP 1:154

After Adam's transgression, God expels him into the earth from which he had been taken. But he does not wish to destroy him in the age to come. Word "28."|

¹"**And I said [to him], 'You are earth, and into the earth once again you will go, out of which I took you [Gen. 3:19b]**. And I will not destroy you, but I will send you away to what I took you from. **Then I can take you once again at my second coming**. And I blessed all my creatures, visible and invisible. And Adam was in paradise for five hours and a half. ²And I blessed the seventh day [which is the Sabbath] in which I rested from all my doings [Gen. 2:2-3].

2 Enoch 65:6-11   OTP 1:192–3

[J]	[A]
⁶And when the whole of creation, visible and invisible, which the Lord has created, shall come to an end, **then each person will go to the Lord's great judgement**. ⁷[And] then [all] time will perish, and afterward there will be neither years nor months nor days or hours. They will be dissipated and after that they will not be reckoned. ⁸But they will constitute a single age. **And all the righteous, who escape from the Lord's great judgement, will be collected together into the great age. And the great age will come about for the righteousness, and it will be eternal.** ⁹And after that there will be among them neither weariness (nor sickness) nor affliction nor worry (nor) want nor debilitation nor night nor darkness. ¹⁰But they will have a great light, a great indestructible light, and paradise, great and incorruptible. For everything corruptible will pass away, and the incorruptible will come into being, and will be the shelter of the eternal residences.	⁶**When the whole of creation, which the Lord has created, shall come to an end, and when each person will go to the Lord's great judgment,** ⁷then the tome periods will perish, and there will be neither years nor months nor days, and hours will no longer be counted; ⁸But they will constitute a single age. **And all the righteous, who escape from the Lord's great judgment, will be collected together with the great age. And <the age> at the same time will unite with the righteous, and they will be eternal.** ⁹And there will be among them neither weariness nor suffering nor affliction nor expectation of violence nor the pain of the night nor darkness. ¹⁰But they will have a great light for eternity, <and> an indestructible wall, and **they will have a great paradise**, the shelter of an eternal residence. ¹¹How **happy are the righteous who will escape the Lord's great judgment, for their faces will shine forth like the sun**

2 Enoch **J 70:1** *OTP* **1:200**

¹And Methusalem began to stand at the altar in front of the face of the Lord, and all the people, from that day for 10 years, **hoping in an eternal inheritance**, and having thoroughly taught all the earth and all his own people. And there was not found one single person turning himself away in vanity from the Lord during all the days that Methusalam lived.

2 Enoch **70:3** *OTP* **1:200–1**

[J]	[A]
³And when the time of the departure days of Methusalam arrived, the Lord appeared to him in a night vision and said to him, "listen, Methusalam! I am the Lord, the God of your father Enoch. I want you to know that the days of your life have come to an end, and **the day of your rest has come close**.	³And after the ending of the days of Methusalom, the LORD appeared to him in a night vision and said to him, "Listen, Methusalom! I am <the LORD>, the God of your father Enoch. <I want you to know> that the days of your life have come to an end, and **the day of your rest has come close**.

3 Enoch

3 Enoch **28:7-10** *OTP* **1:283–4**

⁷Every day when the Holy One, blessed be he, sits on the throne of judgment and judges all the world, with the books of the living and the book of the dead open before him, all the celestials stand before him in fear, dread, terror, and trembling. When the Holy One, blessed be he, sits in judgment on the throne of judgment, his garment is white like snow, the hair of his head is as pure as wool, his whole robe shies like a dazzling light and he is covered all over with righteousness as with a coat of mail [Dan. 7:9 | Rev. 20:11]. ⁸The Watchers and the holy ones stand before him like court officers before the judge; they take up and debate every single matter and they close each case that comes for judgment before the Holy One, blessed be he, as it is written, "Such is the sentence proclaimed by the Watchers, the verdict announced by the holy ones" [Dan. 4:17]. ⁹Some of them decide the cases; some of them issue the verdicts in the great court in 'Arabot; some of them raise the questions in the presence of the Almighty; some complete the cases before the One Above, and some carry out the sentence of the earth beneath, as it is written,

> Behold, a Watcher and a holy one came down from heaven.
> At the top of his voice he shouted,
> "Cut the tree down, lop off its branches,
> strip off its leaves, throw away its fruit;
> let the animals flee from its shelter
> and the birds from its branches" [Dan. 4:10f. (MT)]

¹⁰Why are the names called Watchers and holy ones? Because they sanctify the body and the soul with lashes of fire on the third day of judgment, as it is written, "**After two days he will revive us, on the third day he will raise us and we shall live in his presence**" [Hos. 6:2f]

3 Enoch **44:7-8** *OTP* **1:295**

⁷I saw the souls of the fathers of the world, Abraham, Isaac, and Jacob and **the rest of the righteous, who had been raised from their graves and had ascended into heaven**. They were praying before the Holy One, blessed be he, and saying in prayer, "Lord of the Universe, how long will you sit upon your throne, as a mourner sits in the days of his mourning, with your right hand behind you, and not redeem your sons and reveal your kingdom in the world [Ps. 20:6 (MT 20:7)]? Do you not pity your sons who are enslaved among the nations of the world? Do you not pity your right hand behind you, by which you stretched out and spread the heavens, the earth, and the heaven of heavens [Isa. 42:5; 48:13; Jer. 10:12; Ezek. 1:22]? Have you no pity?" ⁸Then the Holy One, blessed be he, answered each and every one of them and said: "Since these wicked ones have sinned thus and thus, and have transgressed thus and thus before me, how can I deliver my sons from among the nations of the world, reveal my kingdom in the world before the eyes of the gentiles and deliver my great right hand, which has been brought low by them."

Sibylline Oracles

Sibylline Oracles Book 1:324-386 *OTP* 1:342-4

³²⁴Then indeed the son of the great God will come,
incarnate, likened to mortal men on earth,
bearing for vowels, and the consonants in him are two.
I will state explicitly the entire number for you.
For eight units, and equal number of tens in additions to these,
and eight hundreds will reveal the name
³³⁰to men who are sated with faithlessness. But you, consider in your heart
Christ, the son of the most high, immortal God.
He will fulfill the law of God – he will not destroy it – [Mt. 5:17]
bearing a likeness which corresponds to types, and he will teach everything.
Priest will bring gifts to him, bringing forward gold,
³³⁵myrrh, and incense [Mt. 2:11]. For he will also do all these things.
But when a certain voice will come through the desert land
bringing tidings to mortals, and will cry out to all
to make the paths straight and cast away [Mt. 3:1-6; Mk 1:1-6; Lk. 3:1-6; Jn 1:23]
evils from the heart, and that every human person
³⁴⁰be illuminated by waters, so that, being born from above [Jn 3:3]
they may no longer in any respect at all transgress justice
– but a man with barbarous mind, enslaved to dances
will cut out this voice and give it as a reward –
then there will suddenly be a sign to mortals when a beautiful
³⁴⁵stone which have been preserved will come from the land of Egypt.
Against this the people of the Hebrews will stumble [Isa. 8:14ff. | 1 Pet. 2:4]. **But the gentiles will be gathered under his leadership.**

**For they will also recognize God who rules on high
on account of this man's path in common light.
For he will show eternal life to chosen men
[350]but will bring the fire upon the lawless for (all) ages.**
Then indeed he will cure the sick and all who are
blemished, as many as put faith in him.
The blind will see, and the lame will walk.
The deaf will hear; those who cannot speak will speak [Isa. 35:5-6; 26:19; 29:18-19; 61:1 | Mt. 11:2-6; Lk. 7:18-23].
[355]He will drive out demons, **there will be a resurrection of the dead**;
he will walk the waves [Mt. 14:24-27; Mk 6:45-51], and in a desert place
he will satisfy five thousand from five loaves
and a fish of the sea, and the leftovers of these
will fill twelve baskets for the hope of the peoples [Mt. 14:13-21; Mk 6:30-44; 8:1-10; Lk. 9:10-17; Jn 6:1-13].
[360]And then Israel, intoxicated, will not perceive
nor yet will she hear, afflicted with weak ears [Isa. 6:9 f. | Mt. 13:13-15; Mk 4:12; Lk. 8:10; Jn 12:40; Acts 28:26].
But when the raging wrath of the Most High comes upon the Hebrews
it will also take faith away from them
because they did harm to the son of the heavenly God.
[365]Then indeed Israel, with abominable lips
and poisonous spittings, will give this man blows.
For food they will give him gall and for drink
unmixed vinegar [Mt. 27:34], impiously, smitten in breast
and heart with an evil craze, not seeing with their eyes.
[370]more blind than blind rats, more terrible than poisonous
creeping beasts, shackled with heavy sleep.
But when he will stretched out his hands and measure all,
and bear the crown of thorns [Mt. 27:27-31; Mk 15:16-20; Jn 19:1-3] – they will stab
his side with reeds – on account of this, for three hours
[375]there will be monstrous dark night in midday [Mt. 27:45; Mk 15:33; Lk. 23:44].
And then indeed the temple of Solomon will effect
a great sign for men [Mt. 27:51; Mk 15:38; Lk. 23:45], when he goes to the house of Adonis [Hades]
announcing the resurrection to the dead [1 Pet. 3:19].
But when he comes to light again in three days
[380]and shows a model to men and teaches all things,
he will mount on clouds and journey to the house of heaven [Acts 1:9]
leaving to the world the account of the gospel.
Named after him, a new shoot will sprout
from the nations, of those who follow the law of the Great One.
[385]But also after these things there will be wise leaders,
and then there will be thereafter a cessation of prophets.

Sibylline Oracles Book 2:221-251   OTP 1:350–1

²²¹Then the heavenly one will give souls and breath and voice to the dead and bones fastened
with all kinds of joining...flesh and sinews
and veins and skin about the flesh, and the former hairs [Ezek. 37:1-10].
²²⁵Bodies of humans, made solid in heavenly manner. Breathing and set in motion, will be raised on a single day.
Then Uriel, the great angel, will break the gigantic bolts,
of unyielding and unbreakable steel, of the gates
of Hades, not forged of metal; he will throw them wide open
²³⁰and **will lead all the mournful forms to judgement**,
especially those of ancient phantoms, Titans
and the Giants and such as the Flood destroyed.
Also those whom the wave of the sea destroyed in the oceans,
and as many as wild beasts and serpents and birds
²³⁵devoured; all these he will call to the tribunal.
Again, those whom the flesh-devouring fire destroyed by flame,
these also will he gather and set at the tribunal of God.
When Sabaoth Adonai, who thunders on high, dissolves fate
and **raises the dead**, and takes his seat.
²⁴⁰on a heavenly throne, and establishes a great pillar,
Christ, imperishable himself, will come in glory on a cloud [Mt. 16:27; 24:30; 25:31; Mk 8:38; 13:26]
toward the imperishable one with the blameless angels [Lk. 9:26].
He will sit on the right of the Great One [Acts 7:55-56], judging at the tribunal
the life of pious men and the way of impious men.
²⁴⁵**Moses, the great friend of the Most High, also will come, having put on flesh. Great Abraham himself will come, Isaac and Jacob, Joshua, Daniel and Elijah, Habakkuk and Jonah**, and those whom the Hebrews killed [Mt. 23:34, 37; Lk. 11:49-51].
He will destroy all the Hebrews after Jeremiah
²⁵⁰judged on the tribunal, so that they may receive and make
appropriate retribution for as much as anyone did in mortal life.

Sibylline Oracles Book 2:313-338   OTP 1:353

But as for the others [the righteous], as many as were concerned with justice and noble deeds,
and piety and most righteous thoughts,
³¹⁵angels will lift them through the blazing river
and **bring them to light and to life without care**,
in which is the immortal path of the great God
and three springs of wine, honey, and milk.
The earth will belong equally to all, undivided by walls
³²⁰or fences. It will then bear more abundant fruits

spontaneously. Lives will be in common and wealth will have no division.
For there will be no poor man there, no rich, and no tyrant,
no slave. Further, no one will be either great or small anymore.
No kings, no leaders. All will be on a par together.
³²⁵No longer will anyone say at all "night has come" or "tomorrow"
or "it happened yesterday," or worry about many days.
No spring, no summer, no winter, no autumn,
no marriage, no death, no sales, no purchases,
no sunset, no sunrise. For he will make a long day.
³³⁰To these pious ones imperishable God, the universal ruler, will also give
another thing. **Whenever they ask the imperishable God**
to save men from the raging fire and deathless gnashing
he will grant it, and he will do this.
For he will pick them out again from the undying fire
³³⁵**and set them elsewhere and send them on account of his own people**
to another eternal life with the immortals
in the Elysian plain where he has the long waves
of the deep perennial Acherusian lake.

Sibylline Oracles **Book 3:63-74**   *OTP* 1:363

Then Beliar will come from the *sebastēnoi*
and he will raise up the height of mountains, he will raise up the sea,
⁶⁵the great fiery sun and shining moon,
And **he will raise up the dead**, and perform many signs
for men. But they will not be effective in him.
But he will, indeed, also lead men astray, and he will lead astray
many faithful, chosen Hebrews, and also other lawless men
⁷⁰who have not yet listened to the word of God.
But whenever the threats of the great God draws nigh
and the burning power comes through the sea to land
it will also burn Beliar and all overbearing men,
as many as put faith in him.

Sibylline Oracles **Book 3:767-776**   *OTP* 1:379

And then, indeed, he will raise up a kingdom for all
ages among men [Dan. 2:44; 7:27], he who once gave the holy Law
to the pious, to all of **whom he promised to open the earth**
⁷⁷⁰and the world and the gates of the blessed and all joys
and immortal intellect and eternal cheer.
From every land they will bring incense and gifts
to the house of the great God [Isa. 2:3; Mic. 4:2; Zech. 14:16]. There will be no other
house among men, even for future generations to know,
⁷⁷⁵except the one which God gave to faithful men to honor
(for mortal will invoke the son of the great God).

***Sibylline Oracles* Book 4:179-192** *OTP* 1:389

But when everything is already dusty ashes,
¹⁸⁰and God puts to sleep the unspeakable fire, even as he kindled it,
**God himself will again fashion the bones [Ezek. 37:1-10] and ashes of men
And he will raise up mortals again as they were before**.
And then there will be a judgement over which God himself will preside,
Judging the world again. As many as sinned by impiety,
¹⁸⁵these will amount of earth cover,
And broad Tartarus and the repulsive recesses of Gehenna.
**But as many as are pious, they will live on earth again
When God gives spirit and life and favor**
¹⁹⁰**to these pious ones. Then they will all see themselves
Beholding the delightful and pleasant light of the sun**.
Oh most blessed, whatever man will live to that time.

***Sibylline Oracles* Book 6:10-19** *OTP* 1:407

¹⁰He [Christ] will teach all with wise words.
He will come to judgment and persuade a disobedient people,
boasting praiseworthy descent form the Heavenly Father.
He will walk the waves [Mt. 14:26; Mk 6:48; Jn 6:19]; he will undo the sickness of men;
He will raise the dead [Mt. 11:5; Lk. 7:22]. He will repel many woes.
¹⁵From one wallet men will have surfeit of bread
when the house of David brings forth a shoot [Isa. 11:1]. In his hand
are the whole world and earth and heaven and sea.
He will flash like lightening on the earth [Mt. 24:27; Lk. 17:24]
as the two begotten form each other's sides once saw him when he first shone forth [cf. Jn 8:56].

***Sibylline Oracles* Book 7:139-149** *OTP* 1:413

In the third lot of circling years,
¹⁴⁰of the first ogdoad, another world is seen again.
All will be night, long and unyielding,
and then a terrible smell of brimstone will extend
announcing murders, when those men perish
by night and famine. **Then he will beget a pure mind**
¹⁴⁵**of men and will set up your race as it was before you**.
No longer will anyone cut a deep furrow with a crooked blow;
no oxen will plunge down the guiding iron.
There will be no vine branches or ear of corn, but all, at once,
will eat the dewy manna [Exod. 16] with white teeth.

***Sibylline Oracles* Book 8:76-109** *OTP* 1:419–20

No longer will you have the fame of your pride
nor will you ever be lifted up, ill-fated one, but you will be laid low.

For the glory of the eagle-bearing legions will also fall.
Where then is your strength? What sort of land will be an ally
⁸⁰which has been lawlessly enslaved by your vain thoughts?
For then there will be confusion of all the land of mortals,
when the universal ruler himself comes and judges [Dan. 7:9-10] **on the tribunal the souls of the living and dead**, and the whole world.
Neither will parents be friendly to children nor children to parents [Mic. 7:6 | Mt. 10:35-36; Lk. 13:28]
⁸⁵because of impiety and affliction beyond hope.
Then you will have gnashing of teeth [Mt. 8:12; Lk. 13:28] and scattering and capture
when the fall of cities comes and yawning gaps in the earth.
When the purple dragon [Isa. 27:1; Dan. 7 | Rev. 12; 13] comes on the waves,
pregnant with a host, and will nurture your children
⁹⁰when famine and civil war are at hand;
then the end of the world and the last day is near,
and the judgment of the immortal God for the approved elect.
First there will be implacable wrath of Romans.
A bloodthirsty time, and wretched life will come.
⁹⁵Who to you, Italian land, great savage nation.
You did not perceive whence you came, naked and unworthy
to the light of the sun, **so that you might go again naked to the same place** [Job 1:21; Eccl. 5:15] **and later come to judgment because you judged unjustly**...
¹⁰⁰By gigantic hands, alone in the whole world,
you will come from a height and swell under the earth
in naphtha and asphalt and brimstone and much fire,
and you will disappear and will be blazing dust
forever. Everyone who looks will hear a mournful
¹⁰⁵great bellowing from Hades and gnashing of teeth
as you strike your godless breast with your hands.
Night is equal to all at once, to those who have wealth
and to beggars. Coming naked from the earth, going naked again
to the earth, they cease from life, having completed their time.

Sibylline Oracles **Book 8:169-177**   *OTP* 1:422

Then a holy prince will gain control of the scepters of the whole world
¹⁷⁰for all ages, **he who raised the dead**.
Then Most High will lead there, then, in piteous fate at Rome,
all the men will perish in their own dwellings.
But they will not be persuaded, which would be much better.
But whenever there rises upon all the evil day
¹⁷⁵of famine and pestilence, hard to bear, and tumult,
and the again the former wretched lord
will assemble the council and deliberate how he will destroy . . .

Sibylline Oracles Book 8:202-212   *OTP* 1:423

The entire year will be an age turned upside down.
The sun, seeing dimly, shines at night.
Stars will leave the vault of heaven. A raging storm with many hurricane
²⁰⁵will lay the earth desolate. **There will be a resurrection of the dead**
And most swift racing of the lame, and the deaf will hear
The blind will see, those who cannot speak will speak,
And life and wealth will be common to all [Isa. 29:18-19 | Mt. 11:5].
The earth will equally belong to all, not divided
²¹⁰by the walls or fences, and will then bear more abundant fruits.
It will give fountains of sweet wine and white milk
and honey . . .

Sibylline Oracles Book 8:217-250   *OTP* 1:423-4

The earth will sweat when there will be a sing of judgment.
A king will come from heaven who is to judge
all flesh and the whole world forever when he comes.
²²⁰<u>Both faithful and faithless men</u> will see God
the Most High with the holy ones at the end of time.
<u>He will judge the souls of flesh-bearing men</u> on the tribunal
when the whole world becomes barren land and thorns.
Men will throw away idols and all wealth [Isa. 2:18].
²²⁵Fire will burn land, heaven and sea,
pursuing the hunt, **and will break the gates of the confines of Hades.**
Then all the flesh of the dead, of the holy ones, will come
to the free light. The fire will torture the lawless forever.
Whatever one did secretly, he will then say everything,
²³⁰for God will open dark breast with lights.
A lament will rise from all and gnashing of teeth [Mt. 8:12; 13:42; Lk. 13:28].
The light of the sun will be eclipsed and the troupes of stars.
He will roll up heaven. The light of the moon will perish [Isa. 34:4 | Rev. 6:12-14].
He will elevate ravines, and destroy the heights of hills [Isa. 40:4].
²³⁵No longer will mournful height appear among men.
Mountains will be equal to plains, and all the sea
will no longer bear voyage. For earth will then be parched
with its springs. Bubbling rivers will fail.
A trumpet from heaven will issue a most mournful sound [Mt. 24:31; 1 Cor. 15:52; 1 Thess. 4:16],
²⁴⁰wailing for the defilement of limbs and the woes of the world.
The gaping earth will then show the abyss of the nether world.
All will come to the tribunal of God the king.
A river of fire and brimstone will flow from heaven.
There will then be a sign for all men, a most clear seal:
²⁴⁵the wood among the faithful, the desired horn [Lk. 1:69],

the life of pious men, but the scandal of the world [Rom. 9:33; 1 Cor. 1:17-25;
1 Pet. 2:6-8],
illuminating the elect [1 Pet. 2:9] with waters in twelve streams.
An iron shepherd's rod will prevail [Ps. 2:9 | Rev. 2:27; 12:5; 19:15].
This is our God, now proclaimed in acrostics,
[250]the king, the immortal savior, who suffered for us.

Sibylline Oracles **Book 8:251-257**　　　　　　　　　　　　*OTP* **1:424**
Moses prefigured him [Christ], stretching out his holy arms [Exod. 17:11],
concerning Amalek by faith so that the people might know
that he is elect and precious with God his father,
the staff of David and the stone he promised [Isa. 11:1 | Jn. 3:36; 1 Pet. 2:6].
[255]**The one who has believed in him will have eternal life**.
For he will come to creation nor in glory, but as a man,
pitiable, without honor or form, so that he might give hope to the pitiable [Isa. 53:2-3].

Sibylline Oracles **Book 8:282-293**　　　　　　　　　　　　*OTP* **1:424–5**
Perceiving everything and seeing everything and listening to everything,
he [Christ] will observe the heart and lay it bare for trial.
He himself is the hearing and mind and sight and reason
[285]of all, who creates forms, to whim everything is subject,
who saves the dead and cures every disease.
Later he will come into the hands of lawless and faithless men,
and they will give blows to God with unholy hands
and poisonous spittings with polluted mouths.
[290]Then he will stretch out his back and give it to the whips [Isa. 50:6]
(for he will hand over to the world the holy virgin) [Jn 19:26f.].
Beaten, he will be silent, lest anyone recognize
who he is, whose son, and whence he came, **so that he may speak to the dead**;

Sibylline Oracles **Book 8:310-317**　　　　　　　　　　　　*OTP* **1:425**
[310]**He will come to Hades announcing hope for all** [1 Pet. 3:19; 4:6]
the holy ones, the end of the ages and last day,
and he will complete the fate of death when he has slept the third day.
And then, returning from the dead, he will come to light,
first of the resurrection [1 Cor. 15:20], showing a beginning to the elect,
[315]having washed off their former vies with the waters
of an immortal spring, so that, born from above [Jn. 3:3, 7],
they may no longer serve the lawless customs of the world.

Sibylline Oracles **Book 8:412-418**　　　　　　　　　　　　*OTP* **1:427**
For I will melt all things and separate them into clear air.
I will roll up heaven [Isa. 34:4; Rev. 6:14], open the recesses of the earth,
And then I will raise the dead, having undone fate

⁴¹⁵**and the sting of death** [1 Cor. 15:55], **and later I will come to judgement, judging the life of pious and impious men**.
I will set ram by ram and shepherd by shepherd
and calf by calf, near each other for trial.

Sibylline Oracles Fragment 3:41-49   *OTP* 1:471
You are not willing to become sober and come to a prudent mind
And know God the king who oversees all.
Therefore the gleam of blazing fire comes upon you.
You will be burned with torches all day, throughout eternity,
⁴⁵Shamed by lies on account of useless idols.
But those who honour the true eternal God
inherit life, dwelling in the luxuriant garden [Mt. 19:29; Mk 10:17; Lk. 18:18]
of Paradise for the time of eternity,
feasting on sweet bread from starry heaven [Exod. 16:4; Jn 6:31-33].

The Apocryphon of Ezekiel

OTP 1:492–4

The Apocryphon of Ezekiel (*Fragment 1*)
Epiphanius, *Against Heresies* 64.70, 5-17

Leviticus Rabbah 4.5

Introduction
"**For the dead will be raised and those in the tombs will be lifted up**," speaks the prophet [**Isa. 26:19 (LXX)**]. And also, so that I might not pass over in silence **the things mentioned about the resurrection by Ezekiel the prophet in his own apocryphon**, I will present them here also. For speaking enigmatically, he refers to the righteous judgment, in which soul and body share:

Introduction (*b. Sanh.* 91ab)
Antonius said to Rabbi, "The body and spirit are both able to escape from judgment. How? The body says, 'The spirit is sinned, for from the day it separated from me, behold, I have been lying like a silent stone in the grave.' Also the spirit can say, 'The body sinned, for from the day I separated from it, behold I have been flying in the air like a bird.' And he (Rabbi) said to him, "I will give you an illustration:"

The lame and blind mend in the garden

¹A certain king had everyone in his kingdom drafted, and had no civilians except two only: one lame man and one blind man, and each one sat by himself and lived by himself. ²And when the king was preparing a wedding feast for his own son [Mt. 22:2; Lk. 14:16], he invited all those in his kingdom, but he snubbed the two civilians, the lame man and the blind man. ³And they were indignant within themselves and resolved to carry out a plot against the king.

⁴Now the king had a garden and the blind man called out from a distance to the lame man, saying, "How much would our crumb of bread have been among the crows who were invited to the party? So come on, just as he did to us, let us retaliate (against) him." ⁵But the other asked, "In what way?"

Lame and blind men in the garden (*Lev. Rab.* 4.5)
Rabbi Ishmael taught: This may be compared to a king who possessed a garden which had beautiful early figs. And he set in it two guards, one lame man and one blind man to guard it. He said to them, 'Be careful with these figs'.

After a little while the lame man said to the blind man, 'I see beautiful early figs'. He (the blind man) said to him, 'Come and let us eat (them)'. He (the lame man) said to him, 'And am I able to walk?' The blind man said to him, 'And can I see?' What did they do?

⁶And he said, "Let us go into his garden and there destroy the things of the garden." ⁷And the blind one spoke, "But how can I, being lame and unable to crawl?" ⁸And the blind one spoke, "What am I able to do myself, unable to see where I am going? But let us use subterfuge." ⁹Plucking the grass near him and braiding a rope, he threw (it) to the blind man and said, "Take hold and come along the rope to me." ¹⁰And he did as he (the lame man) had urged (and) when he approached, he said, "Come to me, be (my) feet and carry me, and I will be your eyes, guiding you from above to the right and left." ¹¹And doing this they went down into the garden. ¹²Furthermore, whether they damaged or did not damage (anything), nevertheless the footprints were visible in the garden.

The lame man rode upon the shoulders of the blind man and they picked the early figs and they ate them. They left and returned, this one in his place and this one in his place.

¹³Now when the partygoers dispersed from the wedding feast, going down into the garden they were amazed to find footprints in the garden. ¹⁴And they reported these things to the king, saying, "Everyone in the kingdom is a soldier and no one is a civilian. So how then are there footprints of civilians in the garden?" ¹⁵And he was astounded.

After a few days the king came.

Parenthetic remark by Epiphanius
So says the parable of the apocryphon, **making it clear that it refers to a man**, for God is ignorant of nothing. For the story says:

The judgment of the intruders

2 ¹He summoned the lame man and the blind man, and he asked the blind man, "Did you not come down into the garden?" ²And he replied, "Who, me, lord?" You see our inability, you know that I cannot see where I walk." ³Then approaching the lame man, he asked him also, "Did you come down into my garden?" ⁴And answering, he said, "O lord, do you wish to embitter my soul in the matter of my inability?" ⁵And finally the judgment was delayed. ⁶What then does the just judge do [cf. Lk. 20:15]? Realizing in what manner both had been joined, he placed the lame man on the blind man and examines both under the lash. ⁷And they are unable to deny; they each convict the other. ⁸The lame man on the one hand saying to the blind man, "Did you not carry me and lead me away?" ⁹And the blind man to the lame, "Did you yourself not become my eyes?" ¹⁰**In the same way the body is connected to the soul and the soul to the body, to convict (them) of (their) common deeds.** ¹¹**And the judgment becomes final for both body and soul, for the works they have done whether good or evil.**

He said to them, 'Where are those beautiful early figs?' The blind man said to him, 'And can I see?' The lame man said to him, 'And am I able to walk?'

What did the king, who was clever, do? He made the lame man ride upon the shoulders of the blind man and he judged them as one. He (the king) said to them, 'In this way you have done (this) and eaten them'.

In this way in the time to come the Holy One, blessed be He, will say to the soul, 'Why have you sinned against me?' It (the soul) will say to him, 'Master of the Universe, I did not sin against you, the body sinned. From the day that I went out from it, I have not sinned'. He (God) will say to the body, 'Why have you sinned?' And it (the body) will say to him, 'Master of the Universe, the soul sinned. From the day it went out from me, am I not like a piece of pottery thrown upon a dung-heap?'

What did the Holy One, blessed be He do? He will restore the spirit to the body and judge them as one. As it is said, '*He will call to the heavens from above, etc.…*' [Ps. 50:4]. '*He will call to the heavens*' – to bring the spirit. '*And to the earth*', to bring the body. 'And after this to judge his people'.

Apocalypse of Zephaniah

Apocalypse of Zephaniah 8:1–9:5   OTP 1:514

8:1 ...**They helped me and set me on that boat.** ²Thousands of thousands and myriads of myriads of angels gave praise before me. ³**I, myself, put on an angelic garment**, I saw all of those angels praying. ⁴I, myself, prayed together with them, I knew their language, which they spoke with me. ⁵Now, moreover, my sons, this is the trial because it is necessary that the good and the evil be weighted in a balance. 9:1Then a great angel came forth having a golden trumpet in his hand, and he blew it three times over my head, saying, **"Be courageous! O one who has triumphed. Prevail! O one who has prevailed. For you have triumphed over the accuser, and you have escaped from the abyss and Hades. ²You will now cross over the crossing place. For your name is written in the Book of the Living."** ³I wanted to embrace him, (but) I was unable to embrace the great angel because his glory is great.

⁴Then he ran to **all the righteous ones, namely, Abraham and Isaac and Jacob and Enoch and Elijah and David**. ⁵He spoke with them as friend to friend speaking with one another.

Greek Apocalypse of Ezra

Greek Apocalypse of Ezra 1:21–2:3 and 5:20-23   OTP 1:572, 577

1:21And Ezra said, "It were better if man were not born; it were well if he were not alive. ²²The dumb beasts are a better thing than man, for they do not have punishment. ²³[You to]ok us and delivered us to judgment. ²³Woe to the sinners in the world to come, for their condemnation is endless and the flame unquenched."

2:1As I said this to him, Michael and Gabriel and **all the apostles** came and said, "Greetings!" ²[And Ezra said, "Faithful man of God!] ³Arise and come hither with me, O Lord, to judgment." And God said, "Behold I am giving you my covenant, both mine and yours, so that you will accept it."

5:20And the prophet said, "Lord, reveal to me the punishments and Paradise." ²¹And the angels led me away to the east [cf. Gen. 2:8] and I saw the tree of life. ²²And I saw there Enoch and Elijah and Moses and **Peter and Paul and Luke and Matthew and all the righteous and the patriarchs**. ²³And I saw there the [punishment] of the air and the blowing of the winds and the storehouses of the ice and the eternal punishment.

Greek Apocalypse of Ezra 4:35-36   OTP 1:575

³⁵And God said, "Hear, my prophet! He [Antichrist] becomes a child and an old man and let no one believe him that that he is my beloved son. ³⁶**And after these things a trumpet** [Isa. 27:3; Zech. 9:14 | Mt. 24:31; 1 Thess. 4:16f.]**, and the graves will be opened and the dead will rise up uncorrupted** [1 Cor. 15:52].

Greek Apocalypse of Ezra 7:1-4　　　　　　　　　　　　　　　　*OTP* 1:578

¹And God said to him, "Hear, Ezra, my beloved one. I, being immortal, received a cross, I tasted vinegar and gall [Ps. 69:21 | Mt. 27:34; Mk 15:36; Lk. 23:36], I was set down in a grave. ²**And I raised up my elect ones and I summoned up Adam from Hades so that the race of men […]. Therefore, fear not death.** ³For that which is from me, that is the soul, departs for heaven. That which is from the earth, that is the body, departs for the earth from which it was taken [Gen. 3:19b]." ⁴And the prophet said, "woe, woe! What shall I do? How shall I act? I know not."

Questions of Ezra

Questions of Ezra A4-7　　　　　　　　　　　　　　　　　　　*OTP* 1:596

⁴The prophet said to the angel, "Lord, who of the living has not sinned against God? ⁵And if that is so, **then blessed are the beasts and the birds who do not await resurrection and have not expected the end.** ⁶If you will crown the righteous, who have endured all tortures, and the prophets and the martyrs when they were taking stones and with a hammer were pounding their faces until there innards were seen, ⁷they were tortured for your sake. Have mercy upon us sinners who have been occupied and have been seized by Satan."

Questions of Ezra A8-10　　　　　　　　　　　　　　　　　　*OTP* 1:596

⁸The angel replied and said, "If there is someone above you, do not talk with him anymore, otherwise great evil will befall you." ⁹The prophet said to the angel, "Lord, I would speak a little more with you, reply to me! ¹⁰**When the day of the end arrives and he takes the soul, will he assign it to the place of punishment or to the place of honor until the Parousia?** […]

Questions of Ezra B1-14　　　　　　　　　　　　　　　　　　*OTP* 1:599

¹He saw the angel of God and asked concerning the righteous and sinners when they go forth from this world. ²The angel said, "**For the righteous there is light and rest, eternal life, but for the sinners, unending tortures.**" ³Ezra said, "If that is so, then blessed are the animals and the beasts of the field and the creeping things and the birds of heaven who do not await resurrection and judgment." ⁴The angel said, "You sin in saying this, for God has made everything for the sake of man and man for the sake of God. And those things in which God finds man, by those is he judged." ⁵Ezra said, "When you take the souls of men, where will you bring him?" ⁶The angel said, "I bring the souls of the righteous to worship God establish them in the upper atmosphere, and the souls of the sinners are seized by the demons who are imprisoned in the atmosphere." ⁷And Ezra said, "And when will the soul which is seized by Satan be delivered?" ⁸The angel said, "When the soul has someone as a good memorial in this world, (this) one releases it from Satan through prayer and (acts of) mercy." ⁹Ezra said, "By what means?" ¹⁰"If sinner's soul has no good

memorial, which helps him, what will happen to him?" ¹¹The angel said to him, "Such a one is in the hand of Satan until the coming of Christ, when the trumpet of Gabriel sounds. ¹²Then the souls are freed from the hands of Satan and soar down from the atmosphere. ¹³And they come and are united each with its body which had been returned to dust and which the sound of the trumpet [Mt. 24:31; 1 Cor. 15:51f.; 1 Thess. 4:16] had built and aroused and renewed. ¹⁴And it raises (it) up before Christ our God who comes to judge (those on) the earth, that is the righteous and the wicked, and requites each for his deeds."

2 Baruch

2 Baruch 11:4-7   Stone-Henze, 89
⁴**Our fathers lay down without pain, and the righteous, see, they are sleeping in the ground in rest**, ⁵for they did not know this sorrow, nor did they hear about what has befallen us [Eccl. 9:5]. ⁶Would that you had ears, O earth, and you, O dust, a heart, and would go and show in Sheol and say to the dead: ⁷Blessed are you more than us, we who live!'

2 Baruch 14:8-14   Stone-Henze, 91–2
⁸But who, O Lord, my Lord, comprehends your judgment [Job 40:8a]? Or who seeks out the depth of your way [Job 28:23]? Or who thinks about the weight of your path? ⁹Or who is able to think about your incomprehensible mind [Job 38:2]? Or who of those who have been born has ever found the beginning or the end of your wisdom? ¹⁰For all of us have become like a breath [Ps. 146:6]. ¹¹For just as the breath rises unawares, turns back, and vanishes [Job 7:7 | Jas 4:14], so is the nature of human beings, who depart not according to their own will. And what will happen to them in the end they do not know. ¹²**For the righteous wait rightly for the end and without fear depart from this life, because they possess with you the power of the deeds that are kept in reservoirs** [Mt. 6:19-20]. ¹³**For this reason, also, they leave this world [or: age] behind without fear, and trusting with gladness they are waiting to receive the world [or: age] that you have promised them.** ¹⁴But as for us, woe unto us who even now suffer insult and at that time wait for evils.

2 Baruch 15:5-8   Stone-Henze, 93
⁵It is right that man would not understand my judgment, had he not received the Torah and had I not instructed him in understanding. ⁶Now, however, since he transgressed knowingly, therefore he will also be tormented knowingly. ⁷**"And regarding the righteous, about whom you said that for their sake this world has come—but also that the one which is to come [will be] for their sake. ⁸For this world is to them a struggle and labor with much fatigue, but that one, then, which is to come [will be] a crown in great glory"** [Rom. 8:18; 1 Cor. 9:25; 2 Cor. 4:17; 2 Tim. 4:8; Jas 1:12; 1 Pet. 5:4; Rev. 2:10].

2 Baruch **21:12-13, 23-25**   Stone-Henze, 96–7

¹²You know where you preserve the end of those who have sinned, **or the consummation of those who have been found righteous**. ¹³For if there were this life only which is here for everyone, nothing could be more bitter than this.

²³Rebuke, henceforth, the angel of death, let your glory appear, let the greatness of your beauty be known, and let Sheol be sealed, so that from now on it will not receive the dead, **and let the reservoirs of the souls give back those who are held in them**. ²⁴For there have been many years like desolation since the days of Abraham, Isaac, and Jacob, and of all those who are like them **who sleep in the earth**, those, for whose sake, you have said, you created the world [or: age]. ²⁵And now, quickly show your glory, and do not delay anything that has been promised by you!"

2 Baruch **23:4-7**   Stone-Henze, 98

⁴Because when Adam sinned and death was decreed for those who are born, then the abundance of those to be born was counted, and for that number a place was prepared where the living will dwell and where those who have died will be preserved. ⁵**Unless, then, the aforementioned number has been completed, no creature lives [again]** [Rom. 11:25; Rev. 6:11]. For my Spirit is the creator of life, and Sheol is receiving the dead. ⁶And furthermore, you ought to hear what will come after these times. ⁷For truly, my salvation [Lk. 21:28; Jas 5:3; 1 Pet. 4:7] is near to come, and it is not far as before.

2 Baruch **24:1-2**   Stone-Henze, 99

¹"**For, see, days are coming and books will be opened in which are written the sins of all who have sinned** [Dan. 7:10 | Rev. 20:12], **and furthermore also the reservoirs in which the righteousness is gathered of all who have been found righteous in creation**. ²At that time, you and the many who are with you will see the long-suffering of the Most High [Rom. 9:22] that is throughout all generations, who has been long-suffering for the sake of all who are born, **both sinners and righteous**."

2 Baruch **30:1-5**   Stone-Henze, 102

¹"And after these, when the time of the advent of the Messiah [cf. Mt. 24:37] will be fulfilled and he will return in glory, then all those who have fallen asleep in hope of him will rise. ²**At that time, those reservoirs will be opened in which the number of the souls of the righteous have been preserved, and they will come out, and the abundance of the souls will appear together in one assembly, of one mind.** The first will rejoice, and the last will not be saddened [1 Cor. 15:52], ³for they know that the time has arrived of which it is said that it is the consummation of times. ⁴**But the souls of the wicked, while seeing all of these, will then waste away all the more,** ⁵**for they know that their torment has arrived and their ruin has come.**"

2 Baruch 42:7-8   Stone-Henze, 108

⁷For corruption will take those who belong to it, **and life those who belong to it.** ⁸**And the dust will be called, and it will be said to it: "Give back that which is not yours, and raise up all that you have preserved until its time."**

2 Baruch 44:9-15   Stone-Henze, 109–10

⁹For everything that is corruptible will pass by, and everything that is mortal goes away. All the present time will be forgotten, and there will be no memory of the present time, which is soiled by evils. ¹⁰For he who runs now runs into emptiness, and he who prospers falls quickly and is humiliated. ¹¹**For that which is yet to be will be desired, and that which is coming after this—we hope for it. For there is a time that does not pass,** ¹²and that season comes that remains forever, and that new world [or: age] that does not return those to corruption who walk into its beginning, but upon those who walk toward torment, it does not show mercy. And those who live in it, it does not bring to corruption. ¹³For they are the ones who will inherit this time of which was spoken, and theirs is the inheritance of the promised time. ¹⁴They are the ones who have acquired for themselves reservoirs of wisdom and with whom treasures of understanding are found. From mercy they have not withdrawn, and they have kept the truth of the Torah. ¹⁵**For to them will be given the world [or: age] that is coming, whereas the dwelling of the rest, who are many, will be in the fire.**

2 Baruch 48:3-8, 45-50   Stone-Henze, 111–12, 115

³You alone know the extent of the generations,
and you do not reveal your mysteries to many.
⁴You make known the abundance of fire,
and the lightness of the wind you weigh.
⁵You investigate the end of the heights,
and the depths of the darkness you examine.
⁶**You command the time appointed that passes by, and it will be observed, and you prepare a dwelling place for those who will be** [Jn 14:2; 2 Cor. 5:1-2].
⁷You remember the beginning which you created,
and the future destruction you do not forget.
⁸You command the flames through signs of fear and force,
and they change into spirits.
With a word you bring into existence that which was not,
and you hold with great power that which has not yet come.

⁴⁵You, O Lord, my Lord, know what is in your creation, ⁴⁶for formerly you commanded the dust that it should give forth Adam, and you know the number of those who were born of him and how they have sinned before you, those who existed, and they have not confessed you as their creator. ⁴⁷With regard to all of them, their end will be their toll, and your Torah, which they transgressed, will requite them on your day.

A. Classification and Anthology of Resurrection Texts

⁴⁸Now, then, let us leave the wicked and inquire about the righteous. ⁴⁹I will recount their blessedness and will not be silent to proclaim their glory, which is preserved for them. ⁵⁰**For surely, just as in a little time in this world [or: age] that passes by, in which you live, you have endured much labor, so in that world [or: age] that has no end you will receive a great light** [2 Cor. 4:17].

2 Baruch 49-52   Stone-Henze, 115–18
THE NATURE OF THE RESURRECTED BODY
⁴⁹:¹"Nevertheless, I will again ask from you, Mighty One, and I will ask mercy from him who made all [things]. ²Indeed, in what shape will those live who live in your day?
Or how will the splendor of those persist who [will be] after then?
³Will they indeed then take this form of the present, and will they put on these members of chains, those that are now [steeped] in evils and through which evils are wrought?
Or will you perhaps change these, those that are in the world [1 Cor. 15:51], as also the world [or: age] [itself]?

THE RESURRECTION
⁵⁰:¹And he answered and said to me: Hear, Baruch, this word,
and write in the memory of your heart everything that you learn.
²**For surely the earth will then return the dead,
which it now receives to preserve them,
while not changing anything in their form.
But as it has received them, so it returns them,
and as I have handed them over to it, so too it will restore them.**

³**For then it will be necessary to show to the living that the dead are living again and that those have come [back] who had been gone. ⁴And when those who know [each other] now will have recognized each other**, then judgment will be strong, and those [things] that were formerly spoken of will come.

⁵¹:¹And after that appointed day will have passed, then afterward the pride of those who are guilty will be changed and also the glory of those who are righteous [1 Cor. 15:51]. ²For the shape of those who now act wickedly will become worse than it is, as they will endure torment. ³**Also, as for the glory of those who are now righteous in my Torah, those who have had understanding in their lives, and those who have planted in their heart the root of wisdom—then their splendor will be glorified through transformations: the shape of their faces will be turned into the light of their beauty** [Mt. 17:2; 1 Cor. 15:41; Phil. 3:21], **so that they will be able to acquire and receive the world [or: age] that does not die, which was then promised to them.** ⁴For those who will then come will groan even more over this, over [the fact] that they rejected my Torah and have stopped their ears so that they would not hear wisdom or receive understanding [Zech. 7:11]. ⁵Therefore, when they will see that those, over whom they are now exalted, will then be exalted and

glorified more than they, and [that] they have all been transformed, these into the splendor of the angels and those into startling apparitions, [then] at the sight of these shapes they will waste away even more. ⁶For first they will see and afterward they will go to be tormented.
⁷But to those who have been saved by their works,
and to those for whom the Torah now is hope,
and understanding is an expectation,
and wisdom is faith,
to them marvelous things will appear in their time.
⁸For they will see that world [or: age] which is now invisible to them,
and they will see a time which is now hidden from them.
⁹And time will no longer make them older [Lk. 20:36].
¹⁰For on the summits of that world [or: age] they will live,
and they will be like the angels,
and they will be deemed equal to the stars [Dan. 12:3].
They will change themselves into any shape they wish,
from comeliness into beauty
and from light into glorious splendor.
¹¹There the expanses of Paradise will be spread out before them. And they will be shown the comeliness of the majesty of the living creatures that are beneath the throne [Rev. 6:4; 7:11], as well as all the armies of angels who are now held by my word, lest they reveal themselves, and who are held by the command, that they stand in their places until their advent will come. ¹²And then the righteous will be more excellent than the angels. ¹³For the first will receive the last, those for whom they had waited, and the last those of whom they had heard that they had passed on.
¹⁴For they have been saved from this world [or: age] of tribulation,
and they have laid to rest the burden of sorrows.
¹⁵For what, then, have humans lost their lives,
and for what have those who were on earth exchanged their soul [Mt. 16:26]?
¹⁶For then they chose for themselves this time that cannot pass without sorrows,
and they chose for themselves that time whose endings are filled with sighs and evils.
But they renounced the world [or: age] that does not make those older who come into it,
and they rejected the time and glory, so that they will not come to the honor of which I spoke to you before."

⁵²:¹And I answered and said: "How can they forget those for whom the woe is preserved then?
²And why, then, do we mourn further over those who die,
or why do we weep over those who go to Sheol?
³Let the lamentations be preserved for the beginning of that future torment,
and let the tears be laid in place for the advent of that destruction that will then be.
⁴But even in face of these [things], I will say:

⁵The righteous—what will they do now?
⁶Delight in the suffering that you suffer now [Mt. 5:10; Acts 5:41; Jas 1:2]!
Why do you look for the decline of those who hate you?
⁷Prepare yourselves for that which is preserved for you,
and be ready for the reward that is laid up for you." ⁸And when I had said these [things] I fell asleep there.

2 Baruch 57   Stone-Henze, 123

¹"And after these, you saw bright waters: they are the spring of Abraham, also his generations and the advent of his son and of his son's son and of those who are like them. ²**Because at that time, the unwritten Torah was named among them**, the works of the commandments were then fulfilled, **and the belief in a future judgment was then born**, and the hope for a world [or: age] that will be renewed was then built, **and the promise of the life that is coming after this was planted**. ³These are the bright waters that you saw.

2 Baruch 66:3   Stone-Henze, 127

³**Not only did he kill the wicked who were alive, but they also took the bones of those who had died from the graves and burned them with fire.**

2 Baruch 76:1-2   Stone-Henze, 132

¹He answered and said to me: "Since the revelation of this vision has been interpreted to you as you have prayed, hear the word of the Most High so that you will know what will befall you after these: ²**because you will surely leave this world [or: age], nevertheless not unto death but unto the preservation of times**, ³ascend, therefore, to the top of this mountain, and all the places of this world will pass before you, the likeness of the inhabited world, the top of the mountains and the depth of the valley, the depth of the sea and the number of the rivers, that you will see what you are leaving where you are going.

2 Baruch 84:5-6   Stone-Henze, 139

⁵And now, Moses spoke to you beforehand, so that it should not befall you—and see, it has befallen you, for you have forsaken the Torah. ⁶**I, too, see, I say to you, that after you have suffered, if you obey those [things] that were said to you, you will receive from the Mighty One everything that has been set aside and preserved for you.**

2 Baruch 85:8-15   Stone-Henze, 140–1

⁸And furthermore, also, the Most High is patient with us here and has let us know what is to be. He has not hidden from us what will befall in the end. ⁹Therefore, before his judgment will claim its own and truth what is rightfully its due, let us prepare ourselves, so that we will possess and not be possessed, and that we will hope and not be put to shame, **and that we will rest with our fathers** and not be tormented with those who hate us.

¹⁰For the youth of the world [or: age] has passed, and the strength of creation is already consumed. The advent of the times is very near, and they have passed. The pitcher is near to the cistern, the boat to the harbor, the journey of the road to the city, and life to [its] consummation. ¹¹Again, then, prepare yourselves, so that, when you have traveled and ascend from the boat, **you will have rest** and not be condemned when you depart. ¹²See, then, the Most High brings to pass all of these. There will not be there again a place for penitence, nor a limit to the times, nor a duration for the seasons, nor a change in the road, nor a place for petition, nor the sending of requests, nor the receiving of knowledge, nor the giving of love, nor a place of repentance, nor supplications for transgressions, nor intercessions of the fathers, nor a prayer of the prophets, nor the help of the righteous. ¹³Then there is there the decree for the judgment of corruption, for the way of fire, and the path that leads to annihilations [Mt. 7:13]. ¹⁴Therefore there is one, through one Torah, one world [or: age], and an end for all who are in it. ¹⁵**Then he lets those live whom he finds and forgives them, and at the same time, he will destroy those who are polluted with sins.**

Apocalypse of Elijah (Coptic Version)

Apocalypse of Elijah 3:5-13   *OTP* 1:745

⁵But the son of lawlessness [cf. Dan. 9:27; 11:31; 12:11 | Mt. 24:15; Mk 13:14; 2 Thess. 2:4] will begin to stand again in the holy places.

⁶He will say to the sun [cf. 2 Thess. 2:9; Rev. 13:13], "Fall" and it will fall.

He will say, "Shine," and it will do it.

He will say, "Darken," and it will do it.

⁷He will say to the moon, "Become bloody," and it will do it [Joel 2:31 | Mt. 24:29; Rev. 6:12].

⁸He will go forth with them from the sky.

He will walk upon the sea and the rivers as upon dry land [Mk 6:48].

⁹He will cause the lame to walk [Mt. 11:5].

He will cause the dump to speak.

He will cause the blind to see.

¹⁰The lepers he will cleanse.

The ill he will heal.

The demons he will cast out [Mt. 12:24-27].

¹¹He will multiply his sings and his wonders in the presence of everyone. ¹²He will do the works which the Christ did [cf. Jn 2:11; 2:23; 3:2; 4:31], except for raising the dead alone. ¹³**In this you will know that he is the son of lawlessness, because he is unable to give life.**

Apocalypse of Elijah 4:24-29   *OTP* 1:748–9

²⁴Now those who are unable to bear up under the tortures of that king will take gold and flee over the fords to the desert places [cf. Mt. 24:16-20; Mk 13:14-19; Lk. 17:31-33]. **They will lie down as one who sleeps.** ²⁵**The Lord will receive their spirits and their souls** [cf. Eccl. 12:7] **to himself.** ²⁶**Their flesh will petrify.**

No wild animals will eat them until the last day of the great judgement. ²⁷And they will rise up and find a place of rest. But they will not be in the kingdom of the Christ as those who have endured because the Lord said, "I will grant to them that they sit on my right hand" [cf. Ps. 110:1; Mk 12:36]. ²⁸**They will receive favor over others, and they will triumph over the son of lawlessness. And they will witness the dissolution of heaven and earth.** ²⁹**They will receive the thrones of glory and the crowns.**

Apocalypse of Elijah 4:30-31   *OTP* 1:749

³¹Sixty righteous ones who are prepared for this hour will hear. ³¹And they will gird on the breastplate of God [cf. Isa. 59:17 | Eph. 6:14; 1 Thess. 5:8], and they will run to Jerusalem and fight with the shameless one, saying, "All powers which the prophets have done from the beginning you have done. **But you were unable to raise the dead because you have no power to give life**. Therein we have known that you are the son of lawlessness."

Apocalypse of Elijah 5:25-39   *OTP* 1:752–3

²⁵**On that day**, the mountain and the earth will utter speech [Isa. 1:2; Mic. 6:2 | cf. *4 Ezra* 5:11]. The byways will speak with one another, saying, "Have you heard today the voice of a man who walks who has not come to the judgment of the Son of God" [cf. e.g. *1 En.* 105:2; 4QFlor 1,11-13; 4QEzra 12:31-33 | Jn 5:22, 27] ²⁶The sins of each one will stand against him [Cf. Wis. 4:20] in the place where they were committed, whether those of the day or of the night [*1 En.* 104:7f]. ²⁷Those who belong to the righteous [cf. *1 En.* 62:11f.; 108:14f.; *Jub.* 23:30 | Lk. 16:23-26] and . . . will see the sinners and those who persecuted them and those who handed them over to death in their torments. ²⁸Then the sinners [in torment] will see the place of the righteous. ²⁹And thus grace will occur. In those days, that which the righteous will ask for many times will be given to them.

³⁰On that day, the Lord will judge the heaven and the earth.
He will judge those who transgressed in heaven,
and those who did so on earth.
³¹He will judge the shepherds of the people [Ezek. 34; *1 En.* 90:1-26].
He will ask about the flock of sheep,
and they will be given to him,
without any deadly guile existing in them.

³²After these things, Elijah and Enoch will come down. They will lay down the flesh of the world, and they will receive their spiritual flesh [1 Cor. 15:44]. They will pursue the son of lawlessness and kill him since he is not able to speak [cf. Mk 1:34],

³³**On that day**, he will dissolve in their presence like ice which was dissolved by a fire. He will perish like a serpent [cf. *T. Ash.* 7:3; *Ap. Mos.* 15-17] which has no breath in it. ³⁴They will say to him, "Your time has passed by for you. Now therefore you and those who believe you will perish." ³⁵They will be cast into the bottom of the abyss [cf. Rev. 20:3] and it will be closed for them.

³⁶**On that day**, the Christ, the king, and all his saints will come forth from heaven [cf. *4 Ezra* 7:28 | Mt. 24:30; 1 Thess. 4:16]. ³⁷He will burn the earth. He will spend a thousand years [cf. Ps. 94:4 vs. Gen. 2:2 | *2 En.* 32:1–33:2; *Jub.* 4:30 | 2 Pet. 3:8; Rev. 20:6] upon it. ³⁸Because the sinners prevailed over it, he will create a new heaven and a new earth [cf. Isa. 65:17; 66:22 | *1 En.* 91:16; *Jub.* 1:29 | 2 Pet. 3:10-13; Rev. 21:1]. No deadly devil [cf. Isa. 25:8 | *4 Ezra* 8:53 | Rev. 20:14; 21:4] will exist in them. ³⁹He will rule with his saints, ascending and descending [cf. Gen. 28:12 | Jn 1:51], while they are always with the angels and they are with the Christ for a thousand years [Rev. 20:4].

Apocalypse of Elijah (Hebrew Version)[4]

'And he lay down and fell asleep beneath a broom-shrub. Then lo, this angel touched him and said, "Get up, eat!" (1 Kgs 19:5); Michael, 'the great prince' of Israel, revealed this mystery to the prophet Elijah at Mount Carmel; (namely), the eschaton and what was scheduled to transpire at the End of Days at the end of the four empires (and) the things which would take place during the reign of the fourth ruler.

A wind from the Lord lifted me (i.e., Elijah) up and transported me to the southern part of the world, and I saw there a high place burning with fire where no creature was able to enter. Then the wind lifted me up and transported me to the eastern part of the world, and I saw there stars battling one another incessantly. Again the wind lifted me up and transported me to the western part of the world, and **I saw there souls undergoing a painful judgment, each one in accordance with its deeds.**

...

Elijah said: **I behold the dead taking form and their 'dust' being reshaped and made like (the forms they had) when they were formerly alive so that they might render praise to God, as scripture states: 'See now that I indeed am He [and there is no deity other than Me; I put to death and I resurrect, I sicken and I heal: none can escape from My power]' (Deut. 32:39). Also un Ezekiel it says: 'and I looked, and behold, sinews were upon them' (Ezek. 37:8). The ministering angles opened their tombs and injected them with their 'animating breaths,' and they revivified. They (the angels) stood them up on their feet.** They shoved everyone who merited punishment into a large hollow place two hundred cubits long and fifty cubits wide. The eyes of the righteous will witness the downfall of all those who did not take pleasure in (observing) the Torah of the Holy One, blessed be He, as scripture states: 'they will go out and see the corpses of those people who rebelled against Me...' (Isa. 66:24).

4. This translation, used with permission, appears in John C. Reeves' book, *Trajectories in Near Eastern Apocalyptic: A Postrabbinic Jewish Apocalypse Reader*, RBS 45 (Atlanta: Society of Biblical Literature, 2005), 31–2, 37–9.

Elijah said: I behold fire and brimstone coming down upon the wicked from heaven, as scripture says: 'the Lord will rain coals of fire and brimstone upon the wicked' (Ps. 11:6). The Holy One, blessed be He, will move the Temple a great distance from the place of eternal torment so that the righteous will not hear the sound of the cry of the wicked (suffering) and seek to obtain mercy for them. 'They will be as if they never were.'

Elijah said: I saw Abraham, Isaac, Jacob, and all the righteous ones in sitting postures, and the land before them was sown with every sort of delightful vegetation. That tree which the Holy One, blessed be He, had prepared was standing in the middle of the garden, as scripture says: 'and there will grow by the stream on its bank on both sides every kind of fruit tree; their foliage will never wither, nor will their fruit ever fail' (Ezek. 47:12). Boats will come 'from En-gedi as far as' Eglayim bearing wealth and riches for the righteous one.

Elijah (may his memory be for a blessing) said: I behold a great city, both beautiful and glorious, descending from heaven wherein it had been built, as scripture states: 'The already built Jerusalem, like the city associated to it' (Ps. 122:3), perfectly constructed and with its people dwelling within it. It is situated by three thousand towers, with 20,000 *ris* separating each tower. Within the span of every *ris* are 25,000 cubits of emeralds, pearls, and (other) jewels, as scripture says: 'I will inlay your battlements with gemstones' (Isa. 54:12).

Elijah said: I saw the houses and the gates of the righteous with their thresholds and door-frames constructed of precious stones. (I saw) the treasuries of the Temple opened up to their doorways [*sic*], and among them were Torah and peace, as scripture states: 'all your children will be instructed by the Lord;[your children will have great peace]' (Isa. 54:13), and it says: 'those who love Your Torah have great peace' (Ps. 119:165), and it says: 'How great is Your beneficence which You have stored up for those who revere You' (Ps. 31:20).

Appendix B

Resurrection Passages in Qumran, Josephus, New Testament, and Early Rabbinic Judaism

Appendix B provides an analysis of resurrection passages compiled from the Dead Sea Scrolls (Table 28), Josephus (Table 29), New Testament (Table 30), Jewish Liturgy (Table 31), and early rabbinic literature (Table 32). These tables are tentative and the author does not claim that they are complete, but they do give an indication of how prevalent resurrection beliefs are in texts not discussed in this monograph, although several of these texts have been referenced in this monograph when deemed relevant. In research currently being concluded by the author, into the resurrection texts appearing among the Dead Sea Scrolls (Table 28), Josephus (Table 29), and Jewish Liturgy (Table 31)[1] dating will be

---

1. Dating the various resurrection texts found in Josephus' writings would not be helpful for this study since they were written during a fairly short time-period. Josephus was born towards the end of the Second Temple Period, in the year of Gaius Caligula's accession (37/38 CE). His writings dates to the tumultuous political period following the first Jewish Revolt, which effectively ended the Second Temple Period. As such, his writings were composed during the latter part of his life: The *Jewish War* (seven books) dates to the late 70s, the *Jewish Antiquities* (twenty books) dates to the mid-90s, and the appendix to *Jewish Antiquities*, *Life*, was completed shortly after 100 CE – falling within a period of about twenty years (Evans, *Ancient Texts for New Testament Studies*, 173–4).

Dating Jewish Liturgy is difficult since "prayers were not written down during the Talmudic times" (David Instone-Brewer, *Prayer and Agriculture*. TRENT 1 [Grand Rapids: Eerdmans, 2004], 95). In the case of the Amidah prayer, it evolved over centuries. According to traditions, *Shemoneh Esreh* originated during the early Second Temple Period with the "men of the Great Synagogue" (*b. Ber.* 33a) or the "120 elders, prophets among them" (*b. Meg.* 17b). Instone-Brewer notes that "the timing of the Eighteen [Benedictions] appear to be linked to Temple sacrifices, and it is possible that they were part of the private prayer service by the priest before starting their duties (*m. Tam.* 5.1)" (Instone-Brewer, *Prayer and Agriculture*, 107). It was not until the end of the Second Temple Period, according to Rabbinic tradition, that the order, number and the wording of the Amidah was fixed by Rabban Gamaliel II of Yavneh and his two disciples, Simeon of Pakula and Shmuel Hakatan (Instone-Brewer, *Prayer and Agriculture*, 108 and Gershom Bader, *Encyclopedia of Talmudic Sages* [Northvale, N.J.: Jason Aronson, 1988], 191).

taken into consideration. However, for the purpose of this appendix, the dates have been excluded. Due to the complicating factor that rabbinical literature tends to contain a non-chronological collection of oral traditions credited to Rabbis living in multiple generations, Table 32, also, does not include the dating of the Rabbinical resurrection passages. These five tables give various categories by which each passage is analyzed and classified (see Table 27). It should be noted that a category only appears in a given table if it is of relevance for the resurrection passages falling within that category. Table 30 shows the uniqueness of the New Testament writings regarding the resurrection belief, since Jesus' death and resurrection functions as proof for the New Testament community.

Table 27. List of categories used in the five resurrection texts tables

Category		Table					Explanation
		28	29	30	31	32	
Date				×	×		Date the book was written.
Passage		×	×	×	×	×	Passage reference.
Notes			×	×	×	×	Author's notes.
Resurrection	Implied		×	×	×	×	A resurrection belief is implied in the passage.
	Stated		×	×	×	×	A resurrection belief is stated clearly in the passage.
Classification	Reference	×	×	×	×		The resurrection passage refers to a resurrection text in the TaNaKh.
	Allusion	×	×	×	×		The resurrection passage alludes to a resurrection text in the TaNaKh.
	Philo-sophical		×	×	×	×	Resurrection passage uses a philosophical argument as proof of a resurrection belief.
	Assumed		×	×	×	×	Since the resurrection belief is assumed, no attempt is made to prove biblically or philosophically that there will be a resurrection.
	Jesus			×			Reference to Jesus' resurrection.
	Miracle			×			Jesus resurrects a person.
	Eschato-logical			×			Eschatological resurrection.
	Jewish/Christian						Jewish, Christian, or a Jewish-Christian passage [J, C, J/C].

B. *Resurrection Passages*   251

Resurrection Texts in the Dead Sea Scrolls

Table 28. List of resurrection texts: Dead Sea Scrolls

Passage	
1QH (1QHodayot)	XI 19-23
	XII 5-XIII 4
	XIV 34-35
	XV 22-31
	XIX 10-14
1QS (1QRule of the Community)	IV 6-8, 11-14
4Q245 (Pseudo-Daniel ar)	Frag. 2
4Q385 (4QPseudo-Ezekiel[a])	Frag. 1-3, 12
4Q386 (4QPseudo-Ezekiel[b])	Frag. 1 col. i
4Q388 (4QPseudo-Ezekiel[d])	Frag. 8
4Q416 (4QInstruction[b])	Frag 2 col. iii
4Q418 (4QInstruction[d])	Frag 69 ii
4Q504 (4QWords of the Luminaries[a])	Frags 1-2 col. vi
4Q521 (4QMessianic Apocalypse)	Frag 1 col. ii
	Frag 2 col. ii-iii
	Frags 7 + 5 col. ii
4Q548 (4QVisions of Amram[f]? ar)	Frag 1

Resurrection Texts in Josephus

Classification of the Resurrection Passages

Table 29. List of resurrection texts: Josephus

Passage		Notes	Resurrection		Classification			
			Implied	Stated	Ref.	Allude	Phil	Assume
Ant.	18.1.3	Pharisees		×				×
	18.1.4	Sadducees						
	18.1.5	Essenes						
War	2.8.10-11	Essenes	×					×
	2.8.14	Pharisees	×					×
	2.8.14	Sadducees						
	3.8.5	Immortality of the soul/ resurrection		×			×	×

Resurrection Texts in the New Testament
Classification of the Resurrection Passages

Table 30. List of resurrection texts: New Testament

Date		Passage	Notes	Resurrection				Classification				
				Implied	Stated	Ref.	Allude	Phil.	Assume	Jesus	Miracle	Esch.
40–100	Mt.	5:3, 10-12	The Beatitudes	x								x
		5:20	Righteous = enter the kingdom	x								x
		6:19-20	Treasures in Heaven	x								x
		7:13-14	The two ways	x								x
		7:21-23	Day of Judgment	x								x
		8:11-12	Feast in Heaven	x								x
		9:18-25	A dead girl/death ‖ sleep	x							x	
		10:8	Jesus sends out the Twelve		x						x	
		10:28	Body/Soul									
		11:5	John's question								x	
		12:38-42	Sign of Jonah		x	x				x		
		13:43	Parable of the Weed		x							x
		16:1-4	Sign of Jonah	x		x				x		
		16:21-28	Jesus predicts His death		x					x		x
		17:2-4	Moses and Elijah	x					x			
		17:22-23	Jesus predicts His death		x					x		
		19:16-28	Rich young ruler	x						x		
		20:17-19	Jesus predicts His death		x					x		
		22:23, 28, 30	Discussion with the Sadducees		x	x						x
		24:29-31	The End of the Age	x		x						x
		25:31-46	The sheep and the goats	x								x

B. *Resurrection Passages* 253

Table 30 continued

Date		Passage	Notes	Resurrection		Classification						
				Implied	Stated	Ref.	Allude	Phil.	Assume	Jesus	Miracle	Esch.
	Mt.	26:63-64	2nd Coming	x								x
		27:52-53	Resurrection of holy people		x					x	x	
		27:62-66	Guarding the tomb		x					x		
		28:1-15	Jesus resurrection		x					x		
60–70	Mk	5:22, 35-43	Jairus daughter death ǀǀ sleep		x						x	
		6:14, 16	Believed that John had been raised from dead	x								
		8:31	Jesus predicts His death		x					x		
		8:35	He who loses his life will save it	x								
		9:4-5	Moses and Elijah	x					x			
		10:17-31	The rich man	x								
		10:33-34	Jesus predicts His death		x					x		
		12:18-27	Discussion with the Sadducees		x							x
		13:24-27	Signs of the End of the Age	x								x
		14:62	The Son of Man coming on the clouds of Heaven	x								x
		16:6, 9, 12, 14	Jesus' resurrection		x					x		

Table 30 continued

Date	Passage	Notes	Resurrection		Classification						
			Implied	Stated	Ref.	Allude	Phil.	Assume	Jesus	Miracle	Esch.
60–70 Lk.	2:29-32	Simeon's praise	x								x
	3:4-6	John's mission	x								x
	6:22-23	Reward in Heaven	x								x
	7:11-17	Widow's son at Nain		x						x	
	7:18-23	John's question		x		x				x	
	8:40-56	Jairus' daughter		x						x	
	9:7-9, 19	Herod perplexed by potential resurrection		x					x		
	9:22	Jesus predicts his death		x					x		
	9:23-27	He who loses his life will save it	x								
85–90 Jn	2:18-22	Rebuild temple in three days		x					x		x
	3:14-18; 4:36, 14	Belief = eternal life	x					x			x
	5:21-29	Resurrection		x				x			x
	6:33-40, 44, 47, 51, 54	Resurrection		x							
	10:17-18	Jesus' resurrection predicted	x						x		x
	11:24-26, 43-44	Lazarus		x						x	
	12:1, 9-10	Lazarus		x						x	
	12:23-25	The Seed has to die		x					x		x
	14:1-4	Jesus will prepare a place for his people	x								x
	20:9; 21:14	Jesus' resurrection		x					x		

B. *Resurrection Passages* 255

Table 30 continued

Date	Passage	Notes	Resurrection				Classification				
			Implied	Stated	Ref.	Allude	Phil.	Assume	Jesus	Miracle	Esch.
Early 60s	Acts 1:22; 2:31-32; 3:15; 4:2, 10, 33; 5:30; 10:40; 13:30, 34, 37; 17:3, 18, 31; 26:23	Jesus' resurrection		×					×		
	9:37, 40-41	Dorcas' resurrection		×				×		×	
	10:42-43	Jesus, the judge	×								×
	13:46	Belief in Jesus ‖ eternal life	×								×
	17:32	Resurrection/judgment		×				×	×		
	20:7-11	Eutychus raised from the dead		×						×	
	23:6-8	Pharisees and Sadducees on resurrection		×							×
	Resurrection of righteous and wicked		×							×	
	Resurrection belief		×				×				

Table 30 continued

Date	Passage		Notes	Resurrection		Classification						
				Implied	Stated	Ref.	Allude	Phil.	Assume	Jesus	Miracle	Esch.
56–57	Rom.	1:4; 4:24-25; 5:10; 6:9-10; 7:4; 8:11, 34; 10:5-9; 14:9	Jesus' resurrection		X					X		
		1:16-17	Righteousness gives life	X								
		2:5-16	Judgment	X								X
		5:18-19	Righteousness brings life	X								
		6:4-5, 8	Jesus sacrifice gives life		X					X		
		8:11	God will give life to mortal bodies	X								
		8:38-39	Nothing can separate us from His love	X								
		14:10-12	Everyone will be judged	X								X
55–56	1 Cor.	6:14	Resurrection	X						X		X
		9:24-27	Win the crown					X	X			X
		15:4, 12-28, 42	Jesus' resurrection		X					X		X
		15:12-57	General resurrection		X			X		X		X
55–56	2 Cor.	1:9	God raises the dead	X								X
		4:14	Resurrection		X				X	X		X
		5:1-10	Resurrection/judgment		X							X
52	Gal.	1:1	Jesus' resurrection		X					X		X
60–63	Eph.	1:15-23	Jesus' resurrection		X					X		X
		2:1-10	Made alive in Christ	X						X		X
		2:19-22; 3:6	Member of God's household	X								
		4:7-13	Body of Christ	X						X		

B. *Resurrection Passages*   257

Table 30 continued

Date		Passage	Notes	Resurrection				Classification				
				Implied	Stated	Ref.	Allude	Phil.	Assume	Jesus	Miracle	Esch.
c. 61	Phil.	2:6-11	Jesus' resurrection	x		x						
		3:10-11, 14	Resurrection, the Heavenly price		x					x		x
		3:20-21	Citizens of Heaven	x								x
c. 62	Col.	1:9-14	A part of His kingdom	x						x		
		2:12-13, 20; 3:1-4	Jesus' resurrection/our resurrection		x					x		x
50	1 Thes.	1:10	Jesus' resurrection/judgment		x					x		x
		4:13-18	Resurrection		x				x	x		x
50	2 Thes.	1:5-10	God's judgment	x				x	x	x		x
62-66	1 Tim.	6:12, 18-19	Eternal life	x					x	x		x
65-67	2 Tim.	1:10-12	Death destroyed	x						x		x
		2:8-13, 18-19	Resurrection		x				x	x		x
		4:7-8	Crown of righteousness	x				x	x			x
62-66	Tit.	2:11-14; 3:7	God, our savior	x					x	x		x
66-70	Heb.	2:14-15	Freed from death	x						x		x
		6:2	Resurrection		x							x
		9:15, 27-28	Promised eternal inheritance	x					x	x		x
		10:35-39	Receive the promise	x					x			x
		11:4, 6, 10, 13, 16, 19, 35, 39-40	Resurrection		x				x			x
		12:22-24, 28-29	Heavenly Jerusalem	x					x	x		x
		13:20	Jesus' resurrection		x					x		
45-50	Jas	4:10	Sin → Death	x				x	x			x

Table 30 continued

Date	Passage	Notes	Resurrection		Classification						
			Implied	Stated	Ref.	Allude	Phil.	Assume	Jesus	Miracle	Esch.
62–64	1 Pet. 1:3-9, 11, 21	Jesus' resurrection → resurrection		×							×
	3:18-21	Jesus' resurrection saves		×					×		×
	4:5-6	God judges living and dead	×				×	×			×
	4:13, 16-18	Suffering = reward	×				×		×		×
	5:1, 4	Crown of glory	×					×			×
64–68	2 Pet. 1:10-11	Great reward	×					×	×		×
	2:4-22	God's judgment		×				×	×		×
	3:4-13	God's judgment	×				×	×	×		×
c. 90	1 Jn 2:17, 25; 4:17; 5:10-13	Belief in Jesus → life	×						×		
60–65	Jude 6	Judgment	×					×			×
	9	Moses' death/resurrection	×					×			×
	14-15	Judgment	×					×			×
	21	Eternal life	×					×	×		
81–96	Rev. 1:18	Keys of death	×						×		
	2:7; 3:21	The one who conquers will eat from the Tree of Life/sit with Jesus on his throne	×			×					×
	20:4-6, 12-15	The first and second resurrection/judgment		×							×

B. *Resurrection Passages*

Resurrection Texts in Jewish Liturgy

Classification of the Resurrection Passages

Table 31. List of resurrection texts: Jewish liturgy

Passage		Notes	Resurrection		Classification			
			Implied	Stated	Ref.	Allude	Phil.	Assume
18 Benedictions	2nd Benediction	Concerning the resurrection		×				×
	12th Benediction	Birkat HaMinim						

Resurrection Texts in Rabbinic Literature

Classification of the Resurrection Passages

Table 32. List of resurrection texts: Rabbinic literature

Mishnah

Passage		Notes	Resurrection		Classification			
			Implied	Stated	Ref.	Allude	Phil	Assume
Sotah	9:15	The Holy Spirit leads to the resurrection which comes through Elijah		×				×
Sanhedrin	10:1-3	These have no portion in the world to come		×	×			×
Berakhot	5:2	Amidah 2		×				×
Avot	4:21-22	"Those who die are [destined] for resurrection"/ Judgment/ Theodicy		×			×	×

The Tosefta

Passage		Notes	Resurrection		Classification			
			Implied	Stated	Ref.	Allude	Phil	Assume
Berakhot	3:9, 24	Prayers		×				×
Sanhedrin	13:3-5	Three groups of people		×	×			

Jerusalem Talmud

Passage		Notes	Resurrection		Classification			
			Implied	Stated	Ref.	Allude	Phil	Assume
Berakhot	5:2	Amidah 2 Rain ‖ Resurrection		×	×			
Ta'anith	1:1	Amidah 2 Rain ‖ Resurrection		×	×			
Ketubbot	12:3	Rabbi's death and his wishes		×	×			
Sanhedrin	10	All Israelites have a share in the world to come, except…		×	×			

Babylonian Talmud

Passage		Notes	Resurrection		Classification			
			Implied	Stated	Ref.	Allude	Phil	Assume
Berakhot	15b	The grave and the womb		×	×			
	18b	Regarding prayers		×				×
	26b	Regarding prayers		×				×
	29a	Regarding prayers		×				×
	33a	Why the rainfall is mentioned in the benediction of the resurrection		×			×	
	60b	Blessing God for restoring souls to dead corpses		×			×	
Sabbath	152b	God will open the graves		×	×			
Pesachim	68a	The righteous are destined to resurrect the dead/God will resurrect		×	×			
	118a	Resurrection Psalm		×	×			

B. Resurrection Passages

Passage		Notes	Resurrection		Classification			
			Implied	Stated	Ref.	Allude	Phil	Assume
Rosh HaShana	17a	Three groups at the Day of Judgment		×	×			
	31a	Resurrection after 1000 or 2000 years		×	×			
	32a	The order of the blessings		×				×
Megillah	17b	The origin of the Amdiah prayer	×		×			
Chagigah	12b	The dew which will revive the dead		×	×			
Sotah	5a	Arrogant people will not resurrect		×	×			
Kiddushin	39b	Every precept in the Torah depends on the resurrection		×	×			
Baba Bathra	16a	Job denied the resurrection of the dead		×	×			
	16b	Esau denied the resurrection of the dead		×	×			
Ketubbot	111a	Who will resurrect (geographically)		×	×			
	111b	Who will not resurrect (the illiterate)/ Resurrection in Jerusalem		×	×			

Passage		Notes	Resurrection		Classification			
			Implied	Stated	Ref.	Allude	Phil	Assume
Sanhedrin	90a	All Israel have a portion in the world to come, except…		×	×			
	90b	Resurrection is derived from the Torah		×	×			
	91a	Can dust come to life?		×			×	
	91b	The parable about the lame (body) and the blind (spirit) men/ Judgment and the world to come/ Resurrection is derived from the Torah		×	×			
	92a	Resurrection is derived from the Torah		×	×			
	92b	The identity of the people whom Ezekiel resurrected		×	×			
	113a	Elijah asked for the keys of resurrection		×				×
Avodah Zarah	18a	No portion in the world to come		×				×
	20b	The holy spirit leads to life eternal		×				×
Chullin	142a	Every precept in the Torah depends on the resurrection		×	×			
Nidah	70b	What conveys uncleanness		×				×

B. *Resurrection Passages*

Midrash Rabbah

Passage		Notes	Resurrection		Classification			
			Implied	Stated	Ref.	Allude	Phil.	Assume
Genesis	13:3-6	Parallel between rain and resurrection		×	×			
	14:5, 8	Two formations, one in this world and one in the next		×	×			
	20:10	You shall return from the dust		×	×			
	21:1	The decree against Adam has a limit		×	×			
	26:2	There will be no death and Sheol will be destroyed	×		×			
	26:6	The righteous will receive a reward while the wicked will burn	×		×			
	28:3	A person will be resurrected from the nut of the spinal column		×			×	
	32:1	The generation of the Flood will neither be resurrected nor judged		×	×			
	35:3	The last blessing is greater than the first		×	×			
	56:1-2	The third day/ Resurrection a reward for worshiping		×	×			
	63:11, 14	Esau denied the resurrection		×	×			
	73:4	Three keys belong to God		×	×			

264   *Afterlife and Resurrection Beliefs in the Apocrypha*

Passage		Notes	Resurrection		Classification			
			Implied	Stated	Ref.	Allude	Phil.	Assume
Genesis	74:1	The land of the living = resurrection		×	×			
	77:1	All God's deeds have been anticipated: Elijah and Elisha resurrected the dead		×	×			
	78:1	Waking up in the morning ‖ resurrection		×	×			
	84:11	Joseph's dream: sun, *moon*, and stars		×	×			
	94	The importance of being buried in Israel		×	×			
	95:1	A person will be resurrected in the same state as he/she died		×	×			
	96:5	The importance of being buried in Israel		×	×			
	102:2	Burial practices		×				×
Exodus	1:1	Esau denied the resurrection		×				×
	15:21	Ten things which God will renew in the Time to Come	×		×			
	32:2	People buried in Israel will resurrect first		×				×
	40:2	The Book of Adam		×				×
	48:2	The day of death is better than the day of birth since closer to the day of resurrection		×	×			

B. *Resurrection Passages*

Passage		Notes	Resurrection		Classification			
			Implied	Stated	Ref.	Allude	Phil.	Assume
Leviticus	18:1	A person will be resurrected from the nut of the spinal column		×	×			
	27:4	Elijah, Elisha, and Ezekiel resurrected the dead → God will resurrect the dead		×	×			
Numbers	11:2	The Abrahamic promise		×				×
	14:1	God has already revived people		×	×			
	15:13	God has already revived people		×	×			
	19:13	The first wilderness generation also has a share in the world to come		×	×			
Deuteronomy	2:9-10	The reason Moses had to die in the wilderness		×	×			
	3:15	Moses counted the patriarchs among the living righteous		×	×			
	7:6	God's three keys/rain ∥ resurrection		×	×			
	10:3	Everything that God does can also be done by the righteous		×	×			

Passage		Notes	Resurrection		Classification			
			Implied	Stated	Ref.	Allude	Phil.	Assume
Lamenta-tions	1:45	The women who threw themselves into the sea believed in the resurrection		×	×			
	2:6	God gave a resurrection promise to Daniel		×	×			
	3:8	God renews our life each morning → resurrection		×	×			
Ruth	3:2	Some people will never resurrect		×	×			
	6:2	See *Eccl. Rab.* 7:17		×	×			
Ecclesi-astes	1:6-7	People will resurrect with their blemishes		×	×			
	1:19-20	As the river returns to its source so will people resurrect from the dead		×	×			
	3:2	Parallel between birth and death		×	×			
	3:18	God has already revived people		×	×			
	5:11, 17	Secret or a public resurrection?/ Parallel between birth and death		×	×		×	
	7:16	Reward in the Age to Come		×	×			
	9:2	A person will be resurrected from the nut of the spinal column		×			×	

B. *Resurrection Passages*

Passage		Notes	Resurrection		Classification			
			Implied	Stated	Ref.	Allude	Phil.	Assume
Esther	9:2	The dead will come alive after three days		×	×			
Song of Songs	1:9	Holy Spirit → resurrection → Elijah		×	×			
	2:2	The hidden bodies in the ground will resurrect		×	×			
	2:18	Acts of kindness → resurrection		×	×			
	7:15	Ezekiel brought the dead to life in the Valley of Dura		×	×			

Bibliography

Afonso, Laurentino Jose. "Netherworld." *EncJud.*
Alexander, T. "פֶּגֶר." *NIDOTTE* 3:577.
Anderson, Gary A. "The Exaltation of Adam and the Fall of Satan." Pages 83–110 in *Literature on Adam and Eve*. Edited by Gary A. Anderson and Michael E. Stone. Leiden: Brill, 2000.
Aptowitzer, V. "Die Seele als Vogel: Ein Beitrag zu den Anschauungen der Agada." *MGWJ* 69 [1925]: 150–68.
Arenhoevel, D. *Die Theokratie nach dem 1. und 2. Makkabäerbuch*. Mainz: Matthias-Grünewald, 1967.
Attridge, Harold W. "Historiography." *JWSTP* 157–84.
Bloch-Smith, Elizabeth. "Burials." *ABD* 1:785–9.
Block, Daniel I. *By the River Chebar: Historical, Literary, and Theological Studies in the Book of Ezekiel*. Eugene, OR: Cascade, 2013.
Blomberg, Craig L. "Matthew." In *Commentary on the New Testament Use of the Old Testament*. Edited by G. K. Beale and D. A. Carson. Grand Rapids: Baker Academic, 2007.
Bock, Darrel L. "Dating the Parables of Enoch: A Forschungsbericht." Pages 58–13 in *Parables of Enoch: A Paradigm Shift*. Edited by Darrell L. Bock and James H. Charlesworth. Jewish and Christian Texts 11. London: Bloomsbury T&T Clark, 2013.
Bock, Darrel L., and James H. Charlesworth, eds. *Parables of Enoch: A Paradigm Shift*. JCTS 11. London: Bloomsbury T&T Clark, 2013.
Boismard, Emile. *Our Victory Over Death: Resurrection?* Collegeville, MN: Liturgical Press, 1999.
Brand, Miryam T. "1 Enoch." Pages 1359–452 in vol. 2 of *Outside the Bible: Ancient Jewish Writings Related to Scripture*, ed. Louis H. Feldman, James L. Kugel, and Lawrence H. Schiffman. Philadelphia: Jewish Publication Society of America, 2013.
Brown, C. "ψυχή." *NIDOTTE* 3:677.
Brown, M. "רְפָאִים." *NIDOTTE* 3:1173–80
Bruce, Frederick F. *The Letter of Paul to the Romans: An Introduction and Commentary*. 2nd ed. TNTC. Leicester, England: Inter-Varsity; Grand Rapids: Eerdmans, 1985.
Buttenwieser, Moses. *Die hebraische Elias-Apokalypse, Part 1: Und ihre Stellung in der apokalyptischen Litteratur des rabbinischen Schrifttums und der Kirche*. 1897; repr., Whitefish, MT: Kessinger, 2010.
Byron, John. *Cain and Abel in Text and Tradition: Jewish and Christian Interpretations of the First Sibling Rivalry*. TBN 14. Leiden: Brill, 2011.
Callaway, Mary Chilton. "The Apocryphal/Deuterocanonical Books: An Anglican/Episcopal View." Pages xxxv–xxxix in *The Parallel Apocrypha*. Edited by John R. Kohlenberger III. New York: Oxford University Press, 1997.

Carson, D. A. "The Apocryphal/Deuterocanonical Books: An Evangelical View." Pages xliv–xlvii in *The Parallel Apocrypha*. Edited by John R. Kohlenberger III. New York: Oxford University Press, 1997.

Cassuto, U. *A Commentary on the Book of Genesis: From Noah to Adam*. Jerusalem: Magnes, 1949.

Cavallin, Hans Clements Caesarius. *Life After Death: Paul's Argument for the Resurrection of the Dead in 1 Cor 15 – Part 1: An Enquiry into the Jewish Background*. ConBNT 7:1. Lund: CWK Gleerup, 1974.

Charles, R. H., ed. *The Apocrypha and Pseudepigrapha of the Old Testament in English*. 2 vols. Oxford: Clarendon, 1913.

Charlesworth, James H. "The Date and Provenience of the Parables of Enoch." Pages 37–57 in *Parables of Enoch: A Paradigm Shift*. Edited by Darrell L. Bock and James H. Charlesworth. Jewish and Christian Texts 11. London: Bloomsbury T&T Clark, 2013.

———. "Preface. The Book of Enoch: Status Quaestionis." In *Parables of Enoch: A Paradigm Shift*. Edited by Darrell L. Bock and James H. Charlesworth. JCTS 11. London: Bloomsbury T&T Clark, 2013.

———. "A Rare Consensus among Enoch Specialists: The Date of the Earliest Enoch Books." Pages 225–34 in *The Origins of Enochic Judaism: Proceedings of the First Enoch Seminar, University of Michigan, Sesto Fiorentino, Italy, June 19–23, 2001*. Edited by Gabriele Boccaccini. Turin: Zamorani, 2002.

———. "Where Does the Concept of Resurrection Appear and How Do We Know That?" Pages 1–21 in *Resurrection: The Origin and Future of a Biblical Doctrine*. Edited by James H. Charlesworth, C. D. Elledge, James L. Crenshaw, Hendrikus Boers, and W. Waite Willis, Jr. Faith and Scholarship Colloquies Series. New York: T&T Clark, 2006.

Chester, Andrew. "Resurrection and Transformation." Pages 47–78 in *Auferstehung-Resurrection: The Fourth Durham–Tübingen Research Symposium, Resurrection, Transfiguration and Exaltation in Old Testament, Ancient Judaism and Early Christianity (Tübingen, September 1999)*. Edited by F. Avemarie and H. Lichtenberger. WUNT. Second Series 135. Tübingen: Mohr Siebeck, 2001.

Christo, Gordon E. "The Eschatological Judgment in Job 19:21-29: An Exegetical Study." PhD diss., Andrews University, 1992.

Collins, Adela Yarbro. "The Early Christian Apocalypses." *Semeia* 14 (1979): 61–21.

Collins, John J. *The Apocalyptic Imagination: An Introduction to Jewish Apocalyptic Literature*. 2nd ed. The Biblical Resource Series. Grand Rapids: Eerdmans, 1998.

———. "The Apocryphal/Deuterocanonical Books: A Catholic View." Pages xxxi–xxxiv in *The Parallel Apocrypha*. Edited by John R. Kohlenberger III. New York: Oxford University Press, 1997.

———. *Between Athens and Jerusalem: Jewish Identity in the Hellenistic Diaspora*. 2nd ed. The Biblical Resource Series. Grand Rapids: Eerdmans, 2000.

———. *Daniel: A Commentary on the Book of Daniel*. Hermeneia. Minneapolis: Fortress, 1993.

———. "Ecclesiasticus, or the Wisdom of Jesus Son of Sirach." Pages 667–98 in *The Oxford Bible Commentary*. Edited by John Barton and John Muddiman. New York: Oxford University Press, 2001.

———. "Enoch, Book of." *DNTB* 314.

———. "Introduction: Towards the Morphology of a Genre." *Semeia* 14 (1979): 1–20.

———. "The Jewish Apocalypse." *Semeia* 14 (1979): 21–59.

———. *Jewish Wisdom in the Hellenistic Age*. OTL. Louisville: Westminster John Knox, 1997.

———. "The Sibylline Oracles." *JWSTP* 357–81.

Constantelos, Demetrios J. "The Apocryphal/Deuterocanonical Books: An Orthodox View." Pages xxvii–xxx in *The Parallel Apocrypha*. Edited by John R. Kohlenberger III. New York: Oxford University Press, 1997.

Cowley, A. E., and Ad Neubauer. *The Original Hebrew of a Portion of Ecclesiasticus (XXXIX. 15 to XLIX. 11) together with the Early Versions and an English Translation, Followed by the Quotations from Ben Sira in Rabbinical Literature*. Oxford: Clarendon, 1897.

Dahood, Mitchell. *Psalms*. 3 vols. AB 16-17A. Garden City: Doubleday, 1965–70.

Day, John. "A Case of Inner Scriptural Interpretation: The Dependency of Isaiah xxvi.13–xxvii.10 [Eng. 9] and Its Relevance to Some Theories of the Redaction of the 'Isaiah Apocalypse'." *JTS* 31 (1980): 309–19.

DeSilva, David Arthur. "Apocrypha and Pseudepigrapha." *DNTB* 58–64.

———. *Introducing the Apocrypha: Message, Context, and Significance*. Grand Rapids: Baker Academic, 2002.

Di Lella, Alexander A. "Conservative and Progressive Theology: Sirach and Wisdom." *CBQ* 28 (1966): 139–54.

Doran, Robert. *Temple Propaganda: The Purpose and Character of 2 Maccabees*. CBQMS 12. Washington, DC: Catholic Biblical Association, 1981.

Doukhan, Jacques B. "From Dust to Stars: The Vision of Resurrection(s) in Daniel 12, 1-3 and Its Resonance in the Book of Daniel." Pages 85–98 in *Resurrection of the Dead: Biblical Traditions in Dialogue*. Edited by Geert Van Oyen and Tom Shepherd. BETL 249. Walpole, MA: Peeters, 2012.

———. "Radioscopy of a Resurrection: The Meaning of niqqepû sōʼt in Job 19:26." *Andrews University Seminary Studies* 34, no. 2 (1996): 187–93.

Dunn, James D. G. *Romans 1–8*. WBC 38A. Nashville: Nelson, 1988.

Edrei, Arye, and Doron Mendels. "A Split Jewish Diaspora: Its Dramatic Consequences." *JSP* 16, no. 2 (2007): 91–137.

———. "A Split Jewish Diaspora: Its Dramatic Consequences II." *JSP* 17, no. 3 (2008): 163–87.

Elledge, C. D. "Resurrection of the Dead: Exploring Our Earliest Evidence Today." Pages 22–52 in *Resurrection: The Origin and Future of a Biblical Doctrine*. Edited by James H. Charlesworth, C. D. Elledge, J. L. Crenshaw, H. Boers, and W. W. Willis, Jr. Faith and Scholarship Colloquies Series. New York: T&T Clark, 2006.

———. *Resurrection of the Dead in Early Judaism: 200 BCE–CE 200*. Oxford: Oxford University Press, 2017.

Embry, Brad, Archie T. Wright, and Ronald Herms, eds. *Early Jewish Literature: An Anthology*. Grand Rapids: Eerdmans, 2018.

Evans, Craig A. *Ancient Texts for New Testament Studies: A Guide to the Background Literature*. Peabody, MA: Hendrickson, 2005.

Fee, Gordon D. *The First Epistle to the Corinthians*. New International Commentary on the New Testament. Grand Rapids: Eerdmans, 1987.

Feldman, Louis H., James L. Kugel, and Lawrence H. Schiffman, eds. *Outside the Bible: Ancient Jewish Writings Related to Scripture*. 3 vols. Philadelphia: Jewish Publication Society of America, 2013.

Flusser, David. *Judaism and the Origins of Christianity*. Jerusalem: Magnes, 1988.

Frankovic, Joseph. "Treasures in Heaven." Online: http://www.jerusalemperspective.com/4661.

Fritsch, C. T. "Pseudepigrapha." *IDB* 3:960–4.
Galenieks, Eriks. "The Nature, Function, and Purpose of the Term Sheol in the Torah, Prophets and Writings." PhD diss., Andrews University, 2005.
Gane, Roy. *Cult and Character: Purification Offerings, Day of Atonement, and Theodicy.* Winona Lake, IN: Eisenbrauns, 2005.
Geoltrain, Pierre. *Le traité de la Vie Contemplativa de Philon d'Alexandrie.* Sem 10. Paris: Adrien-Maisonneuve, 1960.
Gilbert, Maurice. "Immortalité? Résurrection? Faut-il choisir?" Pages 282–7 in *Le Judaïsme à l'aube de l'ère chrétienne: XVIIIe congrès de l'association catholique fançaise pour l'étude de la bible (Lyon, Septembre 1999).* Paris: Cerf, 1999.
Gillman, Neil. *The Death of Death: Resurrection and Immortality in Jewish Thought.* Woodstock, VT: Jewish Lights, 1997.
Goldstein, Jonathan A. *2 Maccabees.* AB 41A. Garden City, NY: Doubleday, 1983.
―――. "Creation Ex Nihilo: Recantations and Restatement." *Journal of Jewish Studies* 38 (1987): 187–94.
―――. "The Origins of the Doctrine of Creation Ex Nihilo." *Journal of Jewish Studies* 35 (1984): 127–35.
Grabbe, Lester L. *Wisdom of Solomon.* Sheffield: Sheffield Academic, 1997.
Greenspoon, Leonard J. "The Origin of the Idea of Resurrection." Pages 189–240 in *Traditions in Transformation: Turning Points in Biblical Faith.* Edited by B. Halpern and J. Levenson. Winona Lake, IN: Eisenbrauns, 1981.
Haas, Volkert. "Death and Afterlife in Hittite Thought." Pages 2021–30 in vol. 2 of *Civilization of the Ancient Near East.* Edited by Jack M. Sasson. 2 vols. New York: Scribner's Sons, 1995.
Hachlili, Rachel. "Burials: Ancient Jewish." *ABD* 1:789–94.
―――. *Jewish Funerary Customs, Practices and Rites in the Second Temple Period.* JSJSup 94. Leiden/Boston: Brill, 2005.
Halivni, David Weiss. *Revelation Restored: Divine Writ and Critical Responses.* Radical Traditions: Theology in a Postcritical Key. Boulder, CO: Westview, 1997.
Harrelson, Walter J. "The Apocryphal/Deuterocanonical Books: A Protestant View." Pages xl–xliii in *The Parallel Apocrypha.* Edited by John R. Kohlenberger III. New York: Oxford University Press, 1997.
Harrington, Daniel J. *Invitation to the Apocrypha.* Grand Rapids: Eerdmans, 1999.
Hasel, Gerhard F. "Resurrection in the Theology of Old Testament Apocalyptic." *ZAW* 92 (1980): 267–84.
Hillers, Roy. "Burial." *EncJud*[2] 4:291.
Hodgens, David. "Our Resurrection Body: An Exegesis of 1 Corinthians 15:42-49." *MJT* 17 (2001): 65–91.
Horbury, William. "The Wisdom of Solomon." Pages 650–67 in *The Oxford Bible Commentary.* Edited by John Barton and John Muddiman. New York: Oxford University Press, 2001.
Instone-Brewer, David. *Prayer and Agriculture.* TRENT 1. Grand Rapids: Eerdmans, 2004.
Jewish Encyclopedia. "Apocalyptic Literature, Neo-Hebraic." No pages. Cited 17 April 2013. Online: http://www.jewishencyclopedia.com/articles/1643-apocalyptic-literature-neo-hebraic.
Johnston, Philip S. *Shades of Sheol: Death and Afterlife in the Old Testament.* Downers Grove, IL: InterVarsity, 2002.
Judaica, Editorial Staff Encyclopaedia. "Afterlife." *EncJud* 2:337.

Kearns, Conleth. *The Expanded Text of Ecclesiasticus: Its Teaching on the Future Life as a Clue to Its Origin*. DCLS 11. Berlin: de Gruyter, 2011.
Kee, Howard Clark, ed. *Cambridge Annotated Study Apocrypha: New Revised Standard Version*. Cambridge: Cambridge University Press, 1994.
Kim, Daewoong, "Wisdom and Apocalyptic in 2 Baruch." *Hen* 33 (2011): 250–74.
Koenen, L. "Die Prophezeiungen des Töpfers." *ZPE* 2 (1968): 178–209.
Kohlenberger, John R. III., ed. *The Parallel Apocrypha*. New York: Oxford University Press, 1997.
Kolarcik, Michael. *The Ambiguity of Death in the Book of Wisdom 1–6: A Study of Literary Structure and Interpretation*. AnBib 127. Rome: Pontificio Istituto Biblico, 1991.
Kwon, Ohyun. "The Formation and Development of Resurrection Faith in Early Judaism." PhD diss., New York University, 1984.
Laato, Antti, and Johannes C. de Moor, eds. *Theodicy in the World of the Bible: The Goodness of God and the Problem of Evil*. Leiden: Brill, 2003.
Larcher, C. *Études sur le livre de la Sagesse*. Paris: Gabalda, 1969.
Lesko, Leonard H. "Death and Afterlife in Ancient Egyptian Thought." Pages 1763–74 in vol. 2 of *Civilizations of the Ancient Near East*. Edited by Jack M. Sasson. 2 vols. New York: Scribner's Sons, 1995.
Levenson, Jon Douglas. *Resurrection and the Restoration of Israel: The Ultimate Victory of the God of Life*. New Haven: Yale University Press, 2006.
Lied, Liv Ingeborg. "Recognizing the Righteous Remnant? Resurrection, Recognition and Eschatological Reversal in 2 Baruch 47–52." Pages 311–35 in *Metamorphoses: Resurrection, Body and Transformative Practices in Early Christianity*. Edited by Turid Karlsen Seim and Jorunn Økland. New York: de Gruyter, 2009.
Linebaugh, Jonathan A. *God, Grace, and Righteousness in Wisdom of Solomon and Paul's Letter to the Romans: Texts in Conversation*. NovTSup 152. Leiden: Brill, 2013.
Longenecker, Bruce W. *2 Esdras*. Sheffield: Sheffield Academic, 1995.
Martin-Achard, Robert. *From Death to Life: A Study of the Development of the Doctrine of the Resurrection in the Old Testament*. Edinburgh: Oliver & Boyd, 1960.
McCown, C. C. "Egyptian Apocalyptic Literature." *HTR* 8 (1925): 397–400.
McGlynn, Moyna. *Devine Judgement and Divine Benevolence in the Book of Wisdom*. WUNT 2/139. Tübingen: Mohr Siebeck, 2001.
McNamara, Martin. *Targum and Testament Revisited: Aramaic Paraphrases of the Hebrew Bible*. 2nd ed. Grand Rapids: Eerdmans, 2010.
Mendels, Doron. "Why Paul Went West: The Difference Between the Jewish Diasporas." *BAR* 37, no. 1 (2011): 49–54, 68.
Metzger, B. M. "The Fourth Book of Ezra." *OTP* 1:519–20.
Milgrom, Jacob. *Leviticus 1–16: A New Translation with Introduction and Commentary*. AB 3. New York: Doubleday, 1991.
Milik, J. T. *Ten Years of Discovery in the Wilderness of Judea*. SBT 26. London: SCM, 1959.
Mueller, James R. *The Five Fragments of the Apocryphon of Ezekiel: A Critical Study*. JSPSup 5. Sheffield: Sheffield Academic, 1994.
Mueller, James R., and G. Robbins. "Vision of Ezra." *OTP* 1:538.
Mueller, James R., and S. E. Robinson. "Apocryphon of Ezekiel." *OTP* 1:487–90.
Myers, Jacob M. *1 and 2 Esdras*. AB 42. Garden City, NY: Doubleday, 1974.
Nagakubo, Senzo. "Investigation into Jewish Concepts of Afterlife in the Beth She'arim Greek Inscriptions." PhD diss., Duke University, 1974.

Nickelsburg, George W. E. *1 Enoch 1: A Commentary on the Book of 1 Enoch, Chapters 1–36; 81–108*. Hermeneia. Minneapolis: Fortress, 2001.

———. *Jewish Literature Between the Bible and the Mishnah*. Philadelphia: Fortress, 1981.

———. *Resurrection, Immortality, and Eternal Life in Intertestamental Judaism and Early Christianity*. Harvard Theological Studies 56. Cambridge: Harvard University Press, 2006.

Nickelsburg, George W. E., and James C. VanderKam, *1 Enoch: A New Translation*. Minneapolis: Fortress, 2004.

———. *1 Enoch 2: A Commentary on the Book of 1 Enoch, Chapters 37–82*. Hermeneia. Minneapolis: Fortress, 2012.

Odeberg, Hugo. *3 Enoch or the Hebrew Book of Enoch: Edited and Translated for the First Time with Introduction, Commentary & Critical Notes*. Library of Biblical Studies. New York: Ktav, 1973.

Park, Joseph S. *Conceptions of Afterlife in Jewish Inscriptions: With Special Reference to Pauline Literature*. WUNT 2/121. Tübingen: Mohr Siebeck, 2000.

Pfeiffer, Robert H. *History of New Testament Times with an Introduction to the Apocrypha*. New York: Harper, 1949.

Pryce, Bertrand C. "The Resurrection Motif in Hos 5:8–6:6: An Exegetical Study." PhD diss., Andrews University, 1989.

Puech, Émile. "Ben Sira 48:11 et la Résurrection." Pages 81–9 in *Of Scribes and Scrolls: Studies on the Hebrew Bible, Intertestamental Judaism, and Christian Origins, Presented to John Strugnell on the Occasion of His Sixtieth Birthday*. Edited by Harold W. Attridge, John J. Collins, and Thomas H. Tobin. Lanham, MD: University of America, 1990.

———. *La croyance des Esséniens en la vie future: immortalité, résurrection, vie éternelle? Histoire d'une croyance dans le Judaïsme ancien*, 2 vols. Paris: Cerf, 1993.

Reese, J. M. *Hellenistic Influence on the Book of Wisdom and Its Consequences*. Analecta Bible 41; Rome: Pontifical Biblical Institute, 1971.

Reeves, John C. *Trajectories in Near Eastern Apocalyptic: A Postrabbinic Jewish Apocalypse Reader*. Atlanta: Society of Biblical Literature, 2005.

Rodriguez, Angel Manuel. "The Heavenly Book of Life and of Human Deeds." *JATS* 13, no. 1 (2002): 10–26.

Sawyer, John A. "Hebrew Words for the Resurrection of the Dead." *VT* 23 (1973): 18–34.

Schaper, Joachim. *Eschatology in the Greek Psalter*. WUNT 2/76. Tübingen: Mohr Siebeck, 1995.

Scott, J. Julius, Jr. *Jewish Backgrounds of the New Testament*. Grand Rapids: Baker, 1995.

Scurlock, JoAnn. "Death and Afterlife in Ancient Mesopotamian Thought." Pages 1883–93 in vol. 2 of *Civilization of the Ancient Near East*. Edited by Jack M. Sasson. 2 vols. New York: Scribner's Sons, 1995.

Segal, Alan F. *Life After Death: A History of the Afterlife in the Religions of the West*. New York: Doubleday, 2004.

Setzer, Claudia. *Resurrection of the Body in Early Judaism and Early Christianity: Doctrine, Community, and Self-Definition*. Boston: Brill, 2004.

Sigvartsen, Jan A. "The Hierarchical Structures Found in the Books *The Life of Adam and Eve*," forthcoming

Skehan, Patrick W. *Studies in Israelite Poetry and Wisdom*. CBQMS 1. Washington, DC: Catholic Biblical Association, 1971.

Skehan, Patrick W., and Alexander A. Di Lella. *The Wisdom of Ben Sira*. AB 39. New York: Doubleday, 1987.

Steiner, Richard C. *Disembodied Souls: The Nefesh in Israel and Kindred Spirits in the Ancient Near East, with an Appendix on the Katumuwa Inscription.* Society of Biblical Literature: ANEM 11. Atlanta: SBL Press, 2015.

Stele, Artur A. "Resurrection in Daniel 12 and Its Contribution to the Theology of the Book of Daniel." PhD diss., Andrews University, 1996.

Stone, Michael E. "Apocalyptic Literature." *JWSTP* 383–441.

———. "The Fall of Satan and Adam's Penitence." Pages 43–56 in *Literature on Adam and Eve*. Edited by Gary A. Anderson and Michael E. Stone. Leiden: Brill, 2000.

———. *Features of the Eschatology of IV Ezra*. HSS 35. Atlanta: Scholars Press, 1989.

———. *Fourth Ezra: A Commentary on the Book of Fourth Ezra*. Hermeneia. Minneapolis: Fortress, 1990.

———, ed. *Jewish Writings of the Second Temple Period: Apocrypha, Pseudepigrapha, Qumran Sectarian Writings, Philo, Josephus.* Compendia Rerum Iudaicarum ad Novum Testamentum 2. Assen: Van Gorcum; Philadelphia: Fortress, 1984.

Stone, Michael E., and Matthias Henze. *4 Ezra and 2 Baruch: Translation, Introduction, and Notes.* Minneapolis: Fortress, 2013.

Stuart, Douglas. "Malachi." In *Zephaniah, Haggai, Zechariah, and Malachi*, vol. 3 of *The Minor Prophets: An Exegetical and Expository Commentary*. Edited by Thomas Edward McComiskey. Grand Rapids: Baker Books, 1998.

Suriano, Matthew J. *A History of Death in the Hebrew Bible*. Oxford: Oxford University Press, 2018.

Tanzer, Sarah J. "A View from History: The Place of the Apocrypha in the Jewish Community." Pages xxi–xxvi in *The Parallel Apocrypha*. Edited by John R. Kohlenberger III. New York: Oxford University Press, 1997.

Urbach, Efraim E. *The Sages: Their Concepts and Beliefs*, 2nd ed. Cambridge, MA: Harvard University Press, 1979.

VanderKam, James C. *An Introduction to Early Judaism*. Grand Rapids: Eerdmans, 2001.

———. *From Joshua to Caiaphas: High Priests after the Exile*. Minneapolis: Fortress, 2004.

———. "Prophecy and Apocalyptics in the Ancient Near East." Pages 2083–94 in vol. 2 of *Civilization of the Ancient Near East*. Edited by Jack M. Sasson. 2 vols. New York: Scribner's Sons, 1995.

Wacker, Marie-Theres. *Weltordnung und Gericht: Studien zu 1 Henoch 22*. FB 45. Würzburg: Echter, 1982.

Wegner, Paul D. *The Journey from Texts to Translation: The Origin and Development of the Bible*. Grand Rapids: Baker Academic, 1999.

Wenham, G. *Genesis 1–15*. WBC 1. Waco, TX: Word Books, 1987.

Winston, David. "Creation Ex Nihilo Revisited: A Reply to Jonathan Goldstein." *Journal of Jewish Studies* 37 (1986): 88-91.

———. *The Wisdom of Solomon*. AB 43. Garden City, NY: Doubleday, 1979.

Wright, J. Edward. "Baruch, Books of." *DNTB* 149.

———. "Esdras, Books of." *DNTB* 337–40.

———. "The Social Setting of the Syriac Apocalypse of *Baruch*." *JSP* 16 (1997): 81–96.

Wright, N. T. *The Resurrection of the Son of God.* COQG 3. Minneapolis: Fortress, 2003.

Xella, Paolo. "Death and Afterlife in Canaanite and Hebrew Thought." Pages 2059–70 in vol. 2 of *Civilization of the Ancient Near East*. Edited by Jack M. Sasson. 2 vols. New York: Scribner's Sons, 1995.

Yamauchi, Edwin. "Life, Death, and Afterlife in the Ancient Near East." Pages 21–50 in *Life in the Face of Death: The Resurrection Message of the New Testament*. Edited by Richard N. Longenecker. Grand Rapids: Eerdmans, 1998.

Index of References

Hebrew Bible/ Old Testament

Genesis
1–11	139
1	8, 195
1:2	76
1:26-27	173
1:28-29	106
2:2-3	222
2:2	246
2:7	2, 44, 76, 107, 140, 195
2:8	44, 236
2:9	182, 201
2:15	44
2:17	129
3:14-19	127
3:19	2, 7, 76, 128, 129, 146, 147, 159, 190, 222
3:23	190
4:9-10	106, 108, 126
4:9	108
4:10	106–8
4:15	108
5–9	109
5:1	44
5:21-32	127
5:24	1, 97, 156
6:3	102
6:5-7	102
6:5	206
6:11-13	102
6:17	44, 102
7:15	44
7:21–8:1	76
7:22	44
9:1-7	106
9:4-6	106
9:4	107
9:5	106
14:5	77
15:1	198
15:11	32
15:13	76
18:17-32	9
23	3
25:8-9	3
25:8	3
25:17	3
28:12	246
35:18	9
35:29	3
49:29-33	3
49:29	3
49:33	3
50:1-14	3
50:13	3
50:24-25	3
50:25-26	3

Exodus
3:1	200
3:8	199
13:19	3
14:14	199
15:1	151, 153, 154
15:25	58, 196
16	146
16:4	232
17:11	231
32:32	6
34	134
34:29-35	78
35:29-30	172
40:11	44

Leviticus
4:1	151
4:2-35	195
16	9
19:17	191
26:30	32

Numbers
16:33	1
20:24	3
25:2-3	2
27:13	3
31:2	3

Deuteronomy
1:31	44
2:11	77
2:20	77
3:13	77
4:10	200
4:15	200
7:6	199
18:11	2
26:12	1
26:14	1, 12
28–32	41, 48, 81
28–30	167
28:26	3
28:59	44
30:11-20	80
30:19	80, 205
30:20	80
31:21	43, 194

Index of References

Deuteronomy (cont.)		17	34, 37	Esther	
31:26	194	17:1	33, 192	9:2	267
31:30	194	17:17-24	17		
32	41, 45	17:17-22	33	Job	
32:15-30	45	17:21-22	192	1–2	167
32:35	45	18	35	1:21	146, 147, 229
32:36	41, 43, 194	18:37	35		
32:39	45, 48, 171, 181, 246	18:38	33, 192	3	205
		18:39	35	3:13-19	1
32:41-43	45	18:40	35	3:13	7
32:43	42	19:5	246	3:17-19	146
32:50	3	19:8-18	33, 192	5:7	201
		19:15-17	192	7:6-7	167
Joshua		19:15	192	7:7	238
15:8	77	19:16	33, 192	7:11-21	167
18:16	77	21:19-24	33	9:26	198
24:32	3			10:8-12	5
		2 Kings		10:8	206
Judges		1:2-4	33, 192	10:9	7
2:17	191	1:6	33, 192	12:24	198
		1:10	33, 192	14:1	201
1 Samuel		1:12	33, 192	14:12	7
2:6	1, 2	1:16-17	33, 192	14:13	2
2:8	16	2	34, 38	14:14	6
3:18	207	2:1-11	33	19:25-27	5, 6
3:19	192	2:1	192	19:26	5, 6
3:20	192	2:11-12	156	21:18	198
7:7-10	192	2:11	1, 192	21:25	1, 12
10:1	192	4:31-37	17	26:5	77
12:3	192	4:31	7	28:23	167, 238
25:29	9	6:17	192	32:1-2	167
28:7-19	12	8:12-15	192	34:23	43
28:8-19	1	8:24	3	38:1–42:6	167
28:16-19	192	9:1-10	192	38:2	167, 238
		13:20-21	17	38:7	78
2 Samuel		13:21	7	38:16	200
3:31-36	3			40:8	167, 238
5:18	77	1 Chronicles		42:17	6
5:22	77	10:13	2		
23:13	77	11:15	77	Psalms	
		14:9	77	1:1-2	202
2		29:15	200	2	52
3:3-9	50, 52			2:4	197
6:1	76	2 Chronicles		2:9	231
8:27	191	21:12-15	192	8:4-5 ET	173
11:43	3			8:5-6	173

9:6	197	139:16	221	6:9	167
10:16	43	145:13	43	6:11	167
11:5-6	190	145:17	207	7:6	167
11:6	182, 247	145:18	190	7:15	121, 168
13:3	7	146:6	238	8:10	167
15:10 LXX	156	151	27, 28	8:12-14	168
16:10	156			8:14	167
18:7	191	*Proverbs*		8:17	44
18:8	74	1:24-31	59, 197	9:1-10	1
20:6	224	2:18	77	9:5	238
20:7 MT	224	2:31	198	11:5	44, 194, 200
27:1	105	3:18	199	11:8	167
31:20	247	8	52	11:10	167
37:13	197	9:9-10	167	12:1	168
37:25	190	9:18	77	12:6	168
44:25	16	9:27	167	12:7	7, 44, 203, 244
49:19	105	12:28	1		
50:1-6	153, 155	14:27	167	12:8	167
50:4	152-4, 235	16:31	193	12:13-14	168
56:13	105	17:3	58, 196	12:13	46
68:2	198	19:23	167	12:14	202, 207
69:11	198	20:29	193		
69:21	237	21:16	77	*Song of Songs*	
69:28	7, 221	30:19	198	1:9	267
86:15	190	35:2	191	2:2	267
88:10	77			2:18	267
90:15	76	*Ecclesiastes*		5:6	9
94:4	246	1:2	167	7:15	267
97:2	191	1:14	167		
97:3	74	1:26	167	*Isaiah*	
97:5	74	2:1	167	1:2	245
99:6	192	2:11	167	1:17	199
104:29	7	2:15	167	2:3	228
104:32	74, 191	2:17	167	2:18	230
106:28	2	2:19	167	4:2-6	6
107:40	198	2:22-23	205	5:24	58, 60, 196
110:1	245	3:19-21	168	8:14	225
114:4	114	3:19	167	11:1	228, 231
116:7	9	3:20	7	11:4	74
119:2	202	4:4	167	14:9	77
119:165	247	4:7-8	167	14:12-19	46
122:3	247	4:16	167	14:14-19	1
132:3	16	5:7	167	14:19	32, 197
135:14	194	5:9	167	14:20-21	43
138:7	190	5:15	229	17:5	77
139:13-16	194	6:2	167	18:19	2

Isaiah (cont.)
24–27	7
24:18	191
25:8	246
26	47, 78
26:11	47
26:12	44
26:14	43, 77
26:19-21	152, 155
26:19-20	47
26:19	1, 7, 16, 43, 74, 77, 78, 152, 202, 220, 233
26:20-21	78
26:20	44
26:21	47
27:1	229
27:3	236
28:5	198
29:18-19	148, 149, 225, 230
30:15	199
34:3	32
34:4	230, 232
35:4-7	148, 149
35:5-6	225
35:6	171
36:19	225
37:36	32
40–55	7, 52
40:4	230
40:26	44
42:5	224
48:13	224
49:6	37, 38
50:4	48
50:6	48, 231
51:13	44
52–53	47, 52, 62
52:1-2	116
52:2	117
52:13-15	62
52:13	7
52:14	48
53	48
53:2-3	231
53:2	48, 62
53:4	62
53:6	62
53:7-9	62
53:8	48
53:9	48
53:10-12	48
53:11-12	62
53:11	7
54:1	62, 197
54:7	44
54:8	44
54:10	44
54:12	247
54:13	247
54:17	199
56:1	44
56:4-5	62
58:7	199
59:17	245
60:8	199
60:19-20	200, 202
61:1	148, 225
61:10	200
62:3	198
64:4-11	44
65:17-25	109
65:17	203, 246
65:20	109, 197
66	7
66:14	7
66:15-16	74
66:22-24	32
66:22	32, 246
66:24	7, 32, 43, 181, 190, 246

Jeremiah
1:6	201
2:13	105
2:19	197
6:15	59
10:12	224
10:15	59
16:7	12
17:12	105
20:18	205
22:19	3
24:9	198
26:7	1
31:8	171
51:39	7
51:57	7

Lamentations
2:22	44

Ezekiel
1:22	224
1:28	200
3:23	200
13:17-21	9
18:20	205
32:17-32	1
32:18-32	1
34	119, 245
37	4, 7, 119, 142
37:1-14	1
37:1-12	16
37:1-10	140, 141, 143, 145, 226, 228
37:8	181, 246
37:12-13	199
39:9	180
39:12	180
43:7	32
43:9	32
47:12	247

Daniel
1:1-2	76
2	139, 144, 169, 170, 175, 180
2:11	201
2:31-45	169
2:34-35	74
2:37-38	169

2:40	169	7:26-27	72	*Hosea*	
2:44-45	74, 170	7:27	133, 169,	5:8–6:6	4
2:44	169, 227		170, 227	6	7
3:23	28	8:4	43	6:2	4, 133, 135,
3:24	28	8:12	76		223
4	132	8:24-25	43, 44	9:4	1, 12
4:10	223	9:24	76	13:14	7
4:13	132	9:25	76		
4:17	132, 223	9:26	202	*Joel*	
4:23	132	9:27	178, 244	2:31	244
7–12	74, 89–91	10:20	79	3:14	205
7	61, 63, 74,	11:31	244		
	81, 144, 146,	11:36	43	*Obadiah*	
	148, 170,	11:45	79, 180	18	58, 60, 196
	175, 180,	12	5, 6, 61, 63,		
	229		79, 114, 126,	*Micah*	
7:2-28	169		170, 175	1:3-4	74, 191
7:2	74	12:1-3	7, 11, 17, 49,	4:2	228
7:4-5	169		61, 114, 123	6:2	245
7:6	74	12:1-2	7, 207	7:6	147, 229
7:7-8	169	12:1	6, 46, 61, 76,		
7:7	74, 169		79, 114, 123,	*Nahum*	
7:8	169		170, 180	3:18	7
7:9-14	170	12:2-3	4, 61, 63, 74,		
7:9-10	72, 78, 131–		102, 123,	*Zechariah*	
	3, 202, 229		170	2	115
7:9	223	12:2	7, 43, 45, 46,	7:11	241
7:10	136, 175,		49, 61, 77–9,	9:1	43
	239		111, 114,	9:14	236
7:11	146, 169		123, 125,	14:16	228
7:13-14	133		174, 194,		
7:13	74		202, 220	*Malachi*	
7:14	74, 169, 170	12:3	7, 46, 58,	3:5	206
7:18	58, 60, 61,		59, 61, 78,	3:16-18	7
	63, 197		79, 114, 123,	3:19 MT	33, 35
7:19-26	169		126, 130,	3:19-24 MT	38
7:19-20	170		174, 179,	3:19-23 LXX	33
7:19	169		196, 204,	3:19-23	35
7:21	146, 170		242	3:20-22 MT	35
7:22	58, 60, 61,	12:11	244	3:21 MT	35
	63, 170, 175,	12:13	4, 61, 63,	3:22 LXX	33
	197		170	3:23-24 MT	33
7:23	169	12:18	63	3:24 MT	35, 37
7:24-25	169	12:22	63	4:1-6	33, 38
7:25	133, 169,	13	28	4:1	33, 35
	178	14	28	4:2-4	35

Index of References

Malachi (cont.)
4:3 35
4:4 33
4:5-6 33, 193
4:5 34, 192
4:6 35, 37

NEW TESTAMENT
Matthew
2:11 224
2:34 226
2:37 226
3:1-6 224
5:3 252
5:8 204
5:10-12 252
5:10 243
5:17 224
5:20 252
6:19-21 168
6:19-20 238, 252
6:20 203
7:13-14 252
7:13 244
7:14 201, 206
7:21-23 252
8:11-12 252
8:12 105, 229, 230
9:18-25 252
9:24 31
10:8 252
10:28 193, 252
10:32 200, 204
10:35-36 229
11:2-6 225
11:2 200
11:4-5 148
11:5 148, 179, 228, 230, 244, 252
11:9 200
12:24-27 244
12:38-42 252
12:41-42 197
13:13-15 225
13:42 230

13:43 58, 78, 196, 204, 205, 252
14:13-21 225
14:24-27 225
14:26 228
16:1-4 252
16:14 199
16:21-28 252
16:26 242
16:27 202, 226
17:2-4 252
17:2 241
17:22-23 252
19:16-28 252
19:21 168
19:28 199, 203
19:29 232
20:17-19 252
20:23 203
22:2 155, 233
22:13 105
22:23-33 11
22:23 252
22:24-30 174
22:28 252
22:30 78, 252
24:15 244
24:16-20 244
24:22 199
24:27 228
24:29-31 252
24:29 244
24:30 226, 246
24:31 230, 236, 238
24:37 239
25:30 105
25:31-46 12, 252
25:31 202, 226
25:34 199, 203
25:36 199
25:41 203
26:63-64 253
27:27-31 225
27:34 225, 237
27:45-46 105

27:45 225
27:51 225
27:52-53 253
27:52 31, 112
27:62-66 253
28:1-15 253

Mark
1:1-6 224
1:34 245
4:12 225
5:21-43 16
5:22 253
5:35-43 253
5:39 31
6:14 253
6:16 253
6:30-44 225
6:45-51 225
6:48 179, 228, 244
8:1-10 225
8:31 253
8:35 253
8:38 226
9:4-5 253
9:48 190
10:17-31 253
10:17 232
10:21 168
10:30 168
10:33-34 253
10:40 203
12:18-37 11
12:18-27 253
12:25 78
12:36 245
13:14-19 244
13:14 244
13:24-27 253
13:26 226
14:62 253
15:16-20 225
15:33-34 105
15:33 225
15:36 237
15:38 225

16:6	253	20:34-36	174	12:1	254
16:9	253	20:36	78, 242	12:9-10	254
16:12	253	21:28	239	12:23-25	254
16:14	253	21:36	197	12:35	198
		23:36	237	12:40	225
Luke		23:44	225	14:1-4	115, 254
1:17	193	23:45	225	14:2	240
1:69	231			15:10	58, 197
2:29-32	254	*John*		16:20	199
3:1-6	224	1:4-9	105	16:22	199
3:4-6	254	1:23	224	19:1-3	225
6:22-23	254	1:51	246	19:26	231
7:11-17	254	2:11	244	20:9	254
7:18-23	225, 254	2:18-22	254	21:14	254
7:22	228	2:23	244		
8:10	225	3:2	244	*Acts*	
8:40-56	254	3:3	224, 231	1:9	225
8:52	31	3:7	231	1:22	255
9:7-9	254	3:12	200	2:22-24	17
9:10-17	225	3:14-18	254	2:27	12
9:19	254	3:19	198	2:31-32	255
9:22	254	3:36	231	3:15	255
9:23-27	254	4:10	105	3:21	203
9:26	226	4:14	105, 254	4:2	255
9:31	58, 196	4:31	244	4:10	255
11:33-34	168	4:36	254	4:33	255
11:49-51	226	5:21-29	254	5:30	255
12:4-5	193	5:22	245	5:41	243
12:8	200, 204	5:27	245	7:60	112
12:33	203	5:28-29	199	9:37	255
13:24	206	6:1-13	225	9:40-41	255
13:25	202	6:19	228	10:40	255
13:28	197, 229, 230	6:31-33	232	10:42-43	255
		6:33-40	254	13:20	192
14:16	233	6:44	254	13:30	255
15:7	205	6:47	254	13:34	255
15:10	205	6:51	254	13:36	112
16:23-26	245	6:54	254	13:37	255
16:23	12, 202, 203	8:12	105	13:46	255
16:24	105	8:56	228	17:3	255
16:25	207	10:11	200	17:18	255
17:24	228	10:17-18	254	17:31	255
17:31-33	244	11:1-45	17	17:32	255
18:18	232	11:11-14	31	20:7-11	255
19:44	59	11:11	112	22:3-5	19
20:15	235	11:24-26	254	23:6-9	9, 11, 12
20:27-40	11	11:43-44	254	23:6-8	255

Acts (cont.)		6:2-3	58, 197	Ephesians	
24:15	12	6:14	256	1:4	200
24:21	12	7:39	112	1:15-23	256
26:23	255	9:24-27	256	2:1-10	256
26:24	198	9:25	238	2:19-22	256
28:26	225	11:30	112	3:6	256
		15	10, 17	4:7-13	256
Romans		15:4	256	5:1	16
1:4	256	15:6	112	5:7-8	16
1:16-17	256	15:12-57	11, 256	5:14	16
2:4	203	15:12-28	256	6:10-17	205
2:5-16	256	15:18	112	6:14	245
3:28	207	15:20	112, 231		
4:17	195	15:29	41	Philippians	
4:24-25	256	15:30	204	2:6-11	257
5:10	256	15:35-57	126	3:10-11	257
5:18-19	256	15:35-42	78	3:14	257
5:18	205	15:35	171	3:20-21	257
6:3-6	10	15:40-45	116	3:21	241
6:4-5	256	15:41	241		
6:8	256	15:42-44	171	Colossians	
6:9-10	256	15:42	256	1:9-14	257
7:4	256	15:44	245	2:12-13	257
7:24	204	15:51-54	171	2:20	257
8:11	206, 256	15:51	112, 238, 241	3:1-4	257
8:13	206			3:5	206
8:18	204, 238	15:52	160, 230, 236, 239		
8:24	58, 196			1 Thessalonians	
8:34	256	15:53-54	200, 204, 205	1:10	257
8:35	197			2:12	200
8:38-39	256	15:55	232	4:13-18	11, 257
9:22	239			4:13-15	112
9:33	231	2 Corinthians		4:15-17	17
10:5-9	256	1:9	256	4:16	201, 230, 236, 238, 246
10:6-7	200	4:14	256		
11:25	239	4:17	195, 238, 241		
11:33	191			5:8	245
12:1	58, 196	5:1-10	256		
14:9	256	5:1-2	240	2 Thessalonians	
14:10-12	11, 256	5:1	58, 196	1:5-10	257
		12:1-3	16	2:4	244
1 Corinthians		12:2-4	130	2:9	244
1:17-25	231				
3:14	204	Galatians		1 Timothy	
3:22	207	1:1	256	6:12	205, 257
6:1-3	174	6:7-8	205	6:18-19	257

2 Timothy
1:10-12	257
2:8-13	257
2:18-19	257
3:2	206
4:7-8	257
4:8	238

Titus
2:11-14	257
3:7	257

Hebrews
2:7-9	174
6:2	257
9:15	257
9:27-28	257
10:31	193
10:35-39	257
10:37	200, 201
11:3	195
11:4	257
11:6	257
11:10	257
11:13	257
11:16	206, 257
11:19	257
11:35-36	193
11:35	257
11:39-40	257
12:11	58, 196
12:17	207
12:22-24	257
12:28-29	257
13:20	257
2:147-15	257

James
1:2	243
1:10-11	198
1:12	238
4:10	257
4:12	204
4:14	238
5:3	239
5:9	206

1 Peter
1:3-9	258
1:3-4	10
1:7	58, 196
1:11	258
1:21	258
2:4	225
2:6-8	231
2:6	231
2:9	231
2:12	59
3:18-21	258
3:19-20	139
3:19	225, 231
4:5-6	258
4:6	231
4:7	239
4:13	258
4:16-18	258
5:1	258
5:4	198, 238, 258
5:10	200

2 Peter
1:10-11	258
2:4-22	258
3:4-13	258
3:4	112
3:7	191
3:8	246
3:9	201, 203
3:10-13	246
3:10	191

1 John
2:17	258
2:25	258
3:2	204
4:17	258
5:10-13	258

Jude
6	258
9	258
14–15	258
21	258

Revelation
1:4	99
1:18	12, 258
1:20	99
2:7	205, 258
2:10	200, 238
2:27	231
3:5	200, 204, 205
3:21	258
4:1	16
4:4	200
6:4	242
6:9-10	201
6:10-11	73
6:11	200, 201, 239
6:12-14	230
6:12	244
6:14	232
7:4	200
7:9	200
7:11	242
7:13-14	200
9:2	202
12	79, 229
12:5	231
12:7	79
12:8-9	79
13	229
13:13	244
13:18	139
14:1	200
14:10	204
17–18	148
17:21	148
19:15	231
20–22	79
20–21	180
20:1	76
20:2-3	79
20:3	245
20:4-6	12, 79, 165, 166, 258
20:4	246
20:6	165, 180, 246

Revelation (cont.)		2:10-13	69	4:36	200, 206
20:8-9	180	2:11-12	69	4:41	201
20:11	223	2:12	206	4:44	204
20:12-15	12, 258	2:15-32	67	4:52	202
20:12-13	79	2:15	199	5:1-20	67
20:12	79, 239	2:16	69	5:9	201
20:13-14	12	2:17	199	5:21–6:34	67
20:14-15	202	2:18-19	69	5:21-22	67
20:14	207, 246	2:25	199	5:23-30	67
20:15	79	2:29	69	5:23	201
21–22	165	2:30	199	5:31-40	67
21:1-7	79	2:31	69	5:37	201
21:1	166, 203, 246	2:33-41	67	5:38-43	29
		2:33	69	5:38-40	29, 189, 201
21:2	166, 202	2:34-35	69	5:41–6:10	67
21:4	166, 246	2:34	69	5:43	201
21:5	203	2:36	200	5:44	201
21:8	79	2:38	207	5:56	201
21:9-27	166	2:39	69, 200	6:2	202
21:22-25	79	2:40	69	6:5	200
21:23	200	2:41	201	6:11-34	67
22:1-5	104, 166	2:42-48	67	6:11	201
22:2	182, 199, 205	2:43	69	6:25	202, 207
		2:45	69	6:26	206
22:4	204	2:46-47	69	6:27-28	205
22:5	79, 166, 202	2:46	200	6:28	202
22:12	198, 204, 206	3–14	64–6, 85	6:33	202
		3:1–5:19	67	6:34	201
22:14	182, 199, 206	3:1-3	67	6:35–9:25	67
		3:1	65	6:35-37	67
22:19	182	3:4-36	67	6:38-59	67
		3:7	201	6:39	202
APOCRYPHA		3:14	67	6:55	201
2 Esdras		3:20-22	203	7	74
1–2	65–7	3:21	205	7:1-25	67
1:1-11	67	4:1-25	67	7:10-16	29, 189, 201
1:12-23	67	4:2	200	7:11	205
1:24–2:14	69	4:7-11	29, 189, 200	7:17	201
1:24-40	67	4:7	202, 205	7:21-24	203
1:24-27	66	4:12	205	7:26-51	30, 189, 202
1:24	69	4:26-52	67	7:26-44	67
1:32	205	4:28	201	7:26	206
1:33-40	66	4:30-31	203	7:32-38	12, 27
2:1-14	67	4:30	205	7:32	201, 204
2:2	199	4:33-43	29, 189, 201	7:34	205
2:10-47	29, 188, 199	4:33	201	7:36	200, 202
2:10-14	66	4:35	201, 204	7:38	202

7:42	202	9:26-37	68	7:101	203, 204
7:44	205	9:38–10:28	68	7:104	202
7:45-74	67	10:9	206	7:112-115	30, 189, 205
7:46	206	10:10	30, 189, 207	7:116-8:3	68
7:47	206	10:15-17	30, 189, 207	7:117-131	30, 189, 205
7:48	204	10:16	67, 195	7:117	203
7:54	206	10:27	206	7:123	200
7:60-61	205	10:29-59	68	7:125	204
7:60	206	10:41-50	67	7:128	205
7:61	206	10:59	206	7:66-105	189, 203
7:64	203	10:60–12:51	68	7:75-115	67
7:69	205	11–12	65		
7:78	204	11:1–12:3	68	*Tobit*	
7:80	204	12:3-51	68	1:17-18	199
7:85	203, 204	12:7	201	4:9	203
7:91	203	12:23-24	206	4:17	190
7:92	203	12:34	207		
7:95	203, 204	13:1-58	68	*Judith*	
7:97	205	13:1-13	68	16:17	190
8:1-3	30, 189, 206	13:13-58	68		
8:1	202, 203, 206	13:23	207	*Additions to Esther*	
		13:32	202	11:1	28
8:3	206	13:37	202		
8:4-36	68	13:48	207	*Wisdom of Solomon*	
8:12-19	30, 189, 206	13:52	202	1–5	52
8:17	202	13:53	202	1:1–6:21	51, 53
8:33	207	13:56	202, 206	1:1-15	53, 55
8:35	202	14:1-51	68	1:1-11	52
8:37-62	68	14:1-18	68	1:1-2	55, 61
8:37-40	30, 189, 206	14:9	202, 206	1:1	52
8:38	207	14:19-48	68	1:4-5	55
8:42	201	14:23	207	1:6-11	55
8:46-54	30, 189, 206	14:34-35	30, 189, 207	1:12	55
8:52	199, 200	14:35	194	1:13-14	55
8:55	206	14:36-48	206	1:15	55, 57, 62
8:56	207	14:45-47	64	1:16–2:24	53
8:61	206	14:45	207	1:16–2:1	53, 55
8:62–9:25	68	15–16	65, 66, 68	2–4	62
8:62	206	15:1-27	68	2	54, 61, 62
8:63	206	15:28–16:17	68	2:1-20	53
9:7-13	30, 189, 207	16:18-34	68	2:1-8	56
9:8	200	16:19	197	2:1-5	55, 60
9:9	197	16:35-50	68	2:2	59
9:12	206	16:51-67	68	2:5	54, 198
9:15	202, 206, 207	16:68-73	68	2:6-11	55
		16:74-78	68	2:12-20	55, 59
9:26–10:59	67, 68	4:66-105	30	2:13	54, 56, 59

Wisdom of Solomon (cont.)

Reference	Pages
2:16-20	81
2:16	56
2:17-20	56
2:17-18	54, 59
2:20	58, 197
2:21-24	53, 55
2:21-22	81
2:21	59
2:22-23	57
2:22	56, 59
2:24	55, 56, 62
3	62
3:1–4:20	53
3:1-13	29, 52, 56, 188, 196
3:1-12	53
3:1-10	57
3:1-9	51
3:1-4	56-59, 62, 63, 81
3:1	56, 61, 62
3:2	197, 198
3:4	56, 57, 59
3:5-6	57-59, 61–3, 81
3:6	59
3:7-13	60, 81
3:7-10	57
3:7-9	58
3:7	59-61, 63
3:8	60, 61
3:9-13	60
3:10-13	52, 59–61
3:10	60
3:13-19	53
3:13	59, 60, 63
3:18	60, 63, 81
4:1-6	53
4:6	60, 63
4:7-20	53
4:15	58, 59, 197
4:16–5:16	29, 188, 197
4:16	51, 60, 61, 63, 81
4:17	58, 59, 196, 198
4:18–5:14	52
4:18	61
4:20	81
5	54, 60, 62
5:1-23	53
5:1-3	53, 55
5:1	60, 61
5:2	203, 207
5:4-13	53
5:4-5	55
5:4	58, 196
5:5	54, 59
5:6-8	55
5:9-13	55
5:14-23	53, 55
5:14	53, 81
5:15-23	53
5:15-16	51, 61, 63, 81
5:15	60, 207
5:17-23	61, 63
5:21	198
6–19	51
6–9	50, 52
6:1–10:21	53
6:1-21	53, 55
6:1-11	52, 53, 55
6:1-8	53
6:1-2	51
6:1	52, 55
6:9-21	53
6:9-11	52
6:12-25	52, 53
6:16	55
6:17-20	57, 62
6:18-20	55
6:21	52
6:22–10:21	51
7–10	52
7:1-22	53
7:1	207
7:7-12	50
7:18	60, 61
7:22–8:1	53
7:22	60
8:2-16	53
8:2	50
8:10-11	50
8:17–9:18	53
8:19-20	63
8:21	50
9:4-5	50
9:18	52
10–19	51
10:1–19:22	53
10:1-21	53
11–19	50, 52
11	52
11:1-14	53
11:5	54
11:15–12:27	53
11:15-20	53
11:15-16	50
11:16	54
11:20	201
11:21–12:2	53
12:3-11	53
12:11	59, 197
12:12-18	53
12:19-22	53
12:23-27	53
13:1–15:19	54
13:1-9	54
13:10–14:11	54
14:11	59
14:12-31	54
14:16-20	51
14:22	51
15:1-19	54
15:18–16:4	50
16:1–19:22	53
16:1-4	54
16:5-14	54
16:15-29	54
17:1–18:4	54
18:5-25	54
19:1-22	54
19:8	198
19:13-17	50
19:15	59
19:22	54

Ecclesiasticus		47:2-11	34	*1 Maccabees*	
1:1–43:33	33	47:12-22	34	1:47	193
1:11–2:17	31	47:23-25	34	2:18	193, 195
2:7-11	190	48:1-11	34, 35, 37,	2:61	190
2:9	29, 31, 37,		192	3:7	191
	188	48:1	33		
2:17	188	48:2-3	33	*2 Maccabees*	
7:15-17	190	48:3	33, 35	1:1–2:18	38, 39
7:17	29, 32, 37	48:5	33	1:1-9	39
11:14-25	31	48:6	33	1:10–2:18	39
11:26-28	31	48:7	33, 200	1:24	195
12:4-7	190	48:8	33	2:19-32	39
12:6	31, 37	48:9	33	2:23	39
14:1	191	48:10-11	33	3–7	39
14:16-19	31	48:10	33, 36	3:1-40	39
16:12-14	31	48:11	29, 32, 33,	3:3	38
16:17-23	190		37	4–6	40
16:22	29, 31, 37,	48:12-16	34	4:1-50	39
	188	48:13-14	31, 37	4:13	193
17:27-28	31	48:13	192	4:19	195
18:21	190	48:15-16	34	4:48	193
19:13-19	191	48:17-22	34	5:1–6:11	39
19:19	29, 31, 37,	48:23-25	34	5:17	195
	188	49:1-16	34	5:20	195
36:13	193	49:1-3	34	5:21	195
38:19-23	31	49:4-7	34	6:6	196
41:3-4	31	49:6-7	34	6:7	193
41:5-13	31	49:8	34	6:12–7:42	39
41:5	197	49:9	34	6:12-17	39, 40, 194
43:32	191	49:10	34, 191	6:16	195
44:1–50:21	31	49:11	34	6:18–7:42	48
44:1–49:16	33, 34	49:12	34	6:18	193
44:1-15	33, 34	49:13	34	6:19	193
44:16–49:16	33	49:14-16	34	6:21-30	193
44:16	34	49:14	34	6:21-25	48
44:17-18	34	49:15	34	6:26	29, 40, 188
44:19-21	34	49:16	34	6:29	48
44:22-23	34	50:1-24	33	7	27, 29, 40–2,
44:23–45:5	34	50:25–51:30	33		188, 193
45:1	191	50:25-29	33	7:1-42	39
45:6-22	34	51:1-12	33	7:1	48
45:23-26	34	51:12	190	7:2	41, 43
46:1-10	34	51:13-30	33	7:3	195
46:11-20	34, 191	51:30	190	7:4	48
46:13-20	34			7:6	40, 41, 43,
46:19-20	29, 31, 37	*Baruch*			45, 48, 81
47:1	34	6	28	7:7	45, 48

2 Maccabees (cont.)		8:5	40	5:7	98, 109
7:8	194, 195	9:1-12	46	5:8-10	98
7:9	41–43, 45, 46, 48, 81, 195	9:5-12	50	5:8	98
		9:5-8	195	6–11	97
		9:5	194	9:2-3	92, 98, 208
7:10-11	48	9:6	194	9:10	98
7:11	27, 42, 43, 47, 48, 81	9:9	194	10:1-6	208
		9:10	46	10:4-6	92, 98
7:12	48	9:12-17	195	10:11-13	92, 98, 208
7:14	42, 43, 46, 49, 194	9:18-31	39	10:16-17	92, 98, 208
		9:28	46, 50	10:20	92, 98, 208
7:16-17	43	12:37	194, 195	10:3-5-6	121
7:17	42, 46, 195	12:43-45	29, 40, 49, 188, 195	13:6	92, 98, 208
7:18-19	44			14:2-6	92, 208
7:18	42, 195	12:43	196	15:7-10	92, 98, 208
7:19	42, 46, 50	12:44-45	48	16:1	92, 98, 208
7:20	41	14	17	17–36	99
7:21	194, 195	14:3	196	19:1	98
7:22-23	42, 44, 45	14:29	195	20:1-8	201, 215
7:22	47	14:37-46	29, 40, 41, 188, 196	20:3	99
7:23	41, 47, 48, 81, 194, 195			20:8	99, 109, 208
		14:46	41, 47, 48	21–26	99
7:25	40	15:20-37	38	21–23	99
7:26	40, 194	15:29	194, 195	22–27	17
7:27-29	42, 44	15:36	39	22	99, 100, 102–4, 107–10, 113, 115, 124, 126, 208, 215
7:27	194	15:37	195		
7:28-29	45				
7:28	47, 49	*Letter of Jeremiah*			
7:29	41, 47, 48, 81	6:3	28		
				22:1-2	100
7:30	41	PSEUDEPIGRAPHA		22:1	100
7:31	42, 46, 50	*1 Enoch*		22:2-4	101
7:32-33	40, 42	1–36	88–92, 97–99, 208	22:2	100–105, 110
7:32	194				
7:33	49, 194, 195	1–5	98, 102, 103	22:3-4	100
7:34-35	42, 46, 50	1:2	98	22:4	99
7:35	46	1:3-9	92, 208, 214	22:5-7	99, 103, 105, 106
7:36	41, 42, 46, 48, 81, 194	1:7-9	98		
		1:7	98, 112	22:5	100
7:37-38	40, 42, 62	1:8	98	22:6	100
7:37	41	1:9	98	22:7	100, 108
7:38	40, 42, 194	5:4-6	98	22:8-13	101
7:39	193	5:4	98	22:8	101
7:40	41	5:5-10	214	22:9-13	101, 104, 110
7:44-45	41	5:5-9	92, 208		
8–15	40	5:6-8	98	22:9	103, 104
8:1–15:37	39	5:7-10	109	22:10-11	103

22:10	101, 103	51:5	114	84:4	93, 209
22:11	103, 105, 109, 110	51:8	114	84:5-6	118
		52–54	112	84:6	118
22:12	103, 105	54:6	92, 208	85–90	118
22:13	102, 103, 109	54:7–55:2	97	87:2	99
		56:8	92, 208	89:36-38	118
22:14	101, 104	58–69	111	89:36-37	93, 209
24:2–25:6	103	58:1-4	92, 208	89:38	118
25	109	60:6	92, 208	89:75	119
25:1-7	109	60:7-10	97	90:1-26	245
25:3-7	216	60:24	92, 97, 208	90:20-37	118
25:4-6	208	61	117	90:20-36	93, 209, 218
25:4-5	109	61:1-5	114, 115, 217	90:21	99, 119
25:6	109, 110			90:22	119
27:2-3	92, 98, 208	61:1	115	90:23	119
32:1-3	115	61:2-5	115	90:25	119
37–71	88, 92, 97, 111, 208	61:2	115	90:26-27	118, 119
		61:4	115	90:28	119
37	111	61:5	92, 116, 208	90:33	119
37:1	111	61:8-9	116	90:34	119
37:5	111	61:8	92, 208	90:37	119
38–44	111	62–63	116	91-107	93, 209
38	92, 208	62:11	245	91-105	97, 119
40:9-10	216	62:12-16	114, 217	91	119
40:9	92, 111, 208	62:13-16	92, 208	91:1	119
41:1	92, 208	62:13-15	116	91:8-19	219
41:8-9	92, 208	62:15	116, 117	91:8-17	93, 120, 209
45–57	111	62:16	117	91:8-9	120
45:2-6	92, 208	65:1–69:25	97	91:9	120
45:47	92	70:3	115	91:10-17	120
46:3	92, 208	70:4	92, 208	91:10	120, 125
47	208	70:16	92, 208	91:11-17	88, 120
47:5	114	72–82	92, 97, 117, 209	91:16	246
48:7	92, 208			91:19	120
49	216	77:3	115	92–93	119
49:3	92, 111, 208	81–82	99	92-105	17
50:1	92, 208	81:1-4	92, 117, 209, 218	92:2-5	93, 120, 209, 220
51–61	111				
51	92, 112, 114, 117, 208, 217	81:1	99, 117	92:3	120
		81:2	117	93:1-10	88
		81:4	118	93:10	120
51:1	113, 114	81:5	99	94-104	93
51:2	112, 114	83–90	88, 93, 97, 118, 119, 209	94:1-5	124
51:3	112, 114			94:6–104:8	119
51:4-5	78, 112, 114			94:9	93, 209
51:4	114	83–84	118	94:11	93, 209
51:5a-3	112	84:4-6	118	95:3	124

1 Enoch (cont.)

95:5-6	93, 209	104:2	78, 79, 122–4	14:12	176		
96:2-3	93, 209	104:3	122	14:13	166		
96:4	124	104:4	79, 123, 124	14:14	166		
96:8	93, 209	104:5	122, 123	15:1-7	168		
97:4	124	104:6	122, 123	15:5-8	238		
97:6	93, 124, 209	104:7-8	121	15:7-8	96, 166, 168, 213		
98:3	124	104:7	79, 121	21:8	166		
98:6-8	93, 124, 209	104:8	124	21:12-13	166, 239		
98:12	124	105:2	245	21:23-25	239		
98:13-14	120, 220	106-107	97, 119	21:23-24	96, 213		
98:14	93, 120, 209	108	97, 119, 125	21:23	176		
100:10	93, 209	108:1	125	21:24	166, 176		
100:4-5	93, 209	108:10-12	125	23:4-7	239		
100:7	124	108:10	125	23:5	96, 213		
102-104	125	108:11	125	24:1-2	96, 166, 175, 213, 239		
102:1	124	108:12	125, 126				
102:3-8	220	108:14-15	125	24:1	176		
102:3	124	108:14	245	26–27	164		
102:4-8	93, 209	108:15	125	28–29	164		
102:4-5	121	108:2-6	125	29	164		
102:4-104:8	120, 121, 123	108:2-3	93, 221	30	165, 169		
102:4-103:8	123	108:2	125	30:1-5	168, 239		
102:4-103:4	121	108:3	125	30:1-3	96, 213		
102:4	122	108:5-6	125	30:1-2	166, 176		
102:5	113, 124	108:5-15	221	30:1	166, 168, 176		
102:6-11	121	108:7-10	125				
103:1-4	93, 121, 209, 220	108:7	125	30:2	166, 169, 176, 177		
		108:8-15	93, 209	30:3-5	166		
103:3-4	79, 123	*2 Baruch*		30:3	169		
103:3	122	5:2-3	166	30:4-5	169, 176		
103:4	122, 123	8:5-6	243	32:1	176		
103:5-8	121, 122	11:4-7	238	32:2-4	163		
103:5	121	11:4	96, 166, 176, 213	32:6	166, 177		
103:6	122			36–40	169		
103:7-8	79, 121, 122, 125	14	167	36–37	169		
		14:2	176	36:11	166, 176		
103:7	122	14:3-7	167	38:1	176		
103:8	122, 123	14:8-14	238	39:2	169		
103:9-15	121, 122	14:8-9	166	39:5-6	169		
103:9-104:6	121, 122	14:8	167	39:5	169		
103:9	121	14:9	167	39:7	169		
104:1-7	93, 209, 221	14:10-14	166	40:1-2	169		
104:1-5	121	14:10-11	167	40:2	169		
104:1	79, 122	14:12-13	96, 166, 168, 213	40:3	164, 169, 170		
104:2-6	79						

41:1–43:3	169	51:8-9	166	85:8-15	243		
41:1-6	170	51:10	78, 172, 173,	85:9	96, 166, 176,		
42:2	170		177		213		
42:4	170	51:11	166	85:15	96, 166, 213		
42:7-8	96, 169, 170,	51:12	173, 177				
	213, 240	51:16	166, 172	*2 Enoch*			
42:8	166, 169,	52:1-5	166, 172	1–34	127		
	176	52:3	176	1–2	131		
44:8-12	164	52:6-7	166	1:1	131		
44:9-15	240	52:7	172	1:5	78		
44:11-13	166	53–74	164	1:8	16		
44:12	177	54:14	166	2:3	131		
44:13	166	54:15	176	3–16	131		
44:15	166	54:21-22	166	7:1	93, 129, 210		
47:7-8	175	56:2	164	7:3	129		
48:2	166	56:5-16	164	8	16		
48:3-8	240	57	243	8:1–9:1	129		
48:6	166	57:1-3	164	8:5	130		
48:22	170, 176	57:2	96, 166, 177,	10:1-6	130		
48:26-47	170		213	10:1-2	130		
48:27-29	171	58:1-2	164	17–40	131		
48:27	166	59:1-12	164	18:7	93, 210		
48:39	166	59:2	166	18:24	210		
48:40	170, 173,	60:1-2	164	19:5	93, 210		
	175	61:1-8	164	20–22	130		
48:45-50	240	61:7	163	22:8	130		
48:48-50	170	62:1-8	164	22:10	130		
48:50	166	63:1-11	164	23:5	129		
49–52	12, 96, 213,	64:1–65:2	164	24:2	127		
	241	66:1-8	164	28:7-10	210		
49–51	78, 170, 175	66:3	96, 213, 243	28:7	210		
49–50	166	67:1-9	164	30:2	210		
49:2-3	171	68:1-8	164	31:2	210		
50:2-4	171, 172	68:5	163	31:7-9	127		
50:2	176	69:1–71:2	164	31:7	127		
51	180, 181	72:1–74:4	164	32	93, 127, 210,		
51:1	166	73–74	164		222		
51:2	172, 177	76:1-2	243	32:1–33:2	246		
51:3-4	176	76:2	166, 176	32:1	128, 129		
51:3	78, 166, 172,	78:6	166	33:1	210		
	174, 177	78:7	176	35–68	127		
51:5-6	173	82:2	166, 176	39:2	93, 210		
51:5	172, 177	83:2	166, 176	39:5	93, 210		
51:6	166, 172,	83:7	166	40:12-13	130		
	174, 176	84:6	166	41–48	131		
51:7	176	85:3	96, 166, 176,	41:2	130		
51:8-14	172		213	42:1	130		

2 Enoch (cont.)		24:11	137	7:26-44	74
42:3-14	130	26:3	137	7:28-29	72, 166
42:3	93, 210	28	131, 133	7:28	72
42:5	93, 210	28:7-10	94, 131, 223	7:29-35	75
42:7	93, 210	28:7	94, 131, 132	7:30-31	72
44	130	28:8-9	132, 137	7:31-44	81, 95
44:3-5	93, 210	28:10	131, 133–5,	7:32-44	72
44:7-8	210		137	7:32-42	72
48:8-9	93, 210	30:2	94, 137	7:32	73, 74, 77–9,
49:2	93, 129, 134,	31:2	94, 131, 137		81, 113
	210	33:1	94	7:33	78
50:2	93, 210	43–44	134, 135	7:34-35	79
50:4-5	93, 210	43:1	134	7:36	79
51:3	93, 210	43:2	134	7:39-42	79
52:15	93, 210	43:3	134	7:43	76
53:2	129	44	133	7:45-48	80
58:4-6	93, 210	44:2-3	134	7:62-69	80
58:6	129	44:3-6	137	7:75-101	72, 73, 81,
60:4	93, 210	44:3	131, 134,		95
62:3	129		136, 137	7:79-87	72
65:6-11	93, 127, 210,	44:5-6	134	7:81-87	70
	222	44:5	134, 137	7:81	70
65:6	127	44:6	134, 137	7:82	70
65:9	127	44:7-8	94, 224	7:83	70
65:11	127	44:7	135	7:84	70
66:6-7	93, 210	48C:7	131	7:85	70
66:7	130	48D:1	131	7:86	70
69–73	127			7:87	70, 72, 81
70:1	93, 127, 210,	4 Ezra		7:88-98	72
	223	1–11	74	7:92-98	70
70:3	93, 127, 210,	2:16	95	7:95-98	72, 78, 81
	223	2:22-24	95	7:92	70
		2:31	95	7:93	70
3 Baruch		4:7-8	12	7:94	70
4:4-6	12	4:26-31	74	7:95	70, 73
5:3	12	4:35-37	73, 81, 95	7:96	70
		4:41	73	7:97	70, 74, 78,
3 Enoch		4:42-43	95		79
2:1	137	5:40	72	7:98	70, 78
10:3-6	131	5:41-56	74	7:101	73, 81
12:5	131	6:18-20	72	7:102-115	72, 81, 143
15:1	134	6:20	78, 79	7:102-103	80
15B:5	134	6:25-28	74	7:106-111	80
16:1	131	7	74, 78	7:113	72, 81
17–18	99	7:125	79	7:116-126	80
18:24	94	7:17	80	7:116-118	80

7:119-125	78	3:5-13	244	14:5	163
7:125	74, 78	3:8-10	179	14:9	163
7:129	80, 81	3:12-13	144, 179	15:5	163
8:1-3	72, 81	3:13	96, 213	16:3	163
8:39	72, 81	4:1–5:1	178	16:6	163
8:51-54	72, 81	4:5	178		
8:53-54	73	4:15	178	*Apocalypse of Zephaniah*	
8:53	12	4:16-19	178	1–8	156
9:6-12	74	4:24-29	96, 213, 244	1:4-6	158
9:9	72	4:24-26	180	2:7	156, 158
9:12	72	4:25-26	179	2:8-9	156
11–13	74	4:27-29	179	3:2-4	157
11:46	74	4:27	178, 179	3:5-7	157
12:11-12	74	4:30-31	245	3:8-9	157
12:34	74	4:31	96, 144, 179, 213	4:7	157, 158
13	74			5:1-6	156
13:3	74	5:2-6	179	7–8	156
13:4	74	5:6	180	7:1–8:5	157
13:5-7	74	5:7-21	179	7:1-9	157
13:5	74	5:22-24	179	7:8	156
13:6	74	5:25-39	96, 213, 245	7:9	156
13:8	74	5:25-35	179	7:10-11	157
13:10-11	74	5:28-29	180, 181	8:1–9:5	157, 236
14:34-35	72	5:32	178	8:1	156
14:35	81	5:37	180	8:3	156
14:36	95			8:5	157
15–17	74	*Apocryphon of Ezekiel*		9–12	156
		Frag. 1	12, 95, 151, 211, 233	9:4-5	156
4 Maccabees				9:4	156
5:7	193			10:1-9	157
6:27	193	*Apocalypse of Moses*		10:4-9	156
17:1	195	13	12	10:10-14	156, 157
		15–17	245	10:10-11	156
Apocalypse of Abraham				10:11	156, 158
15–32	88	*Apocalypse of Sedrach*		10:12-14	156
		1:21	163	11:2-6	156
Apocalypse of Elijah		2:5	163	12:1	158
1:8	179	4:1	163	12:5-8	158
1:9	179	9:1	163	B6	156
1:10	179, 180	9:2	163		
1:11	179	9:3	163	*Greek Apocalypse of Ezra*	
2:1	178	10:1-4	163		
2:47–3:1	178	11:1-9	163	1:2–2:3	236
2:51	178	11:11	163	1:6	159
2:52	178	11:12-13	163	1:12-14	159
3:1-18	178	12:1	163	1:12	158

Greek Apocalypse of Ezra

1:24	159, 160
2:1	95, 158, 212
2:7	159
4:5-24	158
4:35-36	236
4:36	95, 158, 159, 212
4:37-39	160
4:43	160
5:1	159
5:2-6	158
5:10	159
5:20-28	160
5:20-23	236
5:20-22	158
5:21-22	159
5:22	95, 158, 212
5:23-28	158
6:3-4	159
6:17	159
6:24	159
6:26	160
7:1-4	237
7:2	95, 158, 212
7:20	159

Jubilees

1:26	128
1:29	246
4:30	246
23	89–91
23:29	79
23:30-31	79
23:30	79, 245
23:31	79

Martyrdom and Ascension of Isaiah

3:13–4:22	86
4:14-22	12

Odes of Solomon

42:10-14	16

Pseudo-Philo

3:10	12
3:16	113
12:1	80
18:1–20:11	80

Questions of Ezra

A2-3	162
A3	158, 162
A4-7	237
A5	95, 158, 212
A6-7	162
A6	158
A8–10	237
A10	95, 158, 162, 212
A11	162
A14-15	158, 162
A19-21	162
A20	162
A21	162
A22-26	162
A27-30	162
A31	162
B1-14	95, 212, 237
B2	158, 162
B3	158
B6–14	158
B6	158, 162
B7-9	162
B11-14	158, 162
B14	162

Sibylline Oracles

Prologue line 27	138
Prologue line 30	138
1–2	137
1	139
1.1-4	139
1.5-64	139
1.282	139
1.283	139
1.324-400	139
1.324-386	224
1.326-329	139
1.326	139
1.349	139
1.353-355	148
1.355	94, 139, 211
1.377-378	139
1.378	94, 139, 211
1.379	139
2	138, 140, 143, 145
2.15	140
2.32-347	140
2.45-55	140
2.93-94	140
2.154-173	140
2.174-186	140
2.177-183	140
2.187-195	140
2.190-192	140
2.196-213	140, 144
2.199-200	140
2.200	142
2.212-213	140
2.217-219	140
2.217	142
2.221-51	94
2.221-251	140, 211, 226
2.221-226	140, 145
2.221-222	140
2.221	142
2.226	140
2.227-237	142
2.230	142
2.231-232	143
2.233	143
2.234	143
2.236	143
2.238-251	140
2.238-250	142
2.239	143
2.245-246	142
2.246-248	142
2.252-255	143
2.254	140
2.283-310	143

2.303-306	143	6.14	94, 211	8.248	149
2.311-312	140, 143	7	137, 138	8.251-336	149
2.313-338	143, 226	7.118-151	145	8.251-257	231
2.313-315	211	7.119-123	145	8.255	94, 149, 211
2.313-15	94	7.120-121	146	8.282-293	231
2.332	143	7.124-129	146	8.286	94, 150, 211
2.334	143	7.126-131	146	8.293	94, 150, 211
2.337	143	7.126-129	145	8.310-317	231
3	137, 143	7.139-149	228	8.310-314	211
3.1-96	143	7.140-144	145	8.310-311	150
3.63-74	143, 227	7.144-45	94	8.310-14	94
3.66	94, 211	7.144-151	145	8.313-314	150
3.75-92	148	7.144-145	145, 146, 211	8.350-358	150
3.393	12			8.359-428	150
3.458	12	7.148-149	146	8.399-400	150
3.767-776	144, 227	8	137	8.401	150
3.769-771	144	8.1-126	146	8.404-411	150
3.769	94	8.76-109	229	8.412-418	232
3.796	211	8.81-99	146	8.413-416	150, 211
4	137, 144, 145	8.82-83	94, 211	8.413-16	94
		8.82	146	11–14	137
4.40-47	144	8.84	147	11–13	138
4.43-44	145	8.96-99	146, 147	Frag. 3	150
4.45-46	145	8.104-106	146	Frag. 3.41-49	94, 211, 232
4.46	145	8.169-216	147		
4.49-53	144	8.169-177	229	Frag. 3.41-42	150
4.54-64	144	8.169-170	147, 148	Frag. 3.44	150
4.65-87	144	8.170	94, 211	Frag. 3.46	150
4.88-101	144	8.171	148	Frag. 3.47-49	150
4.102-51	144	8.194-216	148		
4.176-178	145	8.196-197	148	*Testament of Abraham*	
4.179-92	94	8.202-212	230	10–15	89–91
4.179-192	144, 211, 228	8.205-8	94		
		8.205-212	148, 149	*Testament of Asher*	
4.179	145	8.205-208	147, 148, 211	7:3	245
4.181-182	145				
4.181	145	8.205	148	*Testament of Benjamin*	
4.182	145	8.217-500	146, 149	9:5	12
4.183-192	144	8.217-250	149, 230	10:2-11	12
4.184-186	145	8.218-223	149		
4.187	145	8.218	149	*Testament of Judah*	
4.189-190	145	8.226-28	94	20	79
5	137	8.226-228	149, 211	20:1-5	79
5.178	12	8.228-231	149	20:2	79
6	137	8.239-242	149	20:3	79
6.10-19	228	8.242	149	23:3-5	16

Testament of Judah
(cont.)
25	79
25:1	17
25:3	79
25:4-5	79
25:4	17, 79
25:5	79

Testament of Levi
2–5	89-91
4:1	12
8:2	99

Testament of Moses
10:1	79
10:2	79
10:7-10	16
10:9	79
10:10	79

Testament of Reuben
4:5	12

Vision of Ezra
1–2	158
6–7	160
8–55	158
8–22	160, 161
25–26	160
27–55	160, 161
53	161
60–63	160
63–66	158
64–65	161
64	160

DEAD SEA SCROLLS
1QH^a
10	16
11.19-21	16
14.29-30	16
16	16
16.5-6	16
17.4-12	16
19.12-14	16

1QH
XI 19-23	251
XII 5–XIII 4	251
XIV 34-35	251
XV 22-31	251
XIX 10-14	251

1QpHab
5.4	58
7.4-5	16

1QS
4.6-8	16, 251
4.11-14	251

1QS^b
5.23	16

4Q245
Frag. 2	251

4Q385
Frag. 1-3, 12	251
frg. 2	142

4Q386
Frag. 1 col. i	251

4Q388
Frag. 8	251

4Q416
Frag 2 col. iii	251

4Q418
Frag 69 ii	251

4Q504
Frags 1-2 col. vi	251

4Q521
Frag. 1 col. ii	251
Frag. 2 col. ii-iii	251
Frags. 7 + 5 col. ii	251

4QEzra
12.31-33	245

4QFlor.
1,11-13	245

11QPs^a
19.10-11	16

PHILO
On the Contemplative Life
11–13	13

JOSEPHUS
Against Apion
1.7-8 §37-42	23

Jewish Antiquities
10.5.1	150
12.9.7 §387	38
13.5.9	11
18.1.3	12, 251
18.1.4	11, 251
18.1.5	13, 251
20.17-96	168

Jewish War
1.1.1	38
2.8.10-11	251
2.8.11	13
2.8.14	12, 251
2.8.15	11
3.8.5	251
7.10.2-4	38
7.8.7	13

MISHNAH
Avot
4:21-22	259

Berakhot
5:2	259

Sanhedrin
10	17
10:1-3	259
10:1	10

Sotah			Nidah		Tosefta	
9:15	37, 147, 259		70b	262	Berakhot	
15	17				3:9	259
			Pesachim		3:24	259
Tamid			68a	45, 181, 260		
5:1	249		118a	260	Pesahim	
					4:18	168
Yadayim			Rosh HaShana			
4:5	23		17a	261	Sanhedrin	
			31a	261	13:3-5	259
TARGUMIC TEXTS			32a	261		
Pseudo-Jonathan					OTHER RABBINIC WORKS	
Gen. 3:19	128, 147		Sabbath		Deuteronomy Rabbah	
			152b	260	2:9-10	265
BABYLONIAN TALMUD					3:15	45, 181, 265
Avodah Zarah			Sanhedrin		7:6	265
18a	262		5a	261	10:3	265
20b	262		37a	108		
			90a	262	Ecclesiastes Rabbah	
Baba Batra			90b	152, 172	1:6-7	171, 172, 266
14b	6		91a	154, 262		
16a	261		91ab	151	1:6	181
16b	261		91b	45, 153, 171, 181	1:19-20	266
					3:2	266
Berakhot			92a	262	3:11	172
15b	260		92b	142, 262	3:18	266
17a	80		97a	147	5:11	266
18b	260		99a	76	5:17	266
26b	260				7:16	266
29a	260		Sotah		9:2	266
33a	77, 249, 260		49b	147	12:5	142, 172
60b	260		113a	262		
					Esther Rabbah	
Chagigah			JERUSALEM TALMUD		9:2	267
12b	77, 261		Berakhot			
			5:2	77, 260	Exodus Rabbah	
Chullin					1:1	264
142a	262		Kettubot		15:21	264
			12:3	260	32:2	264
Kettubot					40:2	264
111a	116, 261		Sanhedrin		48:2	264
111b	172, 261		4:1	108		
			10	260	Genesis Rabbah	
Megillah					13:3-6	77, 263
17b	249, 261		Ta'anith		14:3-4	173
			1:1	77, 260	14:5	263

Genesis Rabbah (cont.)
14:8   263
20:10   127, 263
20:12   80
21:1   263
23:6   80
26:2   263
26:6   263
28:3   142, 172, 263
32:1   263
35:3   263
48:11   173
56:1-2   133, 263
63:11   263
63:14   263
73:4   263
74:1   264
77:1   264
78:1   264
84:11   264
94   116, 264
95:1   171, 264
96:5   264
102:2   171, 264

Lamentations Rabbah
1:45   266
2:6   266
3:8   266

Leviticus Rabbah
4:5   151, 154
18:1   142, 172, 265
27:4   265

Mek. of R. Simeon ben Yochai
Exod. 15:1 154

Midr. Song
2:13   147

Numbers Rabbah
11:2   265
14:1   265
15:13   265
19:13   265

Pesiqta de Rab Kahana
76a   37

Ruth Rabbah
3:2   266
6:2   266

Sifre Deut.
10[67a]   80

Song Rabbah
1:9   267
2:2   267
2:18   267
7:15   142, 267

APOSTOLIC FATHERS
1 Clement
26:3   6

Barnabas
11:9   163

CLASSICAL AND ANCIENT CHRISTIAN LITERATURE
Augustine
City of God
22.29   6

Epiphanius
Against Heresies
64.70, 5-17 151, 233

Hippolytus of Rome
Refutatio omnium haeresium
27.1   13
28   12

Origen
Commentary on Matthew
17.29   6

JEWISH LITURGICAL TEXTS
Amidah
2   17

Index of Authors

Afonso, L. J. 2
Agourides, S. 162
Alexander, D. 77
Alexander, P. 131
Alexander, T. 32
Andersen, F. I. 126, 127
Anderson, G. A. 173
Aptowitzer, V. 154
Arenhoevel, D. 38
Attridge, H. W. 65

Bader, G. 249
Bloch-Smith, E. 3
Block, D. I. 9
Blomberg, C. L. 147
Bock, D. L. 97, 111
Boismard, M.-E. 56
Brand, M. T. 97
Brown, C. 107
Brown, M. 77
Bruce, F. F. 50, 51
Buttenweiser, M. 177
Byron, J. 106, 108

Callaway, M. C. 21
Carson, D. A. 21
Cassuto, U. 106
Cavallin, H. C. C. 14
Charles, R. H. 21, 187
Charlesworth, J. H. 16, 18, 83, 97, 98, 111, 185
Chester, A. 5
Christo, G. E. 5, 6
Collins, A. Y. 66
Collins, J. J. 4, 5, 7, 21, 31, 32, 37–9, 50, 51, 56, 64, 65, 80, 88, 91, 97, 119, 131, 138, 140, 143, 144, 146, 150, 164, 165
Constantelos, D. J. 21
Cowley, A. E. 36

Dahood, M. 5
Day, J. 7
DeSilva, D. A. 21, 24, 27, 38–40, 50–2, 62, 65, 66, 74, 83, 186
Di Lella, A. A. 31, 37
Doran, R. 38, 39
Doukhan, J. B. 5, 11
Dunn, J. D. G. 51

Edrei, A. 24
Elledge, C. D. 8, 11, 13, 14, 109, 142
Embry, B. 18
Evans, C. A. 19, 24, 28, 84, 127, 131, 138, 150, 155, 158, 186, 249

Fee, G. D. 41
Feldman, L. H. 18
Fiensy, D. 158
Flusser, D. 173
Frankovic, J. 168
Fritsch, C. T. 84

Galenieks, E. 1, 2, 5, 12
Gane, R. 9
Geoltrain, P. 13
Gilbert, M. 57
Gillman, N. 56
Goldstein, J. A. 40, 41, 45–7, 154
Grabbe, L. L. 56
Greenspoon, L. J. 5

Haas, V. 1
Hachlili, R. 3
Halivni, D. W. 64
Harrelson, W. J. 21
Harrington, D. J. 50, 52, 66, 74
Hasel, G. F. 5
Henze, M. 185
Herms, R. 18

Hillers, R. 3
Hodgens, D. 172
Horbury, W. 56

Instone-Brewer, D. 249

Johnston, P. S. 1, 8

Kamlah, E. 107
Kearns, C. 32
Kee, H. C. 32, 46, 52
Kim, D. 166
Klijn, A. 163
Koenen, L. 178
Kohlenberger III, J. R. 21
Kolarcik, M. 54, 56
Kugel, J. L. 18
Kwon, O. 14

Laato, A. 9
Larcher, C. 52, 56, 57
Lesko, L. H. 1
Levenson, J. D. 15
Lied, L. I. 173
Linebaugh, J. A. 51
Longenecker, B. W. 65, 66

Martin-Achard, R. 5
McCown, C. C. 178
McGlynn, M. 50
McNamara, M. 128
Mendels, D. 24
Metzger, B. M. 65
Milgrom, J. 4
Milik, J. T. 13
Moor, J. C. de 9
Mueller, J. R. 150-2, 155, 158
Myers, J. M. 65

Nagakubo, S. 14
Neubauer, A. 36
Nickelsburg, G. W. E. 7, 10, 11, 14, 21, 45, 47, 56, 61, 84, 97, 100, 102, 104, 105, 109, 111, 112, 114, 116-21, 125, 185

Odeberg, H. 132

Park, J. S. 12, 14
Pfeiffer, R. H. 56, 57

Pryce, B. C. 4
Puech, E. 37, 57

Reese, J. M. 51, 57
Reeves, J. C. 185, 246
Robbins, G. 158
Robinson, S. E. 150
Rodriguez, A. M. 7

Sawyer, J. A. 5
Schaper, J. 6
Schiffman, L. H. 18
Scott, J. J., Jr 10
Scurlock, J. 1
Segal, A. F. 1, 7, 11, 13, 14, 69, 74, 80, 104
Setzer, C. 4
Sigvartsen, J. A. 174
Skehan, P. W. 31, 37, 52
Steiner, R. C. 3, 4, 9
Stele, A. A. 4
Stone, M. E. 65, 66, 68, 73, 74, 78, 80, 126, 158, 173, 185
Stuart, D. 35
Suriano, M. J. 2, 11

Tanzer, S. J. 21, 23

Urbach, E. E. 173

VanderKam, J. C. 38, 57, 111, 112, 114, 116, 117, 120, 185

Wacker, M.-T. 99, 102, 104
Wegner, P. D. 23
Wenham, G. J. 106
White, W. 77
Winston, D. 47, 50, 51, 129
Wintermute, O. S. 155, 156, 177, 178
Wright, A. T. 18
Wright, J. E. 158, 162-4
Wright, N. T. 1, 4, 6-8, 57, 60

Xella, P. 1, 3

Yamauchi, E. 8

www.ingramcontent.com/pod-product-compliance
Lightning Source LLC
Chambersburg PA
CBHW070015010526
44117CB00011B/1577